Robyn Crothers

The Pilgrim Way

The Pilgrim Way

By
ROBYN CROTHERS

Beloved, I beg you as sojourners and pilgrims, abstain from fleshly lusts, which war against the soul, having your conduct honourable among the Gentiles, that when they speak against you as evildoers, they may, by your good works which they observe, glorify God in the day of visitation. – 1 Peter 2: 11-12

The Pilgrim Way
Robyn Crothers

Published by Parables
September, 2020

All Rights Reserved. No part of this book may be reproduced or utilized in any form or by any means, electronic or mechanical, including photocopying, recording, or by any information storage and retrieval system, without permission in writing from the author.

    ISBN 978-1-951497-89-7
    Printed in the United States of America

Readers should be aware that Internet Web sites offered as citations and/or sources for further information may have been changed or disappeared between the time this was written and the time it is read.
Unless otherwise stated the NKJ version of the Bible has been used throughout.

The Pilgrim Way

By
Robyn Crothers

Beloved, I beg you as sojourners and pilgrims, abstain from fleshly lusts, which war against the soul, having your conduct honourable among the Gentiles, that when they speak against you as evildoers, they may, by your good works which they observe, glorify God in the day of visitation. – 1 Peter 2: 11-12

The Pilgrim Way

Author's Preface

The Bible – God's Words – to us is truly an amazing book, a book unlike any other. It is many books, yet one. It alone tells us how and why God created all we can see including ourselves and the things which we cannot see as well. It tells us about God, the triune God – Father, Son and Holy Spirit. Many have described the Bible as God's love letter to humanity, those creatures who alone are made in his image, who have fallen, who have rebelled and lost their relationship with him and how he has planned to bring them, us, back into that original personal intimate fellowship.

But the Bible is also a how-to manual for us. It contains all that God wants us to know, all that we need to understand, including warnings that are intended to keep us safe while journeying through this world whose prince is not our Father of lights (James 1:17), but the ruler of darkness (John 14:30, Ephesians 6:11-12 NIV) and the encouragements to keep travelling on his highway, the way.

1Peter was written by Peter the apostle probably sometime around 64-68 AD. His desire was to encourage the church and its individuals, which in his time consisted of both Jewish and gentile converts to Christianity, for they were in danger of losing their way because of being persecuted for their faith. This new found faith had severed the ties which had bound them to their non-Christian relatives and neighbours. They were being tested by the suffering they were experiencing as a result of these fractured relationships and the political upheaval during this time in history. This is probably not what they had expected when they first heard the gospel message and became pilgrims but these challenges are still faced by every believing generation.

Peter answered their needs (and ours) by reminding and reassuring them of the truths of the gospel, of how much Jesus had given up and willingly endured and suffered for them because he trusted in God's loving care. As Christ did so without sinning, remaining holy, Peter instructs these and all hurting pilgrims how they too can live God-pleasing holy lives while in this sinful world, without losing their hope, joy and peace.

The whole Bible *really* needs to be read, studied prayerfully and soaked in before and above any other writings are even glanced at or considered because only the Bible was written, breathed out, by God himself.

However, thank you for looking at *The Pilgrim Way*. This book was birthed as a result of hearing a sermon preached by the Reverend Philip J. Burns on 1Peter 2:11-12. I am indebted to him for both the challenge – "Our text this morning deals with a topic that once used to be a major theme among Christians, but in these days seems to be strangely absent . . . to my knowledge, apart from Bunyan's "Pilgrim Progress" written in 1650, there are even very few books on the subject, though it is one that should always be foremost in our minds . . ."[1] – he unknowingly threw at the writer in me and for his four sermon point outline that I have used for some sections of this book.

This book though would never have reached maturity without my husband's quiet support for which I will be forever grateful. He has been head grocer, chief, cuppa-maker, garbo, cleaner, gardener and grandchild entertainer whenever I turned the computer on and got the books out.

As you, my dear reader apply yourself to my scribblings please keep in mind that because I am a no-body in the world of authors I have quoted fairly heavily from a variety of Christian writers, not that I personally do not know or believe of what I am writing about but because they are affirming what I have learnt but do so more eloquently and clearer than I feel I can. I also hope to show by using authors from different stages of history (so please check the footnotes for dates) that the human nature, its desires and needs, as well as the basic causes of stresses and distresses have

---

[1] Rev. Philip J. Burns (born1961) Sermon: *The daily battle: proving to be true pilgrims* (1Peter 2:11-12) 15 March 2015

not changed and therefore the usefulness and necessity of understanding the Bible is unchanged.

Knowing my own heart and my past I would argue with Paul that I and not he is the small one, the worst of sinners. I too know the guilt and disappointment of failure and the painful distressing tensions of living as a new creation yet with the old nature still kicking, the shock of warfare from the world, the church and within self, the darkness of God's seemingly indifference and absence, and of losing friends and family because I will not let go of this crutch called Christianity. So, if you find any challenging encouragement, any carrot to assist you, in your own pilgrimage, or better still a hunger to search the Bible for yourself, it will only be by our great God's loving graciousness, not the skill (or lack of such) of my pen.

Yours in Christ,

Robyn.

Robyn Crothers

Contents

Authors Preface — p1

Prelude — p7

Part One: A Mindset to Adopt 1Peter 2:11a — p15
Defining words and concepts p21, How Satan messes with our minds p53, All new, what now? p58, Enmity, suffering and obedience p70, The mind of Christ p79, Holiness and habits of p93, Love, but which one? p104, Heed worry and anxiety p 124, Remember rightly p129.

Part Two: A War to Fight 1Peter 2:11b — p133
Temptations vs Trials p148, Crucifying sin and reaping holiness p156, Battle ready p163, Satan again and when God goes A-wall p204, Endurance, how and why? p214, Heed all weights including shame p233, Joy, clouds and the cross p246.

Interlude 1: A word on despondency John 14:1-3, 16, 27. — p253
With extracts from Bunyan's *Heart's Ease in Heart Trouble*

Part Three: A Lifestyle to Maintain 1Peter 2:12 — p291
Differences, sovereignty and decisions p299, Love and holiness p305, Legalism, those top 10 and persecution p318, Joyful cross carrying p331, 1Corinthians 13 p339, Contented (marital) submission p358, Bunyan's pilgrims and Vanity Fair p376, The seven walks of living p398, Heed forgetfulness p403.

Interlude 2: Take heed before that day Luke 13:6-9 — p417
With extracts from Bunyan's *The Barren Fig-Tree*

Part Four: A Day to Remember 1Peter 2:12b — p427
The sheep's homecoming p439, The goat's homecoming p452, Three parables but what's the time Mr. Wolf? p460 and a closing hymn p480.

Finale: the carrot! — p485

Robyn Crothers

Prelude

In the beginning was God. The triune God of creation and history, the author who breathed out our scriptures through his chosen human secretaries.

At some point in his time eternal he began to create. Our time, as we understand time, began then. Part way through the sixth day, when he had finished preparing a suitable universe and earth that was good for his image bearers to dwell in and care for, he made man, male and female. As God's representatives, man, female and male, were blessed by him to fill, subdue and rule his earth. Declaring all was very good at the end of this day God commemorated all that he had done by resting on the seventh for nothing else was needed. The dark chaotic void was filled with his visible order, light and life.

And so, the life of our ancestral parents began eastward of Adam's place of creation, in a garden planted for them by God named Eden. A garden where God, after Adam having named all the living creatures had not found a suitable companion for himself, placed him in a deep sleep, removing a rib, sculptured one and brought her to a rejoicing Adam who named her Woman. Then God commanded them to cling together and become one flesh.

Eden was full of every tree that was pleasant to the senses as well as being good for food.

God, however being a good and loving creator, desiring only what was best for his image bearers, gave instructions about two of these trees. One tree, being the tree of life, they were as free to eat from it as all the other trees, for God's will and desire for them was abundant life and eternal fellowship with him.

The second tree, being a tree that though eating of it would make you knowledgeable of good, which I'd suggest Adam and Woman had buckets of already, they would also know and so experience evil and death, two things that our parents had yet no knowledge of in this very good earth. It was this tree that our God declared to Adam was off limits for food, though he said nothing about not enjoying any other benefits this tree may have held, such as shade and beauty to behold.

Here, almost at the beginning of time, we see that language and therefore words are a gift from God for communicating with him and ourselves. Language 'so that He might communicate with us . . . so that He might tell us both what we need to know and what we need to do . . .The Bible displays God as one who commands and humans as required to practice obedience. This presentation starts in Eden.'[2] Here in this garden man, male and female, walked in the cool of the day, naked and unashamed in joyful fellowship with the LORD God, Yahweh.

Enter Satan the great lying deceiver and tempter masquerading as one of God's good creatures of his creation, "Did God really say that? Did God really mean that? Are you sure that is what God wants, really wants?"

So, Woman who had no want, with a silent Adam at her side, listens, looks, wants, takes and shares.

This is the fall. The fall of our parents from intimate fellowship and friendship with God and one another, from abundant life into immediate spiritual death and a slow physical decay that eventually resulted in their physical death.

The fall from all that was very good into all that is evil.

The beginning of earth's groaning and labouring with the pangs of birthing (Romans 8:20-22), and the beginning of our seemingly

---

[2] J. I. Packer (born 1926) and Carolyn Nystrom (born 1940) God's *Will Finding Guidance for Everyday Decisions* Baker Books 2008 p.87, 89

endless restless search for something to fill the hole, the empty void within.

This is when God pronounces his curse upon Satan and judgement upon mankind for his rebellion, his promise of restoration, his shedding of the first blood to cover Adam and Woman. Adam's subsequent faith in God was shown by him renaming Woman Eve for he believed in God's promise that she would be the mother of all living mankind.

And our God, because of his inmate goodness, banished mankind from the garden, lest Adam or Eve put out their hand and ate also from the tree of life, and by eating lived forever (Genesis 3:22) in this sin damaged state, far removed from what God wanted for us.

All humanity is fallen and on equal footing for it is only through faith in the redeeming work of the Son, Jesus Christ at calvary that any man or woman will become un-fallen and allowed again to eat of this tree and live forever.

      Yes, mankind has a way back.

      But it must be God's way back, not ours.

It must be God's planned way back, the way of the cross and his word alone shows us the way. The Bible contains all that we need to understand this way and what he needs us to do to be restored again into full unashamed, covenantal fellowship with him. It is a salvation by grace, God's grace alone, a message which attacks our pride for it leaves no room for us to get any kudos.

We can do nothing to earn this grace, we can only humbly and gratefully accept it by faith. Faith that believes God exists and his word the Bible is truth. Faith that believes what the Bible says about who Jesus is and what he did for fallen humanity is real, that he alone is the only true saviour humanity has, for he alone fulfils all God's requirements. Faith that knows that if this gift of God is accepted, we are released from Satan and sin's slavery, and though we are promised opposition and persecution in this life, we will also be blessed and rewarded here and in eternity to come as God has promised. Faith looks forward in expectant hope for this eternal life walking with God in a new world where there is no more sickness, pain, tears or death ever, for it will be a world again without sin. This life as a freed person with a personal relationship with the God of the Bible, in this fallen world, living in expectation for that glorious hope is the pilgrim's way.

Question: What or who is a pilgrim?
Answer: Someone who is on pilgrimage.
Question: What then is a pilgrimage?
Answer: The concise Oxford dictionary defines a pilgrim in part as a person who journeys through life, a traveler. The word itself comes from the Latin *peneginus*, which means a *stranger* and has nothing at all to do with penguins. Pilgrimage is defined as a pilgrim's journey where his life is viewed as a journey.

The context that a word appears in the Bible for the first time usually helps us to understand its meaning, its biblical meaning.

In Genesis 47:9 we read, 'And Jacob said to Pharaoh, "The days of the years of my pilgrimage are one hundred and thirty years . . . they have not attained to the days of the years of the life of my fathers in the days of their pilgrimage."'

The margin in my Bible tells me pilgrimage is literally *sojourning*. So, from this reading it appears that these words pilgrim/pilgrimage are referring to the life of a person here on earth but let's look a bit more.

Jacob, his father Isaac and grandfather Abram (who was the twentieth generation from Adam, see Luke 3:34-38) had no permeant residence. They owned no land of their own except for a field, one field which contained a cave and some trees in a land called Canaan, the modern-day location of Lebanon, Syria, Jordan and Israel.

Abram, or Abraham as God later named him, had bought this field in the way business was conducted in his time for a burial place for his wife Sarah. This is the first description in the Bible not only of buying land but of burying and mourning the death of a loved one. Sarah, Abraham, Isaac, Rebekah, Leah (Genesis 49:29-32), Jacob and Joseph (Joshua 24:32) are all buried here. They were all aliens, strangers, wanders, not belonging and not always welcomed by the natives of this or other lands that they travelled through or rested in.

They did however have a convent relationship with Yahweh, the one true God, the creator God, the God above all other gods (Genesis 15).

They believed in this God's promise of a homeland where they would rest from wandering, where they would belong and be welcome, of a city which has foundations whose builder and maker is God, (Hebrews 11:8-10), and by keeping their focus on this invisible reality they persevered in their pilgrimage here as we read in Hebrews 11:1-3, 13-16, 'Now faith is the substance [realization] of things hoped for, the evidence [confidence] of things not seen. For by it the elders obtained a good testimony. By faith we understand that the worlds were framed by the word of God, so that the things which are seen were not made of things which are visible . . . These all died in faith, not having received the promises, but having seen them afar off were assured of them, embraced them and confessed that they were strangers and pilgrims on the earth. For those who say such things declare plainly that they seek a homeland. And truly if they had called to mind that country from which they had come out, they would have had opportunity to return. But now they desire a better, that is, a heavenly country. Therefore, God is not ashamed to be called their God, for He has prepared a city for them.'

The biblical definition of a pilgrim, the definition we need to consider for the purpose of this book, is not of any person on this earth walking through life haphazardly as they see fit but of a person who is in covenant relationship with God. A person who has experienced God's saving grace, his salvation that is in and through Christ, who is no longer a pagan, an uncircumcised gentile but a Christian, a believer in the one true God, a new creation (2Corinthians 5:17), with a renewed mind (Ephesians 4:23) and a whole new life and wardrobe, new goals and walking a new journey by faith not sight (2 Corinthians 5:1-2,7), with a new destination (The Revelation of Jesus Christ 21:10,23-27, 22:14-15) and a new master, the original true and good master of mankind before the fall who's bondage or yolk unlike Satan's is easy and light (Matthew 11:28-30). An individual who has a living personal relationship with Jesus Christ, a person who by looking to Jesus, the founder and perfecter of their faith will run with endurance the pilgrimage set before them bearing the reproach that Christ endured for here, they have no lasting city, but instead seek the city that is to come (Hebrews 12:1-2, 13:13-14).

A pilgrim is an obedient and submissive disciple of Christ, a student, a humble follower, a worshiping cross-carrying Christian focused on the end of his or her wanderings here and being warmly lovingly welcomed home by his or her Father. A stranger to this world, dancing to a different tune who as a result will suffer some form of persecution from those who dance to a different piper.

Now to undertake a journey, any journey, you require some necessary items such as some sort of itinerary, a plan, a guide book, a starting point and a destination to focus on so you don't get off course becoming horribly lost. And if you are anything like me you will need to watch that you do not carry unnecessary stuff like the kitchen sink, stuff that ends up weighing you down so much that you just give up and quit 'cos it's just way too hard. So, let's see . . .

We have our starting point – Salvation, our new birth, our becoming a whole new creation, a Christian whose citizenship is in heaven making us pilgrims on pilgrimage in this world. (If you are unsure you are saved, please keep reading and think about the two choices you have to choose between before it is too late.)

We have our destination – our promised homeland, our King's kingdom and our Father's house which has many mansions.

We have our guide book – the Bible.

And we even have *the* personal travelling companion of all travelling companions, and no, I am not talking GPS, but the one who has promised not only that he will go before us and check out the path but that he will send another friend, the Holy Spirit, who being closer than a brother, will remind us of the way when we get muddled and lost and give us comfort.

So, are you ready to discover what the four parts of 1Peter2:11-12, along with other scriptures, recent biblical scholars' writings as well those of hundreds of years ago can do to guide us in discovering how we are to be as pilgrims and what we need to wear or leave off?

Well then, turn the page and let us begin. . .

Robyn Crothers

Part One: A Mindset to Adopt

Beloved, I beg you as sojourners and pilgrims . . .
1Peter 2:11a

First to live as pilgrims, Peter tells us of a *mindset to adopt*. "Beloved, I urge you as aliens and strangers . . .' (1Pt.2:11) That's how we are to think about ourselves. Beloved by God we are thus aliens and strangers on this earth which is for now under the dominion of the evil one. Thus, we're not simply foreigners, we're on enemy turf! We dare not forget this! Our sense of identity should not be derived from this world, but from our relationship to God and His people, bound for heaven.[3]

Question: What does it mean to adopt a mindset?
Answer: Firstly, let us consider some definitions, mainly from my battered Oxford dictionary.

Mindset
A mindset is the habits of the mind formed by earlier events.

Mind
The mind is the seat of consciousness, or thought, volition, feelings, the intellect, a way of thinking or feeling.

Habit
A habit is a settled or regular tendency or practice that can be hard to give up, a mental constitution or attitude, an automatic reaction to a specific situation.

---

[3] *Sermon: The daily battle: proving to be true pilgrims*

Habits are the thought and emotional patterns engraved on our minds.[4] We are what we repeatedly do. Excellence, then, is not an act, but a habit.[5]

Adopt

The context we are considering is not about taking a person into a relationship but about choosing to follow a course of action, to accept or take on a new, a different way of thinking, feeling and therefore being, as your own.

<u>Question</u>: Is this the most important thing to do first as a pilgrim? Why start with the mind?

<u>Answer</u>: First I decided to check with Google.

"We are what we think", claimed Socrates a Greek philosopher who died in 399BC. My brain started turning over, interestingly this sounds like Proverbs 23:7a, 'For as he thinks in his heart, so is he.'

Mindset influences everything: self-esteem, health, relationships and careers. It's often just as powerful as circumstances in determining the course of your life.[6]

Over 90% of our behaviour is driven by our unconscious motivations, values, assumptions, beliefs and habits.[7]

Okay, so that means that only 10% of me is aware of what all of me is doing?!!

Our thoughts can change the way we behave, the decisions we make, and the feelings we experience. In short, they have a lot of influence over us, more so than we think.[8]

I had discussed my Google searching with a doctor in my congregation and he later presented me with an article from which the following extract comes –

---

[4] Jerry Bridges (1929-2016) *The Pursuit of Holiness* Navpress 1985 p.134

[5] Aristotle Greek philosopher (384-322 BC)

[6] From experiencelife.com published by Jessie Sholl

[7] The site Mindsets Matter: The Neuroscience of Leading Change. https://www.results.wa.gov> default>files

[8] exploringyourmind.com psychology March 28 2017

Neuroscientist Marc Lewis believes that drug dependence or addiction is not a disease of the brain but as NDARC Professor Alison Ritter describes 'a complex cultural, social, psychological and biological phenomenon.' 'Lewis argues that addiction – or dependence, as we would call it in Australia – is the result of "deep learning", probably triggered by stress or alienation. It can duly be unlearned by forging stronger synaptic pathways via better habits.'

He argues that the neurobiological changes seen in the brain as a result of addictions 'are induced by any goal-orientated activity that becomes all-consuming, such as gambling, sex addiction, internet gaming, learning a new language or instrument, and by powerfully valanced activities such as falling in love or religious conversion. And while the American Medical Association may have classified alcoholism as a disease in 1956 and obesity in 2013, it hasn't gone so far as to similarly smote love or Catholicism. "It even applies to making money," Lewis says of this deep learning. "There have been studies showing that people making high-powered decisions in business and politics also have very high levels of dopamine metabolism in the striatum, because they're in a constant state of goal pursuit."

The result of constant stimulating this reward system keeps the user focused only on the moment. "You can't think about tomorrow or next week," says Lewis. "You've lost the idea of yourself being on a line that extends from the past into the future. You're just drawn into this vortex that is the now." . . . Lewis argues that new habits can overwrite old. "People have to really be ready, because there has to be a powerful surge towards other goals . . . Goals about their relationships and feeling whole connected and under control. The striatum is highly activated and looking for those other goals to connect with. There was a study made on addicts of cocaine, alcohol and heroin, and it showed that six months to a year into their abstinence there were regions of the prefrontal cortex that had previously showed a decline in synaptic density from underuse, which had returned to baseline and then gone beyond baseline. That indicates growth of powerful new synaptic networks, and if you're setting up new paths then you're deactivating old paths, because they're being used less." [9]

Then lastly Google put up this gem.

The thoughts we allow into our brains every day shape our lives and determine our future . . . Your thoughts and beliefs contribute to your personality and character. We become what we think about all the day long.[10]

Perhaps I should think about being thinner all day every day, or taller so I could reach the top shelf in the supermarket?

But seriously, if the world sees a mindset as that powerful and that it is formed by earlier events, which for all mankind who are not pilgrims is the fall, then perhaps as pilgrims we do need to adopt a different mindset, the new God glorifying one he desires to give us.

<u>Question</u>: But what does the Bible have to say regarding mindsets and the need of a new one to adopt?

<u>Answer</u>: In Mark 7:14-23 we read, 'When [Jesus] had called all the multitude to Himself, He said to them, "Hear Me, everyone, and understand: There is nothing that enters a man from outside which can defile him; but the things which come out of him, those are the things that defile a man. If anyone has ears to hear, let him hear!" When He had entered a house away from the crowd, His disciples asked Him concerning the parable. So he said to them, "Are you thus without understanding also? Do you not perceive that whatever enters a man from outside cannot defile him, because it does not enter his heart but his stomach, and is eliminated, thus purifying all foods?" And He said, "What comes out of a man, that defiles a man. For from within, out of the heart of men, proceed evil thoughts, adulteries, fornications, murders,

---

[9] Jenny Valentish *Why addiction isn't a disease but instead the result of 'deep learning'* The Age 11:29:2018 https://ndarc.med.unsw.edu.au/blog/why-addiction-isn't-disease-instead-result-deep-learning

[10] *We Become What We Think About – Transcend Your Limits* found at https://ww.transcendyourlimits.com.su

thefts, covetousness, wickedness, deceit, lewdness, an evil eye, blasphemy, pride, foolishness. All these evil things come from within and defile a man."'

> Cleanse first the mind of thy inward man, from evil dispositions and affections, and the outward behaviour will soon follow and show its fruit in all that is virtuous and praise worthy.[11]

In Matthew 5:21-22, 27-28, we read of Jesus saying, '"You have heard that it was said to those of old, 'You shall not murder, and whoever murders will be in danger of judgement.' But I say to you that whoever is angry with his brother without a cause shall be in danger of the judgement. And whoever says to his brother, 'Raca!' [literally in the Aramaic language, 'Empty head'] shall be in danger of the council. But whoever says 'You fool!' [the Greek means saying more, as in worse than Raca, more than already said] shall be in danger of hell fire . . . You have heard that it was said to those of old, 'You shall not commit adultery.' But I say to you that whoever looks at a woman to lust for her has already committed adultery with her in his heart."'

Barnes writes, 'Christ states here what *does* defile the man, or render him a sinner; "Evil thoughts". These are the first things. These are the fountains of all others. Thought precedes action. Thought, or purpose, or motive gives its character to the conduct. All evil thoughts are here intended. Though we labour to suppress them, yet they defile us; they leave pollution behind them. Murders, or taking the life of others with malice. The malice has its seat in the heart, and the murder therefore proceeds from the heart. Theft is taking away the goods of others without their knowledge or consent. They are produced by *coveting* the property of others. They proceed, therefore, from the heart, and violate at the same time two commandments – the *tenth* in thought, and the *eighth* in act. "False witness". Giving wrong testimony. *Concealing* the truth, or stating what we know to be

---

[11] Rev. John Fleetwood. D. D. *Fleetwood's Life of Christ. The Life of our Blessed Lord and Saviour Jesus Christ; together with the Evidences of the Evangelists, Apostles, and Chief Disciples* (First published 1841) Thomson, Niven Publishers. p491

false, contrary to the ninth commandment. It proceeds from a desire to injure others, or to take away their character or property, or to do them injustice. It proceeds thus from the heart. "Blasphemies". Blasphemy proceeds from opposition to God, hatred of his character, and from a *desire* that there should be no God. It proceeds from the heart. "Covetousness", always proceeding from the heart – the unlawful desire of what others possess. "Wickedness." The original here means *malice*, or a *desire of injuring others.* "Deceit"; i.e. fraud, concealment, cheating in trade. This proceeds from a desire to benefit ourselves by doing injustice to others, and this proceeds from the heart. "Lasciviousness." Lust, obscenity, unbridled passion – a strong, evil desire of the heart. "An evil eye." That is, an eye, sour, malignant, proud, devising or purposing evil. "Having eyes full of adultery, that cannot cease from sin." "Pride." An improper estimate of our own importance – thinking that we are of much more consequence than we really are – always the work of an evil heart. "Foolishness." Not want of intellect. Man is not to blame for that. But *moral folly*, consisting in choosing bad ends, and bad means of gaining them; or, in other words, sin and wickedness. All sin is folly. It is foolish for a man to disobey God; and foolish for anyone to go to hell.

"These things defile a man". What an array of crimes to proceed from the heart of man! What proof of guilt! What strictness is therein the law of God! How universal is depravity!'[12]

Can you see from these writings that thoughts, the good which will glorify God and can only come from a new heart, or the evil which defiles us and their corresponding actions arise from within the fallen, natural- born-with heart or mind of a person?

However, before we go any further, I believe it will be to our advantage to define some more words and ideas using a Bible

---

[12] *Fleetwood's Life of Christ* comment from Barnes (Albert Barnes 1798-1870) on the Gospels. p272

dictionary along with verses from the Bible and selected comments.

Defining words and concepts

Heart

Sometimes *heart* means our reason or understanding, sometimes our affections and emotions, and sometimes our will. Generally, it denotes the whole soul of man and all its facilities, not individually, but as they work together in doing good or evil. The mind as it reasons, discerns, and judges; the emotions as they like or dislike; the conscience as it determines and warns; and the will as it chooses or refuses – are all together called the heart. [13]

Packer and Nystrom tell us that 'the heart is the very center, the energy center, of the person. Our desires, purposes, plans, attitudes, according to scripture, all come out of the heart . . . All that constitutes a person (life, energy, attitudes) all of this and more come out of the heart, as if the heart is a factory in which all personal qualities are constituted.'[14]

After the fall mankind's heart grew increasingly evil, so much so that around the nineth generation we read in Genesis 6:5-6, 8, 'Then the LORD saw that the wickedness of man was great in the earth, and that every intent of the thoughts of his heart was only evil continually. And so, the LORD was sorry that He had made man on the earth, and He was grieved in His heart . . . But Noah found grace in the eyes of the LORD.'

Mankind's heart remained stubbornly evil despite experiencing the flooding of the whole earth and God's following tests and chastisements because of their choices and so by the time of Ezekiel (roughly about 2000years after the flood) they were experiencing some of what God had promised in Deuteronomy (very roughly about 1100years after the flood) as a result.

---

[13] *The Pursuit of Holiness* p63-65 Quote adapted from John Owen's (1616-1683) definition of the heart in 1656

[14] *God's Will* p63-4

We read in Ezekiel 18:31 of the Lord God instructing man to '"Cast away from you all the transgressions which you have committed, and get yourselves a new heart and a new spirit. For why should you die . . .?"'

Then the Lord God says in Ezekiel 36:25a, 26-7, '". . . I will sprinkle clean water on you, and you shall be clean . . . I will give you a new heart and put a new spirit within you; I will take the heart of stone out of your flesh and give you a heart of flesh. I will put My Spirit within you and cause you to walk in My statutes, and you will keep My judgements and do them."'

Even as pilgrims with a new heart, our old heart continues to beat, so that we can never be sure, fully know our own motives, let alone anyone else's, only God does therefore it is best we leave the judgmental stuff to him.

David knew this. This is why in Psalm 19:12-14 we read 'Who can understand his errors? Cleanse me from secret faults. Keep back Your servant also from presumptuous sins; let them not have dominion over me. Then I shall be blameless, and I shall be innocent of great transgression. Let the words of my mouth and the meditation of my heart be acceptable in Your sight, O LORD, my strength and my Redeemer.'

Sin

What a tiny word for a very big problem. I have heard definitions like 'missing the mark' – what mark I thought? 'Not being obedient to God's commands', or something I had inherited and something I willed to do, were other ideas, but finding these vague and in the end not always helpful I hesitated as to what to write for you. Then the other day my minster asked me if I had seen the YouTube clip *"What is Sin?"* by the theologian John Piper and as I had not, he played it for me. I could not scribble notes that were readable fast enough so when I was back home, I investigated further and eventually found the original written sermon based on Romans to read and take notes from. As I found it uncomfortably helpful, I have chosen to give you some snippets to consider here with the hope you may check out the full message for yourself at a later time.

Sinning is any feeling or thought or speech or action that comes from a heart that does not treasure God over all other things.

> Sin is:
> The glory of God not honoured.
> The faithfulness of God not trusted.
> The holiness of God not reverenced.
> The promises of God not believed.
> The greatness of God not admired.
> The commandments of God not obeyed.
> The power of God not praised.
> The justice of God not respected.
> The truth of God not sought.
> The wrath of God not feared.
> The wisdom of God not esteemed.
> The grace of God not cherished.
> The beauty of God not treasured.
> The presence of God not prized.
> The goodness of God not savoured.
> The person of God not loved.[15]

Gables, in regards to the devils who believe and tremble, says that they know and believe the things of God but will not submit to his lordship over them. A sinner is a sinner not because he is lacking in knowledge about God, it's simply he won't bow to that knowledge which he has of God in obedience to do the will of God in his life.[16]

Piper continues, 'Once Paul has made clear what the essence or root of sin is in Romans 1-3, he now makes clear in the following chapters the magnitude of its power in us. He speaks of sin *reigning* like a king in death (5:21), holding dominion like a Lord

---

[15] John Piper (born 1946) Sermon: *Sin Prefers Anything to God* audio transcript April 8, 2015. https:// www.desiringgod. org

[16] From notes taken while listening to Pastor Jim Gables' sermon series on Bunyan's Pilgrim's Progress #37 *Talkative – how to expose him* 2.6.99
https://www.sermonaudio.com>Jim

(6:14), *enslaving* like a slave master (6:6, 16f,20), to whom we have been *sold* (7:14), as a *force* that produces other sins (7:8), as a *power* that seizes the law and kills (7:11), as a hostile occupying *tenant* that dwells in us (7:17, 20), and a *law* that takes us captive (7:23) And this powerful presence in us, defines us until we are born again. . . . .

[Sin is] not mainly what you do. It is mainly who you are – until you are a new creature in Christ. And even then, for us who are born of God, it is an ever-present, indwelling enemy to be put to death every day by the Spirit (Romans 8:13) . . . It is who we are to the bottom of our hearts. Until Christ . . . [for] . . . without Christ we cannot do good . . . (Heb. 11:6, Rom. 14:23) . . . What this calls for is a radical God-centeredness in the way you think about everything . . . (Phil. 3:6-8) In other words, unless all those good deeds come from faith in Christ, they are refuse and loss. That was [Paul's] new orientation . . . The reason Paul says that "whatever is not from faith is sin" (Rom. 14:23) is that faith is a receiving of God in Christ as our Saviour, and Lord, and supreme Treasure. Which means that actions which don't come from faith, don't come from treasuring God over all things. And that's what sin *is* – not treasuring God above all things, preferring anything more than God.'[17]

Question: Did Jesus, who is both fully God and fully man, treasure God, his Father, in his heart over all others and all other things, stuff?

Answer: Hebrews 10: 5-7, 'Therefore, when He came into the world, [Jesus] said: "Sacrifice and offering You did not desire, But a body You have prepared for Me. In burnt offerings and sacrifices for sin You had no pleasure. Then I said, 'Behold, I have come – In the volume of the book it is written of Me – To do Your will, O God.'"

---

[17] John Piper Plenary Session – 2015 Conference for Pastors Feb 2, 2015 Sermon: *What Is Sin? The Essence and Root of All Sinning* desiringgod.org

Because the Son loved the Father, he lived in
absolute obedience to him.

Christ became a man, voluntary laying aside the use of his Godness, to live as a human in this fallen world rather than at home with his Father, experiencing like temptations that we do as we read in Hebrews 4:14-15, 'Seeing then that we have a great High Priest who has passed through the heavens, Jesus the Son of God, let us hold fast our confession. For we do not have a High Priest who cannot sympathize with our weaknesses, but was in all points tempted as we are, yet without sin.'

He suffered deep sadness, pain, even homelessness as we learn when a certain scribe promised to follow Jesus wherever he went, 'Jesus said to him, "Foxes have holes and birds of the air have nests, but the Son of Man has nowhere to lay His head' (Matthew 8:20).

Rejected, hated and sentenced to dying accursed for he 'has redeemed us from the curse of the law, having become a curse for us (for it is written, "Cursed is everyone who hangs on a tree")' (Galatians 3:13), all because he chose obedience to God, 'for I have come down from heaven, not to do My own will, but the will of Him who sent Me . . . Therefore, My Father loves Me, because I lay down My life that I may take it again. No one takes it from Me, but I lay it down of Myself. I have power to lay it down, and I have power to take it again. This command I have received from My Father . . . Now My soul is troubled, and what shall I say? 'Father, save me from this hour'? But for this purpose I came to this hour. Father, glorify Your name . . . For I have not spoken on My own authority; but the Father who sent Me gave me a command, what I should say and what I should speak. And I know that His command is everlasting life. Therefore, whatever I speak, just as the Father has told me, so I speak . . . I have glorified You on the earth. I have finished the work which You have given Me to do' (John 6:38, 10:17-18, 12:27-28a and 49-50, 17:4).

The only sinless man to walk this earth for his life time and who did treasure God above all else is Jesus and that is the reason why he alone is the suitable sacrifice for our salvation.

> Have you, my dear reader, loved God this much?
> Me neither!
> Sin does not love to glorify God. Sin does not love to thank God. Do I have a kind of love to Christ and thankfulness for grace that corresponds to the horrors of what I was rescued from and to the price the most beautiful and innocent person paid for that rescue? [18]

Spurgeon writes, 'You must be divorced from your sin or you cannot be married to Christ. Recall the question which flashed into the mind of young Bunyan while playing sports on Sunday: 'Wilt thou have thy sins and go to hell, or wilt thou quit thy sins and go to heaven?' That brought him to a dead stand. That is a question which every man will have to answer, for there is no going on in sin and going to heaven. That cannot be. You must quit sin or quit hope.

Do you reply '. . . To will is present with me, but how to preform that which I would I find not . . .' Come, then, if you have no strength, this text is still true, 'When we were yet without strength, in due time Christ died for the ungodly.'

. . . However many other things may seem to contradict it, will you still believe it? God has said it and it is a fact; therefore, hold on to it tightly, for your only hope lies there. Believe this, trust Jesus, and you will soon find power with which to slay your sin. But apart from Him, the armed strong man will hold you forever his bond slave.'[19]

Idols and idolatry

Someone once said, 'There is a god we want and there is a God who is, and the two are not the same. And if we don't want the God who is, we will invent the god we want, and we will worship him.' In the Old Testament we learn what God thinks of idols and the worship of them which is idolatry.

---

[18] Ibid

[19] C. H. Spurgeon (1834-1892) *All of Grace The infinite love of God* Whitaker House 1981 p80

In Exodus 20:1-5 we read, 'And God spoke all these words, saying: "I am the LORD your God, who brought you out of the land of Egypt, out of the house of bondage. You shall have no other gods before Me. You shall not make for yourselves a carved image– any likeness of anything that is in heaven above, or that is in the earth beneath, or that is in the water under the earth; you shall not bow down to them nor serve them. For I, the LORD your God, am a jealous God . . ."'

God shows us the foolishness of idolizing these idols in passages like Isaiah 44: 14-17 and 46: 6-7, where we read that man 'plants a pine and the rain nourishes it. Then it shall be for a man to burn, for he will take some of it and warm himself; Yes, he kindles it and bakes bread; indeed, he makes a god and worships it; he makes it a carved image, and falls down to it. He burns half of it in the fire; with this half he eats meat; he roasts a roast, and is satisfied . . . And the rest of it he makes into a god, his carved image. He falls down before it and worships it, prays to it and says, "Deliver me, for you are my god!". . . They lavish gold out of the bag, and weigh silver on the scales; they hire a goldsmith, and he makes it a god; . . . they worship . . . they carry it and set it in its place . . . Though one cries out to it, yet it cannot answer nor save him out of his trouble.'

And in Psalm 115:4-8 we read that 'idols are silver and gold, the work of men's hands. They have mouths, but they do not speak; eyes they have, but they do not hear; Noses they have but they do not smell; they have hands, but they do not handle; feet they have, but they do not walk; nor do they mutter through their throat. Those who make them are like them; so is everyone who trusts in them.' Ouch!

Pastor Michael Boyd tells us that today 'we might not physically make an idol to worship. . . we tend to buy them. Things that represent our deep needs . . . An idol is something or someone we look to to answer questions God has already answered. . . Questions like Am I loved? Am I valuable? Am I important? Am I desirable? Am I safe? Am I acceptable? God has already answered those questions to us in Jesus. But we don't believe him. So I'd like to ask you a question. Please consider your answer and you might catch a glimpse of your idol: *When I am not seeking God on these questions, where do I tend to look to find my answers?* What do you look to or cling to, to know that you are loved? Whose opinion do I look to to know that I am acceptable? Jesus is the YES to all these questions. He is the visible representation of God's character . . . And he is the fulfilment of every longing of the human heart . . . idols, in whatever form, are third parties because they are not God . . . the Father is jealous for his Son's glory. When you or I put something or someone as the symbol of what we yearn for we rob Jesus of his rightful place and his glory. It's as though we are saying to God, 'Your Son is not good enough as an answer to my fears.' No wonder God is jealous!'[20] Only God can save us and fulfil us and give life purpose and meaning completely and lastingly, no idol can do this. God will not tolerate being second, he will jealously guard what is his because he knows the destructive power of an idol and because he loves you, he will do whatever is needed to teach you to stay away from them and stay with him.

Good vs evil/bad

First, we need to understand and remember that it is God who decides what is good and evil, not his created beings. And because God never changes, his view of what is good or evil also never changes throughout time, unlike ours.

Jesus tells us in Matthew 7:17-18 that '". . . every good tree bears good fruit, but a bad tree bears bad fruit. A good tree cannot bear bad fruit, nor can a bad tree bear good fruit."'

Then in Matthew 12:35 Jesus instructs that '"A good man out of the good treasure of his heart brings forth good things, and an evil man out of the evil treasure brings forth evil things."'

James writes more pointedly that 'With [our tongue] we bless our God and Father, and with it we curse men, who have been made

---

[20] Reverend Michael Boyd *Sermon series: The 10 Commandments. Commandment #2: The problem of idols.* Colossians 1:9-23 Exodus 20:4-6 2014

in the similitude of God. Out of the same mouth proceed blessing and cursing. My brethren, these things ought not to be so. Does a spring send forth fresh water and bitter from the same opening? Can a fig tree, my brethren, bear olives, or a grapevine bear figs? Thus, no spring yields both salt water and fresh.' (James 3:9-12)

All that is not of God, from God is evil, is bad.
In Exodus 34: 6 we read a part of Yahweh's declaration of his character, 'And the LORD passed before him and proclaimed, "The LORD, the LORD God, merciful and gracious, longsuffering, and abounding in goodness and truth . . .' God's goodness is his glory, there is nothing bad or evil in Yahweh for then he would not be God. Before we were pilgrims, we were evil, our hearts were only evil and to do pure good was not possible. But now what comes out of our new heart should be good.

The world

According to Gables the Bible uses this word in three ways –
- To describe the material universe that God created.
- To describe the human race. As in John 3:16, 'For God so loved the world that He gave His only begotten Son, that whoever believes in Him should not perish but have everlasting life.'
- To describe organized humanity living without God at its center. This is the most used sense of the word, and it is in an evil sense. It is only slightly younger than the created material universe. God created man and placed him in the world with the responsibility to keep his commandments. The devil used creation to take man away from his obedience to God and so destroyed their lives. This is Bunyan's Vanity Fair. All pilgrims have to go thru this world to get to heaven for there is no other way. Though we have to be in the world we do not have to be of the world, we do not have to take on its ways of thinking or doing.[21]

---

[21] Notes from Gables' sermon series on Pilgrim's Progress #40 *Vanity Fair – The Description* 2.9.99

> The doctrine of this world: Get all the gusto out of life you can as you only get one life. Don't let the life hereafter, if there is one, take this life's enjoyment.[22]

The World says: "You have needs – satisfy them. You have as much right as the rich and the mighty. Don't hesitate to satisfy your needs; indeed, expand your needs and demand more." This is the worldly doctrine of today. And they believe that this is freedom. The result for the rich is isolation and suicide, for the poor, envy and murder. [23]

> <u>Warning</u>: Gal.i.4. You cannot be a pilgrim if you are not delivered from this world and its vanities; for if you love the world, if it has your supreme affections, the love of God is not in you, 1John ii.15; you have not one grain of precious faith in precious Jesus. [24]

Spirit

Luke 8:55a reads, 'Then [the little girl's] spirit returned, and she arose immediately . . .'

And Romans 8:16 informs us that, 'The Spirit Himself bears witness with our spirit that we are children of God'.

Soul

Our soul's worth is above what all the world's coffers could pay as Psalm 49: 6-8a tells us, 'Those who trust in their wealth and boast in the multitude of their riches, none of them can by any means redeem his brother, nor give to God a ransom for him – for the redemption of their souls is costly.'

In Ezekiel 18:4, the Lord God says, '"Behold, all souls are Mine; the soul of the father as well as the soul of the son is Mine; the soul who sins shall die."'

---

[22] Ibid #05 *Evangelist exposes Worldly Wiseman 1.5.99*

[23] Fyodor Dostoevsky (1821-1881)

[24] John Bunyan (1628-1688) *The Pilgrim's Progress* comment by Mason (William Mason 1719-1791) *The Pilgrim's Progress and other select works with preface and memoir of the Author.* Henry Cooke Melbourne, Victoria. p140-1

James 1:21 teaches us to, 'Therefore lay aside all filthiness and overflow of wickedness, and receive with meekness the implanted word, which is able to save your souls.'

Body

Matthew 10:28 advises us to 'not fear those who kill the body but cannot kill the soul. But rather fear Him who is able to destroy both soul and body in hell.'

While 1Corinthians 15:35-44 speaks of our different types of bodies, '. . . How are the dead raised up? And with what body do they come? . . . what you sow is not made alive unless it dies . . . you do not sow that body that shall be, but mere grain . . . to each seed its own body . . . So also is the resurrection of the dead. The body is sown in corruption, it is raised in incorruption. It is sown in dishonour, it is raised in glory . . . It is sown a natural body; it is raised a spiritual body.'

Body, soul and spirit, these three constitute a person in their entirety. 1Thessalonians 5:23 reads, 'Now may the God of peace Himself sanctify you completely; and may your whole spirit, soul, and body be preserved blameless at the coming of our Lord Jesus Christ.'

This is the only place in the New Testament where the tripartite being of a person is implied. Our spirit enables us to be in contact with the divine Spirit and is that part of a person which God's Spirit quickens at the time of our salvation and it leaves the physical body at death. The soul equals life, a person's personality or inward animating essence. The body is the physical being separate from spirit and soul. In my years of nursing I dealt with many a corpse and always felt that even though their body may have appeared the same there was something missing that had made them, well them. This was both their spirit and soul.

Faith

Romans 10:17, 'So then faith comes by hearing, and hearing by the word of God.'

James 2: 20-22, 26 'But do you want to know, O foolish man, that faith without works is dead [useless]? Was not Abraham our father justified by works when he offered Isaac his son on the altar? Do you see that faith was working together with his works, and by works faith was made perfect [complete]? . . . For as the body without the spirit is dead, so faith without works is dead also.'

The original Greek means *trust* or *a firm persuasion*. The corresponding verb means *to believe*, as illustrated in Jesus' command to Jairus in Mark. 5:36, 'As soon as Jesus heard the word that [Jairus' daughter was dead], He said to the ruler of the synagogue, "Do not be afraid; only believe."'

The epistle writers occasionally used the same word to refer to what one believes, the content of their faith, God's revelation in scripture as we read in Galatians 1:23, 'But they were hearing only "He who formerly persecuted us now preaches the faith which he once tried to destroy."'

True godly faith shows itself in a pilgrim's righteous works. They are two faces of the same coin; faith is the cause and works the effect. As Elisabeth Elliot wrote, 'Faith is not a feeling. Faith is willed obedience in action.'[25]

What is faith?
Faith is my acceptance of God's facts.[26]

Believe or belief

Genesis 15:6, 'And [Abram] believed in the LORD, and He accounted it to him for righteousness.'

But as with faith, wrong, dead belief is useless.

James 2: 19, 'You believe that there is one God. You do well. Even the demons believe – and tremble!

The Hebrew root used in the Old Testament, from which the English word Amen, used to express approval of what had been said or done came, means *to establish* or *confirm*.

---

[25] Elisabeth Elliot *Suffering is Never for Nothing* B & H Books 2019 goodreads.com

[26] Watchman Nee (1903-1972) *The Normal Christian Life* Tyndale House Publishers 1977 p68

The Greek word used in the New Testament, literally means to *place one's trust in another*, and is used over ninety times in John's gospel. To believe in Jesus is to believe in his person and to trust him completely for salvation as we read in John 3:14-16, 'And as Moses lifted up the serpent in the wilderness, ['. .Moses made a bronze serpent, and put it on a pole; and so it was, if a serpent had bitten anyone, when he looked at the bronze serpent, he lived.' Numbers 21:9] even so must the Son of Man be lifted up, that whoever believes in Him should not perish but have eternal life. For God so loved the world that He gave His only begotten Son, that whoever believes in Him should never perish but have everlasting life.'

Belief is one of the most important ideas in the entire Bible because a person must believe both in and on God in order to be saved from his sin and their way of living must show the evidence of this. Whenever the Old or New Testament state a person *believed in the Lord* it is saying that that person has made a choice, a decision to treat God's word as true and certain and has made a commitment or covenant to be obedient, to do what and as God wants.

> To know is a thing that pleases talkers and boasters but to do is that which pleases God.[27]
>
> As the belief of the truth lies at the foundation of the hope of eternal life, and is the cause of any one becoming a pilgrim; so, the belief of a lie is the cause of anyone's turning out of the way which leads to glory.[28]

Great care must be taken that the Jesus/God/Spirit you believe in and are trusting in and obeying *is* the triune God of the Bible and not of your or someone else's imagination.

Salvation

---

[27] Notes from Gables' sermon series on Pilgrim's Progress #37 *Talkative – how to expose him*. 2.6.99

[28] *The Pilgrim's Progress* comment by Mason p55

He who never became a fool in the eyes of the world for Christ, is not yet made wise unto salvation through the faith of Christ.[29]
Peter, speaking to the rulers and elders of Israel about the Christ Jesus said in Acts 4:12, 'Nor is there salvation in any other for there is no other name under heaven given among men by which we must be saved.'

> "Yes, from my bosom, my Belov'd I give,
> That my lost creatures may return and live;
> He for your sakes shall lay his glory by,
> For you be born and suffer, gasp and die;
> The price of guilt my Holy One shall pay,
> And tread of death and hell the bitterest way."
> -Brooke's Redemption[30].

The Greek word Paul used for salvation literally means *deliverance* or *preservation*. If you would like you can turn back and re-read the first paragraph of Piper's explanation of what sin does to us using Paul's letter to the Romans. This is what Christ has delivered us from and will preserve pilgrims from as John 8:36 tells us, '. . . if the Son makes you free, you shall be free indeed'.
As someone once instructed, 'Cast off the bondage of your body for you were not meant to be led like a dog on the leash of lust or hunger.'
Salvation is one very big gift made up from many smaller gifts, yet none can be received or used alone without all the others. All are essential and as you go through these definitions and explanations see if you can understand how acceptance of this package will make us aliens and pilgrims in this world.
The salvation package involves the following –

Justification

Romans 3:20 and 4:25-5:1, 'Therefore by the deeds of the law no flesh will be justified in His sight, for by the law is the knowledge

---

[29] *The Pilgrim's Progress* comment by Mason p44

[30] Bunyan The *Holy War made by King Shaddai upon Diabolus, for the regaining of the metropolis of the World.* The Pilgrim's Progress and other select works p434

of sin . . . [Christ] was delivered up because of our offences, and was raised because of our justification. Therefore, having been justified by faith, we have peace with God through our Lord Jesus Christ.'

James 2:24-25, 'You see then that a man is justified by works, and not by faith only. Likewise, was not Rahab the harlot also justified by works when she received the messengers and sent them out another way?'

Justification is a legal term used of a favourable verdict. The Greek noun for justification comes from the Greek verb which means *to acquit* or *to declare righteous*. Here God is the judge determining the state of each person according to his law which exposes all our sin. God is also our justifier when we believe in the work of his Son on the cross as he credits his righteousness to us and so can declare us just.

Born again

This birth is explained in John 3: 3-6, 'Jesus answered and said to [Nicodemus], "Most assuredly, I say to you, unless one is born again, he cannot see the kingdom of God." Nicodemus said to Him, "How can a man be born when he is old? Can he enter a second time into his mother's womb and be born?" Jesus answered, "Most assuredly, I say to you, unless one is born of water and the Spirit, he cannot enter the kingdom of God. That which is born of the flesh is flesh, and that which is born of the Spirit is Spirit."'

Campbell writes, 'The word for 'again' can also mean 'from above', so this is describing our birth from above, our second birth by God because of His saving work on the cross.' The expression, "except a man be born again", or born from above, signifies that great change which is wrought on the souls of men by the Spirit of God. The phrase, among the Jews, was often used loosely. Proselytes were said to be 'born again' – brought into the world a second time – and by that means [circumcision] rendered sons of Abraham. The language of the Saviour is peculiarly emphatic, as indicative of the absolute necessity for this change in order to salvation. More was meant than a mere ceremony. It indicated nothing less than being renewed in the spirit of their minds, becoming partakers of the Divine nature, having Christ formed in their hearts, and his image stamped on their souls. The terms 'water' and 'the Spirit' here used, are significant of the same thing, the Holy Spirit, just as baptism with the Holy Ghost and with fire represent the Spirit's purifying influence, and not the addition of literal fire. The work of the Spirit is likened to the motion of the wind. About this fact there can be no doubt, although the mode of action is undiscovered.'[31]

The washing of regeneration and regeneration

Titus 3:5 teaches us that 'not by the works of righteousness which we have done, but according to His mercy He saved us, through the washing of regeneration and renewing of the Holy Spirit.'

And Ephesians 5:26 adds, 'that [Christ] might sanctify and cleanse [the church] with the washing of water by the word.'

The Greek for regeneration literally means being born again, describing the new birth effected by the Spirit. The original word that is only used in these two verses means a full body washing. The regenerative activity of the Holy Spirit is characterized elsewhere as cleansing and purifying, as seen in Ezekiel 36:25, [The LORD speaking to Ezekiel about Israel] 'Then I will sprinkle clean water on you, and you shall be clean; I will cleanse you from all your filthiness and from all your idols.'

God saves us through one process of the Spirit but with two faces, again like a coin – the washing with water [spiritually, not physically] and his invisible work of renewal.

Reconciliation

2Cointhians 5:18, 'Now all things are of God, who has reconciled us to Himself through Jesus Christ, and has given us the ministry of reconciliation'.

---

[31] *Fleetwood's Life of Christ* comment from Dr Campbell's (John Campbell 1794-1867) Expository Bible p131

The Greek basically means a *change* or *exchange*. In the context of relationships between two parties this implies a change in attitude on the part of both involved, *a change from enmity to friendship*. Inherent in the teaching of justification is the changed attitude of God, because of the cross, toward the sinner with declaring a person who was formerly his enemy to be reconciled to him.

Adoption

Galatians 4:4-7, 'But when the fullness of the time had come, God sent forth His Son, born of a woman, born under the law, to redeem those who were under the law, that we might receive the adoption as sons. And because you are sons, God has sent forth the Spirit of His Son into your hearts, crying out, "Abba, Father!" Therefore, you are no longer a slave but a son, and if a son, then an heir of God through Christ.'

Adoption is a legal term, which in this context shows that all pilgrims, male or female, have been given the full privileges of first-born-sonship in God's family. At salvation God places the Spirit of his Son into our hearts so we become in effect his natural born children. As such we are not just adopted in the meaning the word now conveys but genuinely begotten by the Father.

Righteousness

James 2:23, 'And the Scripture was fulfilled which says, "Abraham believed God and it was accounted [credited] to him for righteousness." And he was called the friend of God.'

1John 2:29, 'If you know that He is righteous, you know that everyone who practices righteousness is born of Him.'

Righteousness refers to *a proper or right relationship* between the triune God and a person. In the Old Testament it was seen mostly in Yahweh's relationship with his people Israel and was fundamentally an attribute of God, the one who remains faithful to his promises, his covenant with Israel and his law. God's people had been given the responsibility to exemplify God's righteousness on this earth. Zealous obedience to the law did not, and still does not equal righteousness. God wanted and so still wants repentant humble hearts that truly worshiped him.

David wrote, 'For You do not desire sacrifice, or else I would give it; You do not delight in burnt offering. The sacrifices of God are a broken spirit, a broken and contrite heart – these, O God, You will not despise' (Psalm 51:16-17).

God desires to be the God of our hearts and minds and the center of our devotion but no person can achieve this by self-effort. God forgives and declares us righteous only because of our identification by faith with his righteous Son.

> To be righteous is to line up our lives with the claims and principles of a higher authority. It is to have a sense of moral integrity that reflects the very nature of God. It is to accept eagerly and joyfully the responsibilities God gives us through his word as the essence of productive living.
>
> In the practical sense, righteousness completes assignments, keeps promises, pays bills, honours commitments, keeps appointments, strives to be on time, and establishes a reputation of reliability.[32]

Sanctification or holiness

In Leviticus 20:7-8 we hear God commanding the freed Israelites through Moses, 'Consecrate yourselves therefore [set yourselves apart for the LORD], and be holy, for I am the LORD your God. And you shall keep My statutes, and preform them: I am the LORD who sanctifies you [sets you apart].'

In Hebrews 10: 10 and 14 we read, 'By that will [God's] we have been sanctified through the offering of the body of Jesus Christ once for all . . . For by one offering He has perfected forever those who are being sanctified.'

These verses show us that there is a God-part and an us-part to this process which is a one off and yet an ongoing process while

---

[32] *Quiet Times for Couples A Daily Devotional* H. Norman Wright (born 1937) Harvest House Publishers 1990 *December 8th* p365 Quote Paul Walker *How to keep Your Joy* Oliver-Nelson Books 1987 p 80

we are on pilgrimage here. The word sanctified means *being set apart* for God. That is, we are, through Christ set apart to God and called to be set apart from those who do not believe in the work of Christ in our daily lives. Being set apart also means to be made holy.

Bridges tells us that '. . . the writer of Hebrews is telling us to take seriously the necessity of personal, practical holiness. When the Holy Spirit comes into our lives at our salvation, he comes to make us holy in practice. If there is not then at least a yearning in our hearts to live a holy life pleasing to God we need to seriously question whether our faith in Christ is genuine . . . When God saves us through Christ, He not only saves us from the penalty of sin, but also from its dominion . . . To continue to live in sin as a Christian is to go contrary to God's very purpose for our salvation. One of the writers of three centuries ago put it like this; "What a strange kind of salvation do they desire that care not for holiness . . . They would be saved by Christ and yet be out of Christ in a fleshy state . . . They would have their sins forgiven, not that they may walk with God in love, in time to come, but that they may practice their enmity against Him without any fear of punishment."

Holiness, then, is not necessary as a *condition* of salvation – that would be salvation by works – but as a *part* of salvation that is received by faith in Christ. . . The same grace that brings salvation teaches us to renounce ungodly living. We cannot receive half of God's grace. If we have experienced it at all, we will experience not only forgiveness of our sins but also freedom from sin's dominion.

This is the point James is making in . . . (James2:14-26). He is simply telling us that a 'faith' that does not result in works – in a holy life, in other words – is not a living faith but a dead one, no better than that which the demons possess.

. . . the more we grow in holiness, the more we need assurance that the perfect righteousness of Christ is credited to us. . . The Holy Spirit makes us more aware of our lack of holiness to stimulate us to deeper yearning and striving after holiness. But

Satan will attempt to use the Holy Spirit's work [of making us aware of our lack, of how sinful you are with lusts pride etc. still] to discourage you that you are not a genuine Christian after all.' [33]

To be holy is to live out this righteousness in an observable way so that people will see our good works and glorify God (see 1Peter 2:12). To be holy is to be set apart or consecrated for service in the kingdom. It is a behavioural style that thinks like God, loves what God loves, hates what God hates, relates to other people as God has related to us, and acts like God acts.[34]

Propitiation

Romans 3:24b-25a says, '. . . through the redemption that is in Christ Jesus, whom God set forth as a propitiation by His blood, through faith, to demonstrate His righteousness . . .'

Hebrews 2:17, 'Therefore, in all things He had to be made like His brethren, that He might be a merciful and faithful High Priest in things pertaining to God, to make propitiation for the sins of the people.'

1John 2:2 and 4:10 we read, 'And He Himself is the propitiation for our sins, and not for ours only but also for the whole world . . . In this is love, not that we loved God, but that He loved us and sent His Son to be the propitiation for our sins.'

Propitiation, especially in the verses from Romans where it is alluding to the mercy seat of the Old Testament tabernacle which was behind the veil and sat above the ark of testimony where after it was sprinkled by the blood of a lamb for atonement, his priest could meet with Yahweh without fear of being slain by him. Propitiation is seen as *a merciful gift to placate or appease* God's rightful wrath.

Ransom and redeemed

---

[33] *The Pursuit of Holiness* p.38-40, 48.

[34] *Quiet Times for Couples* p 365 Quote from *How to keep your Joy*

In Mark 10:45 we read of how Jesus viewed his reason for being on the earth the first time, '"For even the Son of man did not come to be served, but to serve, and to give His life a ransom for many.'

1Peter 1:18-19 say, 'knowing that you were not redeemed with corruptible things like silver or gold, from your aimless conduct . . But with the precious blood of Christ, as a lamb without blemish and without spot.'

These two words have the picture behind them of freeing slaves by *paying the set price*, to restore them to how they should be.

Anointing

John wrote his first epistle (letter) because pilgrims were, and still are in danger of being deceived by the many alluring lies of false gospel teachers and wanting to encourage as well as warn he wrote, 'But you have an anointing from the Holy One, and you know all things . . . the anointing which you have received from Him abides in you, and you do not need that anyone teach you; but as the same anointing teaches you concerning all things, and is true, and is not a lie, and just as it has taught you, you will abide in Him.' (1John 2:20, 27)

This anointing is the impartation, the giving or sharing, of the Holy Spirit to a pilgrim joining us to Christ the anointed one. As a result, we can know now all things with respect to discerning God's truth from lies and so are enabled to resist the temptations of these and to live godly lives in this world.

The new man

2Corinthians 5:17 tell us that 'if anyone is in Christ, he is a new creation; old things have passed away; behold all things have become new', and Colossians 3:9-10 instruct us what our responsibilities are as a result, 'Do not lie to one another, since you have put off the old man with his deeds, and have put on the new man who is renewed in knowledge according to the image of Him who created him.'

The Greek for *new* does not mean something more recent as in a new pair of shoes as the old have holes, but something having a *different quality or nature.* This nature is one that all pilgrims partake of individually and as the unified body known as the church.

Divine power and divine nature

2Peter 1:2-4, 'Grace and peace be multiplied to you in the knowledge of God and of Jesus our Lord, as His divine power has given to us all things that pertain to life and godliness, through the knowledge of Him who called us by glory and virtue, by which have been given to us exceedingly great and precious promises, that through these you may be partakers of the divine nature, having escaped the corruption that is in the world through lust.'
This is an expression unique in the New Testament. Divine power is the power God used creating everything as well as raising Christ from death. It is this divine power that he has given us along with his divine nature. It is God's power and God's nature within that our spiritual abilities and the power to live a godly life arise from.
The divine nature is God's essential qualities or character which is unchangeable, it is who God is. As pilgrims have been regenerated with this and indwelt by God, we can exhibit the same characteristics individually and as a church.

Glorification

Philippians 3:20-21, 'For our citizenship is in heaven, from which we also eagerly wait for the Saviour, the Lord Jesus Christ, who will transform our lowly body that it may be conformed to His glorious body, according to the working by which He is able even to subdue all things to Himself.'
The glorification of a pilgrim is the final act of redemption by God's work of saving grace and occurs as they are released from this world to arrive home. It is the *final removal of **all** sin*, of all that remains of the old man's nature. This hope above all others makes the cost of being a pilgrim worthwhile in this world.

Only a couple more words or ideas I think we may benefit from defining. Was that a groan?

Christian

A Christian is one who belongs to Christ, a [person] who has been granted a relationship with the exalted Christ at God's right hand.[35]

The label was first used as a term of contempt against believers at Antioch; Acts 11:26; 'And when [Barnabas] had found [Saul], he brought him to Antioch. So it was that for a whole year they assembled with the church and taught a great many people. And the disciples were first called Christians in Antioch.'

Other titles for pilgrims that are used early on in the formation of the church were –

- Brethren for brothers in Christ. Acts 6:3, 'Therefore, brethren, seek out from among you seven men of good reputation, full of the Holy Spirit and wisdom, who we may appoint over this business'
- Disciples. Acts 2:41, 6: 1, 'Then those who gladly received [Peter's] word were baptized; and that day about three thousand souls were added to them . . . Now in those days, when the number of the disciples was multiplying . . .'
- Believers. 1Timothy 4:12, 'Let no one despise your youth, but be an example to the believers in word, in conduct, in love, in spirit, in faith, in purity.'
- Followers of the Way. Acts 9:2, 'and asked letters from [the high priest] to the synagogues of Damascus, so that if he [Saul] found any who were of the Way, whether men or women, he might bring them bound to Jerusalem.'
- Saints. 1Corinthians 1:2, 'To the church of God which is at Corinth, to those who are sanctified in Christ Jesus, called to be saints, with all who in every place call on the name of Jesus Christ our Lord, both theirs and ours.'
- Nazarene. The Jews who denied Christ was the Messiah called pilgrims Nazarenes. Acts 24:5, 'For we have found this man [Saul now called Paul] a plague, a creator of dissension among all

---

[35] Dick Lucas (born 1925) *The Message of Colossians & Philemon* BST Inter-Varsity Press, 1980 p134.

the Jews throughout the world, and a ringleader of the sect of the Nazarenes.'

Cheever writes that 'the Christian life is represented as a race, a work, a labour, a conflict, a warfare. It needs a strong, constant, unwavering purpose, along with the constant, ever present, omnipotent grace of God. God is our all in all. Christ's strength must be made perfect in our weakness. So David says, I will run in the way of thy commandments when thou shalt enlarge my heart. Here is the purpose, I will run; here is the way, thy commandments; here is the soul's dependence, when thou shalt enlarge my heart; and here is the source of power, the grace of God in the heart; in the deep heart. To this Paul answers, Work out your own salvation, with fear and trembling, for it is God that worketh in you both to will and to do. Blessed harmony of God's working and man's working, of God's grace and man's obedience.'[36]

> We aren't called to *become* Christians; we are called to *be* Christians. Don't ever think that faith in Christ is just a type of 'spiritual life insurance', something we obtain and then put away until we need it to get into heaven. The Christian life is *a new journey* – one that will take us the rest of our lives. [37]

Repentance

Acts 17:30-1, Paul speaking, '"Truly, these times of ignorance God overlooked [before the Christ was fully revealed by his birth, death, resurrection and ascension] but now commands all men everywhere to repent, because He has appointed a day on which He will judge the world in righteousness by the Man whom He has ordained. He has given assurance of this to all by raising Him from the dead."'

---

[36] Dr Cheever (George Barrel Cheever 1807-1890) *Bunyan and His Times* The Pilgrim's Progress and other select works p 4

[37] Billy Graham (1918-2018) *The Journey How to live by Faith in an uncertain world* W Publishing Group 2006 p62

The Revelation of Jesus Christ 3:19, Jesus speaking, '"As many as I love, I rebuke and chasten. Therefore be zealous and repent."'

To receive the salvation package your personal repentance of your sins must be given to God by faith and repentance of your sins must continue while you live in this world for, we will still sin as pilgrims and we need our Father's forgiveness and cleansing to maintain a right relationship with him.

To repent is like an apology as in that you are acknowledging a deep feeling of sorrow over your actions toward an injured party – in this instance God – but it is far more as you are resolving by God's grace to turn around 180^0 and never face that way again, never trod that path of rebellion against him again. It is a change of mind, a change of attitude, a deliberate conscious turning from living in and practicing sin, evil, darkness to seeking God's face.

> Repentance means turning from as much as you know of your sin to give as much as you know of yourself to as much as you know of your God, and as our knowledge grows at these three points so our practice of repentance has to be enlarged.[38]

The fear of God

Because I struggled with this concept as a believer, I have included it just in case you might also. This fear of God is far removed from the fear many of us know of in regards to our earthly fathers.

We must always keep in mind that God is always a good loving God for he cannot deny himself and as believers he is our Abba, our forever good and loving Father.

But he is still the sovereign LORD God, much more and bigger than us in every way. It is in this sense of awe and respectful reverence that we fear him. The upside is because pilgrims do rightly fear God, we have nothing else in this world to fear at all and that includes any other person, be they a gentile or a pilgrim.

---

[38] *God's Will* p104

Psalm 27:1, 'The LORD is my light and my salvation; whom shall I fear? The LORD is the strength of my life; of whom shall I be afraid?'

Psalm 130:3-4, 'If You, LORD should mark iniquities, O Lord, who could stand? But there is forgiveness with You, that You may be feared.'

Luke 12:4-5, '"And I [Jesus] say to you, My friends, do not be afraid of those who kill the body, and after that have no more that they can do. But I will show you whom you should fear: Fear Him, who, after He has killed, has power to cast into hell; yes, I say to you fear Him!"'

> Fear . . . is a worship-word; it means not panic and alarm, but awe and adoration . . . This fear of the Lord is reverence – with boldness, yes – but reverence linked with awe at God's greatness, and an active, deep concern to obey and please Him. . . what the reference to fear and trembling means in Phil. 2:12-13 . . . the reason for the awe and reverence: 'for it is God who works in you, both to will and to work for His good pleasure' . . . Every right thought we manage to think and every right action we manage to preform, is God's work in us and His gift to us. This realization evokes deep awe and deep gratitude and an ongoing sense of humble dependence on the God who thus confirms to us that he is ours and we are His. This state of mind is at the heart of the human reality labelled 'the fear of the Lord'.[39]

The balanced ministry of the Holy Spirit is in giving us a sure fast hope of acceptance in God because of Christ and the awareness that God is a consuming fire, the fear or reverent respect of God and his rights in our lives is the goad to keep us from backsliding,

---

[39] Ibid p125-127

growing cold and apostasy and leads us to look to God's power and willingness to work in us rather than looking within. [40]

God's will

1Timothy 2:4, '[God] desires all men to be saved and to come to the knowledge of the truth.'

1Thessalonians 4:3, 7 and 5:18, 'For this is the will of God, your sanctification: that you should abstain from sexual immorality . . . For God did not call us to uncleanness but in holiness. . . in everything give thanks; for this is the will of God in Christ Jesus for you.'

The big picture of God's revealed will which is shown to us in his word has two parts. Firstly, that all unbelieving sinful rebels would accept his gracious provision of salvation and become pilgrims and secondly, that as pilgrims we would humbly and obediently let his work of sanctification have its perfect work in us by submitting to the leadership of his Spirit to live a morally pure or holy life, using our renewed minds to discern how to apply what his word says to the situations we are faced with each and every day of our pilgrimage here.

God's sovereignty

This is the supreme authority of God to do as he wishes, which is logical when you consider that he is God, creator and ruler of all he has made, which is everything including humanity.

Bridges writes that 'No plan of God's can be thwarted; when He acts, no one can reverse it; no one can hold back His hand or bring Him to account for His actions. God does as He pleases, only as He pleases, and works out every event to bring out the accomplishment of His will. Such a bare unqualified statement of the sovereignty of God would terrify us, if that were all we knew about God. But God is not only sovereign, He is perfect in love and infinite in wisdom . . . Confidence in the sovereignty of God in *all* that affects us is crucial to our trusting Him. *If there is a single*

---

[40] Notes from Gables' sermon series on Pilgrim's Progress #16*The Interpreter's House* #8*The 7th room*. 1.16.1999

event in all of the universe that can occur outside of God's sovereign control, then we cannot trust Him. His love may be infinite, but if His power is limited and His purpose can be thwarted, we cannot trust Him. . . [BUT] . . . Nothing is so small or trivial as to escape the attention of God's sovereign control; nothing is so great as to be beyond His power to control it . . . Philip Hughes said, 'Under God . . .all things are without exception fully controlled – despite all appearances to the contrary. [consider the death and burial of Christ] . . . God has an overarching purpose for all believers: to conform us to the likeness of His Son, Jesus Christ (see Romans 8:29). He also has a specific purpose for each of us that is His unique tailor-made plan for our individual life (see Ephesians 2:10). As Psalm 138:8 says, 'The LORD will fulfil his purpose for me'. Because we know God's directing our lives to an ultimate end and because we know God's sovereignly able to orchestrate the events of our lives toward that end, we can trust Him. We can commit to Him not only the ultimate outcome of our lives, but also all the intermediate events and circumstances that will bring us to that outcome.

Alexander Carson [1776-1844] said

> God's sovereignty is always to his people in wisdom in love. This is the difference between sovereignty in God and sovereignty in man. We dread the sovereignty of man, because we have no security of its being exercised in mercy, or even justice: we rejoice in the sovereignty of God, because we are sure it is always exercised for the good of his people.'[41]

Fleetwood wrote that '[Jesus] taught them [the disciples] that the Almighty Father of the whole was the guardian and protector of every being in the universe; that every action is subject to his will, and nothing is left to the blind determination of chance. And is we

---

[41] Jerry Bridges *Trusting God* Navpress 2008 p 35, 25, 29, 17, 35-36.142

direct our lives according to the divine will, we have surely no reason to be anxious about the necessaries of life.'[42]

Do I trust this God enough to surrender my life into his sovereign hands unconditionally? This does not require me to understand everything about him or his work first, it just requires me to trust in his love.

God's providence

We could just as easily say, 'In God's wisdom he does...'
Bridges tells us that the 'well-known theologian J. I. Packer defines providence as:

> "The unceasing activity of the Creator whereby, in overflowing bounty and good will, he upholds His creatures in ordered existence, guides and governs all events, circumstances, and free acts of angels and men, and directs everything to its appointed goal, for His own glory." ...

For my own sake, I have developed a slightly shorter definition... *God's providence is His constant care for and His absolute rule over all His creation for His own glory and the good of His people..* Nothing, not even the smallest virus, escapes His control... note... the twofold objective of God's providence: His own glory and the good of His people. These two objects ... are always in harmony with each other. God never pursues His glory at the expense of the good of His people, nor does He ever seek our good at the expense of His glory. He has designed His eternal purpose so that His glory and our good are extricably bound together ... If we are going to learn to trust God in adversity, we must believe that just as certainly as God will allow nothing to subvert His glory, so He will allow nothing to spoil the good He is working out in us and for us.'[43]

Prayer

1Thessalonians 5:17, 'pray without ceasing'.

---

[42] *Fleetwood's Life of Christ*. p163
[43] *Trusting God* p13-14

James 1:5-8 and 5:16b, 'If any of you lacks wisdom, let him ask of God, who gives to all liberally and without reproach, and it will be given to him. But let him ask in faith, with no doubting, for he who doubts is like a wave of the sea driven and tossed by the wind. For let not that man suppose that he will receive anything from the Lord; he is a double-minded man unstable in all his ways . . . The effective fervent prayer of a righteous man avails much.'

Romans 8:26, '. . .The Spirit also helps in our weaknesses. For we do not know what we should pray for as we ought, but the Spirit Himself makes intercession for us with groanings which cannot be uttered.'

Prayer is simply a pilgrim or a group of believers talking to God about anything, big or small, or anyone, be they fellow pilgrims, unbelievers or themselves, that they have joy over, concern for, or needs as a result. There is no magic needed for private prayers, no special place, posture, feeling or emotion, words, tone or time, just a need to connect with your Father with the Spirit's help.

Mark 9:24b, '"Lord, I believe; help my unbelief!"', is an example of fervent and effective praying.

Campbell tells us that 'Our Lord is particularly empathic on the importance of importunity in prayer. Prayer is a matter in which for more depends on the spirit than on the letter of the exercise. The expression may be very defective, and yet the prayer be such as has power with God. In prayer, the doctrinal element ought, of course, to be Scripturally correct and thoroughly evangelical, but the great . . . and distinguishing feature ought to be the sentiment, emotional, expression of desire, direct intercourse with God. Mere meditation is not prayer; Scripture exposition is not prayer; the enunciation of a creed is not prayer. All these, however, and much besides of a kindred character, have too frequently occupied the place is, direct intercourse with God; which, however, admits of the utmost variety of thought and expression. As an example of this direct address, the Lord's Prayer is perfect. Devotion makes no account of rhetoric. The attempt at offering "an eloquent prayer" is an abomination. Everything declamatory, and all that savours of display, is an outrage. Simplicity, humility, devoutness, few words and many things, strong faith, and strong feelings – these are among the prime qualities of true devotion. Christians do well to consider the importance which the Saviour attaches to prayer for the Holy Spirit, since on his indwelling presence and almighty power everything turns.'[44]

And Spurgeon advises that 'Prayer is an available resource for all kinds of dilemmas or difficulties. In *The Pilgrims' Progress*, when the City of Mansoul was besieged, it was in the depth of winter and the roads were very bad, but even then prayer could travel on them. I will venture to affirm that if all earthly roads were so bad that they could not be travelled, and if Mansoul were completely, surrounded, so that there was not a gap left through which we could break our way to get to the king, the road upward would always be open. No enemy can barricade that; no blockading ships can sail between our souls and the haven of the mercy seat. The ship of prayer can sail through all temptations, doubts, and fears, straight up to the throne of God, and while she may have left the port with only griefs and groans and sighs, she will return loaded with a wealth of blessings. You have hope . . . for you can always pray.'[45]

Can I hear you wondering why on earth am I putting all this information before you? It is because this is foundational to what we now are, this is what a pilgrim is. These words and concepts are not just letters on paper, they are what makes us citizens of God's kingdom and not of this world any longer and show as a result why we are a peculiar people and why our mindset must be of not belonging, of being in the world but not of the world. These words tell us of our God's vast enabling provisions. These words and concepts tell us that as pilgrims we have been crucified with Christ and the following tale told by Tozer gives us a good picture of what this means for our way of thinking and so being.

---

[44] *Fleetwood's Life of Christ* comment from Dr Campbell's Expository Bible p366
[45] Charles Spurgeon *Finding Peace in Life's Storms* Whitaker House 1997 p90

'A young man came to an old saint and asked him, "What does it mean to be crucified with Christ?

After thinking for a moment, the old saint said, "To be crucified means three things. First, the man who is crucified is facing in only one direction. You cannot turn around to see what is going on behind you. You stopped looking back and look straight ahead. The man on the cross is looking in only one direction, and that is the direction of God, Christ, and the Holy Spirit, in the direction of biblical revelation, of angels, and edifying of the church, the direction of sanctification and the Spirit-filled life. He is looking only in one direction."

Then the old man thought for a moment and said, "One thing more about a man on a cross; he is not going back . . . He is not coming back. When you go out to die on a cross, you say good-bye to your friends, you kiss your friends good-bye, and you are not coming back. . ."

"Another thing about the man on a cross," said the man, "he has no further plans of his own. Someone else has made his plans for him. On the way up the hill, he does not see a friend and say to him, 'Well, Henry, next Saturday afternoon about three we'll go fishing up by the lake.' He is not going fishing. He is finished. He is going out to die; he has no plans at all."' [46]

These words and concepts are why we are expected to and are able to adopt an un-worldly mindset, a new God-glorifying way of thinking and therefore of being. God has freed us and given us the enabling. We pilgrims then are responsible to do the visible works that prove, if you like, the truth of our invisible internal new birth, the truth of these concepts and words. We work out our own, not someone else's, salvation for the watching world to witness.

How Satan messes with our minds

---

[46] A. W. Tozer (1897-1963) *Delighting in God* compiled and edited by James L. Snyder Bethany House Publishers 2015 p86-87.

But a new mindset will never be easy to adopt and one reason for this is that our adversary will be attempting to mess with our minds.

Bridges explains that 'When God originally created man, the reason, the emotions and the will all worked in perfect harmony. Reason led the way in understanding the will of God, the will consented to God's will, and the emotions delighted in doing it. But with the entrance of sin into man's soul, these three faculties began to work at cross purposes to one another and God. The will has become stubborn and rebellious and will not consent to that which reason knows to be the will of God. Or, more commonly, the emotions get the upper hand and draw away both reason and will from obedience to God . . .

With new birth our reason is again enlightened, our affections and desires redirected, and our wills subdued. But . . . this . . . is a growing process. We are told to renew our minds (Rom.12:2) to set our affections on things above (Col.3:1) and to submit our wills to God (Ja. 4:7) . . . While the will is the ultimate determiner of all choices, it is influenced in its choices by the strongest forces brought to bear upon it . . . these . . . forces . . . reach our wills through either our reason or our emotions.

Therefore, we must guard what enters our minds and what influences our emotions . . . David guarded his way with the Word of God (Ps.119:9).

The Bible speaks primarily through our reason, and this is why it is so vitally important for our minds to be constantly brought under its influence . . .

It is helpful first to realize that while God most often appeals to our wills through our reason, sin and Satan usually appeal to us through our desires . . .

In the final analysis it is God who works in us to will and to act according to His good purpose. But we are expressly told by Paul to work at this ourselves (Ph.2:12). Our responsibility regarding our wills is to guard our minds and emotions, being aware of what influences our minds and stimulates our desires.'[47](Italics mine)

Reason determines, that a greater and more permanent good hereafter is preferable to a less and fleeting enjoyment at present: faith realizes, as attainable, a felicity infinitely more valuable than all which this world can possibly propose to us; so that in this respect the life of faith is the reign of reason over passion, while unbelief makes way for the triumph of passion over reason. Nor can anything be more essential to practical religion than an abiding conviction, that it is the only true wisdom, uniformaly and cheerfully to part with every temporal good, whenever it interfers with the grand concerns of eternity.[48]

Now when [Christian] was got up to the top of the hill [called Difficulty] there came two men running against him amain; the name of the one was Timorous, and of the other Mistrust: to whom Christian said, Sirs, what's the matter you run the wrong way? Timorous answered, that they were going to the city of Zion, and had got up that difficult place: but, said he, the further we go the more danger we meet with; wherefore we turned, and are going back again. Yes, said Mistrust, for just before us lie a couple of lions in the way, (whether sleeping or waking we know not;) and we could not think, that is we came within reach, but they would presently pull us in pieces.

Then said Christian, you make me afraid: but whither shall I flee to be safe? If I go back to my own country, *that* is prepared for fire and brimstone, and, I shall certainly perish there: if I can get to the Celestial City, I am sure to be in safety there. I must venture: to go back is nothing but death; to go forward is fear of death, and life everlasting beyond it. I will yet go forward'. So Mistrust and Timorous ran down the hill and Christian went on his way.[49]

---

[47] *The Pursuit of Holiness* p 126-7, 128, 131.
[48] *The Pilgrim's Progress* comment by Scott (Thomas Scott 1747-1821) p67
[49] *The Pilgrims Progress* p83

Christian shakes off fear, by sound scriptural reasoning; even the reasoning of faith, against the fear of the flesh, and mistrust or unbelief. We have always a sure word of prophesy, whereunto we shall do well to take heed. When dangers beset, and fears assault, remember whose ye are, and whom ye serve: look to the way you are in, and the end of your faith, even the salvation of your soul. Study the word of God, and obey it.[50]

Our reason, enlightened by the Holy Spirit through the Word of God, stands in the way of sin gaining mastery over us through our desires. Therefore Satan's great strategy is to deceive our minds . . Deceit of the mind is carried on by degrees little by little. We are first drawn away from watchfulness, then from obedience. [51]

Peter in 1Peter 5:8 instructs us to be 'sober, be vigilant; because your adversary the devil walks about like a roaring lion, seeking whom he may devour.'

Perhaps Peter knew how much this alertness is needed because he personally experienced the consequences of not being watchful, awake and praying like his Lord had instructed on that dark night of Christ's betrayal.

The Greek word used here that is translated as *sober* is also used in 1Peter 1:13 where we read, 'Therefore gird up the loins of your mind, be sober, and rest your hope fully upon the grace that is to be brought to you at the revelation of Jesus Christ', where it means to abstain from wine, to be sober and watchful.

Paul warns pilgrims to be careful what sort of spirit they allow to control them as we read in Ephesians 5:8-11, 15-21, 'For you were once darkness, but now you are light in the Lord. Walk as children of light (for the fruit of the Spirit is in all goodness, righteousness, and truth), finding out what is acceptable to the Lord. And have no fellowship with the unfruitful works of darkness, but rather expose them . . . See then that you walk circumspectly, not as fools but as wise, redeeming the time, because the days are evil.

---

[50] Ibid comment by Mason p83
[51] *The Pursuit of Holiness* p 67

Therefore do not be unwise, but understand what the will of the Lord is. And do not be drunk with wine, in which is dissipation; but be filled with the Spirit, speaking to one another in psalms and hymns and spiritual songs, singing and making melody in your heart to the Lord, giving thanks always for all things to God the Father in the name of our Lord Jesus Christ, submitting to one another in the fear of God.'

Yes, we have been given the Spirit when we became pilgrims, but because the Greek present tense is used here, we learn that the filling is not a once-for-all experience. Jesus has already taught us this is how it will be for pilgrims as we read in John 7:37-39a, 'On the last day, that great day of the feast [of tabernacles], Jesus stood and cried out saying, "If anyone thirsts, let him come to Me to drink. He who believes in Me, as the Scripture has said, out of his heart will flow rivers of living water." But this He spoke concerning the Spirit, whom those believing in Him would receive', that the Spirit will so keep filling us that he will flow out of us as a river, a fountain that never ceases to gush forth so others may drink, be saved and never experience spiritual thirst again.

Question: Why is Paul commanding us to be filled with one and not the other?

Answer: What do you think would be more honouring to our Father for all he has equipped us with, to be so filled with an alcoholic spirit that our brain struggles to fire off coordinated electrical messages for our muscles fibers to twitch in the right way, to work together so we can stand let alone make the Spirit's directed, life choices which honour God, or to be so under the influence of his Spirit that all we think, say or do will be controlled by him?

There is another reason for us to be soberly watchful that has in some ways nothing to do with being in enemy territory yet everything to do with not yet being home. Christ is going to return again to our earth but as judge and King. But more on this much later.

Robyn Crothers

All new, now what?

So no longer a pagan, an uncircumcised gentile, but a Christian, a believer in the one true God, a pilgrim who is a new creation, under a new master with a new journey, a new destination, a new mindset and so a mind needing renewal which leads to new goals, new behaviours, new lifestyle, new . . . new . . . new . . .

If you are anything like me all this new stuff can take a bit of getting used to, a bit like new clothes or shoes that feel restrictive, scratchy even blister making till they've been worn a while. I felt uncomfortable, not sure how to be, how to belong. Home was no longer home as none of my family are Christian. The face in the mirror was the same but the thoughts and feelings swirling behind the eyes were not.

I'm not good at throwing out those seen-better-days things, those shoes or slippers (I've got them on now) that have become soooo comfortable, no longer rubbing or pinching making blisters, the dressing-gown that wraps around you in a warm hug like an old friend, that chair you've always sat in, the old that we have lived with for such a long time that now has many memories attached, that we have become comfortable with, at home with can be very, so very hard to give up, to leave or put aside, yes even those 'somethings' that are not necessarily good for us or nice to us can be hard. All habits, our set ways, good or bad, are hard to change. A mindset is no different. Both require Spirit empowered discipline and prayer to last.

But we are now new, different. We belong to a new master. Not only do we have to adopt the mindset of being a pilgrim here in what had been home but is no longer, we must behave accordingly, after all we have been plucked from the filth and mire of our sin and placed in a kingdom whose city is of pure gold, like clear glass as heirs to the King of Kings! A new way, not the old comfortable-without-thought-ways or habits of our past and to behave differently we must begin to think differently.

<u>Question</u>: So how are we meant to keep and grow this new mindset?

<u>Answer</u>: This is going to be a long and round-a-bout answer with more questions, so make yourself comfortable . . .
I've had several years of counselling for post-traumatic stress disorder some years back, which involved cognitive therapy to give me skills that would enable me to make many changes to the way I thought. My brain was in need of 're-wiring'. I was taught that the responses to stress start in the mind, in the thinking before the brain and body responds. So, the best place to stop wrongful reactions or responses (such as the rush of adrenaline 'cos I've gotta run) was to stop them where they started, in my mind (I'm not safe). For me this was hard and mentally exhausting work that made my body physically tired as well. And slow! Much slower than wearing in a pair of new shoes or jeans!

- Firstly, I had to identify and name the event then acknowledge and name the old painful feelings and beliefs behind them and the inappropriate actions that resulted by jotting them down on paper.
- Secondly, I had to answer four simple, but not easy-to-do-so questions about the old belief or thought I'd named with a 'Yes' or 'No' and 'why'.

    Is it fact – reality or truth?
    Is it nurturing me?
    Is it helping me meet my goals? (This meant I had to now figure out if I even had any!)
    Is it keeping me in inappropriate conflict with others?

- Thirdly, if three of these questions were answered negatively that old belief or thought was irrational and had to be replaced by the truth, by the new rational belief which I had to acknowledge on my bit of paper.
- Fourthly, I had to *put off the old* way of thinking and so behaving.
- Fifthly, I had *to put on the new*, right beliefs, thoughts and resulting feelings and behaviours.

In short, (after you've waded through all that) I was asked to intervene and dispute my old beliefs, choices or thoughts that arose from the event in such a manner that I was given a new feeling, belief therefore a new behaviour which gave a better, a healthier outcome for that event.

Feelings are neither good nor bad, they are just what you are feeling. However, it is how you handle them, how you respond (not react which is done unthinkingly) as a result, the action that your feelings cause is what will be good or bad.

My behaviour arising from my feelings can either have a good or bad result for me and others. However, another's behaviour towards me, or towards another that I see or hear, can stir up feelings within me that may result in me reacting badly if I can't slow things down inside to be able to consider a proper response. For example, someone speaking in a loud aggressively angry tone either at my face or within my hearing can still send me into a flight reaction quicker than I can work out a more normal response. Yet this person's way of conversing may trouble no one else. This scenario can also be true for other activities that may have a more obvious sinful hue to them.

> It may not be the activity itself that determines whether something is sinful for us, but rather our response to that activity . . . Many activities, strictly speaking, are morally neutral, but because of some immoral associations in a person's past may be detrimental to that person, at least for a time. Those of us who do not have that immoral association must be considerate of these people lest we cause them to slip back into an activity that is sinful for them.[52]

<u>Question</u>: How are we to respond in areas where pilgrims have convictions as to what is God's will for a certain situation which are different from their brethren's?

<u>Answer</u>: Paul has laid down three general principals found in Romans 14: 1-4, 5-8, 23 to guide us, which say, 'Receive one who is weak in the faith, but not to disputes over doubtful things. For one believes he may eat all things, but he who is weak eats only

---

[52] *The Pursuit of Holiness* p92, 93

vegetables [this is not about being vegetarian but if a pilgrim should be seen eating meat that he and others knew had been used in worshiping an idol]. Let not him who eats despise him who does not eat, and let not him who does not eat judge him who eats; for God has received [accepted] him. Who are you to judge another's servant? To his own master he stands or falls. Indeed, he will be made to stand, for God is able to make him stand. . . One person esteems one day above another; another esteems every day alike. Let each be fully convinced in his own mind. He who observes the day, observe it to the Lord; and he who does not observe the day, to the Lord he does not observe it. He who eats, eats to the Lord, for he gives God thanks; and he who does not eat, to the Lord he does not eat, and gives God thanks. For none of us lives to himself, and no one dies to himself. For if we live, we live to the Lord; and if we die, we die to the Lord. Therefore, whether we live or die, we are the Lord's. . . But he who doubts is condemned if he eats, because he does not eat from faith; for whatever is not from faith is sin.'

> The first is that we should not judge those whose convictions are different from ours (v.1-4).
>
> The second principle is that whatever our convictions are, they must be 'to the Lord,' that is, developed out of a sense of obedience to Him (verses 5-8).
>
> The third principle is that whatever convictions we have developed as 'to the Lord,' we must be true to them (verse 23).
>
> If we go against our convictions, we are sinning, even though others may have perfect freedom in that particular thing.[53]

Now back to me re-wiring my brain with an example to show the relevance of my disclosure of personal stuff.

One that I still have to work on is to develop a picture of my worth and value from God's point of view (after all it is only his point of

---

[53] Ibid p 93

view that is eternal), what he says about me in his word and not from the many false voices of my past.

This is the doing of Romans 12:2 which tells us, 'And do not be conformed to this world, but be transformed by the renewing of your mind, that you may prove what is that good and acceptable and perfect will of God.'

The verb, being in the present tense, shows that the action will be continuous, a lifelong process while the word *mind* describes the way you think, the way you look at life as a daily process. I had to intentionally choose how to respond to life rather than do the old automatic reactions of my past that kept me in the dirt of 'not good enough'. Being dependant on God's provisions, I still have the responsibility to use my mental capacities, my brain, to work out and show the truth, the proof of God's ways being best, his will for me being good. These new mindsets, discernments are born by spending time, much time regularly and prayerfully in God's word and avoiding things like films and people who speak and treat women or children disrespectfully, contemptuously, like dirt.

Question: Did you notice my italics before in the fourth and fifth steps of my cognitive therapy section . . . *put off* . . . *put on*?

Answer: Well there was a reason.

The apostle Paul in Ephesians 4:17-24 writes, 'This I say, therefore, and testify in the Lord, that you should no longer walk as the rest of the Gentiles walk, in the futility of their mind, having their understanding darkened, being alienated from the life of God, because of the ignorance that is in them, because of the blindness of their heart; who, being past feeling, have given themselves over to lewdness, to work all uncleanness with greediness. But you have not so learned Christ, if indeed you have heard Him and have been taught by Him, as the truth is in Jesus: that you put off, concerning your former conduct, the old man which grows corrupt according to the deceitful lusts, and be renewed in the spirit of your mind, and that you put on the new man which was created according to God, in true righteousness and holiness.'

Did you see my reason?

Paul is teaching us here the foundational basis of our new life by comparing what we were before with what we are now and showing us why this has happened. As pagan gentiles our mind's workings were futile, never good but now with Christ everything is changed, is new.

Stott writes that 'What is immediately noteworthy is the apostle's emphasis on the intellectual factor in everybody's way of life . . . First, we have experienced a new creation, and secondly, in consequence, we have received a new mind which is constantly being renewed . . . It is our new creation which has given us a new mind; and it is our new mind which understands our new creation and its implications . . . .[The theme of this section of Ephesians4:7-5:4] is the integration of Christian experience (what we are), Christian theology (what we believe) and Christian ethics (how we behave). They emphasize that being, thought and action belong together and must never be separated. For what we are governs how we think and how we think determines how we act. We are God's new society, a people who put off the old life and put on the new; that is what he has made us. So we need to recall this by the daily renewal of our minds, remembering how we 'learned Christ . . . as the truth is in Jesus', and thinking Christianly about ourselves And our new status . . . it is only when we have grasped clearly who we are in Christ, that the desire will grow within us to live a life that is worthy of our calling and fitting to our character as God's new society.'[54]

So, put off the old and put on the new. Adopt those new ways of thinking, new attitudes, and new choices leading to new Christ like behaviours.

<u>Question</u>: How can you decide if a course of action is the right, good choice, the best or the worst?

---

[54]John Stott (1921-2011) *The Message of Ephesians God's new Society* The Bible Speaks Today Series IVP 1997 p 175, 183, 193-4

Answer: I read this a long time ago in one of my many books and because it was very helpful to me at that time and still is, I'm passing it on.

How to know right from wrong:
A powerful way of developing convictions.

"Everything is permissible for me' – but not everything is beneficial" (1Cor. 6:12)

1. Is it helpful – physically, spiritually, and mentally?

"Everything is permissible for me' – but I will not be mastered by anything" (1Cor. 6:12)

2. Does it bring me under its power?

"Therefore, if what I eat causes my brother to fall into sin, I will never eat meat again, so that I will not cause him to fall" (1Cor. 8:13)

3. Does it hurt others?

"So whether you eat or drink or whatever you do, do it all for the glory of God" (1Cor. 10:31)

4. Does it glorify God? [55]

Paul has some additional counsel how to keep and grow this new mindset we have been given in another of his letters, Philippians 2:12-16a where we read, 'Therefore, my beloved . . . work out your own salvation with fear and trembling; for it is God who works in you both to will and to do for His good pleasure [or purpose] Do all things without complaining and disputing, that you may become blameless and harmless children of God without fault in the midst of a crooked and perverse generation, among whom you shine as lights in the world, holding fast the word of life.'

Jeremiah writes, '[Therefore . . .] What has Paul said? Paul has said that Jesus Christ came from heaven . . . He was obedient unto the death of the cross. He humbled himself, he died, he was buried, he was resurrected, and he ascended to a high; and every knee shall bow and every tongue confess . . . Therefore, and then he gives us our instructions . . . Doctrine is always the foundation

---

[55] *The Pursuit of Holiness* p91

upon which duty rests. . . He is saying because you're saved, there's somethings you should do. . . We can't do anything to be saved. But once we become Christians, God begins to work in us so that we can have a part both in our own growth and sanctification and also in the opportunity that he gives us to reach the world . . . Who really is responsible for your spiritual growth . . "Timothy exercise yourself toward godliness" [1Timothy 3:7b] And the word exercise . . . It's the word 'gumnasia' in Greek . . . He said to Timothy, 'get into the spiritual gymnasium and work out and grow your faith . . . take this seriously.'
God has given us everything we need for life and godliness. He's put it in us . . . Now, what the Scripture is saying, 'Take what I've given you and develop it and make it work and practice it . . . Notice verse 13 . . . God has worked in us, he's working in us, he will continue to work in us, but we're to work diligently so that we might realize the benefit of all that God has done, and is doing for us . . . Discipline one is, I'm going to do my part. Discipline two is, God's going to do his part . . . third discipline, I will do my part. I will depend on God . . . I will be different from the world . . . we are to be people who have a cheerful life in an unhappy world. What Paul is saying is if you work it out in your own life and you take what God has given you and you develop these disciplines, you won't be a complainer. That'll get off your list . . . next . . . straight living in a crooked world . . . And this doesn't mean we have to live perfectly. He didn't say that you may become perfect. He said blameless and harmless. That means live a life that nobody can point a finger at you . . . 'harmless' means to be pure, unmixed. . . 'crooked' . . . is the word . . . from which we get 'scoliosis' . . . Paul says, 'The world is crooked. Stand up straight . . The Bible says "Shine. Live the right life. Don't be harmful and don't do things that will deny who you are as a Christian. But you have to take it a step further 'cause they're going to come and ask

you, and when they ask you, hold forth the Word of Life. Give them the message of the Gospel.'"[56]

And for Paul the message of the gospel was 'Jesus Christ, and Him crucified' (1Corinthians 2:2).

In Romans 6: 9-13 we read, 'knowing that Christ, having been raised from the dead, dies no more. Death no longer has dominion over Him. For the death that He died, He died to sin once for all; but the life that He lives, He lives to God. Likewise you also, reckon [consider] yourselves to be dead indeed to sin, but alive to God in Christ Jesus our Lord. Therefore do not let sin reign in your mortal body, that you should obey it in its lusts. And do not present your members [as in arms, legs, brain etc.] as instruments of unrighteousness to sin, but present your selves to God as being alive from the dead, and your members as instruments of righteousness to God.'

Bridges writes, '. . . do not let . . . Paul is addressing our wills . . . our dying to sin is the result of union with Christ not something we do but something Christ has done . . . our dying to sin is fact because Christ died to sin all united with him died to sin . . . We are not to let sin reign . . . NOTE this IS NOT THE SAME AS DIE . . . our daily experience with regard to sin is determined . . . by our will – by whether we allow sin to reign . . . But our will must be influenced by the fact that we died to sin . . . Christians tend to sin out of habit . . . Though we have been delivered from the kingdom to sin and its rule we have not been delivered from its attacks . . . You cannot say to a slave, "Live as a free man", but you can say that to someone delivered from slavery. Now that we are in fact dead to sin – to its rule and reign – we are to count on that as being true. We are to keep before us this fact that we are no longer slaves. We can now stand up to sin and say no to it. Before we had no choice; now we have one. When we sin as Christians

---

[56] David Jeremiah (born 1941) sermon on Philippians 2:12-15 *The Joy of Responsibility* sermons.love

we do not sin as slaves but as individuals with the freedom to choose. We sin because we choose to . . .' [57]

So as a pilgrim, you and I sin as Adam and Eve did before the fall. We make the choice to obey Satan rather than God.

Bridges advises that 'We are to put off our old self – our sinful disposition and its habits – and put on the new self – with its character and habits of holiness . . . Breaking sinful habits must be done in co-operation with the Holy Spirit and in dependence upon Him . . . determination . . . based upon sheer human resolve, has never once broken the shackles of sin. But there are practical principles which we can follow to train ourselves in godliness.

<u>Principle 1</u> Habits are developed and reinforced by *frequent repetition* . . . The more we say no to sin, the more we are inclined to say no.

<u>Principle 2</u> In breaking sinful habits and acquiring new ones . . . *never let an exception occur*. When we allow exceptions we are reinforcing old habits, or else failing to reinforce the new one . . . watch the 'just this once' type thinking. [Hmmm that might explain why the diet does not last long.]

<u>Principle 3</u> . . . *diligence in all areas is required to insure success in one area.* . . . We may feel that a particular habit 'isn't too bad' but continually giving in to that habit weakens our wills against the onslaughts of temptation from other directions. This is the reason, for example, that it is so important to develop habits of self-control over physical appetites [the diet again] . . . such indulgences weaken our wills in every other respect of our lives.

Remember however . . . *don't be discouraged by failure*. There is a vast difference between failing and becoming a failure. We become a failure when we give up – when we stop trying. [So back to that diet, again.]' [58]

How condemning are those words we read before, *We sin because we choose to*, after all our Lord has done for us.

---

[57] *The Pursuit of Holiness* p 54-59.
[58] Ibid. p 134-136

How? Why?

I don't know about you but I seem to be rather prone to being forgetful. Forgetting where I put my glasses or the car keys or even parked the car is very frustrating but to forget what we have in Christ now, what we now are in Christ and to live accordingly is far worse, it's putting ourselves back into a mindset of bondage while we are actually free!

In Matthew 16:13-23 we get to read of two questions that Jesus asks the twelve disciples, who men say he is then who they, the disciples say he is. With Simon Peter's answer, "You are the Christ, the Son of the living God." Jesus pronounces him blessed because God the Father has revealed this to him and this statement of who the Christ Jesus is, is the rock which his church will be built upon. As a result, Jesus begins to teach them what is to happen to him, the Son of the living God and Peter cannot handle this, this is not the way it is to be and he tells Jesus so. Jesus responds saying, "Get behind Me, Satan! You are an offense to Me, for you are not mindful of the things of God, but the things of men." Jesus then goes on to tell the disciples that they must give up self, all self to follow him.

Anderson comments, '"Dost thou," as if he had said, "my disciple, so far forget thyself as to become my teacher – my follower, as to become my master? Dost thou so far forget who I am, and whom thou hast just confessed me to be, as to take hold of me? Get thee behind me. If thou wilt be my disciple, *be* it, and not what thou art presuming to be, my teacher and adviser . . ."

From the conduct of Peter, which he found it necessary thus severely to censure, our Lord takes occasion to describe, both for his sake . . . and, indeed, of all who should profess to be such the character of the true disciple . . . must follow him considerately, exclusively, and entirely . . . he must 'deny himself' – his understanding, his will, his affections, his ease, and that which is so dear to man, his own enjoyment and aggrandizement, - self in all its forms and ends; for these he must cease to live as chief

ends, or should they interfere or be inconsistent with making Christ the chief end, live in anyway, or to any degree at all . . .' [59]
We pilgrims must be mindful of who Christ is and who we are in him. We must use our God-given brains and remember. How long, I often wonder, will it take me, us to realize as pilgrims we are free-from-sin's tyranny and control and consistently live like it?
My question has reminded me of something written by Charles R. Swindoll that I once read and copied into my diary some years ago now . . .

> Where did we pick up the idea that God is mad or irritated with us? Knowing that all of God's wrath was poured out on His Son at His death on the cross, how can we think like that? As a matter of fact, the reason he brought Jesus back from the grave is that he was satisfied with His Son. Ponder this: If the Father is satisfied with His Son's full payment for sin, and we are in His Son by grace through faith, then He is satisfied with you and me. How long must we Christians live before we finally believe that?

Yet remember back to Bridges' third principle and the words *don't be discouraged by failure* and remember that our God is a forgiving God, so confess that you have stuffed up yet again and seek his aid to stop doing so in that area of your life.
In 1John1:5-2:2 we read, 'This is the message which we have heard from Him and declared to you, that God is light and in Him is no darkness at all. If we say that we have fellowship with Him, and walk in darkness, we lie and do not practice the truth. But if we walk in the light as He is in the light, we have fellowship with one another, and the blood of Jesus Christ His Son cleanses us from all sin. If we say we have no sin, we deceive ourselves, and the truth is not in us. If we confess our sins, He is faithful and just to forgive us our sins and to cleanse us from all unrighteousness. If we say that we have not sinned, we make Him a liar, and His

---

[59] *Fleetwood's Life of Christ* comment from Anderson's (possibly Henry Tompkins Anderson 1812-1872) Life of Christ. p284

word is not in us. My little children, these things I write to you, so that you may not sin. And if anyone sins, we have an Advocate with the Father, Jesus Christ the righteous. And He Himself is the propitiation for our sins, and not for ours only but also for the whole world.'

Pilgrims, having owned up to their sin state and been washed of their sin by Christ's blood, are to make a disciplined practice of walking in the light of God's truth in the company of other pilgrims and not the darkness of sin anymore with those who love the world and its sinful practices.

However, since we are not yet perfected pilgrims we will sin (though we should not) and our God knows this. O the joy of having an advocate, of being able to confess and have our 'feet' washed! Every new day gives us a chance to fall into the dirt of sin yet again but also a chance to look up to our loving Father anew and seek his forgiveness and strength to get up, dressing our wounds and returning us to our walking of the pilgrimage he has set us on till he welcomes us home.

Enmity, suffering and obedience

It is because of all that we have from God, the transplanting from this world's garden into the kingdom of glory's garden, the freeing from bondage and being adopted by the King and being made citizens of his country that we are now on *enemy turf* as the Reverend Burns said, that we will to varying degrees experience a new enmity.

In 1Peter 4:1-4 we read, 'Therefore, since Christ suffered for us, in the flesh, arm yourselves also with the same mind, for he who has suffered in the flesh has ceased from sin, that he no longer should live the rest of his time in the flesh for the lusts of men, but for the will of God. For we have spent enough of our past lifetime in doing the will of the Gentiles [unbelievers] – when we walked in lewdness, lusts, drunkenness, revelries, drinking parties, and abominable idolatries. In regards to these, they think it strange that you do not run with them in the same flood of dissipation, speaking evil of you.'

We in the western world, will cop at least some flack, be thought weird and gossiped about, maybe even crucified by the media if we are a 'somebody' but we are freed, not to have to 'keep up with the Jones', to not fear how another believes we should live and think. Pilgrims in other areas of the world suffer far worse enmity. But no pilgrim has to listen and follow the many voices of the world that change faster than the wind, we only have to hear and obey the unchanging one.

Proverbs 29:25 tells us that, 'The fear of man brings a snare, but whoever trusts in the LORD shall be safe [secure or literally 'set on high'].

This snare is being trapped by or enslaving ourselves to the whims of what others decide is right and acceptable. Yep, the Bible speaks of the weight of peer pressure for any age.

Whereas Proverbs 8:13 and 9:10a tell us that, 'The fear of the LORD is to hate evil; pride and arrogance and the evil way and the perverse mouth . . . The fear of the LORD is the beginning of wisdom.'

Fearing God brings us good things, keeping us away from that which defile us, which hurt and harm for as Psalm 19:9a tells us 'the fear of the Lord is clean', which is not what the world wants you to know or believe.

Mind you good things, keeping us away from that which hurt and harm, our loving Father can achieve by sending pilgrims home, by decreeing their physical death.

In other areas of our world a pilgrim can be in real peril of losing their physical life for confessing Christ. This is nothing strange or new, it occurred in Bible times and in Bunyan's times.

Question: Does our view of suffering need to be changed?
Answer: I believe so. Mine anyway, if not yours. In John 15:20 and 16:33 Jesus tells us '"Remember the word that I said to you, 'A servant is not greater than his master.' If they persecuted me, they will also persecute you. . . These things I have spoken to you, that in Me you may have peace. In the world you will have tribulation; but be of good cheer, I have overcome the world."'

John xii.27 ["Now My soul is troubled, and what shall I say? 'Father, save Me from this hour'? But for this purpose I came to this hour"] Innocent nature got the first word, but Divine wisdom and love got . . . the last. They who would proceed regularly must go upon the *second thought*. The complainant *speaks first*; but, if we would judge righteously, we must *hear the other side*. With the second thought he checked himself: "For this came I unto this hour"; he does not *silence* himself with this, that he *could not* avoid it, there was no remedy; but *satisfies* himself with this, that he *would not* avoid it, for it was pursuant to his own voluntary engagement, and was to be the crown of his whole undertaking; should he now fly off, it would frustrate all that had been done hitherto. Reference is here had of the Divine counsels concerning his sufferings, by virtue of which, thus it behoveth him to submit and suffer. This should reconcile us to the darkest hours of our lives, that we were all along designed for them (see 1Thess: iii.3 ['that no one should be shaken by these afflictions; for you yourselves know that we are appointed to this.]) [60]

1Peter 2:19-23, 'For this is commendable, if because of conscience toward God one endures grief, suffering wrongfully. For what credit is it if, when you are beaten for your faults, you take it patiently? But when you do good and suffer, if you take it patiently, this is commendable before God. For to this you were called, because Christ also suffered for us, leaving us an example, that you should follow His steps: 'Who committed no sin, nor was deceit found in His mouth'; who, when He was reviled, did not revile in return; when He suffered, he did not threaten, but committed Himself to Him who judges righteously'.

As pilgrims we should not be surprised, tripped up, or spooked by suffering as we journey home. To believe that we will not is to believe a lie. A definition of suffering which when considering our Father's loving sovereignty, I find very challenging is 'Suffering is

---

[60] *Fleetwood's Life of Christ* comment by Matthew Henry p465-6

having what you don't want or wanting what you don't have.'[61] But as Jesus commands in John 14:1, '"Let not your heart be troubled; you believe in God, believe also in Me"' we need to give some serious thought to the reality of suffering as a pilgrim and whether we believe in the practical truth of this verse and so behave in a manner that shows we do, never ever forgetting that the only judgement we need to consider is our Father's and that his is always right and true unlike the world's.

Bunyan writes that 'God had but one Son without sin, but no son without suffering . . .

God never appointed this world to be the place of man's rest, but of our exercise, and only a passage to another world; and in this our passage we must look for storms and tempests . . . man is no sooner brought home to God [become a pilgrim], but he must expect to be hated by the world, assaulted by Satan, chastened by the Lord; our own corrupt hearts will be always vexing; the old man, the flesh, thwarting all the motions of the new nature, lusting against the spirit. The lusts of the flesh will be as pricks in our eyes, and as thorns in our sides; we shall have enemies in our own houses. But this truth is so manifest in all the Scriptures, that I shall insist no longer on it, only shall add this by way of use; let all Christians prepare for affliction, by getting an interest in God through Christ; by getting sin pardoned and purged, by getting peace with God and conscience, by getting hearts crucified to the world; and then, when troubles come, let us bear them as Christians, not murmur nor repine, but in patience possess our souls; not desponding nor fainting; remembering that our troubles are no more, but infinitely less than we have deserved. Job xxxiv.23, 'He will not lay upon man more than right.' God perfectly understands our need, and knows our strength. 1Pet. i.6, 'If need be, ye are in heaviness.' 'He is faithful who will not suffer you to be tempted above that ye are able.' 1Cor. x.13. It is the wise, just, and gracious God and our Father that tempers our cup

---

[61] *Suffering is never for nothing*

for us . . . God knows our need, and our strength, and so suits all his remedies accordingly; therefore let us be patient, bearing our troubles with an equal mind, not suffering as per force, but willingly . . . In our affliction, let us search our hearts, and try our ways; let us fly to God by prayer, and resign up ourselves to him, and trust in him, casting our cares and burdens on him, Psal.Lv.22. 1Pet. v.7.

Most Christians are not mortified and crucified to the world, not acquainted with God and the promises, as they ought to be, nor so resolved to follow God fully, as they ought, and therefore are so dejected and discontented when afflictions come. O that we did count the cost, when we first begin to make profession of Christ; and that we had such full persuasions of the incomparable worth and excellences of the Lord Jesus, as that we could willingly part with all things for his sake! O that we had such believing apprehensions of the wisdom, faithfulness, righteousness and mercy of God, such sights of his reconciled face, and such tastes of his fatherly love to us in Christ, as that we could quietly submit to his holy will, and be well satisfied with all his dispensations toward us . . .

Let us grow weary of our sins, not of our sufferings . . . Let us consider, also the real spiritual benefit of affliction. God aims at our profit; and in good time, in the best time, he will send deliverance. And be sure, those that are not unmindful of their duty, God will not be unmindful of their safety.

This is the language of faith; if God be my God, if I be his child, born of him, reconciled to him, pardoned, justified, sanctified, in covenant with him; why am I troubled, though he give me neither health, nor wealth, nor friends, nor relations? Have I not enough, in having God to be my God?

Trust, then, depend and rely upon God in Christ, and by an holy confidence, resign up your will to his will, to do what he would have us do; to be what he would have us be; to suffer what he would have us suffer; and then heart trouble will cease; and sweet peace cometh, when, having trusted all with God, we can in heart say, Lord, if thou wilt have me poor, disgraced, imprisoned, diseased, deprived of all my dearest friends, I am content to be so; I trust all my concerns with thee. O the sweet peace and quiet that will be in that soul!' [62]

Adopting this other-world mindset, that to suffer is okay, normal in the life of a pilgrim. Keeping it, remembering it and living it out is the pilgrim's task, a basic foundation for all a pilgrim is to be.

This thinking also aids us to be our Father's representatives and ambassadors on this earth.

Ambassadors are expected to obey the laws of the land so as to not be offensive to the natives, but only when they do not conflict with their King's laws.

In Romans 13:1-8 we read, 'Let every soul be subject to the governing authorities. For there is no authority except from God, and the authorities that exist are appointed by God. Therefore whoever resists the authority resists the ordinance of God; and those who resist will bring judgement on themselves. For rulers are not a terror to good works, but to evil. Do you want to be unafraid of the authority? Do what is good, and you will have praise from the same. For he is God's minister to you for good. But if you do evil, be afraid; for he does not bear the sword in vain; for he is God's minister, an avenger to execute wrath on him who practices evil. Therefore you must be subject, not only because of wrath but also for conscience' sake. For because of this you also pay taxes, for they are God's ministers attending continually to this very thing. Render therefore to all their due: taxes to whom taxes are due, customs to whom customs, fear to whom fear, honour to whom honour. Owe no one anything except to love one another, for he who loves another has fulfilled the law.'

Can I hear you protesting?

Do your reasons go along the same vein as mine did once? 'You've gotta be joking! Paul did not live in today's world with

---

[62] Bunyan *Heart's Ease in Heart Trouble*. The Pilgrim's Progress and other selected Works p 827-8, 835, 849, 876.

these authorities we have to put up with. He's got his head in the sand . . . No way!'

Firstly, in this passage God, through Paul, is telling pilgrims how to be therefore think about these things of this world that we still are living in and holding us responsible for how we are obedient to him. He is not telling us how the authorities should do their jobs or the judgement they will be under if they do not carry out their God-assigned positions in a manner pleasing to him.

Chambers once wrote 'To see that my adversary gives me my rights is natural; but . . . from our Lord's standpoint it does not matter if I am defrauded or not; what does matter is that I do not defraud.' [63]

Paul wrote his letter to the Romans around two thousand years ago. So a brief history lesson about the times the apostle Paul and Bunyan lived in should help us see that the good-old-days including their authorities were not that good either.

During the reign of Claudius (41-54AD) agitations in the Roman Jewish community resulted in their expulsion from Rome. This is perhaps the time mentioned in Acts 18:2, 'And [Paul] found a certain Jew named Aquila, born in Pontus, who had recently come from Italy with his wife Priscilla (because Claudius had commanded all the Jews to depart from Rome); and he came to them.'

Historians debate whether or not the Roman government distinguished between Christians and Jews prior to AD96. It is suggested that the Roman magistrates just wanted to maintain law and order and that the reasons underlying their decision to expel the Jews were essentially the same as those which triggered expulsions of other groups such as Isis worshipers, devotees of Bacchus or astrologers.

As God is not the author of confusion [disorder] but of peace (1Cor. 14:33), should Pilgrims behave in ways that

---

[63] Oswald Chambers (1874-1917) *My utmost for His Highest Daily Devotional June* 30th *Do it Now* Barbour 1935

make them no different from worldly groups protesting, rioting about government decisions they don't like?

Should we behave in ways that display hatred and complete disregard for the wellbeing of another made in the same image?[64]

As a form of punishment crucifixion in Rome was banned in the 4th Century AD. In 1401 a law in Britain made being tied to a stake and burnt alive the penalty for heresy. Before it was abolished in 1790 it claimed many Christian lives. Carrying out the full sentence of 'hanging, drawing [where the person while still alive was disemboweled] and quartering' ceased after 1814. Pressing, where a wooden board was placed upon a person lying prone and had increasingly heavy weights placed on it, was last carried out in 1735. Before 1776 many criminals were transported to the North American colonies but from 1787, they were shipped to Australia. The last public hanging was in 1868. The last Pillory (head and hands) sentence was in 1837 and the last one in the Stocks (feet) in 1872.

Bunyan spent twelve years in jail because he refused to stop preaching and praying in a manner that the state church, the Church of England had declared illegal. It has been said of his treatment by the authorities of his times, that it was only by 'a miracle of mercy' that he was not hanged or transported.

Cheever writes that '. . . the age where God placed [Bunyan] . . . was an age of the formation and intrepid action of great minds; it was also an age for the development of apostolic piety and endurance of suffering, on the part of men and ministers who chose to obey God rather than man. If great qualities and great capacities of virtue existed, there were great flames to try them; sharp tools and terrible, to cut and polish the hidden jewels of the Saviour . . . After Bunyan had laid in jail for some time, the justices

---

[64] From *Roman Policy toward the Jews: Expulsions from the City of Rome during the* First *Century.* https://www.jstor.org>stable and *Suetonius on Christians* https://en.m.wikipedia.org

sent their clerk of the peace; Mr Cobb, to admonish him and demand his submission (as in to the decrees of King Charles II – no praying unless from the Common Prayer Book and in a place permitted as per the 1662 Act of Uniformity) . . . "Sir, said Bunyan, Whickliffe saith, that he which leaveth off preaching and hearing of the word of God for fear of excommunication of men, he is already excommunicated of God, and shall, in the day of judgement, be counted, a traitor to Christ . . ." . . . I told him [Mr. Cobb] that Paul did owe the powers that were in his day to be of God; and yet he was often in prison under them for all that. And also, though Jesus Christ told Pilate that he had no power against him but of God, yet he died under the same Pilate; and yet, said I, I hope you will not say that either Paul or Christ did deny magistracy, and so sinned against God in slighting the ordinance. Sir, said I, the law hath provided two ways of obeying; the one to do that which in my conscience I do believe that I am bound to do actively, and where I cannot obey actively, then I am willing to lie down, and to suffer what they shall do unto me.' [65]

So as pilgrims both freed yet constrained by our rightful fear of our LORD we are expected by God to obey the laws of the land as in pay our taxes and bills, obey traffic laws, not rob, defraud or murder, or pay the penalty for breaking them.

I live in regional Victoria, Australia. If I was still working as a registered nurse today I, as a pilgrim, would have to humbly refuse to do some tasks I'd be expected to do and I could find myself unemployed or even facing a court as a result. I believe there is a time coming in Australia where pilgrims could find themselves in jail because they could not obey the law of the state because it means we would have to disobey God's moral and ethical standards, his laws.

---

[65] *Bunyan and His Times* p 8, 23-25

This has already happened to pilgrims in other countries. By accepting the penalty, the authorities have ordained, even if it's just paying a parking fine, we are obeying the law of the land. By becoming aggressive and rude to the council office staffer or policeman who is just doing what they are paid to do or rioting and being a menace or threat to our society we are not being respectful or obedient to the God-ordained authorities.

The mindset that Peter was considering in his letter and that the Reverend Burns talked of having to adopt is that of being a stranger, an alien to this world, the mindset of a pilgrim.

But I have started you on the journey of considering being transformed by the renewing of your old mind that Paul talks of in Romans after he had discussed all we have in Christ.

There is so much in all of scripture of what our renewed mind should look like, so much taking off and putting on that both you, my dear reader and I would be completely exhausted and befuddled. Also, this book would never end and probably look far worse than my room and robe after such a time of changing. So instead I am going to look at what I consider to be the main three foundations this renewed mind rests on (other than the obvious one of suffering in this world just because we are now a peculiar people and aliens, that we have already considered) which I believe all the other stuff that we are called to put on flows from and these are having a Christ-like mindset, a mindset of Christ-like holiness and the habits arising from this and thirdly a mindset of love, Christ-like love.

The mind of Christ

Question: What could be more Christ like than having the mind of our Lord Christ Jesus? But does the Bible tell us we are to have his mind and what his mindset was?

Answer: We have previously considered how our mind influences all else, so that if we want lasting change rather than a mask, an act, we have to be changed from the inside out, transformed; the invisible mind first and the visible behaviour or look last.

John, the beloved disciple, tells us that if we say, claim to live in Christ we should be seen to walk, live as he did.

1John 1:6 reads, 'If we say we have fellowship with Him, and walk in darkness, we lie and do not practice the truth.'

To walk as Christ, pilgrims will need to have the same mind.

In 1Corinthians 2:16b we read, 'But we have the mind of Christ', so as pilgrims we already have the mind of Christ and in verse 12 of this same chapter we read, 'Now we have received, not the spirit of the world, but the Spirit who is from God, that we might know the things that have been freely given to us by God.'

> He does not mean that the Christian is able to understand all the thoughts of the Christ. But he does mean that the indwelling Spirit reveals Christ. The spiritual man accordingly does not see things from the viewpoint of the worldly. He sees them from the viewpoint of Christ.[66]

These provisions given by God at our new birth are for us to use, so I think we had better have a good look at what we can learn about Christ's mindset from scripture for as we have read previously, it is our responsibility to make use of all that our God has provided us with, to adopt and use this radically new way of thinking and walking.

In Philippians 1:27, 2:1-8, Paul the bondservant of Christ writes, '. . . let your conduct be worthy of the gospel of Christ, so that . . . I may hear . . . that you stand fast in one spirit, with one mind striving together for the faith of the gospel . . . Therefore if there is any consolation in Christ, if any comfort of love, if any fellowship of the Spirit, if any affection and mercy fulfil my joy by being like-minded, having the same love, being of one accord, of one mind. Let nothing be done through selfish ambition or conceit, but in lowliness of mind let each esteem others better than himself. Let each of you look out not only for his own

---

[66] Rev. Leon Morris (1914-2006) *The First Epistle of Paul to the Corinthians An Introduction and Commentary* Tyndale Press 1964 p62

interests, but also for the interests of others. Let this mind be in you which was also in Christ Jesus, who, being in the form of God, did not consider it robbery to be equal with God, but made Himself of no reputation, taking the form of a bondservant and coming in the likeness of men. And being found in appearance as a man, he humbled Himself and became obedient to the point of death, even the death of the cross.'

Just think on this!

Christ voluntarily and submissively left the presently unknowable to us, mind-blowing glory of heaven and all that was rightfully his as God's beloved only Son and being the creator and maintainer of all things, found himself confined in what he had created, the skin of an embryo and the womb of Mary and entered this sin-stained earth, being delivered in a cow shed with all its muck and noise, naked, defenseless and fully dependant on those hearts and hands which he had also made. And all for one purpose only – to serve, to suffer, to die on a Roman cross so we might live as his Father willed.

<u>Question</u>: Have you ever noticed how Jesus went that last time to Jerusalem?

<u>Answer</u>: Luke, the physician reporting to his friend Theophilus had and he noted it down for us as the events of that last journey for the Passover feast unfolded.

In Luke 9:51, 53 we read, 'Now it came to pass, when the time had come for [Christ] to be received up, that He steadfastly set His face to go to Jerusalem . . . But they did not receive Him, because His face was set for the journey to Jerusalem.'

Luke 13:22, 34, 'And He went through the cities and villages, teaching, and journeying toward Jerusalem . . . [grieving not for himself but for the city and people of Jerusalem] "O Jerusalem, Jerusalem, the one who kills the prophets and stones those who are sent to her! How often I wanted to gather your children together, as a hen gathers her brood under her wings, but you were not willing!'

Luke 19:28b, 41-47a, '. . . He went on ahead, going up to Jerusalem . . . Now as He draw near, He saw the city and wept over it, saying, "If you had known, even you, especially in this your day, the things that make for your peace! But now they are hidden from your eyes. For days will come upon you when your enemies will build an embankment around you, surround you and close you in on every side, and level you, and your children within you, to the ground; and they will not leave in you one stone upon another, because you did not know the time of your visitation." Then He went into the temple and began to drive out all those who bought and sold in it, saying to them, "It is written, 'My house is a house of prayer', but you have made it a 'den of thieves'." And He was teaching daily in the temple.'

Luke 21:37, 'And in the daytime He was teaching in the temple, but at night He went out and stayed on the mountain called Olivet.'

Luke 22:47-53, 'And while He was still speaking, behold, a multitude [believed to be around 100 people] and he who was called Judas, one of the twelve, went before them and drew near to Jesus to kiss Him. But Jesus said to him, "Judas, are you betraying the Son of Man with a kiss?" When those around Him saw what was going to happen, they said to Him, "Lord, shall we strike with the sword?" And one of them struck the servant of the high priest and cut off his ear. But Jesus answered and said, "Permit even this." And He touched his ear and healed him. Then Jesus said to the chief priests, captains of the temple, and the elders who had come to Him, "Have you come out, as against a robber, with swords and clubs? When I was with you daily in the temple, you did not try to seize Me. But this is your hour, and the power of darkness."'

Christ *steadfastly* set his face.

About seven hundred years before Jesus came, Isaiah gave us a picture of what this was like (the doing) and how (the thinking) Jesus could do it.

Isaiah 50:7, 'For the Lord GOD will help Me; therefore I will not be disgraced; therefore I have set My face like a flint, and I know that I will not be ashamed.'

Flint is a hard, grey stone of nearly pure silica that was used for arrow or spear heads because of its hardness. To set one's face like flint was to be hard and unyielding, there was no thought of not going forwards to his death. And because he knew God was with him, helping him, he did not fear experiencing shame or disgrace, being further humbled.

He is Isaiah's servant King as seen in Isaiah 42:1a, 49:5-7 and 50:5-6, '"Behold! My Servant whom I uphold, My Elect One in whom My soul delights . . . "And now the LORD says, who formed Me from the womb to be His Servant . . . 'It is too small a thing that You should be My Servant to raise up the tribes of Jacob . . . I will also give You as a light to the Gentiles, that You should be My salvation to the ends of the earth.'" Thus says the LORD, the Redeemer of Israel, their Holy One, to Him whom man despises, to Him whom the nation abhors, to the Servant of rulers . . . The Lord GOD has opened My ear; and I was not rebellious, nor did I turn away. I gave My back to those who struck Me, and My cheeks to those who plucked out the beard; I did not hide My face from shame and spitting.'

Christ in – no, not in his incarnation but before time began – had the mindset of a servant willing to suffer because of his willing obedience to his Lord, his Father, regardless of the consequences.

This was not expected or accepted by the Jews or the world at that time and not even now by some. Sadly, for them, the second time Christ appears on this earth it will be as the triumphant, victorious ruler they were or are looking for, which they will realize they also don't want because then he will be coming as ruler to judge.

Jesus served fallen humanity during his life-time walking the earth he'd made, in obedience to his Father. Those who were only interested in the entertainment he provided or what free cure or food he could hand out, as well as those who knew their hunger and thirst and hanged upon every word he spoke, who believed and obeyed, were all served by him. And as the time for his sacrifice drew near, as he felt the dark shadow of his cross, he still had the same mindset. On that very last evening he took the lowest position of any household servant and kneeling washed his disciples' road-filthed feet. He even washed the feet of Judas, knowing him to be his betrayer, his enemy.

Jesus showed us what it is to be humble, to live in humility. And he showed us that being such comes from a proper, a true perspective of self and abilities, our Father's perspective and the knowledge that he is our ever present source of help and strength.

Knowing your value to God, God's view of you now as a pilgrim is the beginning of understanding what true humility is, it is a humbleness from security, from inner strength in knowing God's view of you not the world's and knowing your forever-neediness of the triune God. So, we are going to divert for a little here to consider a part of our mindset that probably needs a tweak but we will return to more on Christ's mindset.

This is a mindset that changes a lot if not everything for a person and I believe in this current world for both females and males it needs exploring. It involves understanding that this creator God is both sovereign over everything and a God of love.

Have you noticed how God loves variety, surprising variety? Consider one of my favourites, the Platypus, an egg-laying, breast feeding, duckbilled, blind, webbed handed and footed yet able to dig a burrow with a spur that would shame the proudest cockerel. The animal kingdom seems to have far more variety than the humans who at a superficial glance look much the same except for colour, size, hair texture and gender. But this look does not do justice to the amazing differences there are in every individual person. For example, you cannot measure someone else's body with your end-of-thumb-knuckle-width (a Chinese length called Cun) and get the same results that you do when measuring your body yet if they measure their body with their Cun they will get your numbers.

<u>Question</u>: Have you ever wondered why you look like you, my dear reader? Have you ever wished you looked different? Have you ever wished to be a different personality or have a skill that someone else has but you haven't? What do the 'voices' inside you tell you about yourself? Have you ever wished you had someone else's experiences of life instead of yours?

<u>Answer</u>: God truly does delight in all the variety seen among people for he in his sovereignty made us that way deliberately and purposefully as Psalm 139 teaches us.

Psalm 139

1. O, You have searched me and known me.
2. You know my sitting down and my rising up;
3. You understand my thought afar off.
   You comprehend my path and my lying down,
   And are acquainted with all my ways.
4. For there is not a word on my tongue,
   But behold, O LORD, You know it altogether.
5. You have hedged me behind and before,
   And laid Your hand upon me.
6. Such knowledge is too wonderful for me;
   It is high, I cannot attain it.
7. Where can I go from Your Spirit?
   Or where can I flee from Your presence?
8. If I ascend into heaven, You are there;
   If I make my bed in hell, behold, You are there.
9. If I take the wings of the morning,
   And dwell in the uttermost parts of the sea,
10. Even there Your hand shall lead me,
    And Your right hand shall hold me.
11. If I say, "Surely the darkness shall fall on me,"
    Even the night shall be light about me;
12. Indeed, the darkness shall not hide from You,
    But the night shines as the day;
    The darkness and the light are both alike to You.

13. For You formed my inward parts;
    You covered me in my mother's womb.
14. I will praise You, for I am fearfully and
    wonderfully made;
    Marvelous are Your works,
    And that my soul knows very well.
15. My frame was not hidden from You,
    When I was made in secret,
    And skillfully wrought in the lowest parts of the earth.
16. Your eyes saw my substance, being yet unformed,
    And in Your book they all were written,
    The days fashioned for me,
    When as yet there were none of them.
17. How precious also are Your thoughts to me, O God!
    How great is the sum of them!
18. If I should count them, they would be more in number
    than the sand;
    When I awake, I am still with You.
19. Oh, that You would slay the wicked, O God!
    Depart from me, therefore, you bloodthirsty men.
20. For they speak against You wickedly;
    Your enemies take Your name in vain.
21. Do I not hate them, O LORD, who hate You?
    And do I not loathe those who rise up against You?
22. I hate them with perfect hatred;
    I count them my enemies.
23. Search me, O God, and know my heart;
    Try me, and know my anxieties;
25. And see if there is any wicked way in me,
    And lead me in the way everlasting.

In my Bible alongside the first verse of this psalm I have written, 'And yet you still died for me!' I also came to realize that I and every other child was conceived primarily because God desired their existence, parental desire, motives came second.
Bridges writes that 'Commenting on this psalm the Rev. James Hufstetler said it well when he said, 'You are the result of the

attentive, careful, thoughtful, intimate, detailed, creative work of God. Your personality, your sex, your height, your features, are what they are because God made them *precisely* that way. He made you the way he did because that is the way he wants you to be. . . If God had wanted you to be basically and creatively different, he would have made you differently. Your genes and chromosomes and creaturely distinctives – even the shape of your nose and ears – are what they are by God's design.

David praised God, not because he was handsome, but because *God made him*. We need to dwell on that thought. The eternal God who is infinite in His wisdom and perfect in His love personally made you and me. He gave you the body, the mental abilities, and the basic personality you have because that is the way He wanted you to be. And He wanted you to be just that way because He loves you and wants to glorify Himself through you.

Bridges writes that, 'This is the believer's foundation for self-acceptance. . . Self-acceptance is basically trusting God for who I am, disabilities or physical flaws and all . . .

If we have physical or mental disabilities or impairments, it is because God in His wisdom and love created us that way. We may not understand why God chose to do that, but that is where our trusting Him has to begin. . .

To [trust God for who I am] though, we must continually keep in mind that the God who created us the way we are is the God who is wise enough to know what is best for us and loving enough to bring it about. Certainly we will sometimes struggle with who we are. Unlike specific incidents of adversity, our disabilities and infirmities are always with us. So we have to learn to trust God in this area continually . . .'[67]

To accept yourself is far better than to esteem yourself. Having a high regard for yourself in the sight of God and others is trouble. Pride is contrary to humility or meekness and always occurs before a fall. To see yourself from God's view is not destructive

---

[67] *Trusting God* p 159, 160-1, 162-3, 165, 167

but transforming. To see yourself as a sinner who a loving God, died for, gives you a worth no one can take from you and for me it sealed the desire to accept his gift of salvation. To see yourself as a child of this God with all the inheritant promises of this relationship, gives you grip to hang on regardless till all is fulfilled in his time.

To accept yourself is to accept God's total sovereignty. To accept God's total sovereignty is to experience what David wrote of in Psalm 131and to desire the same for others because simple, child-like trust in God is so very good.

Psalm 131

1. LORD, my heart is not haughty,
   Nor my eyes lofty.
   Neither do I concern myself with great matters,
   Nor with things too profound for me.
2. Surely I have calmed and quietened my soul,
   Like a weaned child with his mother;
   Like a weaned child is my soul within me.
3. O Israel, hope in the LORD
   From this time forth and forever.

Question: What for you are *great matters* or *things too profound* I wonder? Does having to deal with these things make you anxious or fearful?

Answer: I don't understand electricity, I'm just grateful all I have to do is flick a switch. So how on earth could finite me understand the infinite omnipotence of God? We, I believe, are prone to forget who is God, who is in control, who is directing everything they made from the beginning to the already written end and as a result attempt to do what we cannot and suffer the consequences of our stupidity, for example crippling disease causing stresses.

Question: What is a *weaned child* like?

Answer: Have you ever seen how a two or three-year-old child who is still being breast fed behaves when close to their mum? They most definitely are not contentedly restful, settled, blissfully and quietly at peace without a problem in the world until they have what they seek and then not for long! If we cannot accept God's sovereignty and the power that comes with that we cannot rest, for we cannot feel safe, we cannot trust that our needs will be met if we do not act to secure them ourselves and so pride and arrogance barge in while assurance, contentment and peace quietly slip out the door.

Don't allow anything or anyone make you believe that as a pilgrim you must take on those great matters or things that are too difficult for you for that is not God's plan for you. Now back to Christ's mind set of humble service . . .

John 13:1-17, 'Now before the feast of the Passover, when Jesus knew that His hour had come that He should depart from this world to the Father, having loved His own who were in the world, He loved them to the end. And supper being ended, the devil having already put it into the heart of Judas Iscariot, Simon's son, to betray Him, Jesus knowing that the Father had given all things into His hands, and that He had come from God and was going to God, rose from supper and laid aside His garments, took a towel and girded Himself. After that, He poured water into a basin and began to wash the disciples' feet, and to wipe them with the towel with which He was girded. Then He came to Simon Peter. And Peter said to Him, "Lord are You washing my feet?" Jesus answered and said to him, "What I am doing you do not understand now, but you will know after this." Peter said to Him, "You shall never wash my feet!"

Jesus answered him, "If I do not wash you, you have no part with Me." Simon Peter said to Him, "Lord, not my feet only, but also my hands and my head!" Jesus said to him, "He who is bathed needs only to wash his feet, but is completely clean; and you are clean, but not all of you. . . You call Me Teacher and Lord, and you say well, for so I am. If I then, your Lord and Teacher, have washed your feet, you also ought to wash one another's feet. For I have given you an example, that you should do as I have done to you. Most assuredly, I say to you, a servant is not greater than his

master; nor is he who is sent greater than he who sent him. If you know these things, blessed are you if you do them."'
Jesus showed no rebellious attitude towards his Father, nor did he turn aside in disobedience at any time of his pilgrimage here. If he had his sacrifice in our place would have been a failure, for he would have been no purer or unblemished than you or I.

<u>Question</u>: How could Jesus do this as a man? How can we? How can you and I serve like this, to this degree?
<u>Answer</u>: The answer I believe can be found in the first four verses of John 13 that we have just read, though there are a couple of reasons in the previous Isaiah reading as well, if you want to find them for yourself.
Jesus knew three things about himself and his Father God that I believe gave him the mindset which enabled him to not only kneel and wash those feet but to set his face as flint and go on to Jerusalem, to his cross and by answering three more questions we shall see how we can think similarly.

<u>Question</u>: Does the Bible tell us that the Father will give us all things?
<u>Answer</u>: Romans 8:16-17, 'The Spirit Himself bears witness with our spirit that we are children of God, and if children, then heirs – heirs of God and joint heirs with Christ, if indeed we suffer with Him, that we may also be glorified together.'
The Revelation of Jesus Christ 21:7, 'He who overcomes shall inherit all things, and I will be his God and he shall be My son.' Note, that to overcome one must trust and obey his or her God.
1Corinthians 3:21-23, 'Therefore let no one boast in men. For all things are yours: whether Paul or Apollos or Cephas, or the world of life or death, or things present or things to come – all are yours. And you are Christ's, and Christ is God's.'
According to Henry, Paul in these Corinthian verses is giving us 'an inventory . . . the spiritual riches of a true believer. "*All is yours.* Nay, the world itself is yours. *Life is yours*, that you may prepare for the life of heaven; and *death is yours*, that you may go to the possession of it. It is the kind messenger that will fetch you to

your Father's house. *Things present are yours*, for your support on the road; *things to come* are yours, to enrich you forever at your journey's end" All is ours, time and eternity, earth and heaven, life and death. But it must be remembered . . . all things are ours, upon no other ground that our being Christ's.'[68]

Conclusion: For now, though we are but pilgrims, we Christians are to inherit all things.

Acts 20:32, 'So now, brethren I commend you to God and to the word of His grace, which is able to build you up and give you an inheritance among all those who are sanctified.'

Question: Does the Bible tell us that we come from God?

Answer: Genesis 1:26-28a, 'Then God said, "Let Us make man in Our image, according to Our likeness . . . So God created man in His own image; in the image of God He created him; male and female He created them. Then God blessed them . . .'

We came from God's mind. He made us male or female, in his image as living symbols of himself to live on the earth that he had made and rule as his representatives. Of all that God created, we alone are in his likeness (this is why we are not animals, though an animal can behave obediently to God's design for it far better than many fallen, rebellious humans), we alone are able to have a relationship with him. But we fell with Adam.

1Peter 1:23, 'having been born again, not of corruptible seed but incorruptible, through the word of God which lives and abides forever'.

The new birth, or regeneration as here, is the act by which God gives spiritual life to one who trusts his Son. Without this birth we cannot understand anything spiritual or enter the kingdom of God.

Conclusion: The Bible tells us that God created us pilgrims. He is 'both the former of our bodies and the Father of our spirits'[69]

---

[68] Matthew Henry (1662-1714) *Matthew Henry's Commentary on the whole Bible in one volume*. Zondervan 1960. p1807

[69] Ibid comment from Psalm 100:3 p685

according to Psalm 100:3 which tells us to, 'Know that the Lord, He is God; it is He who has made us, and not we ourselves; we are His people and the sheep of His pasture.'

Question: Does the Bible tell us that we will return to God when we die physically?
Answer: Bear with me and these readings, as they will make sense eventually (I trust).
Isaiah 35:10, 'And the ransomed of the LORD shall return, and come to Zion with singing, with everlasting joy on their heads. They shall obtain joy and gladness, and sorrow and sighing shall flee away.'
2Samuel 5:6-7, 'And the king [David] and his men went to Jerusalem against the Jebusites, the inhabitants of the land . . . Nevertheless, David took the stronghold of Zion (that is, the City of David).'
Psalm 125:1, 'Those who trust in the LORD are like Mount Zion, which cannot be moved, but abides forever.' Literally, Zion is an area in Jerusalem called the City of David where God keeps choosing to build his tabernacle (house) or a word used figuratively for God's kingdom, the heavenly new Jerusalem.
Hebrews 12:22, '. . . you have come to Mount Zion and to the city of the living God, the heavenly Jerusalem, to an innumerable company of angels.'
The Revelation of Jesus Christ 21:2-4, 'Then I, John saw the holy city, New Jerusalem, coming down out of heaven. . . And I heard a loud voice from heaven saying, "Behold the tabernacle of God is with men . . . And God will wipe away every tear from their eyes; there shall be no more death, nor sorrow, nor crying. There shall be no more pain, for the former things have passed away."'
John 13:36-14:6, 'Simon Peter said to Him, "Lord, where are You going?" Jesus answered him, "Where I am going you cannot follow Me now, but you shall follow Me afterward . . . Let not your heart be troubled; you believe in God, believe also in me. In My Father's house are many mansions; if it were not so, I would have told you. I go to prepare a place for you. And if I go and prepare a place for you, I will come again and receive you to Myself; that

where I am, there you may be also. And where I go you know, and the way you know . . . I am the way, the truth, and the life. No one comes to the Father except through Me."
<u>Conclusion</u>: The Bible does tell us that we will return escorted by the Lord Jesus Christ himself and dwell with God for eternity but we must wait patiently for God's right timing.

Is this not the gospel message, the goal of God's redeeming work to right all that has been wrong with his creation since the fall, that we pilgrims might return to walking in the cool of the day with him in a place where sin no longer exists?

We are to follow Christ as our example, using all that we have in him by the Father's grace to display by our works the reality of having this new mindset, the mind of Christ. A mindset marked by an unselfish, sacrificial, humble servant-like attitude of patient obedience that will produce the fruit of the Spirit – which we will consider soon – and the fruit that knowing Christ produces, good works that are pleasing to our Father.

Holiness and habits of

When all capitals were used in the Old Testament for God's name it was shorthand for Jehovah Elohim or Yahweh, the I AM WHO I AM, the personal name of the one who possess all the divine power, the creator, who is also always actively present, faithful and unchangeable, first used in Genesis 2:4, 'This is the history of the heavens and the earth when they were created, in the day that the LORD God made the earth and the heavens'.

In Leviticus 11:44a we read a command of the LORD, 'For I am the LORD your God. You shall therefore concentrate your selves, and you shall be holy; for I am holy . . .'

Peter writes in 1Peter 1:13-16, 'Therefore gird up the loins of your mind, be sober, and rest your hope fully upon the grace that is to be brought to you at the revelation of Jesus Christ; as obedient children, not conforming yourselves to the former lusts, as in your

ignorance; but as He who called you is holy, you also be holy in all your conduct, because it is written, "Be holy, for I am holy."'
And in Hebrews 12:14-16 we read, 'Pursue peace with all people, and holiness, without which no one will see the Lord: looking carefully lest anyone fall short of the grace of God; lest any root of bitterness springing up cause trouble, and by this many become defiled; lest there be any fornicator or profane [godless] person like Esau, who for one morsel of food sold his birthright.'

<u>Question</u>: What does it mean to be holy or have holiness?
<u>Answer</u>: Do you remember the definition for sanctification? Holy, sanctified and righteous are all similar. By faith in Christ's work on the cross pilgrims are already set apart for God, sanctified, holy, declared morally blameless as all our sins have been pardoned. But as with sanctification so is our being holy, becoming as God himself in character, it is a lifelong process as well as a one-off declaration. As you read when we were defining this word, *It is a behavioural style that thinks like God, loves what God loves, hates what God hates, relates to other people as God has related to us, and acts like God acts.* Scripture commands us to grow in holiness, to pursue, to display it in all our behaviours as we live this pilgrim life here, till it is attained, till we are perfected, when we are home.

Heart holiness does not mean sin free but a desire to be free from sin[70]

Wilberforce advises that 'We need to warn . . . that there is no shortcut to holiness. It must be the business of [our] whole lives to grow in grace and continually to add one virtue to another. It is as far as possible, 'to go on towards perfection' (Hebrews 6:1). 'He only that doeth righteousness is righteous' (1John 3:7). Unless they bring forth 'the fruit of the Spirit' (Galatians 5:22), they can have no sufficient evidence that they have actually received the Spirit of Christ, 'without which they are none of His' (Romans 8:9). Unless, then, the root of the

---

[70] Notes from Gables' sermon series on Pilgrim's Progress *#38 Talkative offended by pure grace* 2.7.99

matter is not found in them, they are not adorning the doctrine of God, but disparaging and discrediting it.

The world does not see their secret humiliations nor the exercises of their closets [habits of prayer]. But the world observes that they have the same eagerness in the pursuit of wealth and ambition, the same vain taste for pretentiousness and display, the same ungoverned tempers, which are found in the generality of mankind – then it will treat with contempt their pretences to be superior in sanctity and indifferent to worldly things. Then such a soul will become hardened in its prejudices against the only way which God has provided for our escape of the wrath to come and our attainment in eternal happiness.

Let him, then, who would be indeed a Christian, watch over his ways and over his heart – with unceasing circumspection. Let him endeavour to learn both from the lives of godly men and devotional books . . .

Thus while he studies his own character and observes the more intimate workings of his own mind, he will acquire insights of the human heart in general. This will enable him to guard against all occasions of evil. Such a perspective will also tend, above all things, to promote the growth of humility and to maintain that sobriety of spirit and tenderness of conscience which are the characteristic marks of the true Christian. It is by this unceasing diligence – as the apostle declares it–that the servants of Christ make their calling sure. It is only thus that their labor will ultimately succeed. 'So an entrance shall be ministered unto them abundantly, into the everlasting kingdom of our Lord and Savior Jesus Christ' (2Peter 1:11).'[71]

---

[71] William Wilberforce (1759-1833) *Real Christianity* Multnomah Press abridged edition 1982 based on the 1829 edition entitled *A Practical View of the Prevailing Religious System of Professed Christians, in the Higher and Middle Classes in This Country, Contrasted with Real Christianity* p125-6

Remembering back to even earlier definitions and the word *habit* let's consider some habits which are ours as pilgrims, the fruit of the Spirit which Wilberforce just mentioned.

Galatians 5:19-26 says, 'Now the works of the flesh are evident, which are: adultery, fornication, uncleanness, lewdness, idolatry, sorcery, hatred, contentions, jealousies, outbursts of wrath, selfish ambitions, dissensions, heresies, envy, murders, drunkenness, revelries, and the like; of which I tell you beforehand, just as I also told you in time past, that those who practice such things will not inherit the kingdom of God. But the fruit of the Spirit is love, joy, peace, longsuffering, kindness, goodness, faithfulness, gentleness, self-control. . . And those who are Christ's have crucified the flesh with its passions and desires. If we live in the Spirit, let us also walk in the Spirit. Let us not become conceited, provoking one another, envying one another.'

Packer and Nystrom write, 'These nine habits that Paul called the 'fruit of the Spirit (singular, 'fruit', not 'fruits') . . . are nine facets of Christ-likeness.

Note first that each of them is a fixed habit of behaving as distinct from a passing mood or a fitful gust of feeling. They are aspects of character, life-habits that persist in place of external incentives, or shall we say temptations, to behave differently. Thus, love persists in the face of active hostility; joy, in face of grounds for bitterness; peace, in face of traumatic troubles; patience in face of impatience and panicky pressures; and so, no. Each of these behaviour patterns involves a willingness to swim against the stream of unthinking impulse, as did the Lord Jesus before us.

Note second, that they are expressions of conviction, shaped by knowledge of God's love to us and will for us. As they are not natural virtues, so they are not supernatural endowments wrought in us over our heads, so to speak, that is, while our heads are still empty of this knowledge. The fruit of the Spirit is the outcome of learning and obeying the gospel, consciously trusting Christ as Savior and Master, and resolutely repenting of our sins. . .

Love: Love (*agapē* [about which I have much to say later]) is the habit of seeking some form of greatness for the other party, labouring to do what is truly good for that person. . . When we worship God, it is love seeking to show him to be already great in our estimation, and to encourage others to acknowledge his greatness. . . love aims and works to make the neighbor's, the loved one, great, whether or not this love is recognized and returned. Paul profiles the fundamentals of neighbour-love in 1Corinthians 13.

Joy: Joy is a habit that, like the rest of the fruit, matures into an active attitude. Joy is a discipline – a delightful discipline – of rejoicing, which begins with simply thinking over the things that God has done for us, the commitment that God has made to us, and the service that God renders to us. . . But joy begins with a disciplined habit of thinking of these things until one is freshly thrilled by them. Then one's rejoicing finds natural expression in smiling, singing, and sharing . . . Joy in the Lord can coexist in the Christian's heart even with grief at unhappy things; 'sorrowful, yet always rejoicing' (2Cor. 6:10) is a Spirit-induced state of mind, incomprehensible to the world but well-known among God's saints. [As I can affirm the truth of this, I would like to suggest that you do not allow anyone to make you feel guilty for being able to rejoice when they consider you should only be grieving as even loved ones or brethren may try to do so.]

Peace: One of the great gifts that our Lord has given us is objective, relational peace between us and our God through the achievement at Calvary. Subjective, personal peace flows from the habit of never forgetting the cross, but constantly remembering what our Lord went through in order to bring us pardon for sin and justification through faith. . . The peace of God produces pleasure, praise, and patience under God's hand of providence . . .

Patience: . . . is a habit of mind and heart that grows out of inner peace. Patience trusts God to be at work even in the frustrating events of life, whether it is engorged traffic or crying babies or implacable vendettas or a seemingly unending series of personal disasters. Patience thinks before speaking, aiming to avoid offending. Patience wills the self to see the world from someone else's perspective – and to walk with that person through their world. Patience is rooted in hope because 'if we hope for what we do not see, we wait for it with patience' (Rom. 8:25). Patience takes the long view; unfazed by short-term setbacks, it will carry on unruffled instead of giving up in despair. Patience accepts God's timing and responds to others in a way that reflects the patience that God has toward us. . . Patience sees today in the perspective of eternity – and can laugh.

Kindness: Kindness is a habit that softens the atmosphere. It is an outgoing of neighbour-love that becomes instinctive, and is often unnoticed even by the person who practices it . . . It is a selfless form of thinking that sees a need and meets it, almost by reflex, with no thought of reward. Like the other fruit of the Spirit, kindness comes by receiving and then imitating the kindness of God . . .

Goodness: Goodness and kindness run into each other and so are often confused. Yet goodness has a quality of moral discernment about it that naked kindness might lack. Goodness thinks beyond the present and evaluates what is best in the long term . . . Goodness discerns what is good and what is evil disguised as good. Goodness, we might say, is kindness well-soaked in wisdom. Like the other qualities . . . goodness is a habit or disposition modelled after God's own character. . .

Faithfulness: Faithfulness doesn't quit. . . to the extent that we develop the habit of faithfulness, whether it is in keeping appointments, keeping bills paid when due, or keeping marriage vows, we begin to mirror, even partially, the character of our God who is faithful always.

Gentleness: We rarely see gentleness in a corporate boardroom . . . A . . . Christ-follower is gentle to the core. Gentleness in the Bible is not the opposite of strength; it is not wimpishness, as modern usage might suggest; it is rather, strength under control, harnessed to love and serve. Gentleness is all the more real because every time it is practiced, gentleness is a freely made choice that is backed by strength. . . . It is [Christ's] gentleness that notices and cares. So it is with . . . Christians.

Self-control: An uncontrolled self is a deadly force. It wills to defy or ignore God and tries to take the place of God . . . Idolizing, exalting, celebrating, and indulging oneself as one's god is the root cause of all the shame, folly, decadence, and moral blindness that mark modern Western culture so ruinously. When Jesus declared that the two greatest commands are that we must love God with all of our heart, soul, strength, and mind, and love our neighbour as much as we love ourselves, both of these commands attacked this human idolatry of self in a way that shows us how we are to transcend and overcome it. It we direct our whole being toward love of God, and if we give as much value to our neighbour as to ourselves, if not indeed more, the project of gaining control of self is well under way . . . self-control operates from a position of strength. A strong understanding of oneself, a strong sense of selfhood, even of self-worth (under God's governing), is entirely proper and even necessary for fruitful life in Christ. And a self that knows itself and has embraced self-denial and given itself to God's control can become a powerful force for good. . .

All nine aspects . . . are in essence habits of reaction: habits of benevolent reaction to awkward people and difficult situations, habits of glad reaction toward God in light of his love. These reactions to other people and oneself are not determined by the way people are behaving toward us, but by what we know of the God who made us, loves us, and has saved us.'[72]

The quote of Wilberforce's, now a few pages back, ended with the reference *2Peter1:11*.

2Peter 1 is where Peter, after his greetings to all believers, reminds them of what the triune God has given us and what we have escaped from as a result then in v5-12 writes, '. . . for this very reason, giving all diligence, add to your faith virtue, to virtue

---

[72] *God's Will* p68-73

knowledge, to knowledge self-control, to self-control perseverance, to perseverance godliness, to godliness brotherly kindness, and to brotherly kindness love. For if these things are yours and abound, you will be neither barren not unfruitful in the knowledge of our Lord Jesus Christ. For he who lacks these things is shortsighted, even to blindness, and has forgotten that he was cleansed from his old sins. Therefore, brethren, be even more diligent to make your call and election sure, for if you do these things you will never stumble; for so an entrance will be supplied to you abundantly into the everlasting kingdom of our Lord and Savior Jesus Christ. For this reason I will not be negligent to remind you always of these things, though you know and are established in the present truth.'

Notice how Peter is telling us that it does not matter how long we have been a pilgrim for as we will never have been one long enough to not hear the old, old story over and over again and again. Please do not allow yourself to become bored with the Christmas or Easter Christian facts (stories) for they are why you have abundant and everlasting life.

These verses have been called the *Ladder of Faith* for you begin on the ground rung and over a life time of labour climb to the top rung. Floor or ground level is having the promises and the power, the faith, the enabling, that God gives all pilgrims and then we begin to move, exercise by placing one foot after the other, rung after rung till we find ourselves escorted through heaven's door to a welcome and a home that our minds currently cannot comprehend.

Richards writes, *'Add to your faith. . .* The word translated 'add' means to make abundant provision for. Making every effort to live a Christian life means we begin with faith – but we do not stop there. We go on, and concentrate on developing the following Christian virtues:

Goodness. The Greek word is *arete*, not one of the more familiar words, rendered 'good'. *Arete* is usually translated excellence. It refers to the full development of our potential; to achievement in a chosen sphere of action. We are called to excel as Christians, not to live 'average' lives.

Knowledge. The knowledge that we add to faith is a knowledge of God's will. The 'superior knowledge' claimed by the false teachers Peter was about to discuss was empty and meaningless. What counts is understanding what God wants from us, and doing it.

Self-control. In Scripture this virtue is contrasted to excesses – to greed, to surrender to sexual passions. The Christian who understands the will of God is to discipline himself or herself to do it.

Perseverance. The word in Scripture suggests a distinctive view of time. The Christian takes the long view, and realizes that God does not work by man's timetable. However discouraging the circumstances, the Christian is able to keep on, faithfully doing the Lord's will.

Godliness. This Greek word for piety suggests a constant awareness of God and a commitment to doing things that are appropriate to one devoted to Him.

Brotherly kindness and love. The two words denote affection, and self-sacrifice. We learn to care about others and their welfare. And we are willing to help them, even at a personal cost.

These qualities 'in increasing measure' will keep us from being 'ineffective and unproductive' and as Mathew Henry writes, 'fruitful in the works of righteousness [which] bring much glory to God'.[73]

Question: How does one pursue something, how do you reach a goal a dream, the top rung of a ladder, how do you persist?

Answer: Not by climbing over another, by using another person to propel you upwards. But by self-discipline. That one word is deceptive for the art of being so takes a life time to perfect. However it is a joyful discipline, a yoke that is light, not of teeth

---

[73] Lawrence O. Richards (1931-2016) *The 365 Day Devotional Commentary* Victor Books 1990 p 1120 and *Matthew Henry's Commentary* p1950

gritting grim self-determination for a time but of a life time of living obediently resting in God's loving grace and provisions each day that he gives, of trusting him to provide what you need to become disciplined and single focused, something the world cannot do well in its mentality of microwave instant gratification or else! And a muscle not used soon withers away, as anyone who has had a limb in plaster knows only too well.

In Paul's time, what we know as the Olympic Games now had already began and the prize was a wreath of olive foliage. Other sporting games had wreaths of laurel (bay), wild celery or pine for prizes. How are you at exercising like a professional sportsperson?

Paul, looking forward to being crowned by one that lasts for eternity wrote in 1Corinthians 9:24-27, 'Do you not know that those who run in a race all run, but one receives the prize? Run is such a way that you may obtain it. And everyone who competes for the prize is temperate [exercises self-control] in all things. Now they do it to obtain a perishable crown, but we for an imperishable crown. Therefore I run thus: not with uncertainty. Thus I fight: not as one who beats the air. But I discipline my body and bring it into subjection, lest, when I have preached to others, I myself should become disqualified.'

Gables says that there are warnings in scripture alongside the promises. There is a warning in 1Corinthians 9:24-7. You are to run to obtain, to bring the body into subjection lest you become a castaway (KJ), disapproved. Castaway is translated in other places of the New Testament as reprobate, meaning one forsaken by God, one God has left to self, to go their own way.[74]

In Philippians 4:8 we read this command, 'Finally, brethren, whatever things are true, whatever things are noble, whatever things are just, whatever things are pure, whatever things are lovely, whatever things are of good report, if there is any virtue and if there is anything praiseworthy – meditate on these things.'

---

[74] Notes from Gables' sermon series on Pilgrim's Progress #15 *The Interpreter's house* #7 *The 6th room* 1.5.99.

In Colossians 2: 5b-10, 20-23 Paul tells us of his 'rejoicing to see your good order [discipline] and the steadfastness of your faith in Christ. As you therefore have received Christ Jesus the Lord, so walk in Him, rooted and built up in Him and established in the faith, as you have been taught, abounding in it with thanksgiving. Beware lest anyone cheat you [literally 'plunder you or take you captive'] through philosophy and empty deceit, according to the basic principles of the world, and not according to Christ. For in Him dwells all the fullness of the Godhead bodily [in bodily form]; and you are complete in Him, who is the head of all principality and power [rule and authority] . . .Therefore, if you died with Christ from the basic principles of the world, why, as though living in the world, do you subject yourselves to regulations – "Do not touch, do not taste, do not handle," which concern things which perish with the using – according to the commandments and doctrines of men? These things indeed have an appearance of wisdom in self-imposed religion, false humility, and neglect [severe treatment, asceticism] of the body, but are of no value against the indulgence of the flesh.'

Bridges writes that here Paul is warning 'us against misguided and wrongly motivated attempts to control the body that leave our thought lives unrestrained (Colossians 2:23) . . . Holiness begins in our minds and works out to our actions. This being true, what we allow to enter our minds is critically important.

The television programs we watch, the movies we may attend, the books and magazines we read, the music we listen to, and the conversations we have all affect our minds. We need to evaluate the effects of these avenues honestly, using Philippians 4:8 as a standard. Are the thoughts stimulated by these various avenues true? Are they pure? Lovely? Admirable, excellent, or praiseworthy?

The world around us constantly seeks to conform our minds to its sinful ways. It is earnest and pressing in its endeavours. It will entice and persuade us (Proverbs 1:10-14). When we resist, it will

ridicule and abuse us as 'old-fashioned' and 'puritanical' (1Peter 4:4).
Too many Christians, instead of resisting, are more and more giving ground . . . A friend of mine told me of a young couple in full-time Christian work who came to him wanting to know if it was wrong to attend X-rated movies! That the question should even be entertained illustrates the degree to which the world has infected our minds...
'But among you there must not be even a hint of sexual immorality, or of any kind of impurity, or of greed, because these are improper for God's holy people. Nor should there be obscenity, foolish talk or coarse joking, which is out of place, but rather thanksgiving', (Ephesians 5:3-4) 'Not even a hint of immorality' places any suggestive speech whatsoever outside the bounds of a holy walk.' [75]
What a lot to consider! If we exercised, disciplined ourselves and applied just the standards of Philippians 4:8 to our minds how many of our behaviours would be changed, how different would our way of being be to those watching us compared to the rest of the world's? The mind boggles!

Love, but which one?

John 3:16, 'For God so loved the world that He gave . . .'
1John 3:1, 16, 23, 4: 19, 5:1-3, 'Behold what manner of love the Father has bestowed on us, that we should be called children of God! Therefore the world does not know us, because it did not know Him . . . By this we know love, because He laid down His life for us. And we also ought to lay down our lives for the brethren . . And this is His commandment: that we should believe on the name of His Son Jesus Christ and love one another . . . We love Him because He first loved us . . . Whoever believes that Jesus is the Christ is born of God, and everyone who loves Him who begot also loves him who is begotten of Him. By this we know that we love the children of God, when we love God and keep His

---

[75] *The Pursuit of Holiness* p 118-120.

commandments. For this is the love of God, that we keep His commandments. And His commandments are not burdensome.'

Question: What is love?
Answer: I can tell you what God's love is not. It is not as the world sees love. It is not wishy-washy sentimental cute sayings found in cards, it is not words without action, and it is certainly not cupid with a bow. It is not as these anon feel-good clever sayings claim.
- Love is touching without touching.
- Love is like a battery; it needs the occasional recharge.
- Love is zipping your sleeping bags together,
- Love is the sum total of lots of nice little things.
- Love is a new experience every day.

Question: But before we go any further let's address this – Why would a supposedly good and loving God send anyone to hell?
Answer: The Bible tells us that God created hell not originally for man but for the angels, the head one being now named Satan, who rebelled against their creator and Lord, (Matthew 25:41). Scripture also tells us that the wages (price) of sin, which is ours to pay if we have not repented of and sought forgiveness for our wrongs, our rebellion against God and his rightful place in our lives and accepted from him in return his gracious and free-to-us gift of eternal life in Christ Jesus our Lord that our names may be written in the Lamb's Book of Life (Revelation 12:27), is death.

Physical death and spiritual death which is eternal separation from God in hell, (Romans 6:23, Revelation 20:12-15) occurs when God in fact honours our choice, our decision not to have him ruling our lives, after all we can do very well without him, can't you tell!

God does not send people to hell after death, he grants them what they chose, loved and desired in life here in this world, heaven and eternity with him or hell and eternity without him.

He gives those who spent their lifetime not wanting him eternity without him, honouring their choice. Completely without him, for while here on earth the unrepentant sinners share in the blessings that he sends the righteous which will not happen in hell, (Matthew 4:44-45).

John 3:36 tells us that 'He who believes in the Son has everlasting life; and he who does not believe the Son shall not see life, but the wrath of God abides on him.' Bob Cretney writes of a time someone asked him '"How could a loving God send people to hell?" He answered, "You're right, God is Love. But God is also holy. He hates sin. He cannot allow sin into His heaven. God does not send people to hell. If you choose not to believe on His Son, God simply honours your choice."'[76]

Now back to what love is (not that we really left for honouring one's set-in-cement decision is a love that respects). Love is a verb. A something you do, show by actions from a Christ-like mindset, a God-like character or nature, empowered by the Holy Spirit. It has nothing to do with self but everything to do with the one you are acting towards or for. This is probably why the Greek word *Eros*, meaning a self-centered love that seeks personal satisfaction and pleasure without always considering the welfare of those used to do so, is not found in the New Testament translated as love.

Question: What does the Bible mean by this word love? What is its importance and how does having a specific type of love as another foundational aspect of our new mindset change our behaviours?

Answer: In the English language we really only have one word for love and that is love, whereas the Greek language has many, each emphasizing a different aspect of this multifaceted word. The Greek words used in the New Testament (according to Strong's[77]) are –

- *agapaō* (#25) to love in a social or moral sense

---

[76] Taken from a daily reading in *Choice Gleanings: Wall Calendar* Dates now unknown.

[77] James Strong, LL.D., S.T.D. *The New Strong's Exhaustive Concordance of the Bible* Thomas Nelson Publishers 1995 Please note that I will be using this book for all #numbered words of Greek or Hebrew origin.

Matthew 5:43-44 where Jesus says, '"You have heard that it was said, 'You shall love your neighbour and hate your enemy.' But I say to you, love your enemies..."'
1Peter 2:17, 'Honor all people. Love the brotherhood. Fear God. Honour the king.'

- *agapētŏs* (#27) beloved: - (dearly, well) beloved, dear Matthew 3:17, '... heaven, saying, "This is My beloved Son..."' 1Peter 2:11, 'Dearly beloved I beg you as sojourners...'
- *thĕlō* (#2309) to determine, choose or prefer, to wish, be disposed. Mark 12:38 where Jesus says, '"Beware of the scribes, who desire to go around in long robes, love greetings in the market places..."'
- *prŏsphilēs* (#4375) friendly toward, i.e. ... acceptable: - lovely. Philippians 4:8, '.. are pure, whatever things are lovely..'
- *philagathŏs* (#5358) fond of good, i.e. a promoter of virtue: - love of good men. Titus 1:8, '... a lover of what is good, sober-minded...'
- *philadĕlphia* (#5360) fraternal affection, brotherly love or kindness, love of the brethren. Romans 12:10, 'Be kindly affectionate to one another with brotherly love, in honour giving preference to one another.'
- *philadĕlphŏs* (#5361) fond of brethren, i.e. fraternal: - love as for the brethren. 1Peter 3:8, '... love as brothers, be tenderhearted, be courteous'.
- *philandrŏs*: (#5362) fond of man, i.e. affectionate as a wife: - love their husbands. Titus2:4, '... admonish the young women to love their husbands.'
- *philanthrōpia*: (#5363) fondness of mankind, i.e. benevolence, ("philanthropy"): - kindness, love toward man. Titus 3:4, '... the love of God our Saviour toward man...'
- *philarguria*: (#5365) avarice: - love of money 1Timothy 6:10a, 'For the love of money is a root of all kinds of evil'.
- *philautŏs*: (#5367) fond of self, selfish, lover of own self 2Timothy 3:2, 'For men will be lovers of themselves...'

- *phileō* (#5368) to be a friend to (fond of an individual or an object) i.e. have an affection for (denoting personal attachment, as a matter of sentiment or feeling; while #25 is wider, embracing especially the judgement and the deliberate assent of the will as a matter of principle, duty and propriety: the two thus stand related) specially to kiss (as a mark of tenderness):- kiss, love.

1Corinthians 16:22, 'If anyone does not love the Lord Jesus Christ, let him be accursed. O Lord, come!'

Matthew 6:5 where Jesus says, '"And when you pray, you shall not be like the hypocrites. For they love to pray standing . . . that they may have glory from men . . ."'

Matthew 26:48, 'Now His betrayer had given them a sign, saying, "Whomever I kiss, He is the One; seize Him."'

There are only two other Greek words used in the New Testament that are translated as kiss. *philēma* (#5370) means 'a kiss' as in Luke 7:45, where Jesus says, '"You gave Me no kiss, but . . ."' and 22:48, '. . . Jesus said to him, "Judas, are you betraying the Son of Man with a kiss?"' and 1Peter 5:14, 'Greet one another with a kiss . . .' The other is (#2705) *kataphileō* meaning 'to kiss earnestly' and its only use in the Bible is by Jesus to describe the kisses that the weeping woman covered his feet with in Luke 7:45.

But the gospel writers used *phileō* for the word Judas used for his sign to show the mob who had to be arrested, Matthew 26:48, 'Now His betrayer had given them a sign, saying, "Whomever I kiss, He is the One; seize Him."'

- *philēdŏnŏs (#5369)* fond of pleasure, i.e. voluptuous: - lover of pleasure. 2Timothy 3:4, '. . . haughty, lovers of pleasure rather than . . . God'.
- *philŏthĕŏs* (#5377) fond of God, i.e. pious: - lover of God 2 Timothy 3:4, '. . . rather than lovers of God'.
- *philŏxĕnŏs* (#5382) fond of guests, i.e. hospitable: - given to (lover of, use) hospitality. Titus 1:7-8, 'For a bishop must be blameless . . . not greedy for money, but hospitable . . .'
- *philŏprōtĕuō* (#5383) to be fond of being first, i.e. ambitious of distinction: - love to have the pre-eminence

3John 9, '. . . Diotrephes, who loves to have the pre-eminence among them, does not receive us.'

- *philŏtĕknŏs* (#5388) fond of one's children, i.e. maternal: - love their children. Titus 2:4, '. . . admonish the young women . . . to love their children.'

These loves are all good for us to give out and receive but there is one more that the New Testament uses which I want us to really consider, one that is rarely seen outside of the New Testament, and that is *agapē* (#26) love, i.e. affection or benevolence; specially (plural) a love-feast: - (feast of) charity ([-ably]), dear, love.

This is an 'Unconditional love that is always giving and impossible to take or be a taker. It devotes total commitment to seek your highest best no matter how anyone may respond. This form of love is totally selfless and does not change whether the love given is returned or not.'[78]

When the King James Version of the Bible was written just over four hundred years ago *agapē* was translated as *charity* which may seem odd to us in today's world but pause and consider for a moment. My trusty Oxford dictionary defines charity or the act of being charitable as a voluntary and generous giving to those in need, a tolerance in judging others, an aptness to judge a person's acts and motives favourably. Is this not how God acts towards fallen humanity and pilgrims and their needs of forgiveness and sustaining? And does not the idea of needing charity prick at our pride of self-reliance and ability?

The beloved apostle, John, who loved Jesus liked using love words in his five books, *agapaō* is used around fifty-two times and *agapē*, about twenty-seven times. For example, consider

1John 4:7-12, 16-18, 'Beloved (#27), let us love (#25) one another, for love (#26) is of God; and everyone who loves (#25) is born of God and knows God. He who does not love (#25) does not know God, for God is love (#26). In this the love (#26) of God was

---

[78] http://www.ezilon.com/articles/articles/7657/1/God-is-Agape-Love

manifested toward us, that God has sent His only begotten Son into the world, that we might live through Him. In this is love (#26), not that we loved (#25) God, but that He loved (#25) us and sent His Son to be the propitiation for our sins. Beloved (#27), if God so loved (#25) us, we also ought to love (#25) one another. No one has seen God at any time. If we love (#26) one another, God abides in us, and His love (#25) has been perfected in us . . . And we have known and believed the love (#26) that God has for us. God is love (#26), and he who abides in love (#26) abides in God and God in him. Love (#26) has been perfected among us in this: that we may have boldness in the day of judgement; because as He is, so are we in this world. There is no fear in love (#26); but perfect love (#26) casts out fear, because fear involves torment. But he who fears has not been made perfect in love (#26).

Agapē is presented in these verses as the very nature of God, he not only loves, he is charitable love and in 1Corinthians 13:13 we are told it is the greatest of the Christian virtues, as Paul writes 'And now abide faith, hope, love, these three; but the greatest of these is love.'

Question: A bit of a sideways one but have you ever wondered what we would be without God?

Answer: I skimmed over some pithy sayings from famous people answering this question that Google came up with. However, the ones I saw seemed to forget one very important fact, that without God we could not even take our next breath let alone exist, we would truly be nothing.

But God exits and therefore so do we. The above verse however, seems to be saying that at the end of time, some things will cease to exist. So back to those three words, faith, hope and love from 1Corinthians 13:13.

Faith which Hebrews 1:11 tells us 'is the substance of things hoped for, the evidence of things not seen' will no longer be needed when we see our hope fulfilled at the 'revelation of Jesus Christ', (1Peter 1:13).

Likewise Romans 8:24 tells us that 'we were saved in this hope, but hope that is seen is not hope; for why does one still hope for what he sees?', so hope will cease to be required after God ends time as we know it and all is fulfilled of his word and we receive, see our inheritance.

But love, this love of God that is his very self will always eternally exist, just as it did before time.

With the assistance of a Bible dictionary[79] and other sources we are going to have a closer look at this love that we should be nurturing in our minds till it spills out in words and deeds.

- All human love, whether God-ward or man-ward, has its source in God. Love in its true reality and power is seen only in the light of Calvary.

Considering 1John 4:7-10 again, Tozer tells us that 'The words 'God is love' mean that love is an essential attribute of God. . . It expresses the way God is in His unitary being, as do the words holiness, justice, faithfulness and truth. Because God is immutable, he always acts like Himself, and because He is a unity, He never suspends one of His attributes in order to exercise another.

From God's other known attributes, we may learn much about His love. We can know, for instance, that because God is self-existent, His love had no beginning; because He is eternal, His love can have no end; because He is infinite, it has no limit; because He is holy, it is the quintessence of all spotless purity; because He is immense, His love is an incomprehensibly vast, bottomless, shoreless sea before which we kneel in joyful silence and from which the loftiest eloquence retreats confused and abashed. . . .

[Love] considers nothing its own but gives all freely to the object of its affection . . .

Self-sufficient as He is, He wants our love and will not be satisfied till He gets it. Free as he is, He has let His heart be bound to us

---

[79] J. D. Douglas & Merrill C. Tenney *The New International Dictionary of the Bible* Zondervan 1987 p 603.

forever. 'Herein is love, not that we loved God, but that he loved us, and sent his Son to be the propitiation for our sins'

'For our soul is so specially loved of Him that is highest,' says Julian of Norwich, 'that it overpasseth the knowing of all creatures: that is to say there is no creature that is made that may know how much and how sweetly and how tenderly our Maker loveth us. And therefore we may with grace and His help stand in spiritual beholding, with everlasting marvel of this high, overpassing inestimable Love that Almighty God hath to us of His Goodness.'

Another characteristic of love is that it takes pleasure in its object. God enjoys His creation. . .

The Lord takes peculiar pleasure in His saints. Many think of God as far removed, gloomy and mightily displeased with everything gazing down in a mood of fixed apathy upon a world in which He has long ago lost interest; but this is to think erroneously. . . in Christ all believing souls are objects of God's delight. "The Lord thy God in the midst of thee is mighty; he will save, he will rejoice over thee with joy; he will rest in his love, he will joy over thee with singing." . . . .

Earth is the place where the pleasures of love are mixed with pain, for sin is here, and hate and ill-will. In such a world as ours love must sometimes suffer, as Christ suffered in giving Himself for His own. But we have a certain promise that the causes of sorrow will finally be abolished and the new race enjoy forever a world of selfless, perfect love.

It is of the nature of love that it cannot lie quiescent. It is active, creative, and benign . . .

The love of God is one of the great realities of the universe, a pillar upon which the hope of the world rests. But it is a personal, intimate thing too. God does not love populations, he loves people. He loves not masses, but men. He loves us all with a mighty love that has no beginning and can have no end . . . This love . . . is more than a thing, it is God Himself in the midst of His

The Pilgrim Way

Church singing over His people. True Christian joy is the heart's harmonious response to the Lord's song of love.'[80]

- Love is created in the believer by the Holy Spirit.

Romans 5:5, 'Now hope does not disappoint, because the love of God has been poured out in our hearts by the Holy Spirit who was given to us . . .'

Galatians 5:22, 'But the fruit of the Spirit is love . . .' prompting pilgrims to love both God and man.

2Corinthians 5:14-15, 'For the love of Christ compels us, because we judge thus: that if One died for all, then all died; and He died for all, that those who live should live no longer for themselves, but for Him who died for them and rose again.'

1John 4:20-21, 'if someone says, "I love God," and hates his brother, he is a liar; for he who does not love his brother whom he has seen, how can he love God whom he has not seen? And this commandment we have from Him: that he who loves God must love his brother also.'

- Love finds its expression in service to our fellow human.

Galatians 5:13; 'For you, brethren, have been called to liberty; only do not use liberty as an opportunity for the flesh, but through love serve one another.'

- And love is the chief test of Christian discipleship.

Luke 14:26, 'If anyone comes to Me and does not hate his father and mother, wife and children, brothers and sisters, yes, and his own life also, he cannot be My disciple.' Hate in this context means that compared to how much you love Christ your love for family or your own life seems like hatred. Christ is your first, greatest love. If other loves are not second they have become your idols.

John 13:35, 'By this all will know that you are My disciples, if you have love for one another.'

- Love is vitally related to faith but faith is basic.

---

[80] A. W. Tozer *The Knowledge of the Holy* STL Books Kingsway Publications 1961 p105, 107-9.

John 6:29, 'Jesus answered and said to them, "This is the work of God, that you believe in Him whom He sent."'

Hebrews 11:6, 'But without faith it is impossible to please Him, for he who comes to God must believe that He is, and that He is a rewarder of those who diligently seek Him.'

- But a faith that does not manifest itself in love both toward God and man is dead and worthless.

Galatians 5:6, 13, 'For in Christ Jesus neither circumcision nor uncircumcision avails anything, but faith working through love . . For you, brethren, have been called to liberty; only do not use liberty as an opportunity for the flesh, but through love serve one another.'

- The Christian must love God supremely and his neighbour as himself.

Matthew 22:37-39, 'Jesus said to him, "'You shall love the Lord your God with all your heart, with all your soul, and with all your mind.' This is the first and great commandment. And the second is like it: 'You shall love your neighbour as yourself.'"

- He must love his enemy as well as his brother.

Matthew 5:43-48, 'You have heard that it was said, 'You shall love your neighbour and hate your enemy.' But I say to you, love your enemies, bless those who curse you, do good to those who spitefully use you and persecute you, that you may be sons of your Father in heaven; for He makes His sun rise on the evil and on the good, and sends rain on the just and on the unjust. For if you love those who love you, what reward have you? Do not even the tax collectors do the same? And if you greet your brethren only, what do you do more than others? Do not even the tax collectors do so? Therefore you shall be perfect, just as your Father is heaven is perfect.'

Romans 12:19-20, 'Beloved, do not avenge yourselves, but rather give place to wrath; for it is written, "Vengeance is Mine, I will repay," says the Lord. Therefore "If your enemy is hungry, feed him; If he is thirsty, give him a drink; For is so doing you will heap coals of fire on his head."

1John 3:14, 'We know that we have passed from death to life, because we love the brethren. He who does not love his brother abides in death.'

- And our love must be void of all hypocrisy, (for then it is not God's but man's love) and displayed by truthful, not insincere deeds, deeds done not for love of the person receiving but for the self wanting.

Romans 12:9, 'Let love be without hypocrisy. Abhor what is evil. Cling to what is good.'

1John 3:18,'My little children, let us not love in word or in tongue, but in deed and in truth.'

- Love is the bond uniting all the Christian virtues.

Colossians 3:14, 'But above all these things put on love, which is the bond of perfection.'

- There is no fear involved with this love of God, not even a whiff.

1John 4:18, 'There is no fear in love; but perfect love casts out fear, because fear involves torment. But he who fears has not been made perfect in love.'

Tozer writes 'Love wills the good of all and never wills harm or evil to any. This explains the words of the apostle John, 'There is no fear in love; but perfect love casteth out fear.' Fear is the painful emotion that arises at the thought that we may be harmed of made to suffer. This fear persists while we are subject to the will of someone who does not desire our well-being. The moment we come under the protection of one of goodwill, fear is cast out. . . As long as we are in the hands of chance, as long as we must look for hope to the law of averages, as long as we must trust for survival to our ability to outthink or out manoeuvre the enemy, we have every good reason to be afraid. And fear hath torment.

To know that love is of God . . . this and only this can cast out fear . . . the deep torment of fear is gone forever. God is love and God is sovereign. His love disposes Him to desire our everlasting welfare and His sovereignty enables Him to secure it. . .

God's love tells us that He is friendly and His Word assures us that He is our friend and wants us to be His friends.' [81]

Can you see how this love is not really the way fallen humanity loves at all times? They can't. It is a love that requires the strength and resources of God, of the Holy Spirit himself within us. In fact, it is God's love created within us that loves like this. And can you see how loving this way affects our attitude and our behaviour towards God, fellow pilgrims and those of the world? And can you see that we need to experience God's love for ourselves first before we can love our neighbour correctly, truthfully, in holiness? And can you see the difference this mindset would make to how we lived out our lives here?

But wait, there is more . . .

I have heard many people over the years saying that they don't like studying the Old Testament as it is in the New that we have love, the Old is just full of 'do nots' and a lot of wrath and bloodletting, not much love being shed around. This thinking is really incorrect for the God of the New Testament is the same God of the Old for the nature of God has never and will never change. It is actually in the Old Testament we first learn how different God's love is from man's love and also the love that the nations surrounding Israel exhibited. Being mostly written in Hebrew, not Greek like the New we will be focusing on the Hebrew word *hesedh*. This is usually translated as mercy or lovingkindness in the NKJ or as love and sometimes kindnesses or kindness in the NIV, though those words give a very small picture of the depth of meaning this word carries. *Hesedh* appears around one hundred and eighty times in the Old Testament.

Again, I am using my Bible dictionary to help explore this word more deeply.

- The Hebrew word *hesedh* is one of the most important in the Old Testament and lies at the center of the Lord's self-revelation of his attitude toward mankind.

---

[81] *The Knowledge of the Holy* p105-6

Throughout the Old Testament the meaning remains unchanged from that found in the first examples: as the Lord looks on us, his *hesedh* is rooted in his grace and mercy.

Genesis 19:19, 'Indeed now, your servant [Lot speaking to the two angels, 19:1] has found favour in your sight, and you have increased your mercy which you have shown me by saving my life; but I cannot escape to the mountains, lest some evil overtake me and I die.' Here it combines the ideas of love, commitment, duty, and care.

- It is explicitly linked with "truth"– i.e., being true to oneself, truthfulness, reliability – and so there is a stress on the loyalty with which love acts. Genesis 32:10, [Jacob speaking to God] 'I am not worthy of the least of all the mercies and of all the truth which You have shown Your servant; for I crossed over this Jordan with my staff, and now I have become two companies.'

Exodus 34:6, 'And the LORD passed before [Moses] and proclaimed, "The LORD, the LORD God, merciful and gracious, longsuffering, and abounding in goodness and truth,'

- The Lord's *hesedh* leads him to redeem repentant mankind.

Exodus 15:13, 'You in Your mercy have led forth the people who You have redeemed; You have guided them in Your strength to Your holy habitation.'

- It is an inexhaustible patient attribute of God's divine

nature. Numbers 14:18, 'The LORD is longsuffering and abundant in mercy, forgiving iniquity and transgression . . .'

Psalm 118:1-4, 'Oh give thanks to the LORD, for He is good! For His mercy endures forever. Let Israel now say, "His mercy endures forever." Let the house of Aaron now say, "His mercy endures forever." Let those who fear the LORD now say, "His mercy endures forever."

Psalm 62:12, 'Also to You, O Lord, belongs mercy; for You render to each one according to his work.'

- The word *hesedh* mirrors the word *agapē* in the New

Testament. It is how the Lord feels and acts toward mankind. As a result, it is how pilgrims, following his example, should act toward others and how they should respond to their Lord himself.

Joshua 2:12, 'Now therefore, I [Rahab speaking to the spies Joshua had sent out into the promised land] beg you, swear to me by the LORD, since I have shown you kindness, that you also will show kindness to my father's house, and give me a true token.'

2Samuel 9:1, 'Now David said, "Is there still anyone who is left of the house of Saul, that I may show him kindness for Jonathan's sake?'

Hosea 6:6, 'For I desire mercy and not sacrifice, and the knowledge of God more than burnt offerings.'

Taking the whole evidence of the Old Testament, *hesedh* holds together the ideas of love and loyalty with a strong emphasis on the practical more than the emotional sides of these ideas. It is the loyal love that is displayed when there is no other motive to action except love and loyalty. [82]

> Put simply, *hesedh* is the defining characteristic of God in the Old Testament. Sometimes translated as "loving-kindness", it is a key to understanding who God really is . . . At the heart of understanding *hesedh* lies the crucial notion that it is unmerited, undeserved, unearnable. This facet of *hesed* is what the New Testament often calls "grace" . . . Some other attempts to translate *hesed* include: "enemy-love," "unexpected favour," "surprising grace," "unmerited forgiveness," "unsolicited love," "compassionate grace." Jesus' life teaches us that a supremely untranslatable word can only be understood when it becomes "infleshed," translated into a living person. Through the incarnation of Jesus, *hesedh* was at last perfectly defined. [83]

So, this is love, the love that our pilgrim lives are to display to a watching world, a love that is only possible for us to understand

---

[82] *The new International Dictionary of the Bible* p 603.

[83] Michael Card (born 1957) *A Sacred Sorrow. Experience Guide. Reaching out to God in the Lost language of Lament* Navpress 2005 p23

and show in action to others because it is first the love of God for us, to us and in us right from the beginning, before he started creating. It is a love based on the deliberate choice of the one loving rather than on the loved one being worthy. And it is commanded of us as we have read before by Jesus and as we read in Deuteronomy 6:5 after our LORD had freed his people from slavery by the Egyptians, 'You shall love the LORD your God with all your heart, with all your soul, and with all your strength.' And as Bridges wrote, 'We must see our circumstances through God's love instead of, as we are prone to do, seeing God's love through our circumstances.'[84]

> The great commandment of all, which is indeed inclusive of all, is, that of "loving God with all our hearts". Where this is the commanding principle in the soul, there is a disposition to every other duty. Love is the leading affection of the soul: the love of God is the leading grace in the renewed soul. Where this is not, nothing else that is good is done, or done aright, or accepted, or done long. Loving God with all our hearts will effectually take us off from, and arm us against, all those things that are rivals with him for the throne in our souls, and will engage us to everything by which he may be honoured, and with which he will be pleased; and no commandment will be grievous where this principle commands, and has the ascendant. [85]

Fleetwood considering Mark xii.29, 30, ['Jesus answered him, "The first [foremost] of all the commandments is 'Hear, O Israel, the LORD our God, the LORD is one. And you shall love the LORD your God with all your heart, with all your soul, with all your mind, and with all your strength.' This is the first commandment. And the second, like it, is this: 'You shall love your neighbour as yourself.' There is no other commandment greater than these'"] wrote that, 'The first and chief commandment is, to give God our

---

[84] *Trusting God* p148

[85] *Fleetwood's Life of Christ* comment by Matthew Henry p481

hearts. The divine Being is so transcendently amiable in himself, and hath, by the innumerable benefits conferred upon us, such a title to our utmost affection, that no obligation bears any proportion to that of loving him. The honour assigned to this precept proves, that piety [a devout act arising from one's love of God] is the noblest act of the of the human mind; and that the chief ingredient in piety is love, founded on a clear and extensive view of the divine perfections, a permanent sense of his benefits, and a deep conviction of his being the sovereign good, our portion in time, and our happiness throughout a never ending eternity. But it is essential to love, that there be a delight in contemplating the beauty of the object beloved, whether that beauty be matter of sensation or reflection; that we frequently, and with pleasure, reflect on the benefits conferred on us by the object of our affections; that we have a strong desire of pleasing him, that we stand in awe [reverent fear] of doing anything to offend him, and have a sensible joy in realising to ourselves that we are beloved in return. Hence the duties of devotional exercises, of being much engaged in prayer and praise, as the most natural and genuine exercises, of the love which a creature can show to the Creator. Nor is this virtue so much any single affection, as the continual bent of all the affections and powers of the mind, body, and soul, being in the right direction: consequently, to love God is always to aim at directing the whole soul towards him, and to concentrate all its facilities on him as its chief object.

Accordingly, the love of God is described in scripture by the several operations of the mind, "a following hard after God", namely, by intense contemplation; a sense of his perfections, gratitude for his benefits, trust in his goodness, attachment to his service, resignation to his will in providence, the obeying his commandments, and putting our trust in him for time and for eternity. This must not consist in any of those singly, but in them all united together; for to content ourselves with partial regards to the supreme Being, is not to be affected towards him in the manner we ought to be, and which his perfections claim.

Hence the words of the precept are, "Thou shalt love the Lord thy God with all thy heart, and with all thy soul, and with all thy mind, and with all thy strength," that is, with the joint force of all thy faculties; and therefore, no idol whatsoever must partake of that love and worship that is due to him. But the beauty and excellency of this state of mind is best seen in its effects: for the worship and obedience flowing from such a universal bent of the soul towards God, is as much superior to the worship and obedience arising from partial considerations, as the brightness of the sun is to any picture which could be drawn of that luminary.

For example, if we look upon God only as a stern lawgiver, who can and will punish our rebellion, it may create within us an awe and dread of him, and compel us to give as much obedience to his laws as we think will satisfy him, but can never produce that true fidelity in the performance of our duty, and that earnestness to fulfil it to its utmost extent, which are produced and maintained in the mind, by the sacred fire of divine love, or by the bent of the whole soul turned toward God. This however is the frame of all others the most becoming of any that can be conceived, and also the most to be desired, because it constitutes the highest perfection, and real happiness of the creature.

Again, this commandment requires us to fear God; and certainly we cannot love the Lord our God, unless we fear and reverence him; for as the love, so the fear of God, is the sum of all the commandments, and indeed the substance of all religion. Prayer and praise are the tribute and homage of religion; by the one we acknowledge our dependence upon God; by the other we confess that all our blessings and comforts flow from him. Such, therefore, as neither pray to God, nor give him the praise due to his name, cannot be said to recognise the living God; for they acknowledge none, but are gods to themselves; and as the love and fear of God are often used in scripture for the whole worship and service, so is this invocation of his name; "Pour out thy
fury upon the heathen, and upon the families that have not called upon thy name"; that is, those who do not worship or serve

him . . .'[86]

Barnes adds that '. . . all true obedience depends on the correct knowledge of God. None can keep his commandments who are not acquainted with his nature, his perfections, and his right to command.

The meaning of "Thou shalt love the Lord thy God", is, thou shalt love him with all thy faculties or powers. Thou shalt love him supremely, more than all other beings and things, and with all the ardour possible. To love him with all the heart is to fix the affections supremely on him, more strongly than on anything else, and to be willing to give up all that we hold dear at his command. "With all thy soul", means, to be willing to give up the life to him, and to devote it all to his service; to live to him, and to be willing to die at his command. "With all thy mind". Submit the *intellect* to his will. To love his law and gospel more than we do the decisions of our own minds. To be willing to submit all our faculties to his teaching and guidance, and to devote to him all our intellectual attainments, and all the results of our intellectual efforts. "With all thy strength". With all the faculties of soul and body. To labour and toil for his glory, and to make that the great object of all our efforts.

This commandment is the first and greatest of all; *first*, not in *order of time*, but of *importance*; *greatest* in dignity, in excellence, in extent, and duration. It is the fountain of all others . . . If He is loved aright, then our affections will be directed towards all created objects in a right manner.'[87]

I'm going to side track for a moment but hang in there as I am hoping you will see and feel what I did reading what follows while keeping in mind all you have just read.

In John 6:1-13 we read of how Jesus had twelve full baskets of bread fragments left over after feeding about five thousand men with five barley loaves and two small fish, but in the next two verses we read of the peoples' reaction; 'Then those men, when

---

[86] *Fleetwood's Life of Christ* p481-484
[87] Ibid comment from Barnes on the Gospels p482

they had seen the sign that Jesus did, said, "This is truly the Prophet who is to come into the world." Therefore when Jesus perceived that they were about to come and take Him by force to make Him king, He departed again to the mountain by Himself alone.'

Scott comments that the crowd had 'hoped this might be a fair opportunity of shaking off the Roman yoke, which they were weary of. If they had one to head them who could victual an army cheaper than another could provide for a family, they were sure of the sinews of the war, and could not fail of success, and the recovery of their ancient liberties. Thus is religion often prostituted to a secular interest, and Christ is served only to "serve a turn". "Jesus is usually sought after for something else, not for his own sake." . . . they would take him "by force," whether he would or no. Those who force honours upon Christ, which he has not required at their hands, displease him, and do him the greatest dishonour . . . Here in he has left a testimony against ambition and affectation of worldly honour, to which he was perfectly mortified, and has taught us to be so.' [88]

Yes, we are to mortify, kill any mindset that leads to a hunger, a lust for worldly acclaim just as Christ did here. We are to go alone in prayer to God for help to do so. And we are not to pray to God in a forceful demanding manner for that which we desire with no thought of his desires for such a prayer cannot be expected to be answered in the way we want. But these things are not what I want you to primarily see from this side tracking. It is this thought, *Christ is served only to "serve a turn", only to get what you want, He is sought after for something else, not for his own sake . . .*

How do you feel when you know someone is using you? Is this loving? Is this loving and glorifying Christ? Is this the action of someone who is growing in holiness? What does this sort of motivation say of your knowledge of the person of Christ, of God and the Holy Spirit?

---

[88] Ibid p 256

Now, where were we? Oh, yes . . .

Question: If God is love, then love is God. Can God fail, can love fail, run out?

Answer: Deuteronomy 31:6, 8 reads, 'Be strong and of good courage, do not fear nor be afraid of them; for the LORD your God, He is the One who goes with you. He will not leave you nor forsake you . . . And the LORD, He is the One who goes before you. He will be with you, He will not leave you nor forsake you: do not fear nor be dismayed.'

Here the Hebrew word translated *leave* can also be translated *fail* as it is in the KJ and NLT versions.

Joshua 21:45, 'Not a word failed of any good thing which the LORD had spoken to the house of Israel. All came to pass.'

In Psalm 136 there is a repeated line in every one of the 26 verses which says, 'For His mercy [his *hesedh* love] endures forever'.

Luke 1:37(NLT), 'For the word of God will never fail.'

Luke 1:37(NLT), 'Don't love money; be satisfied with what you have. For God has said, "I will never fail you. I will never abandon you."'

So, no, God cannot fail and neither can his love, unlike ours. As pilgrims we have the triune God abiding within, so we have all we need to not fail, to love as he. Do you not find that incredibly reassuring and encouraging?

John 14:23, 'Jesus answered and said to him, "If anyone loves Me, he will keep My word; and My Father will love him, and We will come to him and make Our home with him."'

The foundational mindset that pilgrims need to adopt, I believe are these that we have looked at – a Christ-like mindset based on his holiness and *agapē/hesedh* love, accompanied by the right fear of God who is our sovereign LORD with an understanding that suffering will occur as we are strangers sojourning through this world on our way home.

Heed worry and anxiety

Scripture has many warnings to pilgrims of how not to appear before the watching world but I am again going to select just one,

one mindset which pilgrims should not have but which we all have to varying degrees and perhaps struggle with more at some parts of our sojourn than others which left unchecked will strangle faith and that is all that gathers under the umbrella of worry. If this is minimized in our lives compared to those outside of Christ, we will stand out from the maddening crowd and show the truth, reality that our God is enough. Easy to write, harder to do.

God tells us that faith comes by hearing his words. Hearing can happen by many ways. You can hear because of someone else reading and preaching from the Bible from the pulpit or through the many forms of media we can use today. You can hear as you silently read to yourself from the words God has given us of himself also. Interestingly the Greek verbs for *obey* and for *disobey* are both compounds of the verb to *hear*. To obey is to hear submissively and to disobey is to hear dismissively. From all this hearing we come to know God personally and relationally and grow in this knowledge and so in our trust and obedience.

Chapter 11 with 12 and its first two verses of the book of Hebrews discusses this faith and how it enables and encourages pilgrims from the dawn of time to us in the now. Even the nameless ones in this passage, who have nothing listed of their doings other than suffering and persecutions to death, of wandering in deserts and living in dens and caves – no degrees, full on evangelistic or missionary programs done here – even these pleased God because they believed he existed and would reward those who were diligent in seeking him.

Faith means clinging, yes even if only by a couple of fingernails, to the sure hope of the reality of God and his promises. But consider this, the process of hearing and faith, like God and his promises are invisible. Remember the earlier definition of faith? Confidence in things invisible.

So perhaps it is understandable that the world scoffs at pilgrims, that faith could be seen almost suicidal, a waste of precious time. This is one reason that can make it hard for pilgrims to sustain faith, another is the fact it can be easily strangled by worry and this world was a cess pool of worry producers in the Bible's time and still is in ours.

Question: What do you think of or picture with this word worry, its causes, its results?

Answer: I am going to throw you a list of random words or ideas but I am sure you can add to them. Words like, anguish, torment, paranoia, difficulty, indecisiveness, crankiness, weariness of spirit, fear, uneasiness, sleeplessness, nervousness, what will people think! scatter-brain, fretting, weight on one's mind, migraine, distressed, shame.

From experience I have discovered that worry leads to fears which when get out of control lead to a paralysis of life and joy, not a good peaceful place to be. Some years back I went through my Bible and underlined all the times God asked us to not fear, not fret, not be anxious and why not. It was a great study.

Let's have a look at the Greek for this word in the New Testament. *merimnao* (#3309) to be anxious about: - (be, have) care (-full), take thought. The root it comes from can give it the idea of dividing or of distraction. In the KJ it is translated careful or thought, worried or worry in the NKJ and worried or anxious in the NASB.

Luke 10:38-42, 'Now it happened as [the disciples and Jesus] went that He entered a certain village; and a certain woman named Martha welcomed Him into her house. And she had a sister called Mary, who also sat at Jesus' feet and heard His word. But Martha was distracted with much serving, and she approached Him and said, "Lord, do You not care that my sister has left me to serve alone? Therefore tell her to help me." And Jesus answered and said to her, "Martha, Martha, you are worried and troubled about many things. But one thing is needed, and Mary has chosen that good part, which will not be taken away from her."'

Matthew 6:24-34 where Jesus is teaching us that '"No one can serve two masters; for either he will hate the one and love the other, or else he will be loyal to the one and despise the other. You cannot serve God and mammon [literally in Aramaic, 'riches']. Therefore I say to you, do not worry about your life, what you will eat or what you will drink; nor about your body, what you will put on. Is not life more than food and the body more than clothing? Look at the birds of the air, for they neither sow nor reap nor gather into barns; yet your heavenly Father feeds them. Are you not of more value than they? Which of you by worrying can add one cubit [about 18inches] to his stature [height]? So why do you worry about clothing? Consider the lilies of the field, how they grow: they neither toil nor spin; and yet I say to you that even Solomon in all his glory was not arrayed [dressed] like one of these. Now if God so clothes the grass of the field, which today is, and tomorrow is thrown into the oven, will He not much more clothe you, O you of little faith? Therefore do not worry, saying, 'What shall we eat? 'or 'What shall we drink?' or 'What shall we wear?' For after all these things the Gentiles seek. For your heavenly Father knows that you need these things. But seek first the kingdom of God and His righteousness, and all these things shall be added to you. Therefore do not worry about tomorrow, for tomorrow will worry about its own things. Sufficient for the day is its own trouble."'

Mark4:18-19 where Jesus is explaining the parable of the sower and seed to his disciples, '"Now these are the ones sown among thorns; they are the ones who hear the word, and the cares of this world, the deceitfulness of riches, and the desires for other things entering in choke the word, and it becomes unfruitful."'

Luke 21:34 where Jesus warns us saying, '"But take heed to yourselves, lest your hearts be weighed down with carousing [dissipation], drunkenness, and cares of this life, and that Day come on you unexpectedly. . ."'

<u>Question</u>: How did Jesus describe Martha's state of mind in the Luke 10 passage?

<u>Answer</u>: Using his NSAB version Mr. Swindoll writes, 'Those two terms He used to describe her attitude are significant . . . The first one, translated 'worried' is the same term found in Mat. 6:25 translated 'anxious' [worried NKJ] . . . *merimnao*. This Greek term means having a divided mind. The English word 'worry' comes

from the German 'worgen', 'to strangle'. See Mk. 4:18-19 . . . Those thorn-like worries [cares NKJ] of the world . . . choke the word . . . Worry strangles the . . . Word of God making it ineffective . . .

"Martha! You are so mentally torn; you are trying to do too many things at once" – that sort of thing. Worry occurs when we assume responsibility for things that are outside of our control.'

Read that last sentence again and sit and think on it for a while if need be.

Worry occurs when we assume responsibility for things that are outside of our control.

My life would be different if I could cement this into my brain and remember it when I need to, and not after my hair has fallen out.

Back to Mr Swindoll (however I will be occasionally butting in) '. . . And . . . His solution – "only a few things are necessary, really only one" . . . . Martha had complicated things by turning the meal into a holiday feast. Not Mary. All Mary wanted was time with Jesus . . Mary's simple faith, in contrast to her sister's panic, won the Saviour's affirmation.

What's wrong with worry? It is incompatible with faith . . . How can we conquer worry? The story of Martha and Mary comes in handy here for in it I find three helpful answers . . .

- Realistic expectations.

[Do not be driven by idealism or what another thinks you should be like but be content to sit and relax in the presence of God.]

- Refusal to play God.

When Mary didn't move toward the kitchen, Martha assumed to role of the 4th member of the Trinity and told Jesus to get with it. [God's game plan is not mine.]

- Remember God's character.

Is God good? Is He just? Fair? Reliable? Faithful? Worriers tend to forget . . .

Contentment with the way things are, even knowing that God could change them if He wished, is a mindset that is foreign to the worrier. What *is*, is not enjoyed because of what *could* be.

Whoever chooses to live like that should be ready for a life time of dissatisfaction.'[89]

How much complaining and grumbling comes from not enjoying life as it is, not being thankful for at least one thing that happened during your day but wishing for something else, something more? How different would our conversations sound if there was an absence of grizzling and moaning about what could have been, or should have been if only _____ ?

Remember rightly

Beveridge advises us that 'Faith is never easy, nor knowing intellectually and experientially that you do not belong anymore in this world, that you can no longer find the enjoyment you once had thinking and doing what you once did as a sinner for your renewed heart/mind as a pilgrim will not allow you to. Yet 'so easy is the yoke of Christ, that, to the faithful Christian, it is a pleasure rather than a trouble to bear it. He is a master who will never require of us more than he will give us grace to preform, nor lay a greater burden upon us than he will give us strength to bear.' [90]

> Mind this. By believing his pardon by the blood, his justification by the righteousness of Christ, the free everlasting love of God to him, by the witness of His Spirit, and the glory of heaven to which he is going, are what strengthens the Christian's heart against all his lusts and corruptions.[91]

Christ's, Paul's, Bunyan's Christian and our focus on our glorious future, on home – just imagine a place where there will never be a reason to cry because our heart will never hurt! – will enable us to

---

[89] Charles R. Swindoll (born 1934) *Simple Faith* W Publishing Group 1996 p198-202.

[90] *Fleetwood's Life of Christ* comment by Beveridge (possibly William/Henry Beveridge baptised 1637 died 1708) p655

[91] *The Pilgrim's Progress* comment by Manson p92

properly assess problems and see how small they are compared to their eternal impact.

Compared to the length of our eternal glory, our sojourn here is extremely temporary.

We should be pleased to know that in the day, the moment that we physically die here, we will immediately be in the place where there is no suffering, no pain and no tears but where we will be face to face with our beloved Jesus.

For his promise to the thief on the cross next to him is for all those who really see him and repent "Today you will be with Me in Paradise" (Luke 23:43).

We will be with God! We will be home! What more could any pilgrim desire? Heaven after all is heaven only because God is there. How much do you desire, long for him, just him?

This is only a mindset of a pilgrim. It is never that of the world, it cannot be.

This new mindset above any other sets us apart from the world, marks us as his and sets us squarely in Satan's sights.

Remember. Remember whose you are now as a pilgrim, remember the new mindset you have been freely given by your Father, remember the hope he has given, remember the promises he has given but remember rightly.

> . . . when Christian was locked up in Doubting Castle, memory formed the club with which the famous giant beat his captives so terribly. They remembered how they had left the right road, how they had been warned not to do so, and how, in rebellion against their better natures, they had wandered into By-path Meadow. They remembered all their past misdeeds, their sins, their evil thoughts and evil words, and all these were like knots of wood in the club, causing sad bruises and wounds in their poor suffering bodies.
>
> However, one night, the same memory that had whipped them, helped to get them free, for it whispered something in Christian's ear. He then cried out as one half-amazed, "What a fool I am to lie in a stinking dungeon when I can walk in freedom! I have a key in my inside coat pocket,

called Promise. It will, I am persuaded, open any lock in Doubting Castle" . . . And so, by this blessed act of memory, poor Christian and Hopeful were set free . . . We may establish, then, as a general principle, that if we would exercise our memories a little more, we could, in our very deepest and darkest distresses, strike a match that would instantaneously light the lantern of comfort . . . and if they would turn to the Book of Truth and the throne of grace, their flame would shine as before . . . [92]

Sadly, heaven is not our focus. We want to enjoy life now and cling to it as long as we're able. We don't view death as the gateway to everything we've been living for. We see it as something to be postponed and avoided at all costs. We don't view ourselves as pilgrims. And because we don't, we can easily hold to a shallow form of Christianity. [93]

O Lord, never allow us to think we can stand by ourselves and not need you, our greatest need.   John Donne 1573-1631

---

[92] *Finding Peace in Life's Storms* p84-5
[93] Sermon *The Daily Battle: proving to be true pilgrims*

Robyn Crothers

Part Two: A War to Fight

. . . abstain from fleshy lusts which war against the soul. 1Peter2: 11b

Abstain from fleshly lusts which wage war against the soul" says verse 11. To abstain means "to hold oneself constantly back from". Waging war, points, not to a single battle, but to a military campaign. Every believer faces a lifelong struggle against these fleshy lusts which, if yielded to, will take a person captive and destroy him . . . The word "war" points to a fierce, constant struggle which implies a fair amount of effort on our part. . . The Christian life is portrayed as effortless and easy. But that's not what Peter says here. He does not urge us to rest, but rather actively abstain from these lusts which war against the soul. [94]

Oh my Mansoul, I [Emmanuel, the Prince of Mansoul] warn you of that, of which, notwithstanding the reformation that is at present wrought among you, you have need to be warned about: wherefore hearken diligently unto me . . . there are yet some Diabolonians [the avowed friends of Diabolus, a mighty giant with a Luciferian heart which was insatiable and enlarged as hell itself] remaining in the town of Mansoul; Diabolonions that are sturdy and implacable, and that . . . plot, contrive, invent, and jointly attempt to bring you to desolation, and so to a state far worse . . . therefore look about you . . . Oh Mansoul, thy work as to this, will be so much the more difficult and hard; that is, to take, mortify, and put them to death, according to the will of my Father. Nor can you utterly rid yourselves of them, unless you should pull down the walls of your town, the which I am by no means willing you should. Do you ask me, What shall we then do? Why, be you diligent, and quit yourselves like men; observe their holds, find out their haunts, assult them, and make no peace with them; wherever they haunt, lurk, or abide, and what terms of peace soever they offer you, abhor; and all shall be well betwixt you and me. And that you may the better know them from the natives of Mansoul, I will give you this brief schedule of the names of the

---

[94] Ibid.

chief of them; and they are these that follow: the lord Fornication, the lord Adultery, the lord Murder, the lord Anger, the lord Lasciviousness, the lord Deceit, the lord Evil-eye, Mr Drunkenness, Mr Revelling, Mr Idolatry, Mr Witchcraft, Mr Variance, Mr Emulation, Mr Wrath, Mr Strife, Mr Sedition, and Mr Heresy. These are some of the chief, O Mansoul, of those that will seek to overthrow thee for ever: . . . but look well into the law of thy king, and thou shalt find their physiognomy, and such other characteristical notes of them, whereby they may be known.

"These, O my Mansoul, and I would gladly that you should certainly know it, if they be suffered to run and range about the town as they wish, would quickly, like vipers, eat up your bowels, yea, poison your captains, cut the sinews of your soldiers, break the bars and bolts of your gates, and turn your now most flourishing Mansoul into a barred desolate wilderness and ruinous heap. Wherefore, that you may take courage to yourselves to apprehend these villains wherever you find them, I give to you . . . full power and commission to seek out, to take, and to cause to be put to death by the cross all manner of Diabolonions, wherever you shall find them lurk within or without the walls of the town of Mansoul.

Nothing can hurt thee but sin; nothing can grieve me but sin; nothing can make thee base before thy foes but sin: take heed of sin, my Mansoul. . . Show me then thy love, my Mansoul, and let not those that are within thy walls, take thy affections off from him that hath redeemed thy soul. Yea, let the sight of a Diabolonion heighten thy love to me. I came . . . to save thee from the posion of those arrows that would have wrought thy death: stand for me, my friend, my Mansoul, against the Diabolonions, and I will stand for thee before my Father and all his court. Love me against temptation; and I will love thee, notwithstanding thine infirmities . . . Nor must though think always to live by sense, thou must live upon my word. Thou must believe, O my Mansoul, when I am for thee, that yet I love and bear thee upon mine heart for ever. Remember therefore, O my Mansoul, that thou art beloved of me; as I have therefore taught thee to watch, to fight, to pray, and to make war against my foes, so now I command thee to believe that my love is constant to thee, O my Mansoul; now have I set my heart and love upon thee, watch: 'Behold I will put upon you none other burden; but that which ye have already, hold fast till I come'. Rev. ii. 24.[95]

There are wars we have to face as pilgrims in this fallen world that as the time draws nearer for Christ's return will increasingly result in the extreme end of persecution, torture and, or physical death, as we refuse to deny our allegiance to our Lord Christ Jesus.

In 2018 the Bible League International stated in their newsletter that 'Christians are the most persecuted group in the world for the past two years running. One Christian is killed for their faith every six minutes.' Yet the Bible does not tell us to fight in these circumstances but how to remain living obediently, trusting fully in our all-powerful and loving God and his promises till the end. This is the perseverance of the saints of which history can teach us much. These types of wars are to be expected and are in fact promised to be experienced by all pilgrims just because we follow Jesus.

In Matthew 5:10-12, Jesus tells us that '"Blessed are those who are persecuted for righteousness' sake, for theirs is the kingdom of heaven. Blessed are you when they revile and persecute you, and say all kinds of evil against you falsely for My sake. Rejoice and be exceedingly glad, for great is your reward in heaven, for so they persecuted the prophets who were before you."'

Then a bit later on in Matthew 5:38-46a we hear Jesus saying, '"You have heard that it was said, 'An eye for an eye and a tooth for a tooth.' But I tell you not to resist an evil person. But whoever slaps you on your right cheek, turn the other to him also. If anyone wants to sue you and take away your tunic, let him have your cloak also. And whoever compels you to go a mile, go with him two. Give to him who asks you, and from him who wants to borrow from you and do not turn away. You have heard that it

---

[95] *The Holy War* p560-62

was said, 'You shall love your neighbour and hate your enemy.' But I say to you, love your enemies, bless those who curse you, do good to those who hate you, and pray for those who spitefully use you and persecute you, that you may be sons of your Father in heaven; for He makes His sun rise on the evil and on the good, and sends rain on the just and on the unjust. For if you love those who love you, what reward have you?'"

<u>Question</u>: How can one pray for those who maliciously and viciously use you for their ends and that's without considering blessing those who curse, hate and persecute you?

<u>Answer</u>: I personally struggle with this. A long back-and-forwards war begins within my head – Do it. NO. Yes. NO. – and regarding all such times that I needed to do the Yeses the Nos have the lead currently. But God and I are working on changing this.

Dietrich Bonhoeffer, a German pastor during WW2 wrote a book titled *The Cost of Discipleship*. He was shot by a camp guard just before the end of the war. His book contains the following quote–

In 1880 A. F. G. Vilmar said of enemies and prayer:

This commandment that we should love our enemies and forgo [sic] revenge will grow even more urgent in the holy struggle which lies before us and in which we partly have already been engaged for years. In it love and hate engage in mortal combat. It is the urgent duty of every Christian soul to prepare itself for it. The time is coming when the confession of the living God will incur not only the hatred and the fury of the world, for on the whole it has come to that already, but complete ostracism from "human society", as they call it. The Christians will be hounded from place to place, subjected to physical assault, maltreatment and death of every kind. We are approaching an age of widespread persecution. Therein lies the true significance of all movements and conflicts of our age. Our adversaries seek to root out the Christian Church and the Christian faith because they cannot live side by side with us, because they see in every word we utter and every deed we do, even when they are not specifically directed against them, a condemnation of their own words and deeds. They are not far wrong. They suspect too that we are indifferent to their condemnation. Indeed they must admit that it is utterly futile to condemn us. We do not reciprocate their hatred and contention, although they would like it better if we did, and so sink to their own level. And how is the battle to be fought? Soon the time will come when we shall pray, not as isolated individuals, but as a corporate body, a congregation, a Church: we shall pray in multitudes (albeit in relatively small multitudes) and among the thousands and thousands of apostates we shall loudly praise and confess the Lord who was crucified and is risen and shall come again. And what prayer, what confession, what hymn of praise will it be? It will be the prayer of earnest love for those very sons of perdition who stand around and gaze at us with eyes aflame with hatred, and who have perhaps already raised their hands to kill us. It will be prayer for the peace of these erring, devastated and bewildered souls, a prayer for the same love and peace which we ourselves enjoy, a prayer which will penetrate to the depths of their souls and rend their hearts more grievously than anything they can do to us. Yes, the Church which is really waiting for its Lord, and which discerns the signs of the times of decision, must fling itself with its utmost power and with the panoply of its holy life into this prayer of love. [96]

1Peter tells us about this internal war pilgrims fight every day of their pilgrimage here. This war is against the old nature within which does not need our adversary's help to cause untold problems. This war is fought by us, our new nature with the Spirit's enabling and God's power.

Titus 2:11-14, 'For the grace of God that brings salvation has appeared to all men, teaching us that, denying ungodliness and worldly lusts, we should live soberly, righteously, and godly in the present age, looking for the blessed hope and glorious appearing of our great God and Saviour Jesus Christ, who gave Himself for

---

[96] Dietrich Bonhoeffer (1906-1945 German concentration camp) *The Cost of Discipleship* Collier Books Macmillon Publishing 1963 p167-69

us, that He might redeem us from every lawless deed and purify for Himself His own special people, zealous for good works.'

Paul wrote these words because people already believed that because of grace they could do and say whatever they felt like. But with grace comes the teaching to deny and to live soberly. The same grace that justifies also provides sanctification, a corresponding change of living. The evidence of having received saving grace is a nature implanted in heart that causes us to be at war with our own sin against God. What is your attitude towards your sin? We can talk about the wrongness and even perhaps admit some but does my sin cause grief in my own heart for what it has done to Christ? [97]

It is also in Ephesians that Paul teaches us of the other warfare we are faced with as God's beloved children. This is a war against spirits, not humanity, and so is not a war that is fought with armoury that governments spend a lot of money on, more than what they spend to feed and shelter those who truly cannot do so for themselves. A pilgrim's armoury cost God his life but is individually fitted and given abundantly, freely to all pilgrims and is mostly invisible and of a protective, defensive nature. In fact, the only offensive armoury we are entrusted with is a smallish sword, more like a paper dagger that has to hit the spot to be effective. But more on this later.

Nor is any of this fighting against our Father.

Romans 5:1, 'Therefore having been justified by faith, we have peace with God through our Lord Jesus Christ.'

Because of Christ's death on the cross, God, in this age of grace, is at peace with mankind not war, not yet, and as pilgrims we are no longer in rebellion, at war with God. We are no longer living against God's will for us but desire to be obedient to it and so

---

[97] Notes from Gables' sermon series on Pilgrim's Progress #37 *Talkative – how to expose him* 2.6.99

with the Spirit's enabling we aim to love, not war against those also made in our Lord's image.

Our God, in this time of grace, is *for* us, not against us regardless of how things may seem. Everything that happened to us before we became pilgrims came from the good and loving hand of the God who desires us to turn back to him, to encourage us to stop our foolish rebellion against him. Everything that happens to us now as his beloved children is allowed by the good hand of our Father because it is good for us, good because it will enable us to become more like Christ and fit for the home he is preparing for us. This good includes his discipline or chastisement of all pilgrims, which we are going to briefly look at because though this is not something we should fight against, it may feel like it.

Chastisement or discipline

Hebrews 12: 5-11, 'And you have forgotten the exhortation which speaks to you as to sons: "My son, do not despise the chastening of the LORD, nor be discouraged when you are rebuked by Him; for whom the LORD loves He chastens, and scourges every son whom He receives." If you endure chastening, God deals with you as with sons; for what son is there whom a father does not chasten? But if you are without chastening, of which all have become partakers, then you are illegitimate and not sons. Furthermore, we have had human fathers who corrected us, and we paid them respect. Shall we not much more readily be in subjection to the Father of spirits and live? For they indeed for a few days chastened us as seemed best to them, but He for our profit, that we may be partakers of His holiness. Now no chastening seems to be joyful for the present, but painful; nevertheless, afterward it yields the peaceable fruit of righteousness to those who have been trained by it.'

These verses follow on from verses we will be considering later but the context is enduring and not becoming soul weary and discouraged because of hostility and hardships. Hostilities, hardships, persecutions and the like can cause us to question our belief, salvation and even God's love for us.

Gables said that though God does use the pain of hardships and sufferings to correct his children, he never chastises a child before letting them know ahead of time through conviction of sin what they are being corrected for. *If you cannot understand why something, some adverse circumstance, is happening to you do not interpret it as God's discipline.* [Bunyan thought similarly which you will read about later.] Job knew the causes of his suffering was not chastisement from God as he knew of no sin within and because we get to read the first chapter, we see that God actually declared him to be a blameless and upright servant who feared him and shunned evil, (Job1: 8). God judges our unconfessed or persistent sinning by disciplining through adversity of many shapes and forms but we will know why because of our conscience. Our Father will not allow us to behave as an unbeliever, an illegitimate child. He will do what never is necessary to bring us to repentance and prevent us from being condemned with unbelievers. Unlike an earthly father God never disciplines in anger, to get even or for any other self-reason, only for our own good, our own holiness and like any good parent he will keep at it till we get it, till we learn the lesson it is intended for.[98]

Firstly, however, let's consider the war Peter is talking about in more detail.

1 Peter 2:11-12 is telling us that we are in a war within ourselves because we have fleshy lusts within waring against our own souls.

These enemies are described differently in different translations, *fleshy lusts* in the NKJ, *evil pleasures of this world* in The Living Bible, *desires of our lower natures* were J. B. Phillips choice for his paraphrasing of the Bible and *sinful desires* in the NIV are a few examples.

These lusts or wants are not of God, they are of the flesh as in our old nature, the world and the devil. They are what please Satan

---

[98] Notes from Gables' sermon series on Pilgrim's Progress #62 *Christian Chastisement* 3.4.99

and our old man not our Father who warns us, saying in 1John 2:15-17, 'Do not love the world or the things in the world. If anyone loves the world, the love of the Father is not in him. For all that is in the world – *the lust of the flesh*, *the lust of the eyes*, and *the pride of life* – is not of the Father but of the world. And the world is passing away, and the lust of it; but he who does the will of God abides forever' (Italics by me).

One could even consider that desiring to live or look as you want regardless, or die how and when you want, could be a fleshy lust. Being tempted to and choosing to deny the Lord's ways and timing to do so, one could be setting themselves on a pathway that may well become soul destroying.

This fallen world of ours whose prince is Satan and our fallen nature are driven by these three lusts. They are the primary three ways that pilgrims can be tempted, lured away from loving obedience to the one triune God.

The lust of the flesh refers to desires for sinful sensual pleasure. This does not necessarily mean sexual pleasures but that seems to be the world's main focus.

The lust of the eyes refers to a desire for more and more stuff, which we call covetousness or materialism.

The pride of life refers to being proud, specifically with getting kudos from your social position, career, marital status, portfolio, house, children etc. To be so focused on this brief life will leave you totally unprepared for the reality of the next.

What a tragedy to invest all our resources or even ourselves in that which will not last as the rich farmer discovered, as we read Jesus' teaching in Luke 12:15-21, '"Take heed and beware of covetousness, for one's life does not consist in the abundance of the things he possesses." Then he spoke a parable to them, saying: "The ground of a certain rich man yielded plentifully. And he thought within himself, saying, 'What shall I do, since I have no room to store my crops?' So he said, 'I will do this: I will pull down my barns and build greater, and there I will store all my crops and my goods. And I will say to my soul, "Soul, you have many goods laid up for many years; take your ease; eat, drink, and be merry."'

But God said to him, 'Fool! This night your soul will be required of you; then whose will those things be which you have provided?' So is he who lays up treasure for himself, and is not rich toward God."'

Considering the seemingly endless, never to be filled or appeased wants, lusts or *appetites*[99] as Mathew Henry called them of the world today for stuff, recognition, acclaim and exotic luxurious getaways but not necessarily with their own spouse and other such things, Peter's Spirit driven words, though written so long ago are still very relevant, as are John's and Christ's. Human nature has not changed since the fall. Only God can change a leopard's spots.

"But", do I hear you say, "we live in a fallen world, nothing is as it should be, it's just so hard!"

Blaming being in this fallen world will not work as we will see by considering Adam and Eve again.

They had everything. They had no needs and no weeds. They lived in the sinless, stress-less, perfection of Eden, where God claimed that all he had made, all that now existed, was very good. The one thing that had not been good, Adam being alone, God had set right and the three of them walked together in the cool of the day. According to God everything was 'yes' for them except for one thing, just one, and that was that they were not to eat from that tree, just one tree, because to do so would cause death.

Genesis 2:16-17 before woman was created tells us that '. .the LORD God commanded the man, saying, "Of every tree of the garden you may freely eat; but of the tree of the knowledge of good and evil you shall not eat, for in the day that you eat of it you shall surely die."'

This phrase *you shall surely die* literally means *dying you shall die*. Dying spiritually, they would later die physically.

---

[99] *Matthew Henry's Commentary* 1John 2:16 p1957

Admittedly they would not have known what death was, but they did know God personally and surely that would be enough to be obedient.

Just one tree of the many, many trees from which they could freely stuff themselves. But – there is always one of these – then enters Satan, as a talking snake with legs, and Eve who has no needs, who has no idea the work weeds would cause, not to mention the pain thorns would bring, listens, looks and wants. They chose to disobey, sin against the God they walked and talked with in the evenings when everything was as it should have been before the fall.

Genesis 3:6, 'So when the woman saw that the tree was good for food, that it was pleasant to the eyes [Can you imagine any of the Eden trees not looking good to eat of, looking unpleasant? No, me neither.] and a tree desirable to make one wise [Who had insinuated they were not already wise? Not God.] she took of its fruit and ate. She also gave to her husband with her, and he ate.'

The questions of why she conversed with a legged snake, added a probation – like the Pharisees would do multiple times many many years later – that God had not given Adam, trusted a stranger over the God they fellowshipped with daily and why Adam was silent, abdicating his God given headship or why he ate are not going to be wrestled with here.

But do you see – *good for food*, is this not a lust of the flesh? *pleasant to the eyes* is equal to the lust of the eyes surely and don't we feel oh so prideful when wiser, or just 'more' than another, owner of more stuff for example, or just 'more' than we were before? Oh, the pride of life, what would advertisers do without you or the other two lusts!

Adam and Eve did not question God's good, rightful loving authority over them till Satan entered into our history before the fall and put that thought into their and so our minds. The two representatives of mankind had not had these desires, these sinful lusts within to fight against till then. We however are born fallen; we are born with these internal lusts. Adam and Eve's desires were only wrong, only sinful because they went against

God's revealed will, known desires for them both. When Adam and Eve sinned by disobeying God, they swapped masters. Disobeying God meant obeying Satan, making him their master as well as master of all the generations of humanity since. Satan, who desires to devour those whom God loves, and especially those who have come to love him back, most definitely has not got our best interests in mind at any time unlike our creator.

Yes, unlike Adam and Eve, we do not live in the good, very good, of Eden, we sojourn in a fallen world where the serpent of old, of Eden, and his companions continue to rage against all the good of God and his bondservants in a similar manner as he did to our first parents and where weeds and thorns flourish. It is Satan and his spirits ultimately who we wage war against, not people or our Father as we learn from Ephesians 6:12, 'For we do not wrestle against flesh and blood, but against principalities, against powers, against the rulers of the darkness of this age, against spiritual hosts of wickedness in the heavenly places.'

It is his wily schemes that along with our eager to participate old man are aimed at tempting pigrims away again from God – and his revealed will for us that we can read and learn of in the Bible – or at least discrediting our witness for him in the world's ever watching eyes, and he starts by messing with our mind, energizing our fallen, old nature. So, though this war can be seen as coming from without us the fighting takes place both without and within.

As David Jeremiah was preparing a message once, a friend sent him a devotional that imagined Satan addressing a worldwide convention of demons and promising them victory in pilgrims' lives if they faithfully did the following twelve things:

   1. Keep them busy with non-essentials.

   2. Tempt them to overspend and go into debt.

   3. Make them work long hours to maintain empty lifestyles.

   4. Discourage them from spending family time, for when homes disintegrate, there's no refuge from work.

   5. Over-stimulate their minds with Television and computers so they can't hear God speaking to them.

6. Fill their coffee tables and their night stands with newspapers and magazines so they've no time to read the Bible.

7. Flood their mailboxes with sweepstakes, and promotions, and get-rich-quick schemes. Keep them chasing material things.

8. Put glamorous models on TV and on magazine covers to keep them focuses on outward appearances; that way they'll be dissatisfied with themselves and dissatisfied with their mates.

9. Make sure couples are too exhausted for physical intimacy, that way they'll be tempted to look elsewhere.

10. Emphasize Santa and the Easter Bunny; that way you'll divert them from the real meaning of the holidays.

11. Involve them in good causes so they won't have time for eternal causes.

12. Make them self-sufficient, keep them busy working in their own strength so they'll never know the joy of God's power working through them.[100]

How many of these twelve strategies cause you to consider your need for God less, tempt you to spend less time with him?

As someone once said, 'A pilgrim who is no threat to Satan, who is not fighting him, will hardly feel as if they are at war with anything, and one could rightfully question the truth of that one's commitment to his pilgrimage'.

If I am not committed to my pilgrimage home, what are my chances of actually getting home? Where's that armour?

> These fleshy lusts are those natural appetites that have their seed in the body and mind. These would be innocent except for sin, but are now enemies of the soul . . . Anyone who is going to make his journey safely and successfully will have to keep himself free from those fleshy lusts that war against the soul. . . The inner life must overcome the flesh or the

---

[100] David Jeremiah *The Great Deceiver who seeks to Destroy* sermons.love>david-jeremiah

flesh will overcome and destroy the inner life . . . one part of us fights against another part of us . . . We are pilgrims journeying home, and the only real enemies, the only dangerous enemies, are within us . . . We have within us temptations which if yielded to would destroy our soul.[101]

What a reason to fight, the protection of my eternal soul!

Pilgrims are facing wars on two overlapping fronts. Our war within does not need any extra outside assistance to be deadly, yet Satan and his army are ever ready to assist our old man once they can find a crack in our armour and make a bloody entrance.

We are in a lifelong war, a bit like my war with weeds in the garden, it will last as long as you are breathing in this world, but not a moment longer. It is a war that begins in a pilgrim's infancy, when we receive our new nature, become a new creation. This is a war that God prepares us for in his word, aids us in and has already won. But don't let this make you think this war, this fighting will be a breeze. It can bring you to your knees, to places you did not know existed, places way past what you think you can cope with despite God knowing you can and his provision of an escape hatch as we learn of in 1Corinthians 10:13 where we read, 'No temptation has overtaken you except such as is common to man; but God is faithful, who will not allow you to be tempted beyond what you are able, but with the temptation will also make the way of escape, that you may be able to bear [endure] it.'

With thanks to Spurgeon here's a reminder of why pilgrims should be actively engaged in a warfare that the world is oblivious to, just in case you've forgotten. He writes, 'Where Christ works a saving work, He casts Satan from his throne and will not let him be master any longer. No man is a true Christian if sin reigns in his mortal body. Sin will be in us; it will never be utterly expelled until the spirit enters glory, but it will never have dominion. There will be a striving for dominion – a lusting against the new law and the new spirit that God has implanted – but sin will never get the

---

[101] A. W. Tozer *Living as a Christian Teachings from First Peter* Regal 2009 p124, 125

upper hand so as to be absolute monarch of our natures. Christ will be the Master of the heart, and sin must be mortified . . . Believer, is sin subdued in you? If your life is unholy, your heart is unchanged; and if your heart is unchanged, you are an unsaved person. If the Saviour has not sanctified you, renewed you, given you a hatred of sin and a love of holiness, He has done nothing in you of a saving character. Grace that does not make a man better than others is a worthless counterfeit . . . "Let every one that nameth the name of Christ depart from iniquity" (2Tim2:19).'[102]

Temptations vs Trials

Paul knew by personal experience the truth of what he penned in Romans 6: 2b, 6-7, 12, 14, 18, 'How shall we who died to sin live any longer in it? . . . knowing this, that our old man was crucified with Him, that the body of sin might be done away with [rendered inoperative], that we should no longer be slaves of sin. For he who has died has been freed [cleared] from sin . . . Therefore do not let sin reign in your mortal body, that you should obey it in its lusts. . . For sin shall not have dominion over you, for you are not under law but under grace . . . And having been set free from sin, you became slaves of righteousness.'

Yet he experienced the truth he described in Romans 7: 15, 20-25, 'For what I am doing, I do not understand. For what I will to do, that I do not practice; but what I hate, that I do. . . Now if I do what I will not to do, it is no longer I who do it, but sin that dwells in me. I find then a law, that evil is present with me, the one who wills to do good. For I delight in the law of God according to the inward man. But I see another law in my members, warring against the law of my mind, and bringing me into captivity to the law of sin which is in my members. O wretched man that I am! Who will deliver me from this body of death? I thank God – through Jesus Christ our Lord! So then, with the mind I myself serve the law of God, but with the flesh the law of sin.'

---

[102] Charles Haddon Spurgeon Morning *& Evening* revised and updated edition Whitaker House 1997 *Evening of Feb 8th* p91

James warns us about these wants which are ours, not God's after encouraging pilgrims to stay on track in James 1:12-16 saying, 'Blessed is the man who endures temptation; for when he has been approved, he will receive the crown of life which the Lord has promised to those who love Him. Let no one say when he is tempted, "I am tempted be God"; for God cannot be tempted by evil, nor does He tempt anyone. But each one is tempted when he is drawn away by his own desires and enticed. Then, when desire has conceived, it gives birth to sin; and sin, when it is full-grown, brings forth death. Do not be deceived, my beloved brethren.' Thomas á Kempis put verse 14 this way –

> At first it is a mere thought confronting the mind; then imagination paints it in stronger colours; only after that do we take pleasure in it, and the will makes a false move, and we give our assent. [103]

Tempt

To entice or incite to do a wrong (remember it is God who declares what is wrong or forbidden, not us his creatures) or forbidden thing, to allure or attract a person to do wrong, to make a trial of something so as to try the resolution of that person. This definition explains why God will never be the source of that which tempts us to sin. Sadly, scripture tells us that we try to tempt him, thinking he is like us in nature.

Temptation

The act or instance of tempting, of inciting to do wrong. Do not grieve God by accusing him of being the source of any temptation. He may allow it as he did with Job, knowing that he can use it for our growth into greater Christ-likeness and Satan is on God's leash, he does not have free-reign even though it may look like it.

---

[103] James B. Adamson in *The New International Commentary on the New Testament: The Epistle of James* Wm. B. Eerdmans Publishing Co. 1976 p72 Quoting Thomas á Kempis (1380-1471) *The Imitation of Christ*

Question: But does not the Lord's Prayer teach us to ask God to not lead us into temptation? I'm confused.
Answer: Yes, you could think that at first when reading Matthew 6:13a, 'And do not lead us into temptation, but deliver us from the evil one.'
Remembering reading what James said consider Matthew 4:1, 'Then Jesus was led up by the Spirit into the wilderness to be tempted by the devil.'
God led Jesus into the wilderness, a place where he was as a human weakened physically, emotionally and spiritually, as we often are, making us easy targets for Satan's temptations. I have long thought that this prayer was asking God not to take us into places where it is most easy for Satan to ensnare us in sin again.

> That is, do not lead us into such temptations as are too hard for human nature; but deliver us, by some means, from the evil; either by removing the temptation, or increasing our strength to resist it. This petition teaches us to preserve a sense of our own inability to repel and overcome the soliatations of the world, and of the necessity there is of our receiving assistance from above, both to regulate our passions, and enable us to prosecute a religious life.[104]

Henry writes that 'Having prayed that the guilt of sin may be removed, we pray, as is fit, that we may never return again to folly – that we may not be tempted to it. It is not as if God tempted any to sin; but, Lord, do not let Satan loose upon us; chain up that "roaring lion," for he is subtle and spiteful; Lord, do not leave us to ourselves, for we are very weak . . . "But deliver us from evil". . . "from the evil one," the devil, the tempter, –" keep us, that either we may not be assaulted by him, or we may not be overcome by these assaults;" or, "from the evil thing, "sin, the worst of evils – an evil, an only evil – that evil thing which God hates, and which Satan tempts men to do and destroys them by."'[105]

---

[104] *Fleetwood's Life of Christ.* p159-160
[105] Ibid comment by Matthew Henry p161

The act of being tempted, having the thought in our head, is not the sin, considering it, conceiving it, growing it, feeding it, indulging it, birthing it, fulfilling it, obeying it, is. As Brooks wrote, 'It is not Satan tempting but my assenting, it is not his enticing but my yielding, that mischiefs me. Temptations may be troubles to my mind, but they are not sins upon my soul whilst I am in arms against them.'[106]

Temptations' ultimate aim is to tempt you away from God and all good that being in relationship with him brings. Satan tailor fits these temptations for each individual as he knows our specific weaknesses. Temptations are not for our good but aim for our destruction and so we are called to protect ourselves from ourselves by crucifying the old man and Satan with what God has provided us with and to stand.

Satan, the prince of this world, works differently than the triune God. Remember what we read in Part 1 about how God usually appeals to our will through our reason while Satan usually gets to us through our sinful desires by confusing and clouding the issues?

> 'We walk by faith, not by appearance' (2Cor 5:7 mg). You probably know the illustration of Fact, Faith and Experience walking along the top of a wall. Fact walked steadily on, turning neither to right nor left and never looking behind. Faith followed, and all went well so long as he kept his eyes focuses upon Fact: but as soon as he became concerned about Experience and turned to see how he was getting on, he lost his balance and tumbled off the wall, and poor old Experience fell down after him. All temptation is primarily to look within; to take our eyes off the Lord and to take account of appearances.[107]

---

[106] Thomas Brooks (1608-1680) *The Mute Christian under the Smarting Rod: with Sovereign Antidotes* (originally published 1659) 8th edition corrected 1684 from *The Complete works of Thomas Brooks* https://archive.org

[107] *The Normal Christian Life* p78

Temptations are not trials. Temptations come from within us, from the old nature we will have to some degree till in heaven. And Satan knowing this is an old master at injecting a subtle anti-God questioning thought into our mind, a little leaven and waiting. And yet, just to confuse us, as the definition said, something that tempts us can become a trial as we struggle to fight against it, a trial to test our resolution to follow hard after God.

Bunyan showed with his characters Christian and Faithful that temptations are fitted individually, as Mason comments 'Christian in great measure escaped the particular temptations that assaulted Faithful, yet he sympathized with him; nor did the later deem the gloomy experiences of his brother visionary or imaginative, though he had been exempted from such trials. One man, from a complication of causes, is exposed to temptations of which another is ignorant; in this case he needs much sympathy, which he seldom meets with; while they who are severe on him are liable to be harassed and baffled in another way, which, for want of coincidence in habit, temperature and situation, he is equally prone to disregard. Thus believers are often led reciprocally to censure, suspect, despise, or dislike each other, on those very grounds which should render them useful and encouraging counsellors and companions.'[108]

Trial

A trial is a process or mode of testing a person's qualities. A test will give you a trial. A trying thing or experience or person, especially hardship or trouble will be felt as a trial. Persecution comes in this box. Trials of all sorts and degrees are individually tailored and sent by God to test us, to refine us, to perfect us. Trials are *always* for the pilgrims' long term good.

God does not change, ever, as James 1:17 teaches, 'Every good gift and every perfect gift is from above, and comes down from the Father of lights, with whom there is no variation or shadow of

---

[108] *The Pilgrim's Progress* comment by Mason p123

turning.' He can only do and give what is perfect and good, and that includes how each trial is fitted for the individual receiving it as with his chastening.

Test
A test is the means of examining, or the circumstances suitable to do this. To try someone severely is to tax their endurance, to test their commitment for example.

Endure
Is to undergo a difficulty or hardship but to last, to finish the race and not succumb, regardless of what comes at you.

Endurance
This is the ability to withstand prolonged strain, regardless.

Perseverance
This is the steadfast pursuit of an object or goal regardless, until it is reached. It may require setting your face like a flint.

Perfect
Being perfect does not mean sin free. The word *perfect* is from the word *teos* or *teleios*, which means *a functional perfection*. In other words, to be perfect is to complete the process, reach the full purpose, or potential of something. As you will see in the passages below it is about allowing the process of pilgrims becoming Christ-like to be completed. You could also say perhaps that it means *full-grown*, for when sin is perfected, reached its full purpose it brings eternal spiritual death. The word of God, perhaps surprisingly, tells us that Jesus needed perfecting also through learning humble obedience to God's will by suffering.

Question: God needing perfecting? Really?
Answer: Yes. In Luke 13:32, Jesus answers some Pharisees saying in part, '. . . Behold, I cast out demons and preform cures today and tomorrow, and the third day I shall be perfected'.
In this verse being perfected is referring to Christ being resurrected, the proof of God's acceptance of all Christ's work,

that it was fully completed. That's around three hundred Old Testament prophesies of the Christ all fulfilled in the Jesus of Nazareth. What's the odds of that occurring?

Considering just eight prophesies, Jesus' place of birth, manner of birth, betrayal, manner of death, people's reactions (mocking, spitting, staring etc.), time of death, piercing and burial, the odds are 1 in 10^{17}. That many American silver dollars would cover the state of Texas to the depth of two feet.[109]

This idea of perfecting is also taught in Hebrews 2:10, 5:9 and 7:28, 'For it was fitting for Him, for whom are all things and by whom are all things, in bringing many sons to glory, to make the captain of their salvation perfect through sufferings. . . And having been perfected, he became the author of eternal salvation to all who obey Him, . . . For the law appoints as high priests men who have weakness, but the word of the oath, which came after the law, appoints the Son who has been perfected forever.'

If the Christ needed perfecting, how much more do we!

<u>Question</u>: What can we learn about God and ourselves through trials and temptations that begin the perfecting, or the sanctifying of us which perhaps we could not learn any other way?

<u>Answer</u>: Job, who before his extreme temptation to curse God began was declared by God to be his servant and that there was 'none like him on the earth, a blameless and upright man, one who fears God and shuns evil' (Job 1:8) declared at its end, 'I have heard of You by the hearing of the ear, but now my eye sees You. Therefore I abhor myself, and repent in dust and ashes' (Job 42:5-6). Job seeing God more clearly that he ever had before as well as his own self, repented and worshipped.

The writer of Psalm 119 writes, 'Before I was afflicted I went astray, but now I keep your word. You are good and do good; teach me Your statutes . . . It is good for me that I have been afflicted, that I may learn Your statutes. The law of Your mouth is better to me than thousands of coins of gold and silver' (v 67-8,

---

[109] Josh McDowell *The New Evidence that Demands a Verdict*. Thomas Nelson 1981 p164 and 193

71-2). He learnt through whatever affliction he had faced that knowing God was worth more than anything the world could give him and so worth the often, painful effort of staying on track.

Peter encourages his persecuted readers by reminding them that they 'are kept [where the original word meant to be garrisoned about by an army] by the power of God through faith for salvation . . . though now for a little while, if need be, you have been grieved by various trials (1Peter 1:5-6).

Though I would rather not experience again what I have in my past, if there was no other way for me to know and love God like I do now than to go through that time of extended dark and lonely affliction again I'd welcome it, especially knowing him to be faithful and loving and understanding by hind-sight the benefits of doing so. Crazy, hey.

Bridges counsels that 'We must remember that 'God does not leave us to do battle alone. Just as He delivered us from the overall reign of sin, so He has made ample provision for us to win the daily skirmishes against sin. . . we are . . . alive to God. (Rom6:11) . . . been brought into the kingdom of Christ . . . *united with Christ in all His power* . . . [Considering Col1:11 and Eph3:16, 20] . . . Where do endurance and patience come from? They come as we are strengthened with God's power . . . To count on the fact that we are dead to sin and alive to God is something we must do actively . . . must form the habit of continually realizing that we are. . . Practically speaking, we do this when by faith in God's Word we resist sin's advances and temptations . . . when by faith we look to Christ for the power we need to do the resisting . . . so we see that God has made provision. . . Through Christ He has delivered us from sin's reign so that we now can resist sin. But the responsibility for resisting is ours. God does not do that for us. To confuse the *potential* for resisting (which God provided) with the *responsibility* for resisting (which is ours) is to court disaster . . .'[110]

---

[110] *The Pursuit of Holiness* p72, 60

While you are in the midst of any affliction, even one that you understand will be good for you, it does not mean that you will always be happy about experiencing it while doing so.

My husband's mother was a very quiet gentle woman of great faith who I'm looking forward to meeting when I get home, once suffered from a severe eye infection for quite a while. One day when it was particularly painful, she'd had enough and said so. Her husband, a lay preacher said, "Well all things work together for the good Dorrie." Her reply was quick, "It's all right for you! You've not got the sore eye!"

As one who also has suffered afflictions that have been made worse when friends spoke unthinkingly like Job's, I'd advise if you have to speak be really tactful. Most times it is far better to listen more and talk less.

Reading through the Old Testament book Ezekiel you get to see that the most common way of knowing, understanding God is by affliction, not ease. And is this not still true today? A safe, self-satisfied, self-reliant, need or want nothing care-free person will not feel the hunger to add God into their life of sunshine and roses. A person's life, emotionally, physically, relationally, seems to have to crack first. Something must make one open their eyes and see that they are not enough, that they need someone far bigger and capable in every way to assist them battle their way through life with a joyful hope and peace instead of despair and emptiness.

Crucifying sin and reaping holiness

As we have read, effort is required from us, it is our responsibility to do so and God has equipped and enabled us to do so. To keep gardens from becoming overgrown by weeds much effort can be needed. Like weeds, sins need to be pulled out, removed, killed and preferably as they appear, when they are just a thought, before they take root and become firmly established requiring much, much more effort and pain. (Oh, my poor back!) Then there are the thorny types. Take baby stinging nettles for an example, I hardly feel them weeding at this stage but I've learnt to wrap my hands and arms in thick tough plastic bags before I tackle the grown-up version.

'Someone may say, "Mr. Tozer, how can a man cleanse his own heart? How can a man purge his own soul?" I might ask you how can a man wash his own hands? He cannot; he can only subject his hands to water and detergents and they do the washing. If he does not subject himself to water and detergent, he will not be cleansed. Just as a man is clean by washing his hands and yet cannot wash his hands, so a man's heart is cleansed when he cleanses himself, and yet he cannot cleanse himself . . .

God says to a sinner, "Cleanse your hands, ye sinners; and purify your hearts, ye double-minded" (Jas. 4:8). What does He mean? Before you sit down at the Father's table, go wash your hands, and yet that sinner cannot wash his hands. Not all the water in the world can wash him clean, only the blood of Christ can do it. Why then is he told to do it? For the same reason the boy is told to go wash. There is water that will cleanse him, but if he does not use water and soap, his hands will still be dirty, and when he rubs them, he only rubs in the dirt.'[111]

> Augustine said that we must pray as though it all depended on God and work as though it all depends on us. [112]

Personally, I don't like warring, fighting with anyone, even myself thought this I am compelled to do because of the Spirit within. Face to face with another I try to avoid it at all costs. It is painful, exhausting and no one seems to ever win. I usually procrastinate by doing an activity related to the degree I need to ignore the problem. Reading, craft, a brisk walk that makes the dog puff or some heavy gardening that produces a lot of sweat and sore muscles and if I am lucky it all blows over before I wash the mud off my hands.

---

[111] *Living as a Christian* p79-80

[112] Warren W. Wiersbe (1929-2019) *With the Word The Chapter-by-Chapter Bible Handbook* Thomas nelson Publishers 1991 p738

But this war of inside-the-head-stuff, is much, much harder to walk away from though I have found some help by attacking the poor garden. I believe the inner thought life causes more problems for a person than any outside attack can.

However, as pilgrims wishing to reach home, zealous to do so, we have no choice but to take up arms against our old self, our old mind set and fight. Procrastinating will only increase the intensity of the battle latter. It's like those weeds, easy to pull out when tiny but as roots grow and stems thicken other equipment is required. And I don't know about you but for me it is painful and terribly exhausting having my old worldly sinful self's thoughts or lusts war against my new self, my renewing mind.

With Satan's happy-to-help lying encouragement and cheer-squad egging on my old self when they have penetrated my armour, messing with my mind, and me forgetting I should be doing in God's strength, not mine, and forgetting his unchanging character towards me as his child, much emotional blood can be shed and as a result even bodily damage can occur. Shoulders so tense they go skywards, past ear level resulting in migraines. A knotted-up stomach leads to all sorts of gastrointestinal problems, some very nasty. Too much adrenaline floating around for too long can cause heart arrhythmias and mental disturbances. Blood pressure raises and blood vessels pop.

But as God's word tells me, and he cannot lie, that I can be victorious in this war one day because of Christ, I, like Paul, press on as he wrote in Philippians 3:12-14, 'Not that I have already attained, or am already perfected; but I press on, . . . forgetting those things which are behind and reaching forward to those things which are ahead, I press toward the goal for the prize of the upward call of God in Christ Jesus.'

These opposing warring voices in my head remind me of an old, Donald Duck cartoon that portrayed Donald's conscious struggling to choose between right and wrong, good and evil. Perched on one of Donald's shoulders, close to an ear was a miniature bright red Donald look-a-like but with horns and a trident (Oh, that Satan was that size and as easy to spot.). On the other shoulder, close to Donald's other ear was a glistening white miniature Donald look-a-like but with a halo. Each was presenting their reasoning for the choice they were counselling him to make. The red duck always seemed to be the loudest and most insistent with the smoothest and most attractive reasoning. Choosing to listen and act upon his advice did give Donald great pleasure – that is until he realized that that acting on that advice was why he was now out of favour with Daisy!

I guess like Donald we have a choice in this war to fight or not to fight, for we always have a choice, but I don't think it's much of a one. If we don't take up the armour provided by God and stand against the wiles, the schemes of Satan and his 'voices', if we procrastinate, giving thought time to him, indulging and feeding our old nature, instead of giving our energies to obeying the Spirit to crucify and render the old man inoperative – well what gets fed and cared for grows and what gets ignored and starved eventually dies, does it not?

As we learn in Galatians 6:7-8, 5:24 'Do not be deceived, God is not mocked; for whatever a man sows, that he will also reap. For he who sows to his flesh will of the flesh reap corruption, but he who sows to the Spirit will of the Spirit reap everlasting life. . . And those who are Christ's have crucified the flesh with its passions and desires.'

Question: What is meant by *to sow to the flesh*?
Answer: To 'sow to the flesh' is to pander to it, to cosset, cuddle and stroke it, instead of crucifying it . . . Every time we allow our mind to harbour a grudge, nurse a grievance, entertain an impure fantasy or wallow in self-pity, we are sowing to the flesh . . . Every time we linger in bad company whose insidious influence we know we cannot resist, every time we read pornographic literature [I would like to respectfully suggest that for some that could be the daily newspaper or the underwear catalogue in today's mailbox.], every time we take a risk which strains our self-control, we are sowing, sowing, sowing to the flesh. Some

Christians sow to the flesh every day and wonder why they do not reap holiness.[113]

It seemed to happen in an instant but on retrospection it had been growing for a long time. Oh, I thought I had killed it, well the bits that really mattered and besides was not God using this to teach me how to relate correctly to a brother in Christ who was not my husband? So as long as it stayed in the recesses of my mind and did not visibly impact my behaviour at church or with my relationship with my husband there surely was no harm in having the very pleasant attention of a Christian brother; right got that sorted.

Do you hear a warning siren? I should have!
Then out of the blue, from left distant field, came the request from a complete stranger, a male from Los Angeles, who liked my profile 'Doing whatever God puts in front of me' and my Granddaughter's first grade drawing of me as my photo and wanted to get to know each other over time yet being unable to wait followed the invite with emails. His studio portrait was stunning – definitely not the work of a child. (Please take note those who are younger than I, that age or marital status are no guarantee for not having these kinds of struggles, believe me.) His profile, career, income and humanitarian achievements matched. Con? Maybe. But that was not what concerned me. I of course did all the right things. If it was friendship, he was looking for my husband and I would be happy to communicate with him. That was the end of contact by email. But he was still 'liking' my posted comments or articles and my mind which in another life time had devoured bags of Mills and Boon novels was really enjoying the fantasies. (This is why I won't read the Christian counterparts, despite others encouraging me to.)

Nothing had been killed, nothing at all.
Around this time, I went down with some sort of bug (pre COVID19 days) that kept me from church for a couple of services and made me so tired I could not concentrate even read so I just

---

[113] John Stott *The Message of Galatians* Inter-Varsity Press 1968 p170

had my thoughts. I watched my loving husband serve me, care for the grandchildren and look after everything without complaint and I thought . . . watched more and thought some more . . . and eventually talked. He had suspected but knew he could not force me or ask me to love him.

WHAT!!!!

And yes, sadly, I had been working on this section.

Sowing to the flesh is not a chore, in many ways it feels very pleasant unlike repentance and the shame you feel.

What does scripture say? Take heed unless you fall. Pride comes before a fall. Watch and pray.

Well that's it. I've discredited myself from continuing writing, for speaking of God and how we should live for above all, this evil I've done was firstly against his goodness to me then against my husband who has never done anything but love me. Strange, scary and confusing how a fantasy could appear better than reality. What my mind had thought of giving up, what I could have lost! I crept into God's presence only to find him like my husband, waiting, knowing and with arms open.

O the joy to be clean again! Remember sinning is not the end of the world, refusing to confess to your ever loving and waiting Father and really repenting is.

Jerry Bridges' statement, 'There is no point praying for victory over temptation if we are not willing to make a commitment to say no to it'[114] is very true. I'd been praying for victory while enjoying my daydreaming.

I am no longer involved with any form of social media platform and it is amazing how much more time I have. I am more aware and less lazy about grabbing those thoughts as they begin to appear and asking for Christ's help to chuck them where they belong.

---

[114] *The Pursuit of Holiness* p96

Question: What is this killing or crucifying of the flesh that we read a couple of pages back in Galatians 5:24 and which Scott's quote mentioned? How are we to do this?

Answer: It is the seeing of sin for what it is, a horrible disfiguring curse on our image and treating it as such. It is a determined active dying to self and an equally determined living and abiding with Christ. It is a conscious deliberate choice all pilgrims must fight to make with every breath they take for in doing so they are giving, letting the Spirit freedom to fight for and with us.

> It is the constant battle against sin which we fight daily – the refusal to allow the eye to wander, the mind to contemplate, the affections to run after anything which will draw us from Christ. It is the deliberate rejection of any sinful thought, suggestion, desire, aspiration, deed, circumstance or provocation at the moment we become conscious of its existence.[115]

There was a day I died. Died to George Mueller, his opinions, preferences, tastes and will; died to the world, its approval or censure; died to the approval or blame of my brethren or friends; and since then I have studied only to show myself approved unto God.[116]

Question: Still thinking on the same quote of Scott's, what's the problem of not reaping holiness?

Answer: Do you remember what we said about holiness and being holy because God is? (I won't know if you need to flick back to those earlier pages and refresh your memory you know, I had to.) This question is a little different. To be able to reap, gather in or harvest a crop you must have had something growing that is producing visible fruit. To reap holiness, you must be growing in your own personal holiness, you must be showing some success in your war against your old man. At the very least, you must be

---

[115] Sinclair Ferguson *The Christian Life* Banner of Truth 1989 p162 quoted by Tim Chester *You Can Change God's transforming power for our sinful behaviours & negative emotions* IVP 2008 p119

[116] George Mueller (1805-1898) https://www.georgemuller.org

fighting to get back up and move forward one step at a time today for if you decide to lie down and quit fighting today tomorrow, if you have a tomorrow, you will have less strength to get up and keep walking, not more.

In 2 Corinthians 6:14, 16b-17, 7:1 we read, 'Do not be unequally yoked together with unbelievers. For what fellowship has righteousness with lawlessness? And what communion has light with darkness? . . . For you are the temple of the living God . . . Therefore "Come out from among them and be separate, says the Lord. Do not touch what is unclean, and I will receive you. I will be a Father to you, and you shall be My sons and daughters", says the LORD Almighty. Therefore, having these promises, beloved, let us cleanse ourselves from all filthiness of the flesh and spirit, perfecting holiness in the fear of God.'

To choose not to be growing in holiness, not to separating ourselves from the sins of this fallen world, not to daily dedicating ourselves to the one true triune God and repenting of any known sin, to not to be conforming to Christ is choosing not to be a Christian, not to be a pilgrim travelling home, not to be fighting against the old man.

Not to be able to have the hope of heaven, of no more pain or tears, of never having eternal peace; is the choice to sow to the flesh, to sow to self, to care for the old nature instead of declaring war against it really a choice you want to make?

Me neither! To arms brethren!

Battle ready

Tozer writes that by 'Going back no further than the times of the founding and early development of our country, we are able to see the wide gulf between our modern attitudes and those of our fathers. In the early days . . . men conceived the world to be a battle ground. Our fathers believed in sin and the devil and hell as constituting one force, and they believed in God and righteousness and heaven as the other. By their very nature, these forces were opposed to each other forever in deep, grave, irreconcilable hostility. Man, our fathers held, had to choose sides – he could not be neutral . . . it must be life or death, heaven or hell, and if he chose to come out on God's side, he could expect open war with God's enemies. The fight would be real and deadly and would last as long as life continued here below. Men looked forward to heaven as a return from the wars, a laying down of the sword to enjoy in peace the home prepared for them.

Sermons and songs in those days often had a martial quality about them, or perhaps a trace of homesickness. The Christian solider thought of home and rest and reunion . . . But whether he was charging into enemy guns or dreaming of war's end and the Father's welcome home, he never forgot what kind of world he lived in – it was a battleground, and many were wounded and slain . . . Man, because of his spiritual nature, is caught in the middle. The evil powers are bent upon destroying him, while Christ is present to save him through the power of the gospel. To obtain deliverance he must come out on God's side in faith and obedience. That in brief is what our fathers thought . . .

How different today. The fact remains the same, but the interpretation has changed completely. Men think of the world not as a battleground but as a playground. We are not here to fight; we are here to frolic. We are not in a foreign land; we are at home. We are not getting ready to live, but we are already living, and the best we can do is to rid ourselves of our inhibitions and our frustrations and live this life to the full . . . The idea that this world is a playground instead of a battleground has now been accepted in practice by the vast majority of fundamentalist Christians . . . their conduct gives them away. They are facing both ways, enjoying Christ and the world, gleefully telling everyone that accepting Jesus does not require them to give up their fun.'[117]

A battleground? Hmmmm . . .

---

[117] A. W. Tozer *Tozer This World: Playground or Battleground?* compiled and edited by Harry Verploeg Authentic 1989 p1-3

Sun Tzu (544-496BC) was a legendary historical figure whose works continue to influence not just modern warfare but also culture, politics, business and sports. For example, he taught –
- If ignorant both of your enemy and yourself, you are certain to be in peril.
- Knowing the enemy enables you to take the offensive, knowing yourself enables you to stand on the defensive.
- If you know yourself but not the enemy, for every victory gained you will also suffer a defeat.
- Begin by seizing something which your opponent holds dear; then he will be amenable to your will.
- If his forces are united, separate them.
- Convince your enemy that he will gain little by attacking you: this will diminish his enthusiasm.[118]

As we have considered the internal lusts both here and in the previous section, we may have some understanding of them now but what of the second type of warfare, the one Paul talks about especially in Ephesians? Let's have a deeper look at this sort of fighting, fighting against external foes. Satan, I believe uses some if not all of these tactics of Sun Tzu so it may be wise to consider them for ourselves.

To begin with do not allow Satan to make you believe he is just a symbol or a cartoon character or even a figment of an overly sensitive imagination. He is real, however, as pilgrims walking in the Spirit, we are not to fear him but respect him and his power for even though it is leashed it is real and he is the one who tempts us to rebel against our Father. We have considered earlier the mindset of seeing ourselves as God does which helps greatly in the fight against how Satan declares you to be. Sadly, I have known of parents who have left the way to follow their children, to keep a relationship with them, giving Satan a victory. He also wins when he manages to divide a church over trivial things like deciding what colour the new carpet should be, forever

---

[118] Sun Tzu quotes from BrainyQuote.com

separating those who had been close, with some never going inside a church again.
We all have weaknesses within ourselves that we, if we know they are there, struggle to strengthen. Satan seems to know about these better than we do and he is quick to gleefully target them.
In Hebrews 4:15-16 we read, 'For we do not have a High Priest who cannot sympathize with our weaknesses, but was in all points tempted as we are, yet without sin. Let us therefore, come boldly to the throne of grace, that we may obtain mercy and find grace to help in time of need.'

Question: How was Christ, God's Son, tempted as we are today some 2000years later yet not sin? Can we do the same as pilgrims?
Answer: Remembering we are called to have the mind of Christ and that while he is fully God, he is also at the same time fully human (What a great mystery!), let us look at my paraphrasing of Luke 4:1-12 and consider how Jesus dealt with being tempted, how he fought and what he fought with.

After the Spirit had led the man Jesus into the wilderness for forty days to have his faith and obedience to the Father tried, he became hungry and the devil appeared and tempted him to sin three times in an effort to break his allegiance to God by saying in effect, "If you are who you say you are make these stones into bread and feed your fleshy lust. . . All the power and glories of the kingdoms of the world that you now see will be yours if you worship me for I have the authority to give to who I please, so go on now and fulfil the lust of your eyes. . . If you are who you claim to be show everyone, prove it to them and jump for God's angels will surely protect you as you are *THE* man (what pride)!"
Remember what Eve and Adam did?
They listened, saw and acted upon their own desires that the serpent ignited within them.
Jesus the man, faced with the same sort of temptations – for into one if not two or all of these three boxes, lust of the eyes, lust of the flesh and pride of life all sins can find a home – did not act as

Satan wanted but wielding scripture in the right context silenced him and he withdrew till another time.

By right context I am referring to the unbiblical idea behind Satan's incorrect quoting, his twisting of Psalm 91:11-12 when he wanted Jesus to jump in his third challenge.

Satan is telling Jesus to throw himself down from the pinnacle of the temple because, God 'shall give His angels charge over you, to keep you and in their hands they shall bear you up, lest you dash your foot against a stone' (v 10-11) and all those watching below will be in awe and know who you are and will worship you as you deserve. This twisting makes a lie about God, the type of God he is, and this is never good. As we will see later careless use of the sword may cause injury to yourself instead of the enemy.

Let's see what this psalm Satan quoted really says and what sort of person it is speaking about that God will protect by considering the relevant verses and the promises of v.14-16.

Psalm 91

1. He who dwells in the secret place of the Most High
   Shall abide under the shadow of the Almighty.
2. I will say of the LORD, "He is my refuge and my fortress;
   My God, in Him I will trust."
3. Surely He shall deliver you from the snare of the fowler
   And from the perilous pestilence.
4. He shall cover you with His feathers,
   And under His wings you shall take refuge;
   His truth shall be your shield and buckler . . .
11. For He shall give His angels charge over you,
    To keep you in all your ways.
12. In their hands they shall bear you up,
    Lest you dash your foot against a stone . . .
14. "Because he has set his love upon Me, therefore I will deliver him;

> I will set him on high, because he has known My name.
> 15. He shall call upon Me, and I will answer him;
> I will be with him in trouble;
> I will deliver him and honour him.
> 16. With long life I will satisfy him,
> And show him My salvation."

Satan seems to have forgotten to quote v.11 in its fullness as he has omitted why the angles have charge over Christ and us and that is *to keep you in all your ways*. These ways are the ways of one *who dwells in the secret place of the Most High*, whose *wings* are his *refuge*, his protection, whose *truth* is God's truth which is his *shield and buckler,* his defense who later on in the psalm we learn has *set his love* upon God. This is not a person who will demand the use of God's protecting ministers to achieve his self-seeking, self-glorifying greedy motives, for he does not, cannot have these sinful ways within him. If a God-loving and name-knowing pilgrim does stumble in the way God has sent her, God will send his angels to help keep her in the way of holiness and righteousness, will deliver and honour her, minimizing any harm.

Jesus answers Satan the third time by quoting from Deuteronomy again (He quoted from Deuteronomy 8:3 to answer Satan's first challenge) but this time from 6:16. Knowing Satan would have been aware of the context of Christ's quote and the background, perhaps more than us, let's have a look and consider both context and verse.

Deuteronomy 6: 13-19, 'You shall fear the LORD your God and serve Him, and shall take oaths in His name. You shall not go after other gods, the gods of the peoples who are all around you (for the LORD your God is a jealous God among you), lest the anger of the LORD your God be aroused against you and destroy you from the face of the earth. You shall not tempt the LORD your God as you tempted Him in Massah.

You shall diligently keep the commandments of the LORD your God, His testimonies, and His statutes which He has commanded you. And you shall do what is right and good in the sight of the

LORD, that it may be well with you, and that you may go in and possess the good land of which the LORD swore to your fathers, to cast out all your enemies from before you, as the LORD has spoken.'

How the Israelites tempted God is told in Exodus 17:1-7, 'Then all the congregation of the children of Israel set out on their journey from the wilderness of Sin, according to the commandment of the LORD, and camped in Rephidim; but there was no water for the people to drink. Therefore the people contended with Moses, and said, "Give us water, that we may drink." So Moses said to them, "Why do you contend with me? Why do you tempt the LORD?" And the people thirsted there for water, and the people complained against Moses, and said, "Why is it you have brought us up out of Egypt, to kill us and our children and our livestock with thirst?" So Moses cried out to the LORD, saying, "What shall I do with this people? They are almost ready to stone me!" And the LORD said to Moses, "Go on before the people, and take with you some of the elders of Israel. Also take in your hand your rod with which you struck the river, and go. Behold, I will stand before you there on the rock in Horeb; and you shall strike the rock, and water will come out of it, that the people may drink." And Moses did so in the sight of the elders of Israel. So he called the name of the place Massah (literally, Tempted) and Meribah (literally, Contention), because of the contention of the children of Israel, and because they tempted the LORD, saying, "Is the LORD among us or not?"'

Jesus was telling Satan that by being obedient to God he would benefit far more than by putting on a display to impress men, to show them who he knew himself to be.

Jesus, like any pilgrim, only has to play for an audience of one, answer to one, and his weapon of choice was scripture. How often are we tempted to put on a display to impress someone, to prove ourselves? Oops!

Anderson writes 'This, which has been said to be an epitome of all the temptations to which man has been subjected from the beginning, though generally spoken of as one, consisted in reality of *three,* which were these -1) The temptation to *distrust*, and *disobedience,* through hunger or the desire for food; 2) To *presumption*, through the desire of distinction; 3) To *pride,* through the desire of power; or as they have been described by others – to *enjoyment, honour,* and *possession.* "By the renunciation of these, when offered to him by the Prince of this world, his obedience," says Stier, "approved itself perfect, and thus he overcame in the abasement of faith, from which he had descended from his divine power, and so led human nature back to God again through the selfsame way by which it had fallen from him." . . . It was as man *for* man that he withstood the temptation and overcame the tempter. Besides his anointing with power by the Spirit, through which he overcame, there is to be considered also the use he made of, and the aid he received from the written Word, which, as Stier profoundly remarks, was not only "written by him, but for him." *"It is written".* Such was the armoury from which he brought his weapons, offensive and defensive, his sword and his shield. . . Besides its importance as a great historical event in the life of Christ, his temptation has an importance to us on other accounts, in being a figure of the conflicts which we must undergo with the same Spirit of evil; of the weapons we are to use, and the way in which we are to overcome; and in being not only a pattern of the conflict, but to all who really engage in it, a pledge of victory!' [119]

Having an understanding of the many ways our enemy works (his wiles) can help our defense as any good general knows, which is one reason for the Bible being written and for us to read it.
In Ephesians 2:1-3 and 4:17-19 for example, we read, 'And you He made alive, who were dead in trespasses and sins, in which you once walked according to the course of this world, according to the prince of the power of the air, the spirit who now works in the sons of disobedience, among whom also we all once conducted ourselves in the lust of our flesh, fulfilling the desires of the flesh

---

[119] *Fleetwood's Life of Christ* comment from Anderson's Life of Christ p118-9

and of the mind, and were by nature children of wrath, just as the others. . . . This I say, therefore, and testify in the Lord, that you should no longer walk as the rest of the Gentiles walk, in the futility of their mind, having their understanding darkened, being alienated from the life of God, because of the blindness of their heart; who being past feeling, have given themselves over to lewdness, to work all uncleanness with greediness.'

Here we see how Satan attempts to alienate both pilgrims and unbelievers from God by disobedience, ignorance and erroneous thinking, all which both fires up and fulfills the lusts and desires of our old natures. Such things all pilgrims should be alert to and ready to resist as we have given ourselves over to God, adopting his new mindset and have the light of Christ, the gospel to send the darkness away.

Then in Ephesians 4:25-32 we read that we are to put '. . away lying, "Let each one of you speak truth with his neighbour," for we are members of one another. "Be angry, and do not sin": do not let the sun go down on your wrath, not give place to the devil. Let him who stole steal no longer, but rather let him labour, working with his hands what is good, that he may have something to give him who has need. Let no corrupt word proceed out of your mouth, but what is good for necessary edification, that it may impart grace to the hearers. And do not grieve the Holy Spirit of God, by whom you were sealed for the day of redemption. Let all bitterness, wrath, anger, clamour, and evil speaking be put away from you, with all malice. And be kind to one another, tenderhearted, forgiving one another, even as God in Christ forgave you.'

Again, we see Satan's attempts to alienate people, but particularly pilgrims, from each other by sins that separate, disrupt or completely sever relationships. Sins like greed – greed for all things, acclaim included, the telling and spreading of lies, anger, theft – which could be taking the credit for someone else's work or good idea, laziness, verbal put-downs, gossip, and arguments especially loud public ones, any attitude or behaviour that is not kind, not loving – like favouring one congregational member over another (James 2:1-9) and where there is no forgiveness specifically given not presumed will fracture relationships. Pilgrims must actively root out and throw in the bin all such thought or feeling before it grows into actions, or thoughtless words that can cause damage like a wild fire and be ready to share the grace and mercy they themselves have received.

Paul here also councils us to not give place to the devil, to not give him an opportunity to make a place for himself in our renewed heart, giving him opportunity to disrupt these precious relationships all pilgrims need. We should not allow anything in our lives that should not be there according to God. Be totally uncompromising, refuse to have anything within that Satan can claim as his because it is not of God and make our life, our witness for God stink. Do not leave it till tomorrow to bin either. Do it before bedtime. We will not always succeed, and so, we learn the importance of prayer, a certain type of prayer, one of confession, repentance seeking forgiveness so we can have the stench washed off our feet and be clean again, uncontaminated.

Question: How do we strengthen our defenses against these ways and any other ways of Satan? How do we stop wrong thoughts becoming sin?

Answer: Know your Bible. It teaches the truth about our opponent, unlike the movies or Donald Duck cartoons and how he ambushes us as we have already briefly considered.

To start with God's word tells us that Satan is a real living being who can think and act but who rebelled against his maker wanting to take his place. Even in my fifty odd years I have noticed a huge shift even among those who consider themselves to be Christian about the reality of Satan and his ability to influence humanity and our ability to control him.

As a child I vividly remember a sermon about the devil and hell where those who belonged with him, those who refused God's grace, would spend eternity. I have never heard such a fire and brimstone approach to preaching since. Though Satan may be able to make himself seem as attractive as an angel of God he is full of darkness and lies. Oh yes, he can tell truths, but only part truths twisted into his lies, as we have seen when he attempted to trip Jesus up. Knowing God's truth, knowing your Bible will equip you to know what is not of God.

According to the Barna Group's definitions, in May of 2017 the USA adult population consisted of 42% nominal-Christians, 23% religious sceptics, 23% non-evangelical born-agains, 6% adherents of non-Christian faiths and 6% evangelical. When asked if Satan was not a symbol but a living being 98% of evangelicals strongly agreed compared with 35% of the non-evangelical born-agains, 34% of the adherents to non-Christian faiths, 16% of the sceptics and 14% of the notional Christians. [120]

In Thomas Chalmer's (1780-1847) sermon, 'The Expulsive Power of a New Affection', he teaches that no one can simply tell himself to stop sinning. The desires that we have, that sinning seemingly satisfies even if briefly, need to be given to God Himself. He alone truly liberates us from their grip and lastingly satisfies us. A renewed affection for God is the prayer that will expel sin. How does one get a 'renewed affection for God'? Read. Read His word to you His book the Bible. Read it more than the glossy mags, the newspaper or more than you sit mindlessly before the TV soaking up worldly morals and behaviours or being on other forms of social media like Facebook. [121]

In his 'brief relation of the exceeding mercy of God in Christ to his poor servant, John Bunyan', titled 'Grace Abounding to the Chief of Sinners', No.70, John writes – 'But I was not without my temptations to go back again; temptations I say, both from Satan, mine own heart, and carnal acquaintance; but I thank God these were out-weighed by that sound sense of death, and of the day of judgement, which abode, as it were, continually in my view; I would often also think on Nebuchadnezzar, of whom it is said, 'He

---

[120] Articles in Faith and Christianity 23.5.2017 https://www.barna.com

[121] I wish to give credit for a paragraph on p152 in *You Can Change* for the ideas just expressed.

had given him all the kingdoms of the earth.' Dan.v.18, 19. Yet, thought I, if this great man had all his portion in this world, one hour in hell-fire would make him forget all. Which consideration was a great help to me...'[122]

John Bunyan's character, Christian spoke of how he got power over his corruptions or annoyances –

> "I think of what I saw at the cross . . . when I look upon my embroidered coat . . . when I look into the roll (For this roll was the assurance of his life, and acceptance at the desired haven) . . . and when my thoughts wax warm about whither I am going." [123]

The knowledge of their Bible (which includes teaching about prayer) the owners of these quotes had allowed them to know their true self, Satan's ways and God's character and this is what enabled them to be overcomers in this war. Never underestimate this book, never let it become dusty. I personally have discovered it to be like no other book I've ever read and I have read a lot, it is truly, as some have said, alive. It is the only full-on and complete how-to manual you really need. True, not every incident one can face is described and advised on but by looking for the underlying basic principles you will have your direction, your answer.

Psalm 119 teaches us a lot about what the Bible does. Read the complete version in your own Bible or by using the internet on your phone. When you see it, you will understand why I have not written it out here in full for you to read.

Verse 9 reads, 'How can a young man cleanse his way? By taking heed according to Your word.'

Verse 105 says, 'Your word is a lamp to my feet and a light to my path'. This means that God gives enough light, understanding for your next step and enough to show you where the following step ahead will be but he will not give more light till you take the next step forward in obedience.

---

[122] *The Pilgrim's Progress* p740
[123] *The Pilgrim's Progress* p91 (85)

Many verses scattered throughout this psalm teach us that we can ask to be taught, to understand, to be led by God. He is eager to help. For example, verses 33-38 and 133, 'Teach me, O LORD, the way of Your statutes, and I shall keep it to the end. Give me understanding, and I shall keep Your law; indeed, I shall observe it with my whole heart. Make me walk in the path of Your commandments, for I delight in it. Incline my heart to Your testimonies, and not to covetousness. Turn away my eyes from worthless things, and revive me in Your way. Establish Your word to Your servant, who is devoted to fearing You. . . Direct my steps by Your word, and let no iniquity have dominion over me.'
Other verses speak of receiving comfort and council.
For example, verses 24, 50 and 52, 'Your testimonies also are my delight and my counsellors . . . This is my comfort in my affliction. For Your word has given me life. . . I remembered Your judgements of old, O LORD, and have comforted myself.'
Then there are the verses that speak of life, affliction and why as seen in verses 75, 92-3 and 116, 'I know, O LORD, that Your judgements are right, and that in faithfulness You have afflicted me. . . Unless Your law had been my delight, I would then have perished in my affliction. I will never forget Your precepts, for by them You have given me life. . . Uphold me according to Your word, that I might live; and do not let me be ashamed of my hope.'

"No time", you say . . .

How edifying is the television, or that magazine, or time spent surfing Google because you are feeling bored? Will those things draw you closer to our God? Do they help you to fight against your lusts or Satan? Hmmmm . . .
This article was published around 1958 about television, black and white television –

> Television in itself is not a sin, but if it robs us of the time we ought to spend with God, then it could become our besetting sin. I have no television in my home, and the reason I do not is that I have no time for it. By the time I get

through with my Lord and doing the things that He wants me to do, I have no time left for anything else. In a matter like this you will have to judge the thing for yourself. If you allow any form of entertainment to hinder your walk with God, then that thing is wrong.[124]

There is so much more that television today is there not? But to encourage you to check out the Bible for yourself instead of the latest news on Google or Facebook, know that the Bible, God's words within the Bible is the paper dagger mentioned earlier, but more on our armoury later.

<u>Question</u>: Does God's word tell us any other ways we are to fight this war? What will this look like?

<u>Answer</u>: I don't know about you but I am not that keen about getting close enough to any sort of snake to do any sort of damage to it, without considering one that talks. I have heard some declare to him that they are binding him so he cannot do some kind of evil to someone or something or so they can rescue something or someone. But I'm not sure about this, I don't want to talk to him, look what happened to Eve! Let's find what scripture says other that the section we have just considered.

1Peter 2:11, 'Beloved, I beg you as sojourners and pilgrims, abstain from fleshy lusts which war against the soul'. Peter uses one word to answer this question in the passage we are considering for the basis of this book, *abstain*. Different translations may use different wording but the idea is the same.

Abstain

Searching my trusty dictionary again, I find word pictures for what abstain looks like – Restrain (check or hold in, keep in check or under control or within bounds, repress, keep down, confine or imprison) oneself; to refrain from (avoid doing) indulging in; to repress (check, restrain, quell, keep under, suppress, prevent from bursting out or actively exclude (an unwelcome thought) from

---

[124] Theodore H. Epp (1907-1985) *Faith in Action* Zondervan 1958 p178

conscious awareness – and in considering them I came to realize that society worldwide as pictured in all forms of media show very few of these pictures of abstaining in a complementary good-for-your-health-or-personhood idea or even for society as a whole if at all.

Looking for inspiration of what to write next I carried out a brief bit of experimental research using Google on my smart phone to answer the question, 'What happens if you abstain?'

Was that a giggle?

Most sites I looked at dealt with sexual stuff, though a few dealt with foods, especially sugar, alcohol or coffee. For my few minutes on line I saw nothing about things such as outbursts of wrath, lying, unedifying words etc. So, I guess I found out what we as a worldwide society prioritize with the word abstain and that the word itself is not viewed as something to practice for our personal benefit. By the way if you are interested Google informed me that 'abstaining from sex will not kill you but . . .'

Since Google brought sexual relationships up let us consider one of the most powerful emotions God has given us for our delight within marriage that Satan has twisted almost beyond recognition and uses for our destruction and why Paul commands us to flee from the ungodly use of it.

1Corinthians 6: 12-20, 'All things are lawful for me, but all things are not helpful. All things are lawful for me, but I will not be brought under the power of any. Foods for the stomach and the stomach for foods, but God will destroy both it and them. Now the body is not for sexual immorality but for the Lord, and the Lord for the body. And God both raised up the Lord and will also raise us up by His power. Do you not know that your bodies are members of Christ? Shall I then take the members of Christ and make them members of a harlot? Certainly not! Or do you not know that he who is joined to a harlot is one body with her? For "the two," He says, "shall become one flesh." But he who is joined to the Lord is one spirit with Him. Flee sexual immorality. Every sin that a man [or woman] does is outside the body, but he who commits sexual immorality sins against his own body. Or do you not know that your body is the temple of the Holy Spirit who is in you, whom you have from God, and you are not your own? For you were bought at a price; therefore glorify God in your body and in your spirit, which are God's.'

This section of scripture teaches us that *any* sexual activity which God has declared as a sin, that is any thought, sight or action *outside of marriage* , the joining of one man to one woman, that causes sexual arousal, that is anything or person or creature other than your spouse, that is causing you to become aroused, that sexually stimulates you in any way, are the *only* sins that you commit against your *own* body, yours, rather than someone else's.

Paul is reminding us that as a pilgrim, our body as well as our spirit, our whole self, now belongs to God for he bought it at a great price uniting us to Christ in the closest and most intimate way, and so the Christian's life should be determined by God's design for it, which does not allow for the specific evil of sexual sin, or any other sin for that matter. This is a basic principle that when considered and applied enables us to choose the right way, a God glorifying walk. However, a war against the powerful sexual lusts of the old nature is guaranteed, and lust does not equal a love that is good for you or the object you are lusting after.

Morris writes, 'The word rendered *take* (verse 15) *airō* means 'take away'. The horrible thing about this sin is that *the members of Christ* are taken away from their proper use . . . There is a horrible profanation of that which should be used only for Christ . . . Paul . . . uses the. . . strong word, *kollōmenos* for *joined*. The verb is used of close bonds of various kinds. In the literal sense it refers to the process of glueing . . . *Flee fornication* . . . the present imperative indicates the habitual action, 'Make it your habit to flee.' That is the only way . . . cannot be satisfactory dealt with by any less drastic measures. The Christian must not temporize with it, but flee the very thought . . . Paul . . . does not say this is the most serious of all sins . . . But this sin, and this sin only, means that a man takes that body which is 'a member of Christ' and puts it into a union which 'blasts his own body'(Way) . . . .fornication involves a man in what God yet calls 'a degrading physical solidarity, incompatible with the believer's spiritual solidarity with Christ' . . worth noting the interpretation suggested by Moule, that 'every sin that a man doeth is without the body' is the slogan of some of the Corinthians, meaning 'physical lust cannot touch the secure "personality" of the initiated.' To this Paul retorts: 'on the contrary: anyone who commits fornication *is* committing an offence against his very "personality"'. The use of *humartēma* for *sin,* rather than the more usual *hamartia,* puts the emphasis on the result, rather than the act . . . Nothing that would be amiss in God's temple is seemly in the body of the child of God. . . Because he is God's temple, the believer cannot think of himself as independent, as belonging to himself. . . we are God's slaves . . . He has bought us to be His own . . . The obligation resting upon believers as a consequence is that they should *glorify God* . . . The prime motive in the service of the Christian must not be the accomplishing of purposes which seem to him to be desirable, but the glory of God.'[125]

With temptations, especially of the sexual sort the Biblical advice is to abstain from or flee from. And later on when we learn what the Bible considers is shameful you will understand that this action is never seen by God as such and remember it is his opinion that matters eternally, not your mates'.

It is okay to run physically just as Joseph did. In Genesis 39:7-12 we read, 'And it came to pass after these things that his master's wife cast longing eyes on Joseph, and she said, "Lie with me." But he refused and said to his master's wife, "Look, my master does not know what is with me in the house, and he has committed all that he has to my hand. There is no one greater in this house than I, nor has he kept back anything from me but you, because you are his wife. How then can I do this great wickedness, and sin against God?" So it was, as she spoke to Joseph day by day, that

---

[125] *The First epistle of Paul to the Corinthians* p 98-104

he did not heed her, to lie with her or to be with her. But it happened about this time, when Joseph went into the house to do his work, and none of the men of the house was inside, that she caught him by his garment, saying, "Lie with me." But he left his garment in her hand, and fled and ran outside.'
I like this idea of how to fight, it seems sensible, a good reason for having adrenaline, though I'd prefer to be able to keep my clothes on. And mentally fleeing from those fleshy lusts, instead of indulging in daydreaming, is excellent pictorial advice (that I should have taken earlier) and I'd be assured of keeping my clothes.
A personal sidetrack here. Even if you are not a pilgrim, being sexually active outside of marriage is damaging to the self, this is not *agapē* but lust. This is not what God wanted for you. Have you ever had your legs waxed, or any other part of your body? Remember the first time? Every time you have sex with someone a bit of you is torn away and lost forever when that relationship is broken, as when the wax is pulled from your skin removing hair by its roots. Even worse if the trusted other commits adultery, a part of you that's been exposed in faith has been ripped away and given to a stranger. Once your trust has been discarded as irrelevant it is hard to give freely again. Sex between a man and a woman is a deeply intimate and personal knowing, far, far more than the mindless instinctive biologically driven act of an animal. We are the only creatures created by God who have sex by choice involving the whole self physically, mentally, spiritually and normally face-to-face. Misuse this gift from God and you will, without his healing and renewing salvation, become hardened and cold and eventually destroy yourself. If you can't take the teaching of God on this as truth, can you please take my personal knowledge from experience, that this is truth and refuse to lose out on the fulfilling goodness of this gift and sell yourself to the empty never satisfied darkness? If you have been ensnared this way, please know that when God makes you all new as a pilgrim, he does make you *all* new. I could have worn white for my second

marriage. I chose to wear blue because that was my husband-to-be's favourite colour but I was all white inside.

We have considered how our God usually appeals to us through our wills while Satan through our desires or lusts. James 1:13-15 told us how temptations worked and 1John 2:16 was on the three lusts of the world. And we know that it is only when we are drawn away by our own mind's desires, lusts, and assent or give into them, putting down our arms and acting upon them, it is only then that we sin. These feelings, desires that begin in our mind, sometimes with something external lighting their flame, are only thoughts, wishes and it is not till we act upon them and do something to satisfy them that we sin. It is while they are silent thoughts, ideas, in our mind that they need to be heard for what they are and silenced, stopped, not acted upon, abstained from.

Be aware here how the world and its media do the tempter's work by peer-pressure, altering the harshness of words, removing ones once used and making what was considered evil or shameful, abnormal to be acceptable, even desirable for today's modern society mostly by films of some sort. For example, compare words like fornicator, adulterer, harlot, bastard, sexual sinner, deviant, abortionist with partner, lover, escort, love child, gay, pro-choicer.

I am going to take you on another sidetrack here though it is still considering how meanings of words have changed so please stay with me. We have seen how scripture teaches us that God is love but we are also taught that our God is a jealous God. Deuteronomy 4:24 reads, 'For the LORD your God is a consuming fire, a jealous God' which should make us pilgrims feel very safe but the meaning and understanding of this word has been twisted and is no longer seen as an acceptable emotion for God or anyone else to express whereas no one seems to be troubled by feeling envy or expressing it, in fact it seems to be actively encouraged since it incites us to spend money. So here we have a feeling that is actually good made evil, not okay, which may cause us to misunderstand God's character; never a good thing to do.

Merill Periman writes, "Jealousy' and 'envy' have very similar meanings and are often confused. In many ways the difference is whether you have some claim on the object of your desire [well God did make us and he does enable us to breath and move . . .] Jealous is defined as 'very watchful or careful in guarding and keeping' [ah, that's the job of our shepherd King] and 'resentfully envious'. Envy is defined as 'a feeling of discontent and ill will because of another's advantages, possessions etc., resentful dislike of another who has something that one desires' [that counts God out for there is nothing that he has not created, besides his will can never be ill or he would no longer be God]. 'Jealousy' has stronger emotions attached. It is no coincidence that 'jealous' comes from 'zealous', which means 'ardent devotion'. The first uses of 'jealous' in English were attached to biblical devotion, then to lovers. If you have, or had, something, and are trying to protect it, you are 'jealous' of it. You can be 'jealous' of your reputation [that's God's glory], your wayward lover . . . 'Envy' on the other hand, is more like 'want' and 'desire' than 'zeal'. It's sometimes considered a 'nice' word for 'jealousy'. The Biblical sin, thought is 'envy' not 'jealousy'. When you 'covet thy neighbour's wife' you are resentful that your neighbour has her and you don't. (If she was yours first then you can be 'jealous' [all mankind belonged to God before the appearance of that talking snake with legs] . . .) 'Envy' derives from the Latin word 'invidere', which means to 'look askance upon' as in 'give someone the evil eyes'. Its previous uses include 'malice' and 'spite'. So 'envy' isn't as benign as some might have it . . .' [126]

Does reading through this help correct your understanding of our God's jealousy, to see it in a good, healthy light that is consistent with his type of love for us, complementary in fact?

Now, where were we? Oh, yes, abstaining . . .

We can abstain, we can make that effort. We can say 'NO' – Yes, we really can! – in the same was as Jesus, the Son of man did. We

---

[126] Merill Periman *Covetous: The difference between 'Jealousy' and 'Envy'* March 21 2013 www.visualthesauras.com

can resist, refusing to yield to our fleshy worldly appetites and stand, to be more than conquerors through him who loves us, using the same tools Christ did, the only ones he and pilgrims have, God's word, the Holy Spirit and God's armour which after all is Christ himself.

"Finally," do I hear you say, "we have got to the armour!"
Yes, and it is found in Ephesians 6:10-18 which says, 'Finally my brethren, be strong in the Lord and in the power of His might. Put on the whole armour of God that you may be able to stand against the wiles of the devil. For we do not wrestle against flesh and blood, but against principalities, against powers, against the rulers of the darkness of this age, against spiritual hosts of wickedness in the heavenly places. Therefore take up the whole armour of God, that you may be able to withstand in the evil day, and having done all, to stand. Stand therefore, having girded your waist with truth, having put on the breastplate of righteousness, and having shod your feet with the preparation of the gospel of peace; above all, taking the shield of faith with which you will be able to quench all the fiery darts of the wicked one. And take the helmet of salvation, and the sword of the Spirit, which is the word of God; praying always with all prayer and supplication in the Spirit, being watchful to this end with all perseverance and supplication for all the saints'

This armour is for those attacks that come from without, that are external to us, not those lusts from within, though our armour will help prevent these being ignited by Satan and additional ones from entering.

But first I want you to note several things which God expects of us before we look at the individual bits and pieces. And we will begin with the rallying cry for all saints and pilgrims to *be strong*. This one is younger than the one Paul penned being written by William Gurnall only about four hundred years ago –

'My brethren be strong . . .

Let this then exhort you, Christians, to labour for this holy resolution and prowess, which is so needful for your Christian profession, that without it you cannot be what you profess. *The fearful* are in the flor not those that march for hell, Rev. 21; the violent and valiant are they which take heaven by force: cowards never won heaven. Say not that thou hast royal blood running in thy veins, and art begotten of God, except thou canst prove thy pedigree by this heroic spirit, to dare to be holy despite men and devils. . . Christ tries his children by their courage, that dare to look on the face of death and danger for his sake, Mark 8:34, 35. O how uncomely a sight is it to see, a bold sinner and a fearful saint, one resolved to be wicked, and a Christian wavering in his holy course; to see guilt put innocence to flight, and hell to keep the field impudently braving it with displayed banners of open profaneness; [to see] saints hide their colours for shame, or run from them for fear, who should rather wrap themselves in them, and die upon the place, than thus betray the glorious name of God, which is called upon by them to the scorn of the uncircumcised. Take heart therefore, O ye saints, and be strong; your cause is good, God himself espouseth your quarrel, who hath appointed you his own Son, General of the field, called 'the Captain of our salvation,' Heb. 2:10. He shall lead you on with courage, and bring you off with honour. He lived and died for you; he will live and die with you; for mercy and tenderness to his soldiers, none like him. Trajon, it is said, rent his clothes to bind up his soldiers' wounds: Christ poured out his blood as balm to heal his saints' wounds; tears off his flesh to bind them up. For prowess, none to compare with him: he never turned his head from danger: no, not when hell's malice and heaven's justice appeared in field against him; knowing all that should come upon him, [he] went forth and said, 'Whom seek ye?' John 18:4. For success insuperable: he never lost battle even when he lost his life: he won the field, carrying the spoils thereof in the triumphant chariot of his ascension, to heaven with him: where he makes an open show of them to the unspeakable joy of saints and angels . . .'[127]

Secondly note what is expected of us, it is to *stand*, just to stand. The word *fight* is not here but stand is four times. We are told to just stand alert, refusing to quit and this is what the armour enables us to do.

The Israelites having escaped from slavery in Egypt, are facing the Red Sea fearing for their lives as Pharaoh and his army are bearing down and we read in Exodus 14: 13-14, that '. . . Moses said to the people, "Do not be afraid. Stand still [firm], and see the salvation [deliverance] of the LORD, which He will accomplish for you today. For the Egyptians whom you see today, you shall see again no more for ever. The LORD will fight for you, and you shall hold your peace."'

In second Chronicles we learn that a great army was coming against the nation of Judah and their king Jehoshaphat who having no power to fight such a multitude knew of nothing they could do but look to their LORD. In 20:14-17, 20, 22 we read, 'Then the Spirit of the LORD came upon Jahaziel . . . and he said, ". . . Thus says the LORD to you: Do not be afraid nor dismayed because of this great multitude, for the battle is not yours, but God's. Tomorrow go down against them . . . You will not need to fight . . . position yourselves, stand still and see the salvation of the LORD, who is with you . .". . So they rose early in the morning and went out . . . Now when they began to sing and to praise, the LORD set ambushes against the people . . . and they were defeated.'

Psalm 46:1-2a, 10, 'God is our refuge and strength, a very present help in trouble [an abundantly available help]. Therefore we will not fear . . . Be still, and know that I am God; I will be exalted among the nations, I will be exalted in the earth!'

Stand

---

[127] William Gurnall (1617-1679) *A Treatise of the Whole Armour of God. Volume 1* Note: no page numbers recorded. Google books https://books.google.com

To stand is to avoid falling or moving or being moved off a base. Endure without yielding or complaining. To tolerate. Nautically it means to hold a specific course. A position taken up; an attitude adopted. To meet or face an opponent courageously and be resistant to any harmful effects of doing so. A stationary condition assumed for the purpose of resistance. Or as the verses we have just considered suggest, cease striving in your own strength, be obedient and trust God.

No complaining?

Oops!

That makes standing a bit harder.

Question: How can I stand? And keep on doing till my sojourning is completed, that could be tomorrow or in 40years and I've been fighting for so long already.

Answer: I believe that there are three main things required to answer this question and Paul tells us what they are.

- First in Philippians 3:13b-14, 17-4:1, '. . . one thing I do, forgetting those things which are behind and reaching forward to those things [v.12, things for which Christ has a hold on me for] which are ahead, I press [strain] toward the goal for the prize of the upward call of God in Christ Jesus . . .Brethren, join in following my example, and note those who so walk, as you have us for a pattern. For many walk, of whom I have told you often, and now tell you even weeping, that they are the enemies of the cross of Christ: whose end is destruction, whose god is their belly, and whose glory is in their shame – who set their mind on earthly things. For our citizenship is in heaven, from which we also eagerly wait for the Saviour, the Lord Jesus Christ, who will transform our lowly body that it may be conformed to His glorious body, according to the working by which he is able even to subdue all things to Himself. Therefore, my beloved and longed-for brethren, my joy and crown, so stand fast in the Lord, beloved.'

Paul is telling us to forget all that is behind, everything, all the pains, griefs, and regrets, all before we became pilgrims and all to this moment as pilgrims, for they have all been wiped away by Christ's sacrifice, and never moving away from the Lord reach towards the promised day when all will be made right, when we will be home and as Christ is.

- Secondly in Romans 15:4, '. . . whatever things were

written before were written for our learning, that we through the patience [perseverance] and comfort of the Scriptures might have hope.'

Dust off your Bible, read all of it, study it, own its truths and promises, and seeing that others have had similar challenges to you yet kept the faith and their hope, wrap its comforts about you like a warm eiderdown.

- Thirdly back in Philippians 4:6-7, 'Be anxious for nothing,

but in everything by prayer and supplication, with thanksgiving, let your requests be made known to God; and the peace of God, which surpasses all understanding, will guard your hearts and minds through Christ Jesus.'

Pray! Pray, pray to God more often than you talk to your best friend on this earth. Tell God all that you feel and think, he can take it, and he alone can do something about either the situation or your attitude towards it. He is the only one who can truly destroy you but he is not against you so let your heart and mind be guarded by his peace.

Gurnall suggests that to stand refers to the saints' ability to stand on that last day, the day of judgement.

Psalm 1:5a tells us that 'the ungodly shall not stand in the judgement' and Psalm 130:3 asks, 'If You, LORD, should mark iniquities, O Lord, who could stand?'

He goes on to write of what it means to stand, 'To stand amounts to as much as, to stand everyone in his rank and proper station, and here is opposed to all disorder, or straggling from our place . . it should be the care of every Christian to stand orderly in the particular place wherein God hath set him . . . when every wheel moves in its place without clashing, when everyone contributes by preforming the duty of his place to the benefit of the whole . .

It is not knowing another's duty, no nor censuring the negligence of another, but doing our own [duty, that] will bring us safely and comfortably to our journey's end. . . [With] some, their declining appears first in a negligence of duties about their peculiar callings, and the duties they owe, by their place and relation, to man, though all this while they may seem very forward and zealous in the duties of worship to God, much in hearing, praying, and such like; while others falter first in these, and at the same time seem very strict in the other. Both are alike destructive to the soul; they both meet in the ruin of the power of godliness. He stands orderly that makes conscience of the whole duty that lies on him in his place to God or man . . .

Our walk must be in that path which our call bleats out. We are therefore commanded everyone to 'do his own business' 1Thes. 4:11 . . . our own things – [things] that come within the compass of our general or particular calling . . . O what a quiet world should we have, if everything and person knew his own place! God will not thank thee for doing that which he did not set thee about. Possibly thou hast good intentions. So had Uzzah (see 2Sam. 6:6-7) . . . It concerns us not only to ask ourselves what the thing is we do, but also who requireth this at our hands? To be sure, God will at last put us upon that question, and it will go ill with us if we cannot show our commission. So long must we needs neglect what is our duty, as we are busy about that which is not . . . And this must needs be displeasing to God – to leave the work God sets us about, to do what he never commanded . . . We shall never be charged for not doing another's work . . . it is not our sin that we do not supply another's negligence, by doing that which belongs not to our place . . . God requires no more than faithfulness in our [own] place . . . many think they may do a thing, because they can do it . . .' [128]

Thirdly notice that we have to take up this armour, put it on and use all of it, not just the bits we feel like when we think we may need them, feel like putting them on. We are to have every item

---

[128] Ibid

on standing at the ready from the moment we become his and find ourselves on enemy turf, till he sends us home and our warring days are over. By having every item on we will be strong in him *and in* the power of his might – which by the way happens to be omnipotent, for there is nothing or nobody more powerful – and not in ourselves.

Gurnall noting two things about this armour tells us of its substance –

FIRST. They are most *defensive arms*. Indeed, there is but one of all the pieces in the whole panoply for offence, *i.e.* 'the sword'. It may be to give us this hint, that this spiritual war of the Christian lies chiefly on the defence, and therefore requires arms most of this kind to wag it. God hath deposited a rich treasure of grace in every saint's heart. At this is the devil's great spite; to plunder him of it, and with it of his happiness, he commenceth a bloody war against him. He wins the day when he doth not lose his grace, his work belong rather to keep what is his own than to get what is his enemy's. And truly this one thing well headed, that the saint's war lies chiefly on the defence, would be of singular use to direct the Christian how to manage his combats both with Satan and also with his instruments. . .

Look, Christian, thou standest always in a defensive posture, with thy armour on, as a soldier, upon thy works, ready to defend the castle of thy soul which God hath set thee to keep, and valiantly to repel Satan's assults whenever he makes his approach. But be not persuaded out of line of thy place and calling that God hath drawn about thee; no, not under the specious pretence of zeal and hope to get the greater victory by falling into the enemies' quarters. Let Satan be the assailant, and come if he will to tempt thee; but go not thou in a bravado to tempt him to do it . . .

May be they revile and reproach thee. Remember now thy part lies on the defence. Give not railing for railing, reproach for reproach. The gospel allows thee no liberty to use their weapons, and return them *quid pro quo* – stroke for stroke. 'Be pitiful, be courteous; not rendering evil for evil, or railing for railing, but contrariwise blessing,' 1Pe. iii. 8, 9. Thou hast here a girdle and breastplate to defend thee from their bullets – the comfort of thy own sincerity and holy walking, with which thou mayst wipe off the dirt thrown upon thy own face – but no weapon for self-revenge. A shield is put into thy hand, which thou mayst lift up to quench their fiery darts, but no darts of bitter words to retort upon them. Thou art *'shod with peace'*, that thou mayst walk safely upon the injuries they do thee, without any prick or pain to thy spirit, but not with pride to trample upon the persons that wrong thee.

SECOND. As most of the pieces are defensive, so all of them *to defend from sin, none to secure the Christian from suffering*. They are to defend him in suffering, not privilege him from it. He must prepare the more for suffering, because he is so well furnished with armour to bear it. Armour is not given for men to wear by the firesides at home, but in the field. How shall the maker be praised, if the metal of his arms be not known? And where shall it be put to the proof, but admist swords and bullets? . . . Resolve for hardship, or lay down thine arms . . . Most men are more tender of their skin than conscience; and had rather the gospel had provided armour to defend their bodies from death and danger, than their souls from sin and Satan. [129]

> By armour is meant Christ. We need of putting on the 'Lord Jesus,' Rom. 13:14, where Christ is set forth under the notion of armour . . . The graces of Christ, these are armour, as 'the girdle of truth, the breast and plate of righteousness,' and the rest. Hence we are bid also [to] 'put on the new man' Eph. 4:24, which is made up of all the several graces, as its parts and members.[130]

---

[129] William Guranll M.A. *The Christian in Complete Armour; A Treatise of the Saint's War against the Devil: Whereis a Discovery is made of that grand Enemy of God and his People, in his Policies, Power, Seat of his Empire, Wickedness, and chief design he hath against the Saints. A Magazine Opened, from whence the Christian is furnished with Spiritual Arms for the Battle, helped on with his Armour, and taught the use of his Weapon: together with the happy issue of the whole War.* Volume II p124-5

[130] Ibid. Volume I

Now after all these observations let's finally consider the actual pieces of our God-given and made armour.

The shield of faith

Question: I can understand why I need faith but why as a shield, and why above all?

Answer: 1John 5:4-5, 'For whatever is born of God overcomes the world. And this is the victory that has overcome the world – our faith. Who is he who overcomes the world, but he who believes that Jesus is the Son of God?'

Jesus tells us in John 16:33 that ". . . in Me you will have peace. In the world you will have tribulation; but be of good cheer, I have overcome the world."

As a pilgrim's faith is evident in our hope of things yet invisible (Hebrews 11:1) I am called above all to believe in a shield that will put out all Satan's fire directed at me that cannot yet be seen? Thanks be to God for his gift of faith.

Paul could have been thinking of the *Scutum* as he wrote, a light one-hand-needed shield that was big enough to cover the entire wielder. And if there were a group with these shields, they could join the shields and resting their left knees on the ground they became like a giant tortoise shell, well protected from fiery arrows or burning missiles. Perhaps this is a good reason for not going it alone as a Christian but to fellowship with others?

Gurnall seeing this shield as *representing our justifying faith* writes, 'Of all graces faith is the chief, and is chiefly to be laboured for. There is a precedency or pre-eminence peculiar to this above all other . . . The apostle indeed gives the precedency to love, and sets faith on the lower hand. 'Now abideth faith, hope, charity, these three; but the greatest of these is charity.' 1Co. xiii. 13. Yet, you may observe, that this prelation of it before faith hath a particular respect to the saints' blissful state in heaven, where love remains, and faith ceaseth. In that regard love is indeed is the greater, because it is the end of our faith. We apprehend by faith that we may enjoy by love. But, if we consider the Christian's present state, while militant on earth, in this respect love must give place to faith. It is true, love is the grace that shall triumph in heaven. But it is faith, not love, which is the conquering grace on earth. This is the victory that overcameth the world, even our faith, 1Jn. v. 4. Love indeed hath its place in the battle, and doth excellent service, but it is under faith its leader. 'Faith which worketh by love', Ga. v. 6. Even as the captain figheth by his soldiers whom he leads on, so faith works by love which it excites. Love, it is true, is the grace that at last posseth the inheritance, but it is faith that gives the Christian right unto it. Without this he should never have enjoyed it, Jn. i. 12. In a word, it is love that unites God and glorified saints together in heaven; but is was faith that first united them to Christ while they were on earth – 'That Christ may dwell in your hearts by faith', Ep. iii. 17.

And if Christ had not dwelt in them by faith on earth, they should never have dwelt with God in heaven . . . 'being justified by faith, we have peace with God', Ro. v. 1. Not justified by love, repentance, patience, or any other grace beside faith . . . 'the righteousness of faith', Ro. iv. 11, 13 – not the righteousness of repentance, love, or any other grace . . .

Faith is the only grace whose office is to lay hold on Christ; and so to appropriate his righteousness for justification to our souls. Christ be the treasure and faith the hand which receives it. . .

Faith defends the Christian in the exercise of all his graces. 'By faith we stand', Ro. xi. 20. As a soldier under the protection of his shield stands his ground and doth his duty, notwithstanding all the shot that are made against him to drive him back. When faith fails, then every grace is put to the run and rout.'[131]

This being so it is easy to understand why this piece of armour goes on first, is it not?

The girdle of truth

<u>Question</u>: What is truth? And why around my waist as a girdle?

---

[131] Ibid. Volume II p11-12, 14, 18

Answer: In John 18:38a we read, 'Pilate said to [Jesus], "What is truth?" Not much has changed has it, for in today's world it is very hard to know who is talking truth or what is truth, but truth is not a *what* but a *who*.
John tells us in John 1:14 and 14:6a, that '. . . the Word became flesh and dwelt among us, and we beheld His glory, the glory as of the only begotten of the Father, full of grace and truth . . . Jesus said to [Thomas and the other disciples], "I am the way, the truth, and the life. . . "
So, we gird Jesus around our waists? Why?
Think of a belt or better still one of those lace up girdles or corsets of an earlier era. A belt keeps our shirt in our trousers or skirt and our trousers or skirt from falling around our ankles and tripping us up. It is, I believe a bit hard to stand when all undone, uncovered, and apart, so better gird quickly. A lace-up girdle however actually supported and strengthened the lady especially her spine (we won't go into how it messed up her internal organs, analogies can only go so far).
Jesus and the Holy Spirit help to keep a pilgrim all together, strengthened in wisdom, knowing which way is up and forward, and this girdle of scripture gives a secure place for hanging the scarab of the sword.
Gurnall adds, 'Gird up the loins of your mind', 1Peter 1:13. . . . The loins are the chief seat of bodily strength . . . Thus as the actings of our minds and spirits are in their faculties and powers, so we are weak or strong Christians. If the understanding be clear in its apprehensions of truth, and the will sincere, vigorous and fixed in its purposes for that which is holy and good, then he is a strong Christian; but if the understanding be dark or uncertain in its notions, as a distempered eye that cannot well discern its object – not able to bring its thoughts to an issue, which to close with, and the will be wavering and unsteady, like a needle that trembles between two lodestones – here the man is weak, and all he doth will be so. . . so want of strength in the mind to know truth and

want of resolution in the will to pursue that which he knows to be holy and good, cause a man to falter in his course . . .
Labour to get a heart inflamed with a sincere love to the truth . . To an heart inflamed with the love of truth, labour to add a heart with the fear of that wrath which God hath in store for all that apostatize from the truth.'[132]

The breastplate of righteousness

<u>Question</u>: What is righteousness and why have it as a breastplate?
<u>Answer</u>: Paul writes in Philippians 3:8b-9, '. . . that I may gain Christ and be found in Him, not having my own righteousness, which is from the law, but that which is through faith in Christ, the righteousness which is from God by Faith . . .'
In Jeremiah 23:5a and 6b we read that the LORD said, 'Behold . . . I will raise to David a Branch of righteousness . . . Now this is His name by which He will be called: THE LORD OUR RIGHTEOUSNESS.'
Then lastly, this from Isaiah 59:14-17a, 'Justice is turned back, and righteousness stands afar off; for truth is fallen in the street, and equity cannot enter. So truth fails, and he who departs from evil makes himself a prey. Then the LORD saw it and it displeased Him that there was no man, and wondered that there was no intercessor; therefore His own arm brought salvation for Him; and His own righteousness, it sustained Him. For He put on righteousness as a breastplate, and a helmet of salvation on His head . . .' Christ saw fit to make righteousness a breastplate so why not us?
The Roman breastplate was designed to protect the vital organs found in the thorax, the heart and lungs especially, so making a death blow difficult. Christ is our righteousness. Use him, what he has given us of himself to protect our heart from the father of lies unlike Ananias (see Acts 5:1-5).
According to Gurnall this breastplate represents *the righteousness of our sanctification* and he adds, 'A man may outlive many wounds received in the arms and legs, but a stab in the heart or

---

[132] Ibid. Volume 1

other vital parts is the certain messenger of death approaching. Thus righteousness and holiness preserve the principal part of a Christian – his soul and conscience . . . righteousness, by defending the conscience, fills the creature with courage in the face of death and danger, whereas guilt – which is the nakedness of the soul – puts the stoutest sinner into a shaking fit of fear. . .

. . . the copulative *'and'* with which this piece of armour is so closely buckled to the former, bids us make a little stand, to take notice how lovingly truth and holiness are here conjoined . . .

Take truth, for *truth of doctrine*. An orthodox judgement, with an unholy heart and an ungodly life, is as uncomely as a man's head would be on a beast's shoulders . . .

Take it for *truth of heart*; and so truth and holiness must go together. In vain do men pretend to sincerity, if they be unholy in their lives . . . Sincerity teacheth the soul to point at the right end of all its actions – the glory of God. . . Thy heart upright, and thy meanings good, when all that proceeds from thy heart in thy life is wicked! How can it be? . . .'[133]

Foot protection

Question: What does the preparation of the gospel of peace mean and why is it on our feet?

Answer: Preparation is the process of being prepared, of getting ready, perhaps like getting the right marks to enable you to enter university. The gospel of peace is the good news that God, now through a work of his own, is at peace with mankind in this age of grace (until the word of God appears on a white horse to judge in righteousness and make war with the nations when fire comes down from God out of heaven and devours the nations gathered together against him, Revelation 19:11-21, 20:7-10) and has given us peace. The war has ended between God and all repentant sinners, as we read in Colossians 1:19-20, 'For it pleased the Father that in [Christ] all the fullness should dwell, and by Him to reconcile all things to Himself, by Him, whether things on earth or

---

[133] Ibid

things in heaven, having made peace through the blood of His cross'.

This peace is what we have to have before we can walk anywhere and tell others of Christ's gospel. This is where our preparation begins, this is our foundation from which we can fulfil Christ's commission. And like the Roman army footwear it is specific footwear to give grip so we can stand, it is the sure knowledge that we have peace with God, we have been forgiven and he now is at war with those who oppose us. So, get these shoes on, work out what to pack and go.

Gurnall has much to add about this peace as we read, *'True peace is the blessing of the gospel, and only of the gospel . . .*

FIRST. Peace with God which we may call *peace of reconciliation*.

SECOND. Peace with ourselves, or *peace of conscience*.

THIRD. Peace with one another, or *peace of love and unity*.

FOURTH. Peace with the other creatures, even the most hurtful, which may be called a *peace of indemnity and service*. . . Go, fire, [remember this is the age of burning people on the stake!] and be the chariot in which such a saint may be brought home from earth to heavenly glory. . . Not a creature comes on a worse message to a saint. It is true they are sharp corrections as to the present smart they bring; but they are ever mercies, and do a friendly office in the intention of God and happy issue to the believer. 'All things work together for good to them that love God . . .' Rom. 8:28.

QUESTION FIRST. What is meant by this preparation of the gospel of peace?

. . . will best appear by considering . . . 'the foot', the only member of the body to be shod – and the piece of armour it is compared to, and that is the soldier's shoe, which (if right) is to be of the strongest make, being not so much intended for finery as defence. So necessarily is this piece of armour indeed, that, for want of it alone, the solider in some cases is disabled for service . . . How long will he go, if not shod, without wounding or floundering? Or, if the way be good, but the weather bad, and his feet not fenced from the wet and cold . . . [may] bring a disease on the whole body. . . Now, what the foot is to the body, that the will is to the soul. The foot carries the whole body, and the will the soul; yea, the whole man, body and soul also. *Voluntas est loco motiva facultas* – we go whither our will sends us. And what the shoe is to the foot, that 'preparation', or, if you please, a readiness and alacrity, is to the will. The man whose feet are well shod fears no ways . . . while the barefooted man . . . shrinks . . . and shrieks . . . Thus, when the will and heart of a man is prompt, and ready to do any work, the man is, as it were, shod and armed against all trouble and difficulty which he is to go over in the doing of it.

QUESTION SECOND. –But why is it called *'the preparation of the gospel of peace'*?

Because the gospel of peace is the great instrument by which God works the will and heart of man into this readiness and preparation to do or suffer what he calls to. It is the business we are set about, when preaching the gospel, to make 'a willing people,' Ps 110 – 'to make ready a people prepared for the Lord,' Luke 1:17. As a captain is sent to beat up his drum in a city, to call in a company that will voluntarily list themselves to follow the prince's wars, and be in readiness to take the field and march at an hour's warning, – thus the gospel comes to call over the hearts of men to the foot of God, to stand ready for his service whatever it costs them. Now this it doth, as it is a 'gospel of peace'. It brings the joyful tidings of peace concluded betwixt God and man by the blood of Jesus. And this is so welcome to the trembling conscience of poor sinners, who before melted away their sorrowful days in a fearful looking for of judgement and fiery indignation from the Lord to devour them as his adversaries; that no sooner [is] the report of a peace concluded betwixt God and them, sounded in their ears by the preaching of the gospel, and certainly confirmed to be true in their own consciences by the Spirit – who is sent from heaven to seal it to them, and give them some sweet gust [taste] of it, by shedding abroad the sense of it in their souls – but instantly there appears a new life in them; to the effect that they, who before were so fearful and shy of every petty trouble as to start and boggle at the thought of it – knowing it could bring no good news to them – are now 'shod with the preparation of the gospel of peace', able to go out smilingly to meet the greatest sufferings that are, or can be, on the way towards them, and say undauntedly to them, as once Christ did to those that came with swords and staves to attack him, 'Whom seek yea?' . . . .

[To consider:] When we are prepared to deny ourselves in any comfort we may enjoy, *then, and not till then, is that which hinders the enjoyment of our lives taken away*; and that is *fear*. . . The more ready and prepared the Christian is to suffer from God, or for God, *the more God is engaged to take care for him and of him.*

The great question I expect now to fall from thy mouth, Christian, is not how mayst thou escape these troubles and trials which, as the evil genius of the gospel, do always attend it? But rather, how thou mayst get this shoe on, thy heart ready for a march to go and meet them when they come, and cheerfully wade through them, whatever they be, or how long soever they stay with thee?

First Directive. Look carefully to the ground of thy active obedience, that it be sound and sincere.

Second Directive. Pray for a suffering spirit.

Third Directive. Be much in the meditation of a suffering state. . . 'Come my people,' saith God, 'enter thou into thy chambers' Isa 26:20. He is showing them their lodgings in his attributes and promises, before it is night and their sufferings be come, that they may readily find the way to them in the dark.

Fourth Directive. Make a daily resignation of thyself up to the will of God.

Fifth Directive. Make self-denial appear as rational and reasonable as thou canst to thy soul.

Sixth Directive. Labour to carry on the work of mortification every day to further degrees than others.'[134]

The helmet of salvation

---

[134] Ibid.

Question: Why is salvation a helmet?
Answer: Bike helmets protect us and our children from brain injury and death. One common result of a brain injury is some form of forgetfulness. I have enough trouble with what is already in my head without having something from the outside adding trouble or snatching away what I need to keep.

Stott reminds us that 'Many of our spiritual troubles arise from our failure to remember we are citizens of two kingdoms. We tend either to pursue Christ and withdraw from the world, or to become preoccupied with the world and forget that we are also in Christ.'[135]

Our mind needs protection from the temptations and lies of Satan as we already covered.

Being able to know and remember the truth of our salvation and all that we have and are as a result is worth protecting also, is it not, for what would happen if we forgot?

There were various types of Roman helmets used over time. During the late 1st century BC to early 2nd century AD the Imperial Gallic helmet was used which came with added ear protection for those who wished to attach it. Between the 1st and 3rd century the Imperial Italic helmet was also used which had projecting ear guards. Ear protection, guards . . .[136]

> When Christians unto carnal men give ear,
> Out of their way they go, and pay for't dear;
> For Master Worldly-Wiseman can but show
> A saint the way to bondage and to woe.[137]

The knowledge of having been saved, being a child of the King and our future hope of resurrection, receiving the fulfilment of all our God's promises and being with Christ for eternity in a new sinless world works like a helmet to protect our minds and our ability to

---

[135] *Message of Ephesians* p23

[136] http://m.tribunesandtriumphs.org

[137] *The Pilgrim's progress* comment by Scott p55

hear the voice of the good shepherd (John 10:1-30) from the effects of sojourning thru this fallen world.

And Gurnall adds, '1Th. v. 8. 'And for a helmet, the hope of salvation.' . . . Hope is a supernatural grace of God, whereby the believer, through Christ, expects and waits for all those good things of the promise, which of present he hath not received, or not fully. . . The promise is, as it were, God's love-letter to his church and spouse, in which he opens his very heart, and tells all he means to do for her. Faith reads and embraceth it with joy, whereupon the believing soul by hope looks out at this window with a longing expectation to see her husband's chariot come in the accomplishment thereof.

The helmet defends the head, a principal part of the body, from dint of bullet and sword; so this 'hope of salvation' defends the soul, the principal part of man, and the principal faculties of that, whereby no dangerous, to be sure no deadly, impression can by Satan or sin be made on it. Temptations may trouble but cannot hurt, except their darts enter the will and leave a wound there, by drawing it to some consent and liking them; from which this helmet of hope, if it be the right make, and fits sure on the Christian's head, will defend him. It is hard to draw him into any treasonable practice against his prince, who is both well satisfied of his favour at present, and stands also upon the stairs of hope, expecting assuredly to be called up within a while to the highest preferment that the court can afford or his king give. No, the weapons of rebellion and treason are usually forged and fashioned in discontent's shop. When subjects take themselves to be neglected and slighted by their prince – think their preferments are now at an end, and [that they] must look for no great favours more to come from him – this softens them to receive every impression of disloyalty that any enemy to the king shall attempt to stamp them withal.

Two things make the head hang down – fear and shame. Hope easeth the Christian's heart of both these; and so forbids him to give any sign of a desponding mind by a dejected countance.

'Be sober, and hope to the end,' is the apostle Peter's counsel, 1Pe. i. 13. There are some engines of war that are of use but now and then, as ladders for scaling of a town or fort; which done [they] are laid aside for a long time and not missed. But the helmet is of continual use. We shall need it as long as our war with sin and Satan lasts. The Christian is not beneath hope so long as above ground, nor above hope so long as he is beneath heaven. Indeed when once he enters the gates of that glorious city, then 'farewell hope and welcome love forever.' He may say, with the holy martyr, Armour becomes earth, but robes heaven. Hope goes into the field and waits on the Christian till the last battle be fought and the field cleared, and then faith and hope together carry him in the chariot of the promise to heaven door, where they deliver up his soul into the hands of love and joy, which stand ready to conduct him into the blissful presence of God.

There are two graces which Christ useth above any other to fill the soul with joy; and they are faith and hope . . . Faith tells the soul what Christ hath done for it, and so comforts it. Hope revives the soul with the news of what Christ will do. Both draw at one tap – Christ and his promise.

It cannot be denied, but all inordinate fears of death betray great unbelief and little hope. We do not look upon death under a right notion, and so we start at it; which, were we by faith but able to see through, and assure ourselves it comes to do us a good turn, we should feel as comfortably on the thoughts of it, as now we are scared at the apparition of it . . . Christian, understand aright what message death brings to thee, and the fear of it will be over. It snatcheth thee from this world's enjoyments, but it leads thee to the felicities of another incomparably better.'[138]

The sword of the Spirit, the word of God

<u>Question</u>: The verse tells us that the sword of the Spirit is the word of God so do I need to understand anything else?

---

[138] *The Christian in Complete Armour Volume II* p129, 130, 132, 133, 134, 144, 171

Answer: The word for sword here and in Hebrews 4:12 is referring to the *machaira*, a knife or dirk. Easy to manoeuvre and used for one-on-one combat to inflict damage or deflect the enemy's weapon away from you. Remember when we considered how Jesus used scripture to answer Satan in the wilderness? Well this is how we are meant to use scripture, specifically and to the point, which means we have to know it better than we probably do (speaking for myself here). I for one do not remember often enough how powerful the words of scripture can be, as Hebrews 4:12 says, 'For the word of God is living and powerful, and sharper than any two-edged sword, piercing even to the division of soul and spirit, and of joints and marrow, and is a discerner of the thoughts and intents of the heart.' So, take care, you would not want to be clumsy and mishandle this sword injuring yourself instead of your enemy.

Gurnall writes, 'Easily might the solider be disarmed of all his other furniture, how glistening and glorious soever, had he not a sword in his hand to life up against his enemies' assaults. And with as little ado would the Christian be stripped of all his graces, had he not this sword to defend them and himself to from Satan's fury. 'Unless thy law had been my delight, I should then have perished in my affliction,' Ps. cxix. 92 . . . O, this word of God is a terror to [Satan]; he cannot for his life overcome the dread of it. Let Christ but say 'It is written, 'and the foul fiend runs away with more confusion and terror than Caligula at a crack of thunder. And that which was of such force coming from Christ's blessed lips to drive him away, the saints have always found the most successful instrument to defend them against his fiercest and most impetuous temptations. . .

. . . The sword, as it defends the soldier, so it offends his enemy. Thus the word of God is, as a keeping, so a killing sword. It doth not only keep and restrain him from yielding to the force of temptations without, but also by it he kills and mortifies his lusts within, and this makes the victory complete. We read of some that for a while escaped the pollutions of the world, yet because their lusts were never put to the sword, and mortified in them by the power of the word applied to their hearts, were at last themselves overcome and slain by this secret enemy that lay skulking within their bosoms, 2Pe. ii. 20, compared with ver. 22.'[139]

Just another thought, the sword of the Spirit is the word of God and the word of God is Christ as John1:1, 14a says, 'In the beginning was the Word, and the Word was with God, and the Word was God . . . And the Word became flesh and dwelt among us . . .' Christ is an offence to all those who will not believe, those who are enemies but for the pilgrim he is our beloved and our defense, our complete armoury against all that desires to destroy or enslave us. He is also our mediator; he is between us and God interceding for us as does the Spirit in regards to our prayers (Romans 8:26).

Prayer and supplication

<u>Question</u>: Why are these included with the armour? How do they protect us against all those dark things of verse 12?

<u>Answer</u>: These habitual disciplines connect us directly to our head commander, no internet, radio or runner required, though we have the Spirits aid and Christ's mediations to ensure our message is heard correctly.

Gurnall writes, '. . . 'the prayer of faith,' Ja. v. 15. Prayer, it is the very natural breath of faith. . . [This is] as if he had said, 'You have now, Christian, the armour of God; but take heed thou forgettest not to engage the God of this armour by humble prayer for your assistance, lest for all this you be worsted in the fight. He that gives you the arms, can only teach you to use them, and enable you to overcome by their use.' . . . The Christian's armour will rust except it be furbished and scoured with the oil of prayer. What the key is to the watch that [is] prayer to our graces – it winds them up and sets them going.' [140]

Prayer is you conversing with God. It is always necessary, but how much more when way above your depth and sinking fast! There is

---

[139] Ibid. p194-5
[140] Ibid. p 36, 288

no special position or words needed for God to hear you. Supplication is usually considered as praying for somebody else's stuff, concerns or needs. An example of prayer and supplication during a war emergency that I know works is "HELP!!!" It can be whispered or screamed, either way God still hears.

Keep in mind that God, being the good Father, (Never had one? Well, as I have learnt he is all you ever wished for and more.) loves to hear from his child in their good times too, not just when they are desperate. But that said, being a good Father, he is politely waiting for you to ask (this shows your humble dependence upon him) for the help he is not only eagerly waiting to give but capable of providing. Prayer is enlisting the aid of the most high God, all his power, all his knowledge, all that Yahweh alone is, and he alone is the only one suited to and capable of attacking the darkness and winning, for the darkness has nothing in him. And he always answers. A 'No' is an answer with a reason. Paul understood why he got a 'No', and Job discovered he did not need an answer and why he did not need one. 'Wait' is an answer expectant of your trust that he alone knows what as well as when is best. And be warned that the consequences of a 'Yes' answer may not always what you would like or expect.

Satan again and when God goes A-wall

<u>Question</u>: Have you noticed which section of our body is not protected by this armour? Can you think of a reason why?

<u>Answer</u>: A pilgrim has nothing to protect her back. If he decides to turn back and run away from the fight, away from an enemy bent on total destruction if not captivity, I do not think the result will be pretty. Turning back means turning your face away from God, turning away from walking, facing towards home and going back into the world you had left behind.

> . . .the well instructed believer sees no safety, except in facing his enemy. If there appear to be danger in persevering, ruin is inevitable if he desist (for Christian "had no armour for his back"); even fear, therefore, will in that case induce a man to stand his ground, and the more

resolutely he resists temptation, the sooner will he regain his tranquillity: for when the suggestions of Satan excite us to pray more fervently, and to be more diligent in every service, that enemy will "flee from us".[141]

Remember that Satan's aim is to destroy. If he cannot do that, he will try to get you to renounce your faith and trust in God or at the very least disable you in your service and witness. [142]

Bunyan believed the devil is real and so should every other pilgrim. We walk upon dangerous ground when we lose sight of the personalities of God and the devil, believing only in the existence of their adjectives – Go(o)d and (d)evil. Bunyan wrote very cleverly of how our arch enemy fights and how he most often picks a downhill time after a mountain top experience. You go into the Valley of Humiliation alone, no one else can go for you or protect you.

Christian saw off in the distance thoughts that troubled him but having no armour for his back he resolved to venture forth and stand his ground, to meet head on whatever was before him for it was not safe for him to turn and run.

This is not a physical battle [though from personal experience it may feel like one], but a battle for your faith. "Who do you think you are to call yourself a Christian?" says that little voice.

Doubts of self and God arise. Satan is a fearful foe, full of pride, fire and destruction. He attacks through thought patterns, leading to you questioning, then doubting, which leads to a life of problems; a subtle beginning that progresses.

Thoughts you have of quitting your pilgrimage come from Satan. You fight back, answering "I like being a Christian more than a non-Christian. I like being in God's service, company etc. so leave off!"

---

[141] *The Pilgrim's Progress* comment by Scott p98

[142] I wish to give credit to *Pilgrim's Progress* p99-113 and Gables' sermons *#27, 29 & 30* for the ideas and some wording through this section on *Satan again and when God goes A-wall*.

Satan changes tack a little, "Christians suffer more than my people."

As a pilgrim you will see over time professing Christians turn back. This can be very discouraging as I well know from experience. If you consider those who you had looked up to who have gone back you will wonder why you should not. You must settle within yourself, glory now with probably less suffering or glory later with Christ and no suffering.

Again, Satan changes tack trying to get a foot in the door, by reminding you of your past sins, "Remember Christian those sins on The Way, remember your wrong motives for serving and yet you think you have a hope of entering heaven!"

Here Christian affirmed the truth of these charges by Satan and then said "there are many more you have neglected to mention, BUT the Prince I serve is merciful and ready to forgive, in fact I have my pardon already . . ."

In regards to this Valley of Humiliation and Apollyon Mason writes, 'In our present mixed state the Lord knows it would not be best for us always to dwell on the mount of spiritual joy; therefore, for the good of the soul, the flesh must be humbled, and kept low, lest spiritual pride prevail. It is hard going down into the Valley of Humiliation without slipping into murmuring and discount, and calling into question the dealings of God with us.'

Scott adds, 'Under discouraging circumstances the believer will often be tempted to murmur, despond, or seek relief from the world. Finding that his too sanguine expectations are not answered, that he grows worse rather than better in his own opinion of himself, that his comforts are transitory, and that much reproach, contempt and loss, are incurred by his professions of religion, discontent will often rise up in his heart, and weakness of faith will expose him to sharp conflicts . . . Apollyon signifies the destroyer, Rev lx. 11; and in carrying on the work of destruction, fallen angels endeavour by various devices to deter men from prayer, and to render them afraid of those things, without which the life of faith cannot be maintained; in order that, after convictions, they may be led to give up religion, as the only method of recovering composure of mind . . . the well instructed believer sees no safety, except in facing his enemy. If there appear to be danger in persevering, ruin is inevitable if he desist (for Christian "had no armour for his back"); even fear, therefore, will in that case induce a man to stand his ground, and the more resolutely he resists temptation, the sooner will he regain his tranquillity for, when the suggestions of Satan excite us to pray more fervently, and be more diligent in every service, that enemy will "flee from us" . . .' [143]

Satan as an angel of light tempts in the three ways we have just described above, by reasoning firstly to return to the pleasures of sin that you still can remember, secondly by magnifying the difficulties – sorrows, sadness and tribulations – of the Christian way of life and thirdly by reminding you of past sins and how you have dishonoured God.

Christian withstood these temptations by using his Bible and God's promises within it.

So now Satan changes into a roaring lion, breaking into a full rage, releasing his full true nature upon Christian, his full hate of God and Christ and all who identify with him.

Our mind can deal intellectually with the first three ways but the last method swamps our mind with confusion. This method is not something that can be dealt with on an intellectual basis. You can become so overwhelmed by something for which you can think of no reason or explanation for, that you fear you are going to drown, blow a fuse or be committed to the funny-farm.

In chapter one of Job we read how Satan told God that Job only feared God and shunned evil because he had hedged him from adverse circumstances but if this changed, he would curse God. So, in verse 12 of that chapter we read that 'the LORD said to Satan, "Behold, all that he has is in your power; only do not lay a hand on his person." So Satan went out from the presence of the LORD'. In one day, in twelve hours Job lost all his 500 yoke of

---

[143] *The Pilgrim's Progress* p98-100

oxen, 500 female donkeys, a multitude of servants, 7,000 sheep, 3,000 camels and 7sons and 3daughters, what then was considered the perfect number and mix of children.

But Job did not react as Satan had hoped so he went back before God and said in 2:5, 'stretch out Your hand now, and touch his flesh, and he will surely curse You to Your face!' Satan went out and not being allowed to take Job's life he struck him with boils from head to toe and Job moved to the city dump with a bit of broken pottery to scrape himself with, cursing the day he was born after his wife told him to curse God and die.

This is an Old Testament example of being sifted by Satan. Peter, the apostle knew how this felt also though his experience was different.

Luke 22:31-32, 'And the Lord said, "Simon, Simon! Indeed, Satan has asked for you, that he may sift you as wheat. But I have prayed for you, that your faith should not fail; and when you have returned to Me, strengthen your brethren."'

Peter, whose confession of who Jesus was, was to be the rock that the church was to be built upon, Peter who was willing to die for his Lord denied even knowing him when questioned by a servant girl on the night of his Christ's arrest. Peter knew the rage of Satan.

Bunyan's Christian, despite having his armour on, was wounded in his head, his understanding of salvation was weakened and doubts entered; wounded in his hand and so he could not properly wield the Sword of the Spirit, he loses confidence in the Word and begins to question it. With his foot laming he questions the gospel of peace, the manner of the Christian's walk. He backs up a little, the wounds causing increasing weakness as time passes.

This is a war!

The Sword flew out of his hand. Satan sure that he had him now, tells him to curse God and die, get it over and done with for Christian bleeding and struggling to stand, despaired of going on, even of living. But as God would have it when he reached out his hand with the last remnant of his strength he caught the Sword.

Crying out "When I fall I shall arise" he inflicted a mortal wound to Satan and then hitting him again Christian sent him speeding away to be seen no more.

Satan was defeated through the work of Christ, his Sword. A re-examination of the gospel enabled Christian to fight back. Don't write someone like Job off during their conflict with Satan, this war is a serious thing. Christian had no *pleasant face* till Satan was wounded. You will not feel like flashing a Hollywood smile for those watching while fighting for real.

James 4:7 tells us to 'submit to God. Resist the devil and he will flee from you.' We resist by refusing to compromise the truth, refusing to turn back, to take the easier way, to get out of the circumstances, to go around the devil, we resist by meeting head on.

Bunyan now moves on to another type of warfare we have not covered till now. It is from within but different for in this battle you are not fighting lusts but real feelings that arise from a real experience that for all purposes appears true, and that is that God has left you, ceased from dwelling within.

Not all pilgrims will experience it as Christian [Bunyan or others] did, but all to some degree will for The Way goes through this Valley of the Shadow of Death after the Valley of Humiliation. This is a different testing; it is worse than the encounter with Satan in regards to the state of the mind. This is a very lonely place to be, and is almost impossible for anyone who has not been here to believe it exists for a pilgrim in armour.

This Valley of Bunyan's represents the dark night of the soul of a true believer from which God has withdrawn the manifestation of himself from and a darkness or night comes to dwell in the relationship between them. God seems to not be there, you feel forsaken, you believe you are, there is no light within just darkness and emptiness.

Prayers seem ridiculous as they just bounced off the ceiling and returned to slap you mockingly across your confused tear stained face. Confused because as hard as you search you can find no known unconfessed sin that could be the cause of this distance and you have covered all unknown as David did in Psalm 19:12, 'Who can understand his errors? Cleanse me from secret faults.'

For me I see being stubborn as a gift from God, as well as being able to remember my past life. I knew I knew him. I'd seen prayers answered. I was not the same as before he had entered my life and kept me from worse dangers and given me a desire to live, I had known peace, I had known hope and joy, so I refused to quit despite God not being there, despite the thick, heavy, darkness and wondering feeling I was going mad.

Each morning I'd force myself to read a psalm and just stay there waiting and attempting to pray looking at that ceiling. My darkness began to crack when the eighteenth day saw me reading Psalm 18 and verse 11, '[God] made darkness His secret place; His canopy around Him was dark waters and thick clouds of the sky.'

I began to think on the idea that God having made the darkness and being in it made the darkness okay, not something to stress over. Sometime later I was hanging the clothes out, the sky was thick with smoke from bushfires making the sun sort of invisible but that did not mean the sun was not there and so my darkness cracked a bit more.

What I learnt through this experience where I was certain that God had left me completely, never to return, was that I needed him, his presence, his face far, far more than any extra gift he could or had given me, I just wanted *him* and that I never ever want to go back into that terrifying feeling of oppressive lonely darkness again.

Mason writes that 'None but the heart of a Christian knows the bitterness of God's hiding away his face. It is death to all his comforts; his mourning under a sense of it, manifests his love to the Lord, and delight in his presence.' [144]

Bunyan's Christian experienced much the same, God seemed not to be real. Sword drawn he walked a very narrow path with a ditch one side and a mire the other and without enough light for

---

[144] *The Pilgrim's Progress* p106

each step to be surefooted. Christian however discovering his Sword was not as effective here as had been with Satan still resolved to go forward and so cried out, "I will walk in the strength of God." Christian experienced most vile thoughts against God, desires that would destroy him and all he held dear which caused him to wonder if he was indeed a Christian especially when this trial seemed to have no end. Know O pilgrim these are not your thoughts, they are suggestions to your much overwrought mind from demonic powers and principalities.

When Christian began to understand that God was with him though he was in a dark and dismal state with no hope, his hope began to grow and morning began to arise. As Christian went out into the light of the rising sun, he looked back, not that he wanted to go back but because he needed to see where he had travelled, what he had experienced back there in the darkness and learn from it.

According to Scott, 'The Valley of the Shadow of Death seems intended to represent a variation of inward distress, conflict, and alarm, which arise from prevailing darkness and insensibility of mind, rendering a man reluctant to religious duties, and dull in the performance of them, which makes way for manifold apprehensions and temptations . . . author meant in general, that such dreary seasons may be expected; as very few believers wholly escape them; but . . . not . . . all experience these trials in the same order or degree . . . the spiritual worshipper at some times, find his soul filled with clear light and holy affection; "it is good for him to draw nigh to God"; and "his soul is satisfied as with marrow and fatness, while he praises his God with joyful lips": at other times, dullness and heaviness oppresses him; he feels little exercise of faith, hope, desire, reverence, love, or gratitude; he seems to address an unknown or absent God, and rather to mock than worship him; divine things appear obscure and almost unreal; and every returning season of devotion, or reiterated effort to lift up his heart to God, ends in disappointment; so that religion becomes his burden instead of his delight. Evils before unnoticed are now perceived to mingle with his services; for his self-knowledge is advanced; his remedy seems to increase his disease; he suspects that all his former joy was a delusion, and is ready to conclude that "God hath forgotten to be gracious, and hath shut up his loving-kindness is displeasure." These experiences, sufficiently painful in themselves, are often rendered more distressing, be erroneous expectations of uninterrupted comfort, or by reading books, or hearkening to instructions, which state things unscriptually; representing comfort as the evidence of acceptance, assurance as the essence of faith, impressions or visions as the witness of the Spirit; or perfection as attainable in this life, nay, actually attained by all the regenerate; as if this was the church triumphant, and not the church militant. The state of the body also, as disordered by nervous or hypochondrical affections, gives energy to the distressing inferences which men often draw from their dark frame of mind; and indeed indisposition may often operate as a direct cause of it; though the influences of the Holy Spirit will overcome this, and all other impediments to comfort, when "he sheds abroad the love of God in the heart". Evil spirits never fail, when permitted, to take advantage of a disordered state, whether of the body or mind, to mislead, entangle, perplex, or defile the soul. Persons of a melancholic temperament, when not aware of the particular causes whence their gloom originates, are apt to ascribe it wholly to desertion, which exceedingly enhances their distress.' [145]

Isaiah 50:10-11, '"Who among you fears the LORD? Who obeys the voice of His Servant? Who walks in darkness and has no light? Let him trust in the name of the LORD and rely upon his God. Look, all you who kindle a fire, who encircle yourselves with sparks; walk in the light of your fire and in the sparks you have kindled – This you shall have from My hand: You shall lie down in torment."'

---

[145] Ibid. comment by Scott

To trust God, you do not have to understand why he does something but who he is. Do not go off his way and go your own way in the light you make regardless of temptations, tests, or how hard the battle is, it is just not worth it.

Scott reminding us of who pilgrims are and how Satan works to undo us comments, 'As all have been overcome by the temptations of the devil, and "of whom a man is overcome, of the same is he brought into bondage"; so by usurpation he is become the god and prince of this world, and we have all been his slaves. But believers, having been redeemed by the blood of Christ, "are made free from sin and become the servants of God": and the abiding conviction, that all the subjects of sin and Satan must perish, concurs with their experience of its hard bondage, in fortifying them against every temptation to return to it. Sensible of their obligations to God as their Creator and Governor, they have deeply repented of their past rebellions; and, having obtained mercy, feel themselves bound by gratitude and the most solemn engagements to cleave to him and his service. Their difficulties and discouragements cannot induce them to believe that they 'have changed for the worse': nor will they be influenced by the numbers who apostatize from love to the world and dread of the cross; for they are "rooted and grounded in love", and not merely moved by fears and hopes. They are sure that the Lord is able to deliver them from their enemies; and should the wicked be permitted to prosper in their malicious devices, they know enough of his plan to rely on his wisdom, truth, and love, in the midst of sufferings . . . If such temptations prove ineffectual, Satan will perhaps assault the believer by representing to his mind, with every possible aggravation, the several instances of his misconduct since he professed the gospel, in order to heighten his apprehensions of being found at last a hypocrite: when the soul is discouraged and gloomy, he will be as assiduous in representing every false step to be a horrid crime inconsistent with a state of grace, as he is at other times in persuading men, that the most flagrant violations of the Divine law are mere trifles. In repelling such suggestions the well-instructed believer will neither deny the charge, or extenuate his guilt; but he will flee for refuge to the free grace of the gospel, and take comfort from the consciousness that he now hates, and groans under the remains of those evils, which once he wholly lived in without remorse; thence inferring, that "his sins, though many, are forgiven".' [146]

Endurance, how and why

A few pages back we considered briefly how to keep going, fighting all our days of pilgrimage here. This is worthy of further consideration, but first a section from Bunyan that for me highlights the difference of a God-given time-out rest and a me-taken one and the dangers of not knowing the difference.

Now their way lay just upon the bank of the river: here therefore Christian and his companion [Hopeful] walked with great delight; they drank also of the water of the river, which was pleasant, and enlivening to their weary spirits. Besides, on the banks of this river, on either side, were green trees for all manner of fruit; and the leaves they ate to prevent surfeits, and other diseases that are incident to those that heat their blood by travels. On either side of the river was also a meadow, curiously beautiful with lilies; and it was green all the year long. In this meadow they lay down and slept . . . When they awoke they gathered again of the fruits of the trees, and drank again of the water of the river, and then lay down again to sleep. Thus they did several days and nights. . . .

So when they were disposed to go on (for they were not as yet at their journey's end), they ate, and drank, and departed.

Now I beheld in my dream, that they had not journeyed far, but the river and the way for a time parted; at which they were not a little sorry, yet they durst not go out of the way. Now the way from the river was rough, and their feet tender by reason of their travels: so the souls of the pilgrims were much discouraged

---

[146] Ibid. p99-100

because of the way. Numb. Xxi.4. Wherefore still as they went on they wished for a better way. Now a little before them, there was on the left hand of the road a meadow, and a stile to go over into it; and that meadow is called By-path-meadow. Then said Christian to his fellow, If this meadow lieth along by our way-side let us go over into it. Then he went to the stile to see, and behold a path lay along by the way on the other side of the fence. 'Tis according to my wish, said Christian, here is the easiest going; come good Hopeful, and let us go over. [147]

Scott writes, 'Believers, even when in the path of duty, walking by faith, and supported by the sanctifying influences of the Spirit, may be abridged of those holy consolations which they have experienced; and if this trial be accompanied with temporal losses, poverty, sickness, the unkindness of friends, or ill usage from the world, they may be greatly discouraged; and Satan may have a special advantage in tempting them to discontent, distrust, envy, or coveting. Thus, being more disposed to "wish for a better way", than to pray earnestly for an increase of faith and patience, they will be tempted to look out for some method of declining the cross, or shifting the difficulty which wearies them: nor will it be long before some expedient for a temporary relief will be suggested. The path of duty being rough, a by-path is discovered, which seems to lead the same way; but if they will thus turn aside (though they need not break through a hedge) they must go over a stile. The commandments of God mark out the path of holiness and safety; but a deviation from the exact strictness of them may sometimes be plausibly made, and circumstances seem to invite to it. Men imagine some providential interposition, giving ease to the weary; and they think that the precept may be interpreted with some latitude; that prudence should be exercised; and that scrupulousness about little things is a mark of legality. Thus, by leaning to their own understanding, and trusting in their own hearts instead of asking counsel of the Lord, they hearken to the

---

[147] Ibid. p168-70

tempter. Nor is it uncommon for Christians of deeper experience, and more established reputation, to mislead their juniors, by turning aside from the direct line of obedience. For the Lord leaves them to themselves to repress their self-confidence, and keep them entirely dependent on him; and thus teaches young converts to follow no man farther than he follows Christ . . .

It would not be politic in Satan to tempt believers at first to flagrant crimes, at which their hearts would revolt; but he draws them aside, under specious pretences, into such plausible deviations as seem to be of no bad repute or material consequence; but every wrong step makes way for father temptations, and tends to render other sins apparently necessary; and if it be a deliberate violation of the least precept in the smallest instance, from carnal motives, it involves such self-will, unbelief, ingratitude, and worldly idolatry, as will most certainly expose the believer to sharp rebukes and painful corrections. The example also of professors, of whom perhaps at the first interview too favourable an opinion has been formed, helps to bolster up the vain confidence of him who has departed from the path of obedience; for these men express the strongest assurance, and venture to violate the precepts of Christ, under pretence of honouring his free grace, and knowing their liberty and privilege! But darkness must soon envelop those who follow such guides, and the most extreme distress and danger are directly in the way they take.'[148]

God knows that our frames are weak and that rest is needed, that is one reason he gave us the Sabbath day, a day of rest every week of our lives. Take his times of rest and refreshment that lie within the path he has ordained, not the path your fleshy or old nature prefers.

<u>Question</u>: Is there any way we can prevent burn-out serving God? Should a pilgrim even experience this? Will a pilgrim?
<u>Answer</u>: Briefly: Yes, No and Yes because God has made provision for our recovery.

---

[148] Ibid. p168-171

Consider what Galatians 6:8-10 says, 'For he who sows to his flesh will of the flesh reap corruption, but he who sows to the Spirit will of the Spirit reap everlasting life. And let us not grow weary while doing good, for in due season we shall reap if we do not lose heart. Therefore, as we have opportunity, let us do good to all, especially to those who are of the household of faith.'

Here we can see encouragements to keep going, a hint of resting for a time when needed, and warnings of going about serving God wrongly. See if you come to similar answers as I as we pull this verse apart.

1. *Flesh* or *Spirit*?

Ensure what and who you are working for, why you are doing whatever you are doing. What kind of seed have you got to plant and what will it become when grown? What is motivating you, self-glory from men which is fickle and short lived or God's glory and his 'well done' echoing throughout eternity?

Colossians 3:23-24, 'And whatever you do, do it heartily, as to the Lord and not to men, knowing that from the Lord you will receive the reward of the inheritance; for you serve the Lord Christ.'

2. *And let us not*

Do not allow, do not permit yourself (or another if they will heed you) over time to become so bone-tired of doing good that you just want to lie down and quit as it's just all too much. This is a matter of the will, a choice to not let something happen. Remember why you are doing this work, who you are serving and his promises to those who do truly serve him for as we read in 2Corinthians 9:8, '. . . God is able to make all grace abound toward you, that you always having all sufficiency in all things, may have an abundance for every good work.'

Knowing this, asking for this and acting in faith on this promise no pilgrim should experience burn out, but then no pilgrim is yet perfected and our loving Father knows this better than we do. Also, the simple good we are called to do, that you will read about soon is hard enough to do, so why do we always seem to want to do the harder, the more? Who are we wanting to impress? There is no point trying to impress God for he cannot love you anymore or any less than he already does. Let us just keep our doing simple, not complicated and we will be less likely to experience the rest of these verses from Galatians.

   3. *Grow weary*

To grow has the ideas of to become, to develop, increase or cultivate, sink into or be transformed into rather than something that happens in an instant. Weariness comes from three basic sources, heavy toil that one tires of, fatigue from any cause or the boredom from just having to keep doing.

One can think of words or phrases like, crushing killing, laborious, burdensome, brain fog, jadedness, washed up washed out, overtax one's strength, fed up to the back teeth, unenjoyable, getting one down. I suggest that to sink into or allow yourself to be overcome by continually exposing yourself to what is the source of any of these feelings is not healthy, not necessarily something God would desire.

What did Jesus do when he grew weary? He slept. Once he was so weary that until he was woken by the disciples he slept through a life-threatening storm while in a boat on the sea. We are meant to sleep during our sojourning here, it is okay, it is not laziness, it is necessary and a gift of God's for this time of grace.

Jesus regularly drew apart from the crowds of needy people who followed him for a time of solitude and prayer. Make time for yourself, for whatever will help you recharge, a time of pleasure without pressure (stress) my counsellor described it. A time of pleasure, enjoyment with your Father without having to do.

   4. *Doing good*

Remember good is defined by God, not you, me or any other human. Someone once said, 'Don't let the urgent take place of the important in your life. The important is neither noisy nor demanding. It patiently and quietly waits for us to recognise its significance. The urgent fights, claws and screams for attention, pleading for our time and makes us think we've done the right thing by calming its nerves. The tragedy is that while on a daily basis we put out the fires of the urgent the important is again left in a holding pattern.'

I often struggle against the lie that whispers I'm being lazy sitting praying when there are several loads of washing to do and whatever and whatever and, well you get the idea. Or that as I don't do, serve as much as others there is something lacking in me. Remember how we looked at Martha and Mary towards the end of Part 1, and how Jesus told Martha that Mary had chosen the good part of the one needful thing, hearing his word, spending time with him, that which lasts for eternity? Well, why do you think we are not good at giving ourselves permission to hang up the apron and sit for a change?

Martin Luther's barber and long-time friend, Peter Beskendorf, asked him if he would teach him how to pray. Luther responded by writing a letter which he called *A Simple Way to Pray*

> . . . Guard yourself carefully against those false, deluding ideas which tell you, 'Wait a little while. I will pray in an hour; first I must attend to this or that.' Such thoughts get you away from prayer into other affairs which so hold your attention and involve you that nothing comes of prayer for that day . . . We must be careful not to break the habit of true prayer and imagine other works to be necessary which, after all, are nothing of the kind . . .[149]

And yet there is good we are commanded to do towards all humanity without forgetting to do the same for our brothers and sisters in Christ. Micah 6:8 says, 'He has shown you, O man, what is good; and what does the LORD require of you but to do justly, to love mercy and to walk humbly with your God?'

The good we can now do as pilgrims with a new heart is simple and basic but not easy and that is to show love, have mercy or lovingkindness (*agapē/hesedh*) toward all mankind for this fulfils all the law and commandments as Romans 13:8 states, 'Owe no

---

[149] Nick Aufenkamp *A Simple Way to Pray Every Day* 6.2.2017 desiringgod.org

one anything except to love one another, for he who loves another has fulfilled the law.'

David also had a simple, though again not easy, idea of longevity and doing good which he shared in Psalm 34: 11-14, 'Come, you children, listen to me; I will teach you the fear of the LORD. Who is the man who desires life, and loves many days, that he may see good? Keep your tongue from evil, and your lips from speaking evil, and your lips from deceit. Depart from evil and do good; seek peace and pursue it.'

The good does not have to be specular feats of faithful service that result in you collapsing but can be quiet unseen continuous plodding that only God and you know of.

5. Lose heart

This is serious and is the result of weariness fully grown. This is to lose hope, give way to despair, to give up as experiencing deep sadness, fatigue or joylessness, to be stuck in the *Slough of Despond* as Bunyan called it. If a person loses all hope, they are close to losing the desire to live. I've been here, it is not pleasant and many speak thoughtlessly for you can truly no longer pull your socks up and keep going. This state needs loving care and compassion, not judgement, from fellow pilgrims who should instead come alongside and silently help carry some of the burden, listening carefully, give hope and encouragement till you are back on track and then not vanish but stay in touch.

If you are in this state tell God. He does hear, does understand and can do something about your circumstances.

Moses did as we read in Numbers 11:11-17, 'So Moses said to the LORD, "Why have You afflicted Your servant? And why have I not found favour in Your sight, that You have laid the burden [responsibility] of all these people on me? Did I conceive all these people? [around 600,000 men, then there were the women children and foreigners] Did I begat them, that You should say to me, 'Carry them in your bosom, as a guardian carries a nursing child', to the land which You swore to their fathers? Where am I to get meat to give all these people? For they weep all over me, saying, 'Give us meat that we may eat.' I am not able to bear all

these people alone, because the burden is too heavy for me. If You treat me like this, please kill me here and now – if I have found favour in Your sight – and do not let me see my wretchedness!"
So, the LORD said to Moses; "Gather to me seventy men of the elders of Israel, whom you know to be the elders of the people and officers over them; bring them to the tabernacle of meeting, that they may stand there with you. Then I will come down and talk with you there. I will take of the Spirit that is upon you and will put the same upon them; and they shall bear the burden of the people with you, that you may not bear it yourself alone."'

6. *As we have opportunity*

We only have opportunity while alive, before the second coming of Christ and while today is today. I believe this refers to those opportunities that come across our paths or to our attention daily, rather than us going out deliberately searching for them, though that does not mean we cannot ask God to send us some. Jesus did not regularly search for or chase people down to help them, to do good for. They came to him. But it does not hurt to pray that your eyes and heart will be open to see these opportunities and respond unlike the disciples who most probably had walked past the woman of Samaria and not seen her as being ready to harvest, gather into the kingdom of God, (John 4:3-43).

7. *In due season we shall reap.*

In God's timing we shall be blessed for the good we have sown here and in eternity. God's promise that we shall reap, that in time there will be a harvest ripe to gather in is a strong incentive to endure till the end.

8. *Will of the Spirit reap everlasting life*

And what a promise to gather in, to harvest, eternal life. Keep on plodding dear pilgrim, sowing or watering or reaping, you have Yahweh's guarantee of a harvest reaping beyond your comprehension. The Spirit within us does so very much for the pilgrim in this world, more that I think we can fully understand here, yet as if that is not enough, he, being our down-payment is also instrumental in bringing us face to face with our beloved when our sojourn here is over.

Romans 8:11, 'But if the Spirit of Him who raised Jesus from the dead dwells in you, He who raised Christ from the dead will also give life to your mortal bodies through His Spirit who dwells in you.'

Question: We have looked at how Jesus fought temptations earlier but how did he endure? Can we endure the same way?

Answer: Hebrews 12:1-4, 'Therefore we also, since we are surrounded by so great a cloud of witnesses, let us lay aside every weight, and the sin which so easily ensnares us, and let us run with endurance the race that is set before us, looking unto Jesus, the author and finisher of our faith, who for the joy that was set before Him endured the cross, despising the shame, and has sat down at the right hand of the throne of God. For consider Him who endured such hostility from sinners against Himself, lest you become weary and discouraged in your souls. You have not yet resisted to bloodshed, striving against sin.'

There is a lot in this short passage (which we will be returning to again) to unpack so we will begin by trying to consider what Christ endured according to this passage before we consider the how.

Question: What does it mean that we have not yet resisted to bloodshed, striving against sin?

Answer: Using Matthew 26:36-56, Mark 14:32-50, Luke 22:39-53 and John18:1-11 we learn what those last few hours of freedom for our Lord and saviour were like.

They unfolded something like this –

Jesus and the twelve disciples had finished what is called the Last Supper and walked to the garden of Gethsemane singing psalms as darkness fell. Taking Peter, James and John, he leaves the others and goes a little way away from them. Telling these three to stay, watch and pray with him that they would not enter into temptation Jesus begins to be very sorrowful and deeply distressed. Telling them that his soul was exceedingly sorrowful, even to death, he moves about a stone's throw away from them and falls to the ground praying that if possible, the coming hour might pass from him saying, 'Abba, Father, all things are possible for You. Take this cup away from Me; nevertheless, not what I will, but what You will.'

Then he went to the three and finding them asleep said to Peter, 'What? Could you not watch with Me one hour? Watch and pray, lest you enter into temptation. The spirit indeed is willing but the flesh is weak.'

A second time Jesus goes from them and prays, 'O My Father, if it is possible, let this cup pass from Me; nevertheless, not as I will but as You will.' When he returned, he again found them asleep, for their eyes were heavy and they did not know what to answer him.

Leaving them and praying a third time Jesus is in extreme agony, his sweat becoming like great drops of blood falling down to the ground as he prays even more earnestly saying, 'O My Father, if this cup cannot pass away from Me unless I drink it, Your will be done.' An angel then appears before him from heaven and strengthens him.

Rising from praying Jesus finds the disciples still sleeping from sorrow and says, 'Are you still sleeping and resting? It is enough! The hour has come: behold the Son of Man is being betrayed into the hands of sinners.'

While he is speaking Judas with the detachment of troops and officers armed with lanterns, torches, swords and clubs (probably around a hundred men) that he had received from the chief priests, Pharisees and elders of the people arrive. As Judas goes forward to kiss Jesus, Jesus knowing all things that would now come upon him moved forward to meet his betrayer saying, 'Friend why have you come? Are you betraying the Son of Man with a kiss?' and addressing the crowd he asks, 'Whom are you seeking?' They answered him, 'Jesus of Nazareth'. Replying 'I AM', an invisible force pushes the mob away from him knocking them onto the ground. Undeterred they again state they are looking for Jesus of Nazareth and Jesus answers, 'I have told you that I AM. Therefore, if you seek Me let these go their way', that the saying might be fulfilled which he spoke, 'Of those whom You gave Me I have lost none.'

Simon Peter, having a sword, now draws it and strikes the high priest's servant, and his right ear is cut off. But Jesus asking, 'Permit even this' touches the wound, healing the servant while speaking to Peter saying, 'Put your sword in its place, for all who take the sword will perish by the sword. Or do you think that I cannot now pray to My Father, and He will provide Me with more than twelve legions of angels? (That's 72,000 angelic soldiers. In 2Kings 19:35 we learn that just one angel killed 185,000 men.) How then could the Scriptures be fulfilled, that it must happen thus? Shall I not drink the cup which My Father has given Me?'

Then addressing the mob also, he said, 'Have you come out, as against a robber, with swords and clubs? When I was with you daily in the temple teaching, you did not try to seize Me. But this is your hour, and the power of darkness, all this was done that the Scriptures of the prophets might be fulfilled.' With this all the disciples forsook Jesus and fled, one even losing his clothing in his haste to escape.

Question: Can a person really sweat blood?
Answer: Yes, and note it is Luke the physician who gives us this detail. *Hematridrosis* is the medical term for this rare condition where the tiny blood vessels in the sweat glands apparently burst when one is under extreme physical or emotional stress, mixing blood with sweat, causing the sweat to appear as blood. It's probably where the saying that 'one is sweating blood', meaning a great effort is being made, comes from. Only a few handfuls of cases were confirmed in medical studies in the 20th century.[150]

Question: What was it about a cup that caused this to happen? Should I care?
Answer: Second question first. Knowing what Jesus went through to obtain all that we as pilgrims have now and look forward to in

---

[150] https://www.webmd.com

hope can only deepen our understanding of the awfulness of our sin and how deeply we are loved by God.

Now the first question.

Snatches of verses from Jeremiah 25:15-38 may help paint an idea of this cup, '. . . says the LORD God of Israel [to Jeremiah]: "Take this wine cup of fury [wrath] from My hand, and cause all the nations, to whom I send you, to drink of it. And they will drink and stagger and go mad because of the sword that I shall send among them." . . . 'Thus says the LORD of hosts, the God of Israel: Drink, be drunk, and vomit! Fall and rise no more, because of the sword which I will send among you. And it shall be, if they refuse to take the cup from your hand to drink, then you shall say to them, 'Thus says the LORD of hosts: "You shall certainly drink! For behold, I begin to bring calamity on the city which is called by My name, and should you be utterly unpunished? You shall not be unpunished, for I will call for a sword on all the inhabitants of the earth," says the LORD of hosts . . . And at that day the slain of the LORD shall be from one end of the earth to the other end of the earth. They shall not be lamented, or gathered, or buried; they shall become refuse on the ground.'

The Revelation of Jesus Christ 14:6-20 speaks of future events when God has called an end to this time of grace and increasing sinfulness, 'Then I saw another angel flying in the midst of heaven, having the everlasting gospel to preach to those who dwell on the earth . . . "Fear God and give glory to Him, for the hour of His judgement has come; and worship Him who made heaven and earth, the sea and springs of water." And another angel followed, saying, "Babylon is fallen, is fallen, that great city, because she has made all nations drink of the wine of wrath of her fornication."

Then a third angel followed them, saying . . . "If anyone worships the beast and his image, and receives his mark on his forehead or on his hand, he himself shall also drink of the wine of the wrath of God, which is poured out full strength into the cup of His indignation. He shall be tormented with fire and brimstone in the presence of the holy angels and in the presence of the Lamb . . ."

So, the angel thrust his sickle into the earth and gathered the vine of the earth, and threw it into the great winepress of the wrath of God. And the winepress was trampled outside the city [Christ was crucified outside the city], and blood came out of the winepress, up to the horses' bridles, for one thousand six hundred furlongs [about 184 miles in all].'

This cup is the judgement of God which he makes all the wicked drink, "You like sin? Fine! Drink your fill and more!" He forces them to drink all the consequences of their own sins so that what they chose to love becomes what makes them sick and destroys them.

Jesus, fully man but without anything in him that Satan could use, completely without sin experienced all of history's collective sins, the full strength and quota of his Abba's wrath against all of mankind's wickedness and evil while on the cross as though he had wrestled as a man with the thought of draining this cup, with Satan encouraging the 'No' side, as a man his desire to obey and his love for the Father won. Jesus accepted this cup. God did not force it upon him.

He was so sin laden that his holy Father had to turn his face away from his only Son, forsaking him while he was hanging dying and cursed on the tree for us.

We do not know, cannot know, what it will be like to live without sin in us and around us for we have been born into this fallen world with a sin-desiring-nature. So though not yet fully able to understand how truly awful sin is even as pilgrims, we will never experience the level of anguish that the never-tainted-by-sin Christ did on the cross when the Father turned away from him. This cup of wrath would have been ours to drain had we not become pilgrims by the loving grace of our God and washed clean by his Son's sinless blood and it would have been us experiencing God's turned face. As pilgrims, we will never ever experience our Abba turning his face away from us as we die because we will not be laden by sin, ours or the world's.

Question: Other than resisting, striving against sin, so much that he sweated blood, what else did Jesus endure according to the Hebrews passage?

Answer: The battle for the work which only Christ could do, that could only be done on the cross was actually won in the garden when Christ accepted God's will and took his cup. A garden was where all had been lost and a garden was where all was won. But though won the cross still had to be endured, a bit like our lives, we are victorious because of Christ's work but we still have to endure, persevere till we are home.

When the gospels were written certain things were known by the people, by the readers, seeing crucifixions and the injuries from whippings were a part of life then. We who thankfully do not witness such things do not have that knowledge so do not necessarily understand as easily.

It was not just his death on the cross that Jesus had to endure, that came last, after desertion, sleep deprivation, facial blows, soldiers' version of blind-man's bluff, taunts and mockery, being passed around like an unwanted parcel to be gawked at, dehydration, being spat upon and seen to be in a world of unclean shame.

The story of Miriam in Numbers 12 links the public shaming of being spat upon with the shame of being an unclean because of leprosy as we read in verses 10b, 12a-14, and '. . . Aaron turned toward Miriam, and there she was, a leper . . . "Please do not let her be as one dead . . . So Moses cried out to the LORD, saying, "Please heal her, O God, I pray!" Then the LORD said to Moses, "If her father had but spat in her face, would she not be shamed seven days? Let her be shut out of the camp seven days and afterward she may be received again."'

There are some scholars who think that Pilate may have hoped that by having Christ scourged he would have pacified the mob and been able to release him in whom he found no wrong. Scourging was done by the flagrum, a short heavy whip consisting of several leather throngs with lead balls and sometimes pieces of bone attached near the ends being brought down across naked shoulders, back and legs of the criminal whose hands were tied to a post above his head. The beating was stopped only when the centurion in charge felt the prisoner was near death having his deep muscle layers and even skeletal structures exposed causing spurting arterial bleeding and strips of flesh to hang like frayed ribbons. Having the cloak which the soldiers dressed Christ with ripped off these wounds before nailing him to the cross, would have been excruciating as well as restarting the bleeding.

But when the mob was not appeased and started to suggest that Pilate was not showing proper reverence for the lordship of Caesar the sentence of crucifixion was given. Death by crucifixion appeared in the Persian culture between 300-400 BC but it was perfected by the Romans, despite having more than one way to carry it out in the first century BC it is the most slow, painful (it is where our word *excruciating* comes from) gruesome, humiliating and public form of capital punishment ever invented –

- Bound to the cross-bar which weighed roughly 30-60kg

Jesus was unable to carry it the 360meters or thereabouts so he was already quite weak physically. If you stumbled you would most likely land flat on your face in the dirt and whatever else was on the road.

- Nails, thick and long, maximum pain, minimum bleeding.

In popular depictions of Christ's crucifixion, the nails are shown in his hands possibly because of the translated wording of John 20:25. But in Greek the word χειρ usually translated as *hand*, could refer to the entire portion of the arm below the elbow. To denote the *hand* as distinct from the *arm* some other word could be added. [151] Going between the bones of the forearm at the wrist would have stopped the nails from ripping throughout the length of your hand when the weight of your sagging body dragged down on them but by severing the median nerve there was constant severe burning pain like lightening and painful contractures of the hands. Feet were extended and one nail went

---

[151] Crucifixion – Wikipedia *Nail placement*

through both arches (probably involving the tarsal or calcaneus bones so that the nail would not rip out when pressure applied downwards), more damaged nerves, more agony that intensified with any downward movement or pressure.

- With knees flexed at about 45 degrees the thigh muscles have to support all your weight. How long can you stand with your knees flexed? Try it. When the legs give out, your weight, if hanging is taken by the arms and shoulders so it is only minutes before these joints dislocate, followed by your elbows and wrists. More torn muscle and nerve fibers. Arms can now as much as 15-23cm longer than usual.

- Considerable weight is now taken by the chest muscles causing the rib cage to elevate. Ribs stuck in the position of inhalation makes exhalation almost impossible. To do so you must push down on your feet to relax the chest muscles, every movement re-wounding that scoured back, but the thighs are too fatigued, so more dislocation of joints, more elevation of chest, increased difficulty to exhale so unable to inhale, decreasing oxygen blood levels, increasing carbon dioxide blood levels, stimulating increased heart rate. Increasing dehydration, increasing viscosity of blood, increasing heart pressure . . . a vicious cycle begins. Heart begins to fail. Lungs begin to fill with fluid restricting breathing even more and other organs start to fail. It is a slow death by suffocation, which with a 'seat' can take up to nine days. Before then you will be way past caring that you are naked before all the passing public and have soiled yourself.

Christ however did not die because of suffocation, he died before the other two hanging beside him who had to have their legs broken to speed up the process. Our Lord died of heart failure, a broken heart, from pericardial effusion or tamponade as the post-mortem evidence of John 19:34 which reads, 'But one of the soldiers pierced His side with a spear, and immediately blood and water came out' showed.

<u>Question</u>: The Hebrews passage said that Christ endured hostilities from sinners, don't we as pilgrims? Why will it help us

not to become weary and discouraged by considering these hostilities that Christ endured?

Answer: Scripture, as we shall see in the verses below, teaches us that all hostility against pilgrims throughout the ages of time because of our refusal to deny our saviour and Lord, are really against him. That is a lot of hostility, a lot of rejection and denial. That's more than we will ever face, besides we deserve to, he doesn't.

Proverbs 14:31, 'He who oppresses the poor reproaches his Maker, but he who honours Him has mercy on the needy.'

Proverbs 17:5, 'He who mocks the poor reproaches his Maker; he who is glad at calamity will not go unpunished.'

Luke 10:16, 'He who hears you hears Me, he who rejects you rejects Me, and he who rejects Me rejects Him who sent Me.'

1Thessalonians 4:8, 'Therefore he who rejects this [God's call to holiness not uncleanness, v7] does not reject man, but God who has also given us His Holy Spirit.'

The types of hostilities we can be called to face are many and varied, from the ego destroying glare someone flashes us or a tightening of their lips, be they a beloved one or stranger to real physical danger as in actions that result in death. But one thing is sure, Christ suffered and persevered despite them and so will every pilgrim, there is nothing here in this world that should terrify us off the way.

In Philippians 1:28, Paul tells us to 'not in any way [be] terrified by [our] adversaries.' If we are he tells us, in the mind of those who are hostile it proves we are not genuine Pilgrims but as they are, bound for hell. However if we are not terrified yet continue to suffer hostilities it is proof to us that we are saved and that God is enabling us to not be spooked off course. The word 'terrified' is only used once in the New Testament and it is here in this passage. It is used to describe horses that become spooked and stampede uncontrollably; it describes and inward fear caused by an outward stimulus. Paul is saying to the believers, 'Don't get spooked be those who come after you. Don't get blown off course.' [152]

Jesus overcame far more than we pilgrims ever will have to face and as he is with us as the victor and for us, we will overcome also as we keep our trust and hope in God rather than our abilities.

Bunyan warns pilgrims early on about the miry Slough of Despond and Scott writes that, 'Increasing knowledge produces deeper self-abasement: hence discouraging fears arise in men's minds lest they should at last perish; and objections against themselves continually accumulate, till they fall into habitual despondency, unless they constantly attend to the encouragements of the Scripture, or in the apostle's language, have their 'feet shod with the preparation of the gospel of peace' . . . Our author, in a marginal note, explains the steps to mean. 'the promises of forgivness and acceptance to life by faith in Christ'; which include the general invitations and the various encouragements given in Scripture to all who seek the salvation of the Lord, and diligently use the appointed means . . . Faith in Christ and in the mercy of God through him, can only set the pilgrim's feet on good ground.' [153]

Further on in their pilgrimage Christian and Hopeful went off the path into By-path-meadow and found themselves prisoners in Doubting-castle, the owner being giant Despair who informed the pair 'that since they were never like to come out of that place, their only way would be forthwith to make an end of themselves, either with knife, halter, or poison; for why, said he, should you choose life, seeing it is attended with so much bitterness? . . . Brother, said Christian, what shall we do? The life that we now live is miserable: for my part, I know not wither it is best to live thus, or die out of hand . . . the grave is more easy for me than this dungeon'

---

[152] David Jeremiah *The Joy of Integrity.* https://sermons.love-the sermons archive

[153] *The Pilgrim's Progress* comment by Scott p48

Hope. Indeed our present condition is dreadful, and death would be far more welcome to me than thus for ever to abide; but yet let us consider the Lord of the country to which we are going . . . And moreover, my brother, though talkest of ease in the grave, but hast thou forgotten . . . hell . . . And let us consider again, that all the law is not in the hand of giant Despair . . . who knows but that God, that made the world may cause that giant Despair may die. . . . That evening on finding them still alive though only just, giant Despair 'fell into a grievous rage, and told them, that, seeing they had disobeyed his counsel, it should be worse with them than if, they had never been born . . . Now Christian again seemed to be for doing it, but Hopeful . . . reminded Christian what he had already had come through so far on his pilgrimage and counselled patience . . . about midnight they began to pray . . . a little before it was day, good Christian, as one half amazed, break out . . . What a fool . . . I am, thus to lay in a stinking dungeon, when I may as well walk at liberty? I have a key in my bosom, called Promise, that will, I am persuaded, open any lock in Doubting-castle.'[154]

Scott writes that 'Peter and the other disciples "slept for sorrow", when they were more especially required "to watch and pray, that they might not enter into temptations" Such repeatdeth sins and mistakes bring believers into deep distresses. Growing more and more heartless in religion, and insensible in a most perilous situation, they are led habitually to infer that they are hypocrites; that the encouragements of Scripture belong not to them; that prayer itself will be of no use to them; and, when they are at length brought to reflection, they are taken prisoners by Despair, and shut up in Doubting-castle . . . Whenever we deliberately quit the plain path of duty, to avoid hardship and self-denial, we trespass on giant Despair's grounds, and are never out of his reach till renewed exercises of deep repentance, and faith in Christ, producing unreserved obedience, especially in that instance where before we refused it, have set our feet in the highway we had forsaken . . . Serious recollection of past conflicts,

---

[154] Ibid p173-181

dangers, and deliverances, is peculiarly useful to encourage confidence in the power and mercy of God, and patient waiting for him in the most difficult and perilous situations; and conference with our brethren, even if they, too, are under similar trials, is a very important means of resisting the devil, when he would tempt us to renounce our hope, and have recourse to desperate measures . . . the assurance of hope is inseparably connected with the self-denying obedience of faith and love.'[155]

Pilgrims are to grow in knowledge but with more knowledge showing up more sin and greater evils in our sins we can begin to despair and begin to think we are but hypocrites and not a true pilgrim. How much knowledge do you think Jesus had? Why did he not doubt himself? Could it be that he knew his Father and spent a lot of time with him? Keep studying your Bible, keep spending time talking and listening to your Father, keep practicing self-denying faithful loving obedience. Spend time with other pilgrims, and God recalling his past graces and mercies to you, to others and to Christ knowing that they are forever new each morning and as they were sufficient for everything Christ faced, they will be for anything you face.

Heed all weights including shame

<u>Question</u>: Returning to Hebrews 12:1-4 and considering the first two verses where it talks about the need to lay aside all and any weight that entangles, catches, trips you up in your sojourning here, what weight do you think pilgrims need to get rid of so their way is easier?

<u>Answer</u>: I have read that this image that the writer to Hebrews uses of a runner being weighed down and throwing the weight off came from that time for runners then did strip their clothes off so they could run unhindered but I am fairly sure that is not what we are being asked to do!

---

[155] Ibid. comment by Scott

We are not specifically told what the weight is, as we are not told what Paul's thorn was (see 2Corinthians 12:7-10) which I consider opens it up to be not a specific thing that all pilgrims may need to avoid at all times but whatever affects an individual pilgrim in this fashion at a certain point in their race, but perhaps not at another time when something different may be have become their snare. A weight could be anything that will attempt to take away your hope or joy of being in Christ, of being a pilgrim on pilgrimage. It cannot be a sin as that is added separately in v1, '. . . lay aside every weight, and the sin which so easily ensnares us . . .'

Proverbs 12:25 (NIV) reads, 'An anxious heart weighs a man down, but a kind word cheers him up.' The NKJ reads, 'Anxiety in the heart of man causes depression, but a good word makes it glad.'

Have you experienced the truth of this at some point in your life? Anxiety or the depression that can result because of it is not a nice weight to be encumbered with, it brings you down. Kindness, even a wolf whistle to a lady weighed down this way, even from a stranger may lighten it for a moment and that can make a long-term difference. And we have, back a few pages, looked at when Moses wanted out as he was so weighed down by responsibilities.

What do you think is a weight for you presently?

It took many years before I started to say 'No' to helping out with church stuff, all good and necessary things that had to be done but that did not mean I had to be the one that said 'Yes'. Yes, we need to be Martha's but never at the expense of being a Mary. If you are too busy to read your Bible, pray or just sit quietly before God listening you are far too busy. Act now. Declutter your life. You will be a contented, more settled, and a better person to be around, to sojourn with.

Someone once said, 'The will of God does not send you where the grace of God cannot keep you' and Hudson Taylor (1832-1905), a missionary in China, said, 'When God's work is done in God's way for God's glory it will not lack for God's supply.'

I am learning a hard lesson in my pilgrimage and though it has been several years of not always comfortable disciplining instruction I still seem to get it not quite right. If this statement of

Taylor's is not true for me, I am not doing his work but mine or someone else's, it is then I burn out, become over tired, over stressed and over doing it (as in I want to quit) and usually God pulls the plug taking any choice away from me because I waited too long to do so, leaving me to withdraw licking my self-inflicted wounds and recover.

I am me, not someone else. The same goes for you.

Remember reading the discussion around Psalm 139 when we were considering mindsets? We should only be doing what God asks of us individually, when he asks, how he asks, for only as long he asks and then we will be able to do whatever he has asked because it will be by his ability in his strength to his glory.

This is discernment, know yourself, your God-given abilities and limits and be sure the desire to do whatever is coming from God and not a want you or someone else has.

Jesus warns us not to get our hearts weighed down by this life, by this world and not be ready for his coming in judgement. The desire to be affirmed by those close to you can be a terrible weight which ensnares you. A weight which increases, tightening its strangling grip if that affirmation, or for that matter anything else that you need from another person to feel whole, is never given. In truth it is only God who can supply and does supply all we need to be whole and therefore feel whole. Whatever makes your heart, your soul heavy, distracted from God, even forgetful of him and his way for you needs to be discarded for though it may not seem a sin, it has become one and it is not good for you. Only Christ's yoke is suited for us to bear and it is as tailor made for the individual as were the ones crafted for oxen.

Something else that can weigh you down is shame.

Have you felt this? The shame of never being enough or doing enough, of not being right can make you want to hide from people and at its extreme make you suicidal.

<u>Question</u>: What is shame? What was shameful that Jesus had to despise? How did he despise it, how can we? Lots of questions,

and more will arise so this is going to be another long answer but hopefully a worthwhile exercise.

Answer: Shame was the final character that Faithful met in Bunyan's Pilgrim's Progress. Faithful found he could not argue against this character unlike Old Man, Madam Wanton or Discontent as shame makes you remain silent and not able to stand for the Lord. Whether it be three hundred years ago [when Bunyan lived] or now the causes of being ashamed of the gospel are the same in spirit that Christ and the apostles faced. Most of the world's objections against religion are shame based –

Objection 1: It is a pitiful low sneaking business for a man to mine religion. It is a sissy thing, not something for 'real' men to consider as it is humiliating. It is a shame for a man to go to church and hear a preacher preach but then to take what he says seriously and go and do it . . .!! It's all right for women and children but men and dogs stay home.

Objection 2: A tender conscious is unmanly.
That is a conscious that wants the will of God, that seeks God's will is not manly. A 'real' man does his own will, he is master of self. It is a shame to ask forgiveness; a man does not say sorry, does not acknowledge he has wronged someone.

Objection 3: For a man to watch over his words and ways and so tie self from liberty will make him a ridicule of the times. The discipline of it, to have to watch what you say and how you act, goes against the way the whole multitude is going.
Have you ever been tempted by someone to do the wrong thing just to prove to them that you are a man? That's what shame makes you do.

Objection 4: Few of the mighty, rich or wise are ever of this opinion to go to church and see who is there. So why would you want to be a Christian then? There are no 'somebodies' that go to church, it is full of 'nobodies', widows, janitors, sinners . . . Religion, the need for it, is a mark of weakness, it makes a man grow strange to the great, you fall out with the influent people, the important or beautiful people in school, at work, at the club . .

Objection 5: Tis a foolish thing to be, you have to give money to the church, wasting your life. And restitution, how stupid!

Objection 6: Think on the base and lower state of a pilgrims' life. There is suffering, persecution, humiliation and all under providence. Look at the person in hospital, look at what God's allowed in his life! Look at how they have to live!

Objection 7: There is ignorance and a want of understanding in all the natural sciences. You're ignorant that science has now disproved the Bible, it's made all religion obsolete. Don't you know that the Bible was okay in the primitive ages but this is the 20th century, it's all outdated like you! The Greek's in Christ's time in their wisdom considered the gospel message and the cross to be pure foolishness.[156]

So that's a picture of how shame affects, can challenge your choice of action, but what is it?

Yep, I'm bringing out my trusty Oxford dictionary that has needed some repairs lately as it is getting too much use lately.

Shame

A feeling of distress or humiliation caused by a consciousness of the guilt or folly of oneself or an associate, a state of disgrace, a person, thing or action that brings disgrace, embarrassment, dishonour, indignity, ignominy.

The first thing that comes to mind of what may have been shameful for Christ after reading this definition is the cross which we have just considered. But could Jesus have felt shame when his family wanted to lock him up for the things he was saying? I would have. How about you? How about as a growing youth being aware that the neighbours and their kids knew that Joseph was not who had fathered him? What of being homeless? What about being accused of keeping the wrong sort of company?

Question: How does the Bible see shame? What according to God's word should we feel shame for?

---

[156] Notes from Gables' sermon series on Pilgrim's Progress #34 *Conversation with Faithful #3* 2.3.99

Answer: The feeling of guilt is about something wrong whereas shame is about being wrong at the core. Shame tells me what men are but nothing of what God or the word of God is or what he can do.[157]

Shame or the feeling of being ashamed is the first negative feeling mentioned in the Bible along with how we react to it and how it is quickly followed by another feeling.

Genesis 2:25 tells us that Adam and Eve 'were both naked . . . and were not ashamed.' But things were very different after they rebelled. Genesis 3:7-10 in part reads, 'Then the eyes of both of them were opened, and they knew that they were naked; and they sewed fig leaves together and made themselves coverings . . and Adam and his wife hid themselves from the presence of the LORD God . . . 'I was afraid because I was naked; and I hid myself.' After the fall Adam and Eve were truly *wrong at the core* because of their sin not because of someone else's actions. they hid from the God who loved them and from one another because of fear of being exposed. They reacted to shame by wanting to hide, hide from the God who they knew loved them and from each other. Fear followed rapidly, almost instantaneously.

> Shame feelings are a threat to the integrity of the self. It keeps us caught in fear of being found out by others. The perceived deficit is so humiliating that the person goes to great lengths of hide the flawed self.[158]

I've done this. Have you?

Hiding, repressing yourself and putting on a mask is not biblical but worldly sinful hypocritical behaviour that will destroy you. This is where pride, sinful pride comes in, something the world does not consider.

Sinful pride makes us ashamed of failures and weaknesses.
Pride fuelled shame can wield great power over us. It

---

[157] https://www.huffpost.comsentry Why we feel shame and how to conquer it/ HuffPost Life.

[158] https://lynnenamka.com Talk Trust and feel therapeutics. Lynne Namka. Ed.D President.

controls significant parts of our lives and consumes precious energy and time in avoiding exposure.[159]

The unbearable weight of shame however, can cause it to become a godly motivator for change, gospel change.

God killed, shed the first blood in his creation to cover Adam and Eve. Jesus shed his blood to cover all who come to him. To completely and finally hide from shame, cover ourselves, we have to hide in Christ, as Romans 10:11 tell us, 'For the Scripture says, "Whoever believes on Him will not be put to shame." And as we will see later Jesus' taught a parable to show that to get into his heaven we must be covered, clothed with the wedding garment of his righteousness. If you have experienced the removal of this weight you know the freedom of Christ's yoke, his peace and rest.

A Bible dictionary tells us that, 'The word group for shame (disconcerted, disappointed, confounded) occurs in the Old Testament most frequently in the Wisdom Literature and in the prophets (especially Isaiah and Jeremiah) . . . The New Testament deepens and expands the concept of shame. A disciple of Christ stands with him unashamedly in a world that finds the cross (Heb. 12:2), God's ways (1Cor. 1:23), and God's persecuted messengers (2Tim. 1:8, 12) shameful. Those ashamed of him now will find Christ ashamed of them on the day of judgement (Mk. 8:38, Lk. 9:26). Conversely, God is not ashamed to call the faithful 'brothers' of Christ (Heb. 2:11).

Suffering for Christ is identification with Christ, glory not shame (Acts 5:41, 1Pt. 4:16). Paul was not ashamed of the Gospel because it is the only antidote for humanity's shame (Rom. 1:16). Ultimately, the Christian who trusts in Christ need not be ashamed of anything (Phil. 1:20; cf Isa. 28:16 Rom. 9:33, 10:11, 1Pt 2:6). When one confesses Christ and openly rebels against him, however the work of Christ is publically shamed (Heb. 6:6).

---

[159] Jon Bloom *Breaking the Power of Shame* 15.7.2016 desiringgod.org

Christians must be diligent to renounce shameful behaviour; though tempting because of its hidden character (2Cor. 4:2).[160]
God's idea of what is and what is not shame is upside down and inside-out compared to the world's understanding.
2Timothy 1:6-12, 'Therefore I remind you to stir up the gift of God [genuine faith v.5] which is in you . . . For God has not given us a spirit of fear, but of power and of love and of a sound mind. Therefore do not be ashamed of the testimony of our Lord, nor of me His prisoner, but share with me in the sufferings for the gospel according to the power of God, who has saved us and called us with a holy calling, not according to our works, but according to His own purpose and grace which was given us in Christ Jesus before time began, but has now been revealed by the appearing of our Saviour Jesus Christ, who has abolished death and brought life and immortality to light through the gospel, to which I was appointed a preacher, an apostle, and a teacher of the Gentiles. For this reason I also suffer these things; nevertheless I am not ashamed, for I know whom I have believed and am persuaded that he is able to keep that which I have committed to Him until that Day.'
Piper teaches that, 'Misplaced shame (the kind we ought not to have) is the shame you feel when there is no good reason to feel it. Biblically, that means the thing you feel ashamed of is not dishonouring to God; or that it is dishonouring to God, but you didn't have a hand in it. . . misplaced shame is shame for something that's good – something that doesn't dishonour God. Or it's shame for something bad but which you didn't have any sinful hand in.
Well- placed shame (the kind you ought to have) is the shame you feel when there is good reason to feel it. Biblically, that means we feel ashamed of something because our involvement in it was dishonouring to God. We ought to feel shame when we have a hand in bringing dishonour upon God by our attitudes or actions.

---

[160] Baker's Evangelical Dictionary of Biblical Theology. Edited by Walter A. Elwell *Shame* Baker Books 1996 from biblestudytools.com

. . . If we want to battle shame at the root, we have to know how it relates to God. And we do need to battle shame at the root – all shame. Because both misplaced shame and well-placed shame can cripple us if we don't know how to deal with them at the root. 2Tim 1:8 . . . If you feel shame for testifying about Jesus you have misplaced shame . . . Christ is honoured when we speak well of him. And he is dishonoured by fearful silence. . . Secondly the text says that if you feel shame that a friend is in trouble (in this case: prison) for Jesus's sake, then your shame is misplaced. The world may see this as a sign of weakness and defeat. But Christians know better. God's honoured by the courage of his servants to go to prison for his name. We ought not to feel shame that we are associated with something that honours God in this way, no matter how much scorn the world heaps on.

Mk 8:38 ["For whoever is ashamed of Me and My words in this adulterous and sinful generation, of him the Son of Man also will be ashamed when He comes in the glory of His Father with the holy angels."] Shame is misplaced when we feel it because of the person or the work of Jesus. If Jesus says, "Love your enemies," and others laugh and call it unrealistic, we should not feel ashamed. If Jesus says, "Fornication is evil," and liberated yuppies label it out of date, we should not feel shame to stand with Jesus.

1Pt 4:16 [Yet if anyone suffers as a Christian, let him not be ashamed, but let him glorify God in this matter.] Suffering and being reproached and made fun of as a Christian is not an occasion for shame, because it is an occasion for glorifying God . . In the Bible the criterion for what is well-placed shame and what is misplaced shame is not how foolish or how bad you look to men, but whether you in fact bring honour to God.

This is so important to grasp, because much of what makes us feel shame is not that we have brought dishonour on God by our actions, but that we have failed to give the appearance that other people admire. Much of our shame is not God-centered, but self-centered . . .

Rom1:16 [For I am not ashamed of the gospel of Christ, for it is the power of God to salvation for everyone who believes, for the Jew first and also for the Greek.] The reason shame in the gospel would be a misplaced shame is that the gospel is the very power of God unto salvation . . .

2Cor 12:9-10 [And He said to me, "My grace is sufficient for you, for My strength is made perfect in weakness." Therefore most gladly I will rather boast in my infirmities, that the power of Christ may rest upon me. Therefore I take pleasure in infirmities, in reproaches, in needs, in persecutions, in distresses, for Christ's sake. For when I am weak, then I am strong.] Now ordinarily weaknesses and insults are occasions for shame. But for Paul they were occasions for exultation . . . don't feel shame for something that honours God no matter how weak or foolish it makes you look in the eyes of unbelievers . . .

1Cor 15:34 [Awake to righteousness, and do not sin; for some do not have the knowledge of God. I speak this to your shame.] . . . Their shame would be well-placed if they saw their deplorable ignorance of God and how it was leading to false doctrine (no resurrection) and sin in the church.

1Cor 6:5 [I say this to your shame. Is it so, that there is not a wise man among you, not even one, who will be able to judge between his brethren?] . . . Their shame would be well-placed because their behaviour is bringing such disrepute upon their God as they fight one another and seek help from the godless to settle their disputes. . . And let's not miss this implication: these people were trying their best to appear strong and right. They wanted to be vindicated by men. They wanted to be winners in court. They didn't want anyone to run over them as though they had no rights. That would look weak and shameful. So, in the very act of wanting to avoid shame as the world sees it, they fell into the very behaviour that God counts shameful.

The point is: when you are dishonouring God, you ought to feel shame, no matter how strong or wise or right you are in the eyes of men.

. . . we battle it by battling the unbelief that feeds its life. And we fight for faith in the promises of God that overcome shame and relieve us from its pain.

   1.   When well-placed shame lingers too long.

. . . The pain ought to be there but it ought not to stay there. If it does, it's owing to unbelief in the promises of God. [Luke 7:36-50, the story of a woman who was a sinner who washed Jesus' feet with her tears and dried them with her hair during a meal at a house of a Pharisee] . . . Indeed she was a sinner. There was a place for true shame, but not for too long. Jesus said, "Your sins are forgiven" . . . And when the guests murmured about this, he helped her faith again by saying, "Your faith has saved you; go in peace."

How did Jesus help her battle the crippling effects of shame? He gave her a promise: 'Your sins are forgiven! Your faith has saved you. Your future will be one of peace.' So the issue for her was belief. Would she believe the glowering condemnation of the guests? Or would she believe the reassuring words of Jesus that her shame was enough? . . . And that is the way every one of us must battle the effects of a well-placed shame that threatens to linger too long and cripple us. We must battle unbelief by taking hold of promises like, Ps 130:4 [But there is forgiveness with You, that You may be feared], Isa 55:6 [Seek the LORD while He may be found. Call upon Him while He is near], 1Jn 1:9 [If we confess our sins, He is faithful and just to forgive us our sins and to cleanse us from all unrighteousness.], 1Tim 1:15 [This is a faithful saying and worthy of all acceptance, that Christ Jesus came into the world to save sinners, of whom I am chief], Acts 10:43 [To Him all the prophets witness that, through His name, whoever believes in Him will receive remission of sins] and 13:39 [and by Him everyone who believes is justified from all things from which you could not be justified by the law of Moses].

   2.   Feeling shame for something that glorifies God.

Our text shows how Paul battled against this misplaced shame. In verse 12 he says, "Therefore I suffer as I do. But I am not ashamed, for I know whom I have believed, I am sure that he is able to guard until that Day what has been entrusted to me." Paul makes very clear here that the battle against misplaced shame is a battle against unbelief . . . We fight against feelings of shame in Christ and the gospel and the Christian ethic by battling unbelief in the promises of God. Do we believe that the gospel is the power of God unto salvation? Do we believe that Christ's power is made perfect in our weakness?

3. Feeling shame for something we didn't do.

Finally, the last instance of battling shame is the instance where others try to load us with shame for evil circumstances when in fact we had no part in dishonouring God.

It happened to Jesus. They called him a winebibber and a glutton. They called him a temple destroyer . . . a hypocrite: He healed others but he can't heal himself. In all this the goal was to load Jesus with a shame that was not his to bear.

The same with Paul. They called him mad when he defended himself in court. They called him an enemy of the Jewish customs and a breaker of the Mosaic law. They said he taught that you should sin that grace may abound. All this to load him with a shame that was not his to bear.

And it has happened to you. And it will happen again. How do you battle this misplaced shame? By believing the promises of God that in the end all the efforts to put us to shame will fail. We may struggle now to know what is our shame to bear and what is not. But God has a promise for us in either case:

> Israel is saved by the Lord with
> Everlasting salvation; you shall not be
> Put to shame or confounded to all eternity.
> (Is 45:17; 49:23)
> No one who believes in the Lord will be
> Put to shame. (Rom 10:11; 9:33)

In other words, for all the evil and deceit, judgement and criticism that others may use to heap on us a shame that is not ours to bear, and for all the distress and spiritual warfare it brings, the promise stands sure that they will not succeed in the end. All the children of God will be vindicated. The truth will be known. And no one who banks this hope on the promises of God will be put to shame.'[161]

<u>Question</u>: After reading all that how should we view Christ's despising the shame now? What was the shame? How did Christ despise the shame?

<u>Answer</u>: The context of the phrase suggests that the shame is connected to the cross but even if connected to Jesus' life here it does not really alter anything. Death by crucifixion was designed to be as painful and as shameful as possible to deter the worst criminals from committing the worst crimes especially against the empire of Rome. Crimes like assassination, treason or defection. Jesus had not committed any crime against Rome but even the innocent experience shame, especially if sentenced as a criminal.

But this is worldly shame as was any shame connected to being a bastard in the world's eyes or homeless or insane.

By going to the cross Jesus was fulfilling all that he had left his Father and his kingdom to do, he was going to glorify, honour the Father and there is no shame in this ever regardless of how we are called to do it, regardless of how men see it. And so, there was never any shame connected to Christ's life, his birth circumstances or how he behaved for he did all things for his Father's glory alone.

Christ despised the shame because he saw, he knew what was really unfolding, he looked upon it from God's view not from man's. This was what he had been confined in skin for. Once his time had come, he did nothing to prevent it. He set his face like flint and allowed nothing to slow his journey to this last Passover where he was to be the sacrificial lamb.

Isaiah 53:7 says, '[Christ] was oppressed and He was afflicted, yet He opened not His mouth; He was led as a lamb to the slaughter,

---

[161] John Piper *Battling the unbelief of Misplaced Shame* Oct 2:1988 2Tim 1:6-12 Topic: Killing Sin desiringgod.org

and as a sheep before its shearers is silent, so He opened not His mouth.'

Christ demanded no rights, he voiced no opinion on the illegality of his trial, he did not resist.

Mark 15:3-5 tells us how this lack of voice astounded Pilate, '. . . the chief priests accused Him of many things, but He answered nothing. Then Pilate asked Him again, saying, "Do You answer nothing? See how many things they testify against You!" But Jesus still answered nothing, so that Pilate marveled.'

In fact, in one of the rare times he did speak it was to give evidence that the council could use to ask Pilate for the death penalty, as we read in Luke 22:70-71, 'Then they all said, "Are You then the Son of God?" So He said to them, "You rightly say that I am." And they said, "What further testimony do we need? For we have heard it ourselves from His own mouth."

Christ's reply 'You say I am' is a Greek idiom meaning 'Yes I am'. Jesus condemned himself as the Jewish council could not find any suitable witness statements that would.

Christ, and as a result all pilgrims can scorn shame, misplaced or well-placed that has lingered too long, once we have the biblical understanding in our heads, for we know as he where we have come from, where we are going and that all will be ours.

Joy, clouds and the cross

<u>Question</u>: What was the joy that was set before Christ mentioned in Hebrews 12:2, that enabled him to endure the cross and despise the shame? Do we as pilgrims have that same joy before us?

<u>Answer</u>: Luke 24: 25-26 reads, 'Then He said to them, "O foolish ones, and slow of heart to believe in all that the prophets have spoken! Ought not the Christ to have suffered these things and to enter into His glory?' Christ had glory with his Father before he put on skin and after he had fulfilled all that God had willed, he returned to that same state of glory though he kept his resurrected skin, the nail prints and spear wound. What joy to be

home! What joy to have had the victory, to have endured, to have finished the work assigned, to hear the Father's well done.

In the original languages of the Bible, capitalizing pronouns referring to God was not an issue. In Hebrew, there was no such thing as upper-case and lower-case letters. There was simply an alphabet, no capital letters at all. In Greek, there were capital (upper-case) letters and lower-case letters. However, in all of the earliest copies of the Greek New Testament, the text is written in all capital letters. When God inspired the human authors of Scripture to write His Word, He did not lead them to give any special attention to pronouns that refer to Him.[162]

Keeping this in mind, let's read Psalm 16:9-11, 'Therefore my heart is glad, and my glory rejoices; my flesh also will rest in hope. For You will not leave my soul in Sheol [the abode of the dead], nor will You allow Your Holy One to see corruption. You will show me the path of life; in Your presence is fullness of joy. At Your right hand are pleasures forevermore.'

Reading that *Your Holy One* will not see, undergo corruption, we know David is referring to Christ. But if those capitals are absent, we could think that David is referring to himself and so us for we are holy ones as pilgrims. This is New Testament teaching. When we as pilgrims physically die in this world it is but like going to sleep here and awaking in our Father's eternal kingdom but quicker. We will not be altered by death, corrupted, we will still be saved sinners by God's grace, having completed walking his path of life here, been perfected and moved on to there, to his presence and a fullness of joy we cannot comprehend while here and when there it will take us an eternity to grasp the joy and the pleasures that will be ours. O what joy to be home, surely that in itself would be enough. But what more joy to have no more sin to wage war against! What more joy to no longer live with the effects of being in a sinful world full of pain, suffering and tears!

---

[162] Should all pronouns referring to God be capitalized? https:// www.gotquestions.or

What joys upon joys to finally see our beloved Lord face to face and know him as he knows us – there are no words for such joy!!
Before we finish with this Hebrews passage 12:1-4, Theodore Epp has some concluding thoughts about this race, weights, sins, witnesses and clouds for you to think on –
Consider, first of all, the word "cloud" as it is used here. The word in the original . . . speaks . . .of a cloud mass that covers the heavens. These witnesses, then, are pictured as surrounding us like a cloud that covers the skies.
. . . the word "witnesses" . . . is speaking of those who have borne witness to the truth and, without question, it has reference to those individuals of faith spoken of in the eleventh chapter of Hebrews. So the picture is not so much that of persons watching us, but rather of those who have seen something and are bearing testimony to it. They have each witnessed in one way or another to their faith in Christ, and their witness gives inspiration to us as we fight the good fight of faith on the field of the Christian life.
In order to inspire and encourage us, these great witnesses to the faith who have gone before us have laid the foundation for every phase of the Christian life. There is no essential element in it that has not been covered by them, so that we can well say that the Bible has the answer for every problem that may face us. . . ..
Through the Word and through those who have witnessed to the truth, we have illustration, example, and inspiration in this great fight of faith. Therefore, the vast cloud of witnesses literally surrounds us wherever we may look.
. . . These witnesses do not illustrate what men and women have become on their own, but what men and women have become through the power of Christ working in them. We can even begin with the first phase of salvation and say that a person who is an all-out sinner can take heart in hearing the testimony of Rahab, the harlot, who by faith believed God and was saved [and included in Jesus' family tree, see Mat.1:5] . . .

The expression "let us lay aside every weight" is translated by Phillips in these words: "Strip off everything that hinders." . . .

Here are some of the weights that hinder us. Again and again they may seek to fasten themselves on us, but we must by prayer and faith lay them aside. One of these is selfish motives. Selfish motives may hinder because we want to impress others with ourselves rather than with Christ. We ought to look away unto Jesus and not seek things for ourselves. If we are seeking to make an impression on people to win applause for ourselves, we will be hindered in our race. A person running a foot race does not have time to think about the spectators and the effect he may be having upon them. If he tries to, he may break stride and lose the race. So it is in the spiritual race. . .

Another weight is that of touchiness. We run the race with Christians running alongside of us and often we are overly sensitive. If someone does not give us the recognition we think we ought to have, or applaud us when we have done something that we think is unusually good, we get our feelings hurt.

Jealousy could be another of those weights which we must set aside. Jealousy can hold us down and cause us to sit around and mope and pout, thinking that some others are getting ahead of us or maybe getting more recognition than we are. Such things exclude the power of God in His fullness in our lives, and for that very reason we are hindered from running the race. From these unchristian attitudes spring up factions which divide the people of God, and in place of the fruit of the Spirit is seen envy, evil temper, etc.

How can such things be set aside? If we follow our instructions by "looking unto Jesus the author and finisher of our faith," these things will drop off. . . "For if ye live after the flesh, ye shall die: but if ye through the Spirit do mortify the deeds of the body, ye shall live." [Rom.8:13] . . . "Likewise reckon ye also yourselves to be dead indeed unto sin, but alive unto God through Jesus Christ our Lord." [Rom6:11] We have to reckon ourselves to have died with Jesus Christ before the Spirit of God can work this victory in us. This calls for the exercise of faith in what God has said.

So it is by faith that we lay aside the weights. By faith we know that we have died with Jesus and that we are now alive unto God [because God has told us it is so]. We look to the Holy Spirit to make effective in our daily experience what is already true with regard to our position before God...

We are next told to lay aside the sin which doth so easily beset us. Phillips translates this as the "sin that dogs our feet." . . . as if we were running a race and something were hanging on our feet. . . a specific sin . . . a sin to which we easily succumb.

The first sin that would be suggested to us in the light of the study we have had in the eleventh chapter of Hebrews is unbelief. "Without faith it is impossible to please Him". Unbelief is the opposite of faith, and it is a sin which constantly dogs the Christian. Faith, on the other hand, is simply taking God at His Word. A good brother in the Lord often said, "I have the Word for it; the Word says it; that settles it." What the Word says should always settle matters for the Christian. . . . Our faith will grow as we meditate on the Word of God day and night.

This race is to be run with patience . . . a spiritual virtue that needs to be cultivated. . . "Strengthened with all might, according to his glorious power, unto all patience and longsuffering with joyfulness" (Col.1:11) . . . There is no lack [to God's power] . . . our competition is not with other believers, but with the forces of sin and Satan.

. . . "looking unto Jesus" . . . we see Jesus with the eye of faith. This is the light for our soul. Now if our eye is single, that is, if it has but one aim or one purpose in life, one delight, one direction, then we shall be filled with light. The singleness of aim is due to our attitude of heart . . . To Paul, there was one great aim in life. He said, "For me to live is Christ." He had no other purpose in living.

On the other hand, the eye that is evil will throw us off balance. If we try to keep one eye on God, and the other eye on self or on the world, then we will run into difficulties. It is then that covetousness, hardness of heart, envy, complaining, grudge-carrying, and all of these other things show up in our conduct.

This is how light becomes darkness. We try to see two things at the same time, but only the single eye that sees Jesus can bring light into the soul. We cannot serve two masters. If we serve God for His approval and at the same time the applause of men, then our eye is double. Darkness is in our hearts.

Our Saviour is described as the Author and Finisher of our faith. . . Our faith originates in Him and is a gift from Him . . . [and He finishes what He starts] ". . . bringing many sons to glory . . ." [Heb.2:10]

In this [Christ's death on the cross, Phil 2:6-8] He is our greatest witness or example of faith. To benefit from His example we must by faith renounce the things this world may hold for the glory that He has set before us. The love of Christ will constrain us to reach this goal. Let us then, look away, to Jesus. Let us consider Him who endured such contradiction of sinners against Himself, lest we be wearied and faint in our minds.[163]

> Mind this. By believing his pardon by the blood, his justification by the righteousness of Christ, the free everlasting love of God to him, by the witness of His Spirit, and the glory of heaven to which he is going, are what strengthens the Christian's heart against all his lusts and corruptions. [164]

Spurgeon writes that 'In every believer's heart there is a constant struggle between the old nature and the new . . . Grace within us will employ prayer, faith, hope and love to cast out the evil. It takes to it the *'whole armour of God'* (Eph 6:11) and wrestles earnestly. These two opposing natures will never cease to struggle as long as we are in this world. Bunyan's pilgrim, Christian, battled with Apollyan for three hours, but Christian's battle with himself lasted all the way from the Wicket gate to the river Jordan. . .

---

[163] *Faith in Action* p172-183

[164] *The Pilgrim's Progress* comment by Mason p92

Although we are troubled, and often in sore conflict, we have an almighty Helper, even Jesus, the Captain of our salvation. He is ever with us and assures us that we will eventually be 'more than conquerors through him' (Rom 8:37). With such assistance the newborn nature is more than a match for its foes . . . Are Satan, the world, and the flesh all against you? Do not be discouraged or dismayed. Fight on, for God Himself is with you! Jehovah-Nissi is your banner, and Jehovah-Rophi is the healer of your wounds. Fear not, for you will overcome. Who can defeat Omnipotence? Fight on, *'looking unto Jesus'* (Heb 12:2). Though the conflict is long and stern, sweet will be the victory and glorious the promised reward.'[165]

Our fleshy lusts or appetites may desire to destroy our soul, they may succeed in killing our body in their attempts to destroy our soul but they cannot kill our soul, only God can do that but he has promised pilgrims eternal life. In fact, as pilgrims here we already have entered into eternal life and the Holy Spirit is our guarantee and witness to the truth of this. So, my dear reader, may you fight with vigour and patient endurance for you are, as a pilgrim, on the winning side with nothing but joy and pleasure ahead of you. Let us thank God – through Jesus Christ our Lord.

---

[165] *Morning and Evening* Morning *June 2nd* p320

Interlude 1: A word on despondency

Just thinking . . .
You my dear reader may breeze through this life here whether you are a pilgrim or not, I do not now, nor did I before I became a pilgrim. Many a time I have felt confused about the circumstances of life and how best to negotiate my way through while causing the least damage to others and myself. There have been times where my motives or facial expressions were misunderstood and I was erroneously judged by those who I had presumed knew me well enough to not do so. This has caused my heart to pain, to become so despondent that I considered quitting the struggle to live simply because it was too painful and confusing. Other times I considered leaving the church I attended, but if the minister is not preaching heresy, one church is as good (or as bad) as another for all pilgrims are a work in progress. And then other times I have considered quitting believing in God, but Peter's words were mine, there was nowhere else to go (John 6:67-69).

<u>Question</u>: But is this the way a pilgrim should be? How can I, how can you, fight against these thoughts and feelings that seem to give a lie to the sufficiency of my Lord for all needs?
Did Jesus ever show any signs of depression? What makes you feel fearfully anxious? As a human Jesus had plenty of reasons why he could have been, few seemed to understand what he was about, the Jews (his people) wanted him ran out of town at first then later dead, he was in demand for what he could do and provide but not many seemed to care about his person. How would you have felt living with these circumstances? How can we be like Christ in this, is it possible, are we meant to?

Answer: Have you realized that most of your unhappiness in life is due to the fact that you are listening to yourself instead of talking to yourself.[166]

Now, please, do not hear me wrongly on this subject. Not only have I had to have several years of counselling I am also taking medication for the rest of my life to fight depression, fears and worries, being told I have probably suffered from this for most of my childhood and adulthood without it being diagnosed. I find the medication actually helps me to think more clearly and gives me more energy to fight rather than flap against what I know to be wrong. I believe what I am putting up for you to read rings true and so is worthwhile considering even if it is an uncomfortable challenge to my, your way of thinking.

After Christ's final Passover meal where he instigated what we now call Communion or the Lord's Supper and after Judas had left the room to betray him and having just informed Peter that he would not be laying his life down for his master's sake as wished but instead would deny him not once but three times, Jesus had much to say to the remaining eleven disciples including these verses, "Let not your heart be troubled; you believe in God, believe also in Me. In My Father's house are many mansions; if it were not so, I would have not told you. I go to prepare a place for you. And if I go and prepare a place for you, I will come again and receive you to Myself; that where I am, there you may be also. . ..
And I will pray the Father, and He will give you another Helper, that He may abide with you forever. . . . Peace I leave with you,
My peace I give to you; not as the world gives do I give to you.
Let not your heart be troubled, neither let it be afraid." (John 14:1-3, 16, 27)

That's a big ask, do you not think, to have peace, to be untroubled and unafraid within your heart as you witness the arrest, trial, the walk out of Jerusalem, and crucifixion of the one you have left all

---

[166] Dr Martyn Lloyd-Jones (1899-1981) *Spiritual Depression* Pickering& Inglis 1965 p20

for? Thinking of some of these verses and of the many tribulations, trials, from the mild to the potentially terminal, John Bunyan set out to answer his similar questions and how to apply them to self and life from the Bible in great detail in his writing titled *Heart's Ease in Heart Trouble* from which the following pages are quoted.

Quest. But is it possible that we should be afflicted, deprived of liberty, of estate, of loving relations, of the desire of our eyes, and of the delight of our hearts, (for such, in a most eminent manner, was Jesus Christ to his disciples – he was "the desire of all nations,") and not be troubled at our very hearts? . . . May we arrive to such a temper; may we get such a calm, quiet, tranquil, and submissive frame of spirit? It is admirable, but is it attainable?

Doct. "That the lively acting of true faith upon God and Christ, or upon God in Christ, is the best preventative of, and remedy against heart trouble, under the greatest loss whatever.

Or,

Faith acted on God in Christ, is the sovereign cure of heart trouble." [Consider the following]

God had but one Son without sin, but no son without suffering . . . Job xiv. 1, "Man that is born of a woman is full of trouble." As our relations and comforts increase, so do the occasions of trouble. If we can, through mercy, obtain a tolerable passage through this world, and a comfortable passage out of it into that better above, we shall have cause to bless the Lord to all eternity.

And much more, as Christians, must we expect troubles. . .

. . . So it must be our care to provide for afflictions; for to prevent them altogether we cannot; but prepare for them we may, and must . . . ; to treasure up God's promises, and store our souls with graces, and spiritual comforts, and firm resolutions in God's strength, to bear up and hold on: we had need be well "shod with the preparation of the gospel of peace." Eph. vi. 15.

. . . David, Psal. xlii. 5, "Why art thou cast down, O my soul? Why art thou disquieted within me?" He was sensible of his afflictions, and that disquieted him, and cast him down. God's people are subject to such disquietments, because they are flesh and blood, subject to the same mould, subject to the same impressions without as other men, and their natures are upheld with the same supports and refreshments as others, the withdrawings and want of which affecteth them as well as others. And besides those troubles they suffer in common with others, by reason of their being called out of the world, the world hates them, and they are therefore more exposed to tribulation than others, and so are apt to be cast down and discouraged: this our Lord foresaw . . . and therefore he counsels them against the same; "Let not your hearts be troubled."

Quest. But it may be demanded, "Whence ariseth this heart trouble and disquietment of mind under affliction?

Answ. There are many causes of it, which is necessary for us to know, that so, knowing the causes, we may the better find the cure; there are outward and inward causes.

First, Outward causes. . . . the first may be God himself. He sometimes withdraws the beams of his countenance, with-holds the sense of his love, hideth his face from his children: (which the saints in Scripture so bitterly complain of and so earnestly pray against.) . . .

. . . The devil is the cause sometimes . . . For he being a cursed spirit cast out of heaven, full of disquietment and discontent himself labours all he can to trouble and disquiet others, to bring others, (as much as in him lies,) into the same cursed condition with himself. . .

Two main designs the devil hath upon men; the one is, if possible, by all imaginable slights, temptations, and enticements, he may keep men in a course of ungodliness, to hinder them from coming to Christ be faith and repentance, to deter them from his holy ways. And when he is not able to do this, but that unsearchable rich and free grace takes hold of some poor souls, and they are snatched out of his hands, their captivity led captive by that mighty Redeemer, then all the devil's labour is to hinder their comfort, and to interrupt their peace, and to make their way to heaven as hard and uncomfortable to them as possible, pursuing them with all dejecting and heart-troubling temptations.

. . . Wicked men are also active in the troubling of God's people . . with reproaches . . . reproachful scorn shows an utter disrespect of a man, which flows from the very superfluity of malice. "Reproach hath broken my heart," saith David, Psal. lxxix. 20, and nothing more doth he complain of than reproach . . .

Secondly, There are inward causes also . . .: when God's people are in affliction, most time that black cloud of melanchloly also surrounds them, and darkness makes men fearful and dejected.

There are many causes within ourselves, as ignorance of God, and of Christ, of the covenant of grace, of the name of God. They that know the name of God, will trust him and not be dejected. Also, forgetfulness of God, and of what he hath done for us. We forget God when we are afraid of man. Our overlooking, and passing by the many comforts we enjoy, even while we are under affliction, taking little notice of our mercies, but let them be all swallowed up in our miseries . . .

It is an evil thing for us to be wedded to our own wills. None more subject to discontent, than those who would have all things after their own way, and are mere strangers to self-denial. Likewise, false apprehension of things . . .; to think God hates us because he corrects us, and when he takes from us, that it is all in wrath. Another common cause is our own watchlessness and carelessness, our neglect of keeping our hearts and consciences pure and clean; and in time of affliction, these former neglects of duty come to our minds; then conscience awakes, and tells our former faults, and this brings trouble of heart. . .

Moreover, unnecessary scruples cause disquietness, solitariness, idleness; when persons will not do what is needful, they are troubled with that which is needless; and idleness tempts the devil to tempt us and trouble us: if we cannot find work for ourselves, the devil will make work for us.

Inconstantly wavering in the ways of God . . . And our inordinate love of creature-comforts, our setting of our hearts on friends, estates, and the like, letting out our hearts on husbands, wives, children, &c., this is to build castles in the air, expecting contentment in and from those things that cannot yield it. Also, multitude of worldly business, and too much pouring on our afflictions, and forecasting the events of things . . .

Q. . . . What is this heart trouble which Christ here forbids his people, and that he would fortify them against?

A. This heart trouble is such a sense of evils felt or feared, as creates to us heart disquietment, dejection, despondency, depriving us of that tranquillity, peace, and comfort which we had in ourselves, or otherwise might have: it is such a disturbance of our passions, such a storm and tempest in our spirits, as causeth inward motions, emotions, and commotions of mind, putting all things in the soul out of order, and it carries in it several evil things . . .

First, Sinful sorrow, worldly sorrow . . . The ground of this sorrow is from ourselves, from our own hearts, though Satan will have a hand in it; and it comes . . . from pride; because we cannot have our wills, therefore we are discontented. We may thank ourselves not only for our troubles, but for our overmuch troubling ourselves in our troubles. If we ward and guard against this worldly sorrow, our troubles would not lie so heavy on us as they do; for as the joy of the Lord doth raise and strengthen the soul, so doth sorrow deject and weaken it. Sorrow and grief doth lie like lead to the heart, cold and heavy, and sinks it downward still; sorrow contracteth and draweth the soul into itself, from that communion and comfort it might have with God and man; and it weakeneth the execution of the offices of it because it drinketh up the spirits, it melteth the soul, it causeth it to drop away. Yea, in this kind of heart trouble, God's own people are many times more excessive than others . . . as their joys are unspeakable and glorious, so their sorrows are sometimes above expression . . . They have a greater sense than others . . . also a clearer judgement than others, and see more into the nature of things . . . they see a greater evil in sin, and in the displeasure of God . . . they value God's favour more . . . They observe more of the displeasure of God in afflictive providences . . . and therefore they have more sorrow . . .

Quest. But is this worldly sorrow lawful and commendable?
Answ. No . . . there are many evils in it, which we should avoid. .

1. Impatience and murmuring against God . . . when our wills are crossed . . .

2. Quarrelling at instruments.

3. Using indirect means for our relief. It is better to pine away in our afflictions, than to be freed from them by sinning.

4. Desponding and distrustful thoughts of God . . .

5. Questioning our interest in God, merely because of the afflictions upon us.

6. Sometimes atheistical thoughts do arise, as if there were no God, no Providence, . . . as if it were in vain to serve the Lord.

7. . . . indisposeth to all good duties; it makes a man like an instrument out of tune, or a bone out of joint: which makes the body move both uncomely and painfully; it unfits for duty to God and man.

8. It makes a man forget former mercies, and overlook present mercies . . .

9. It makes us unfit to receive, mercies, and embrace the best counsels: such plasters will not stick; they refuse to be comforted.

10. It disposeth us to receive any temptation. Satan hath never more advantage than upon discontent.

11. It hinders beginners from coming unto the ways of God.

12. It rejoiceth and hardeneth the wicked . . . Let our sins lie heavy upon us, and then our afflictions will lie light. Let us grow weary of our sins, not of our sufferings. . . consider, also, the real spiritual benefit of affliction. God aims at our profit; and in good time, in the best time, he will send deliverance.

... Lam. iii. 65, "Give them sorrow of heart, thy curse." As godly sorrow is God's blessing, a grace of God's Spirit, a fruit of faith, Zech. xii. 10, so worldly sorrow is God's curse, and a bitter fruit of unbelief...

Secondly, Another piece of heart-trouble is sinful fear... as verse 27. As if he had said, Let not that distemper of base slavish fear seize your hearts...

This fear is a tyrant where is comes, and it tyrannizeth where it prevails...

But we must distinguish of fear.

1. There is a natural, lawful fear, when evils are approaching to our bodies, or names, of friends, or the like dangers are apparent... it was in Christ himself. Mark xii. 14, 15. Also, it is said, "he feared, and was sore amazed," Mark xiv. 33, yet without sin.

2. There is a lawful filial fear of God's judgements, which ariseth from the consideration of the evil of sin, and of God's righteousness; and of his hatred of sin, and his wrath against it: which fear produceth repentance, self-examination, a repentance, self-examination, a turning to God with our whole hearts, through reformation, and an endeavour to secure ourselves in God's covenant, and hide ourselves...

3. There is a base, slavish fear of approaching evils, arising from our misapprehensions of God producing in us unworthy thoughts, sinking into despondency, and inciting to murmuring and impatience, and putting us upon sinful shifts, the use of unlawful means to prevent or excape dangers; a fear of despondency, a vexatious, distracting fear, that drives from God, and unfits for service; a tormenting, disquieting fear, that unsettles and discomposeth our minds, disturbs our peace, suspends our acts of faith, and disposeth us to diffidence, distrust, and impatience: this is the fear that Christ would not have his people's hearts troubled with.

Thirdly, Another... is care, vexatious distracting care, which our Lord would not have his disciples trouble themselves with, and therefore he useth so many powerful arguments to dissuade them from it. Matt. vi., from ver. 25 onward. 1. He assures us, it is

God that takes care for our bodily life; we trust him with that; how much more should we for food and raiment. 2. Saith he, your Father takes care for the fowls, and provides for them; "are ye not much better than they?" 3. He clotheth the lilies, "and will he not clothe you?" 4. You cannot, by all your care, make your condition better than God hath appointed it shall be, ver. 27. 5. Your heavenly Father knows you want all these things. 6. They that are ignorant of God, and of his fatherly care and good providence, . . . they trouble themselves with those cares; therefore you should not do so who have a heavenly Father that dearly loves you, and looks after you. 7. You have the promise of the faithful God, to have all necessaries provided for you, while you make it your care to serve, and please, and trust him; ver. 33, "All these things shall be added unto you." 8. We have no cause to be thoughtful for time to come, because every day brings evil enough with it; and therefore it is no wisdom to perplex ourselves with cares . . . Our Lord also shows us how prejudicial such cares are to our profiting by the word, Matt. xiii. 22; and expressly commands us, "to cast our cares upon him, for he careth for us." 1Peter v. 7.

Fourthly, Despondency of spirit, dejectedness, distrust, discouragement, are other pieces of heart trouble . . . Casting down breeds disquietiness, because it springs from pride, which is a turbulent passion; and everything that crosseth and disappoints it, causeth a combustion in the mind. When a man cannot come down, and stoop to that condition that God casts him into, then is he discontented; and this comes from his pride. . . It is the Lord that appoints all our conditions for us . . . To like our condition, to be pleased with it, and with the holy will of God in it; that is, to be content, content with sickness, poverty, shame, prison, loss of relations and friends, &c. . . . when our wills lie even with God's wills, (as in reason they should,) and our minds lie even with our conditions, then have we inward peace, and tranquillity, quietness, and contentment, and never till then . . .

This distrust of God's providence is a grand evil; when we think we cannot live, unless we have a greater portion of earthly things, and this sets us upon carking cares, we know not how we and ours will be provided for . . . Now this we may cure, by casting ourselves upon God's promises . . . Let us cast ourselves on God's providence. Will he provide for ravens, lilies, and neglect his own children? It cannot be imagined.

Earthly things are but a vain show, they can give us no joy of heart, nor peace of conscience: they cannot add one cubit to our stature, nor one moment to our lives.

Fifthly, Persecution may cause heart trouble, when men are offended. . . . Our Lord did on purpose foretell his disciples what persecutions they should undergo, that they might not be offended, John xvi. 1; forewarned, forearmed. It is a blessed thing not to be offended at persecution for Christ. . . To be troubled at persecution for Christ's sake, is to be offended at the cross of Christ . . .

Sixthly, Temptations from Satan . . . Satan's suggestions, his fiery darts, those tormenting thoughts which he casts into the minds of Christ's disciples, create to them much disturbance . . . Christ hath overcome the world, and therefore bids his disciples be of good cheer, John xvi. 33, so hath he also overcome the devil; he hath trodden this serpent under his feet already, and this prince of peace will tread him under your feet also shortly. . .

Seventhly, Desertion . . . Sometimes God but doth seem to hide his face . . . Sometimes God doth really forsake his people, as to the sense of his favour . . . God's people may lose the sense of his love, but never lose his love, for that is everlasting. But to lose the sense of his love, is a grievous trouble to a . . . soul, that hath tasted and felt the love of God and his favour; for their great happiness is to have the favour of God: "In his favour is life, and his lovingkindness is better than life." This is the joy of their lives. (Psal. cxix. 135) . . . No such as have found this, must needs be troubled when they lose it.

Two things chiefly cause God to hide . . .

1. When their hearts are too much set upon, and carried out after earthly comforts . . . When a man smiles so much on the world, and gives it so much room in his heart, God frowns, and is

offended that the gift should be so much loved, and the giver so neglected.

2. When their hearts are let out too little after God, and there grows a strangeness between God and them, and they begin to grow cold, dull and dead in duty . . .

Q. But how is it so [that believing in God and in Christ, is the best antidote against this sinful heart trouble]?

A. . . . What this faith in God is; . . . Heb. xi. 6 . . . to believe that God is that, which he hath revealed himself in his word to be; viz., that he is an all-sufficent, almighty, only-wise God; a righteous, gracious, merciful God; a holy God, a loving God . . . Exod. xxxiv. 6, 7 . . . To believe that he is wonderful in counsel, and excellent in working. Isa. xxviii. Last. That he is the Father of mercies, the true and faithful God of all grace, and of all consolation; with many more admirable attributes of God doth the Scripture furnish us, that we may build our faith, and place our trust in him, to prevent heart trouble. . .

Also this faith in God, is to believe that "he is a rewarder of them that diligently seek him."

That he being God all-sufficent, he is able to support, to supply, to deliver his people out of all their troubles, and that he is willing to do so, as well as able, for he has promised; and he is a rewarder, a God that will abundantly, plentifully, reward all his suffering ones; great shall be their reward in heaven. Matt. v. 12. And to believe God to be a rewarder, is to lay hold on his covenant, wherein he promiseth so to be . . . I will give thee grace and glory, and will with-hold no good thing from thee. I that am the infinite first and best being of all things, the living fountain of all mercy, the original of all power and goodness: I will be a God to thee, thy God, thy Father, if thou wilt take me for thy God, and place all thy happiness in me, and wilt become my servant, and give up thyself sincerely to me, to serve and obey, to love and fear, and trust me only. This is to believe in God, to accept of God for our God, and yield up ourselves to be his people. . . Gen. xii. 1, 2, 3, Gen. xv. 1, and Gen. xvii. 1, I am God all-sufficient; all sufficient to support thee in thy way, and work, and all-sufficient to reward thee in the end; therefore, be thou upright and faithful; let not your heart be troubled, whatever dangers and difficulties thou meetest with in my way and work, and what losses soever thou sustainest for my sake, believe, I am God all-sufficient; I will sufficiently reward thee; thou shalt be no loser by following and serving me . . . act your faith in God, and seriously consider what God that is in whom you believe; and believing also your interest in that God, that he is your God, this God all-sufficient is your God . . . Your acting of faith on God, your God, will prevent and cure your heart trouble, and that these several ways.

First more generally.

He that believes in God as his God, believes God is always present with him, according to his promises. . . God is always present with his people, and that for gracious purposes, (and not as a bare spectator) as to proportion and measure out their afflictions to them, that they may not be above their strength, nor more than need. 1Cor. x. 13; 1Pet. i. 6. All the afflictions of God's people are measured by the hand of the most wise, most merciful, and gracious God; all the malice of men and devils cannot add a drachm to the weight, nor a drop to the measure, beyond God's appointment. He is present to order and fix the time of our sufferings . . . It is our loving Father that sets up the glass of the time of our troubles; he appoints their beginning, their duration, their end . . . All the powers of earth cannot bring trouble on us, till the hour come . . . nor continue our troubles longer than his time. . . God is present to mix some comforts with the cross, thereby to allay the bitterness of it; present to support the soul with inward strength . . . present to sanctify afflictions for good, and at length, in his good time, which is the best time, when he hath perfected his own work in his people, he is present or their full deliverance. . . .

More particularly . . . When he gives to his people, he gives in love; when he takes, he takes in love. Now, when a soul believes that all is from love, and all in love, he is supported. When a man can believe that all his troubles come to him from the Father of mercies, and his Father in Christ, he cannot but bear them patiently...

Q. But how shall I know that God loves me when he afflicts me?
I answer, when we can discern that we have received any spiritual benefit by any affliction, we may certainly conclude that the love of God was in that affliction. Fury is not in God toward his people. Isa. xxvii. 4. And he intends nothing but our good: to purge away our sins, to wean us from the world, to draw us nearer to himself, to humble us, to try us, to conform us to Christ, to prepare us for glory, &c. . .

Secondly, Faith acted upon God's glorious attributes will fortify against heart trouble... upon this all-sufficiency ... all-mighty... absolute sovereignty and supremacy ... his unchangeableness .. his wisdom... righteousness ... faithfulness

Thirdly, Faith acted on the covenant of grace, God's everlasting covenant, will help to support under trouble... This acting of faith in God's covenant supported David in his greatest troubles; 2Sam. xxiii. 5 . . . though his family was wasted and blasted, this answered all, that "he was in covenant with God." . . .

Fourthly, Faith acted upon the word of God, will support the soul. . . . believe God's word, the word of truth; . . . the word of promise; . . . the word of threatening, Matt. x. 37. . .we should consider that when these are removed, that Christ remains ours still, and with us still; our relation to him is not broken; and Christ will be instead of all and better than all to us . . ; the examples of God's saints in the world . . . "to be followers of them who through faith and patience inherit the promises." Heb. vi. 12.; the word of experience. David tells us his experience, and saith, "It was good for him that he had been afflicted." And many Christians living can, and do bless God for their afflictions, and that God, by taking away of their relations from them, he made more room in their hearts fro himself, and communicated more of himself to their souls.

Fifthly, Faith acted upon the work of God . . . he that doeth whatsoever he pleaseth.

Sixthly, Faith acted on the will of God. . . Luke xxii. 42; and so we pray continually, "Thy will be done:" and therefore when it is done, our hearts must not be troubled.

Lastly, Faith acted on the gracious ends and designs of God in afflicting us, and removing our earthly comforts from us, will prevent heart trouble. . . Such ends as these,

1. . . . to discover and purge away our sins. Isa. xxvii. 9. . .

2. To try and exercise our graces. Job xxiii. 10; 1Pet. i. 6, 7.

3. To crucify our hearts unto, and to estrange our affections from the things of this world.

4. To draw our hearts nearer to himself . . .

5. To bestow greater, and better mercies upon us. God never takes away any darling comfort from his people, but his design is, to give a better in the room of it . . . John xiv. 7.

6. To make them partakers of his holiness. Heb. xii. 10.

7. To fit and prepare them for that far more exceeding and eternal weight of glory. 2Cor. iv. 17..

THE SECOND QUESTION

. . . . What is it to believe in Christ?

In general, it is to believe all that which is revealed in the holy Scriptures concerning Christ; to believe the record that God hath given of him in his word, as 1John v. 10-13. To believe that Jesus Christ is the eternal Son of God. John i. 18. That he came out from the Father; was made flesh; took upon him our nature; was born of a virgin; lived on earth in the form of a servant, a poor despicable life; preached the gospel, working miracles, &c. That he suffered upon the cross, with all the sins of his people upon his soul and body; that he bore the cross of the law, the wrath of God, which was due to man for sin. That he died a most painful, shameful, and cruel death, dying as a sacrifice, to satisfy God's justice, to atone and pacify his wrath, to make our peace, and to reconcile us to God. That he rose again from the dead, ascended into heaven, to prepare a place there for his people; that he sitteth at the right hand of God everlasting, to make continual intercession for us: and that he shall come to judge the world at the last day: and while he is absent from us in person here on earth, he promised to send his Spirit the Comforter into the world, to convince and convert all those which his Father hath given him, to call them by his word, to quicken, strengthen, establish, comfort, and confirm them, until he come again, "to take them to himself, that where he is, they may be also." John xiv. 1, 2. This is the record that God hath given of his Son; "that whosoever believeth in him, should not perish, but have everlasting life." John iii. 16, 36. Now to believe in Christ, is to believe all this testimony of him. And . . . to come unto him weary and heavy laden with our sins, heartly willing to accept of the Lord Jesus upon his own terms, to take him for our only Lord, to give up our whole selves, souls and bodies, to his blessed government by his word and Spirit in all things, and unfeignedly and unreservedly to enter into covenant with him, to become his, and his alone, and his forever; and to rely upon him for life, for grace and salvation; this is to believe in Christ. . . .

Q. But what is that in Christ which faith must act upon, to effect this cure of heart trouble when afflictions come upon us?

A. Such like things (as I showed before) as are in God for faith to act upon, which are these, that follow:

First, Faith must be acted upon the loving gracious sweet nature of Jesus Christ. . . His thoughts of us who believe in him, were thoughts of love from everlasting. . . He loved us, and gave himself for us . . . He is one of our nature, our kinsman . . .

Act your faith on Christ as yours, your Jesus, he that died for you, he that sweated great drops of blood for you in the garden, wrestling and grappling with his Father's wrath for you in your name and stead there, an upon the cross. Consider, that this your dearest Jesus now in glory, knows your souls in adversity; he seeth all the trouble of your hearts, he sympathizeth with you in all your afflictions, his heart now in heaven, "is touched with the feeling of your infirmities" on earth. Heb. iv. 15. He hath human nature still, though glorified. He feels our losses, crosses, griefs, pains, and sorrows; his heart, his most tender heart, is affected. O that we could but believe this! . . . believe in Jesus, look up by faith unto Jesus your dear Lord; whatsoever, whosoever you have lost, you have not lost your Jesus, your best friend, your heavenly husband:: you have his heart, his bowels towards you still; you have his eye, his tender, watchful, provident eye upon you still; you have his ear open to your cries still; yea, you have his everlasting arms underneath you to sustain you still, for else you would sink . . .

If we read these things, or hear them read, and do not apply them to our own souls by faith; if we do not meditate on them, and let them sink down into our hearts, if we do not pray earnestly that the holy Spirit would bring them home, and lay them close to and fix them on our hearts, they will do us no good, yield us no comfort; therefore meditate on them, apply them, and act faith upon them.

Secondly, We must act faith upon the many precious attributes of Jesus Christ . . . these are exceeding many. I shall mention only some.

First, Jesus Christ is our advocate with the Father. 1John ii. 1,2. . . when men accuse us, and our own consciences too; when we are deprived of our near and dear relations, distressed with pains and sicknesses, pinched with wants and necessities . . .

To have a friend in heaven, and such a friend, so wise, so powerful, so faithful, so merciful, so sensibly affected with all our misery, so tender, so able, and so willing to bear and help us; I say, this is infinitely better than all the friends that ever we had, or could have on earth; and this friend liveth; and maketh continual intercession for us. . .

Secondly, Jesus Christ is bread from heaven: the true bread for souls, the bread of life, the water of life. John vi. 35, 48, 51. Now when poor saints are fed with the bread of affliction, and with the water of adversity, let them look up to Christ, and act faith upon him, he will be living bread, life-giving bread, living water to their souls, to revive their drooping, and to refresh their fainting spirits.

. . When your souls want strength to bear your burdens, want comfort in your distresses, act faith on this Jesus, this bread of life, this water of life, and you shall be refreshed, you shall have joy and peace in believing. Rom. xv. 13.

Thirdly, Jesus Christ is called "the sun of righteousness, and the bright morning star." Mal. iv.2. Rev. xxii. 16. He is the fountain of righteousness and life, as the sun is of light; he hath healing in his wings. "he was wounded for our transgressions, that by his stripes we might be healed." Isa. liii. 4,5, and lxi. 1,2. He was appointed to heal the broken hearted. Luke iv. He will heal our backslidings. Hos. xiv. 4. . . . He is the bright and morning star. We are in darkness, clouds and darkness upon our spirits; many dark providences befall us, we see not our way many times, know not what to do: now, let us act faith on Jesus, he will bring light out of darkness. We are under black fears and sorrows, and all dark night sometimes with us: but if we can look up to this bright morning star, he will enlighten our darkness, he will shine In upon our hearts, and scatter all the clouds . . .

Fourthly, Jesus Christ is called the "captain of the Lord's hosts, and the captain of our salvation." Josh. v.14,15; Heb. ii. 10. He hath the command of all the creatures, for he is "head over all things", Eph. i. 22, over men and devils; "all power in heaven and on earth is his." Matt. xxviii. 18. . . . What can hurt us? What should we fear? . . . No creature, no man, no devil, can act anything against us without our Lord's leave. . . Let us make him our leader, and by faith in him we shall be more that conquerors. He hath overcome the devil and the world for us, and he will overcome all our corruptions, fears and sorrows in us, and will shortly set his crown upon our heads. . . "and in bringing of many sons to glory, he was made perfect through suffering." Heb. ii. 14; John xvi. last. Act faith in him who hath perfected our salvation for us. That work is done, and it was done through suffering . . . And then have we any cause to let our hearts be troubled with sinful fears, cares, and sorrows? Have we any cause to be cast down and discouraged while we are walking conformable to him, travelling the same way to heaven that he went hither, the same way to glory, the way of reproach, shame, grief, sorrow, fear, poverty, persecution, tribulation, desertion, the same steps that our Lord went to glory? O that we could but still keep our eye on Jesus, and often consider what way he went to heaven! And being our captain, we should show ourselves his good soldiers, and be content to go the same way.

Fifthly, Jesus Christ is called the "consolation of Israel," Luke ii. 25 . . .He is the only person that brings true comfort being the fountain of the spring of all consolation . . . And it is his promise, that when he hath brought his people into the wilderness of fears and troubles, that they know not which way to turn, that then he will speak comfortably to them, will speak to their hearts, as the word in the original signifies. Hos. ii. 14.

Sixthly, Jesus Christ is called a counsellor. Isa. ix. 6. He is most wise; he is the "wisdom of the Father: in him are hid all the treasures of wisdom and knowledge." Col. ii. 3. Yes, he is made of God our wisdom. 1Cor. i. 30. So that when we are in doubts and darkness, perplexed with temptations, and know not what to do; when we are under sad and dark providences, and know not how to interpret them; when we are under various exercises, and know not how to answer God's ends in them, nor how to improve them; when we are in the dark, and know not the meaning of God's dispensations, nor the design of God in them: now are our hearts troubled in all such cases: but here is our remedy, this is the course we must take: act faith now upon Jesus; he is wisdom, he is a most wise and faithful counsellor; we may freely open all our cases and conditions to him; he will not betray us or bewray us; we may safely trust him with all the secrets of our hearts; and let us labour by faith to trust him for counsel in all cases; let us wait for his counsel, trust to it, and "let not your hearts be troubled."

Seventhly, Jesus is a Redeemer, that is his name: he came into the world on this very business, to redeem his people from all iniquity, Tit. ii. 14, "from this present evil world, from our vain conversations." He hath shed his precious blood to purchase us:

"we are bought with a price." 1Cor. vi. 20. We are none of our own; we are his, the purchase of his blood; and we may be confident that he dearly loves us, for he dearly bought us; and if he had not dearly loved us, he would never have given himself for us. Gal. ii. 20. That was the highest testimony of his love: "He loved us, and washed us from our sins in his blood." Rev. i. 5. He will redeem us from the wrath to come. O! then, let us act faith on our sweet Redeemer, as Job did in the midst of all his troubles. "I know," saith he, "that my Redeemer liveth," &c. So may every believer say, although my friends and dearest relations die, my credit and estate dies; though my outward comforts all die, this supports me, that "me Redeemer liveth," and this our Redeemer is mighty, mighty to save, able to save to the uttermost. Heb. vii. 25.

Therefore, let us act faith on our dear Redeemer, and upon his redemption, and let us believe that shortly the day of our full redemption will come, when we shall be delivered fully and for ever from sin, Satan, and the world: from all our burdens, fears, and sorrows, temptations and tribulations.

I might mention many other sweet names and titles of Jesus Christ, which would be food for faith to feed upon: as, that he is the everlasting Father, Isa. ix. 6, . . . the Prince of peace . . . Isa. lvii. 19. He is also our Shepherd, therefore (said David) I shall want nothing. Psal. xxiii. 1. He is a fountain opened, a fountain of light, life, love, grace, and truth. He is the head of his body, the church. The husband, the bridegroom . . . He is the "heir of all things." Heb. i. 2. . . . He is the "King of saints, the rock of ages." Yea, he is all and in all." O beloved! Had we but faith to act on this blessed Jesus . . . Let our faith but apprehend, apply, and appropriate Jesus as our blessed head, our most dear husband, and then consider in earnest who he is, and what he is : how mighty, how full, loving, pitiful, compassionate, tender-hearted, and kind; how ready to help, how engaged to us by many promises, and can we then take up such unworthy thoughts of him, as to think he hath forgotten us? Will he not timely support and supply us? Hath he shed his blood for us, and will he forget us? . . . Surely it is our want, or the weakness of our faith, that causeth all our heart trouble. . . apply and appropriate Christ to our souls, and act faith upon those precious names of Christ, which are not as so many empty titles which are sometimes given to men, but they are real representations of that most dear love and tender affection, of that special care, mercy, and loving-kindness that is in Jesus towards all his poor children, that they might draw out the same for their strong consolation; and that they might trust in him, and not despond, nor be dejected . . .

Thirdly, Faith acted on the covenant of grace, whereof Christ is the mediator, and upon all his exceeding great and precious promises, will prevent all heart trouble. Believe in the blessed Mediator of the new covenant, who hath undertaken, not only on God's part, to see that his part be performed to us, but also is become our surety; undertaking for us, and by himself, to fulfil the whole law of God, both actively and passively; "to fulfil all righteousness" for us, and by his Spirit to enable us to fulfil the conditions of the covenant, working in us faith, love, obedience, and all grace.

In this sense God hath given Christ to be a covenant to us, Isa. xlii. 6; and his blood is the blood of the covenant, by which he rescueth poor souls that were prisoners of sin and Satan, out of the pit of destruction. Zec. ix. 11. By this covenant, upon Christ's shedding of his blood as a sacrifice for sin, and his preforming all the work of mediation, and upon our receiving of him, and believing in him as he is offered to us in the gospel, God is pleased to promise to become our God, our reconciled Father, to pardon all our sins, to give us his Spirit and all grace here, and glory hereafter. . .

Besides, let us consider, there is not a passage of providence from God to us, but it comes through the hand of this Mediator. 1Cor. viii. 6, "All things are by him." Put what you will in the hand of a mediator, and in his power, it must needs turn to the good of him for whom he is a mediator. . .

1. This mediator steps in between God's wrath and us, in all

our afflictions, that no fury, or effects of it, may break forth from God on his people, for whom he is the Mediator, that nothing but fatherly love may be in the chastisement; and if love send the affliction, whatever it be, to try and purge, &c., there can be no hurt in that affliction. Again, our mediator interposeth, either to hold off the smart, or to allay and mitigate it, that it shall not distract, Dan. iii. 25, no nor hurt.

2. He steps in to uphold us, and to strengthen our weaknesses, enabling us to endure. Phil. iv. 4, 12, 13. . . Faith acted on this blessed Mediator, eying him, and believing that our afflictions come through his hands, even his who loved us, and died for us, our dearest friend, and who hath all power in heaven and earth, must be a mighty support to us in all our troubles.

Fourthly, Let faith be acted upon the word of Christ also. Ye believe the word of God, believe the word of Christ . . . Christ's word of precept. His word of command in time of trouble: "Fear not him that can kill the body, but him that can cast both soul and body into hell." Luke xii. 4, 32. . . acted upon the promises of Christ . . . to be always with us, to send the Comforter . . . that he "will not break the bruised reed, nor quench the smoking flax." Matt. xix. 29. That he will give an hundred-fold for all our losses for his sake. That he will carry us in his bosom; that he will hear our prayers, that he will give us a crown, a kingdom, everlasting life, with many more. . . acted on the word of threatening . . . Jesus Christ hath dreadfully threatrened those that love father or mother, son or daughter, more than him, or their own lives; and those that are ashamed of him, or his word, and those that fall from him, and those that hear his sayings and do them not; and those that are fruitless branches, &c. Matt. x. 37; Luke xiv. 26; Mark viii. last; John xv.2. . .

Fifthly, Faith acted on the work of Christ, will either prevent or cure heart trouble. And that again if faith be acted upon the work he hath done for us already, and upon the work he is now doing for us in heaven, and upon the work he is now doing in us on earth, and upon the work he will do for us, and in us, and upon us at the last day: all which works of Christ. If we act our faith on them, we shall not be much troubled in our hearts...

... acted upon that great and glorious work of Christ for us when he was upon earth, that work which his Father gave him to do in the days of his flesh, as our Redeemer...

Let us consider, that our blessed Lord denied himself on earth, and was well pleased not to have his own will, but referred himself entirely to his Father's, what reason have we poor worms, to be troubled when our wills are crossed? Let us in heart and life say as we pray, "Thy will be done on earth as it is in heaven." Matt. vi. 10. And when the will of God is done upon our families, and relations, let not your hearts be troubled, but let us imitate Jesus Christ in our submission to the will of God, making it our work on earth to be doping all the good we can, and so to put him on, and walking as he walked, and not to be troubled.

... Faith acted on Christ's suffering work on earth, will greatly contribute to our support: "he was a man of sorrows," Isa. liii. 1,2, 3, so that is we meet with sorrows on earth, we do but drink of our Master's own cup, and that should quiet us.

Christ's sufferings on earth were of two kinds, ...

1. For our imitation. His patent suffering of reproaches, scorns, revilings, contradictions of sinners, temptations, persecutions, bonds, poverty, shame, loss of friends, &c., suffering all with invincible patience, and meekness, without the least murmuring, repining, disquiet, or discontent, without any retaliation; for when he was reviled, he reviled not again: he prayed for his enemies, &c., and all this as our "example, that we should follow his steps." 1Pet. ii. 21, 22, 23. And if our Lord, the Lord of heaven and earth, suffered such things, what reason or cause have we to be troubled in our hearts when we are persecuted, reviled, forsaken of all our friends, impoverished, exposed to shame and sorrow, seeing our blessed Lord was so exposed, and so exercised upon earth? ... Shall we think to fare better than he? ... his whole life being a life of suffering, he knew what trouble meant ... He hath a feeling of all our infirmities ...

2. But his great suffering work for us, was his work of

satisfaction. . . O blessed Jesus! When our sins were upon him, he was sore amazed, groaned, was exceeding sorrowful, even unto death; he was in a bloody sweat, in a bitter agony in the garden; he was falsely accused, unjustly condemned, and then barbarously crucified, suffering that cursed and cruel, shameful, and painful death of the cross, and all as our surety, and as a sacrifice to God for our sins. "Christ, our Passover, was sacrificed for us," 1Cor. v. 7, to make atonement and satisfaction to the law and justice of God for us. Rom. iii. 25. . .

. . . faith must be acted upon the work of Christ, which he is now doing for us in heaven. . . as our advocate to plead our cause, and manage all our business there, presenting his blood, in the virtue of it, to his Father for our pardon, presenting our persons and services perfumed with the incense of his own righteousness, and by his Spirit applying the virtue of all to our souls. . .

. . . Christ is doing a work in us on earth, while he himself is in heaven. He is humbling us, purging us, teaching us, mortifying our corruptions, crucifying our inordinate affections, sanctifying us, and so preparing us for heaven: . . . he is fitting us for his Father's house, by all his providences, by every loss and cross; by all our afflictions, as 2Cor. iv. 17, "Our light afflictions, which are but for a moment, work for us (that is by the way of preparation) a far more exceeding and eternal weight of glory." . . . he is still forming, squaring, fashioning, and working by his Spirit, word, and rod, upon his people, to make them more and more conformable to himself, to square them as stones for his building, to make them habitations for himself, temples for the holy God to dwell in, and that he himself may delight to dwell in them here, and to make them fit to dwell with him for ever in glory. . .

Moreover, our faith should be acted upon the work that Christ is now doing for us in heaven. Besides his intercession for us there, he is preparing for us a place in heaven, as he told his disciples, to comfort them . . . A place in heaven is infinitely better, and more to be desired than the best place on earth. . . Here below all places are full of darkness, snares, temptations, fears, dangers, persecutions; but [heaven] is a place of perfect peace, perfect rest, of light, comfort, joy, and consolation. Here we are pilgrims and strangers, there is our home, our Father's house. . .

. . . Our faith must be acted upon the work that Christ will do for us, and in us, and upon us, in heaven at the last. It is above all our understanding to conceive what glorious works Christ will do for us and in us at the last day. "It doth not yet appear what we shall be." 1John iii. 2. There shall be a day of the manifestation of the sons of God. The poor despised saints, all black and cloudy here, covered with shame and reproach now, shall then be manifested to be the Lord's jewels: that will be a day of their full redemption, both of soul and body, their wedding and their solemn coronation day; then their blessed Redeemer shall publicly own them, and bid them welcome to his Father's house . .

Sixthly, Our faith must act upon the will of Christ, in order to the preventing and curing our heart troubles, fears, and sorrows. . . It is his will, that in the world they [his people] should have tribulation, but yet, that they should be of good cheer. It is his will, that in their patience they should possess their souls, and not faint nor be discouraged. It is his will they should be sanctified, and that all their afflictions should promote their sanctification. It is his will, that although he love them, yet to rebuke and chasten them; and when he doth so, that they shall be zealous and repent. It is his will, that they should deny themselves, and take up their cross daily, and follow him. That they should fear none of those things that they should suffer. That they should walk in his steps, hold fast to the end, be faithful unto death. That they should overcome. It is his will, that they should not love father or mother, son or daughter, more that himself; no, nor their lives, but be willing to part with all for his sake. Yea, it is his will, his last will, that all his poor disciples, after they have suffered a while, may be with him where he is, to behold his glory. . .

Lastly, Our faith must be acted upon the ends and designs of Christ is all his afflictive providences towards us; and these his ends are all very good and gracious. With this argument he himself used to cure the heart trouble of his disciples for his departure from them, viz., that he had good ends in his going away from them; his end was, to prepare a place for them, a better place than any to be found here, a place in heaven, in the Father's house. And his end was to send the Spirit, the Comforter, unto them, which would not come if he did not go away. John xvi. 6, 7. . . Now, if we can act faith upon the blessed ends of Christ, in removing our earthly comforts from us, which are, to bestow upon us better mercies, to give us more of his Spirit, and of the graces and comforts of it, our hearts would not be troubled, could we believe, that Christ's end in all his chastisements, is, to prepare us for that place in his father's house, it would comfort and support us. . . . So long as the people of Christ enjoy most of the comforts of this world, (I speak it by sad experience) commonly they enjoy least of God, and of his Spirit; and usually when Christ takes away their earthly comforts, then he manifests most of himself, and of his tender love to them: he brings them into the wilderness, and then speaks comfortably to them, Hos. ii. 14: then he speaks to their hearts, and not to the ears only, as in time of prosperity; then he gives out most of the graces and comforts of his Spirit. Christ never takes away these outward mercies from his people, but with design to bestow better, if our discontent and unbelief do not hinder. . .

Two ways, principally faith acted on God and Christ, doth effect this great cure of heart trouble, and procure heart's ease.
First, By applying and appropriating God and Christ to the soul, and all that God is, and all that Christ is, and all that God hath, and all that Christ hath, and all that God and Christ have promised: faith applieth and appropriateth all this to the soul, faith gives the soul right, title, claim, propriety, and interest to, and in God and Christ; faith makes all the believers own. . . This is the language of faith: My God, my Lord, my Christ, my Saviour, my Redeemer; and this quiets and satisfies the soul fully, or nothing in heaven or earth can do it. . .
Either God is ours, or he is not; either Christ is ours, or he is not. If God and Christ be not ours, we have cause enough of heart

trouble, cause enough to mind our danger, and to be troubled at our very hearts, that we are in such a woeful case; and should now, above all things labour after an interest in God and in Christ; whatever our losses in the world be, this dangerous state of our souls should be most minded, and speedily looked after above all things.

But if God be ours, and if Christ be ours: if we have chosen God for our portion in Christ; and if we have rightly and truly received Jesus Christ the Lord, for our only Lord and Saviour; and have unfeignedly given up our whole selves to him; then may we act our faith upon God, as our God, and upon Jesus Christ as ours, and may claim our right in God and in Christ, and in all that God and Christ is and hath, as our own; and then what cause of any heart trouble? If God be ours, if Christ be ours, all is ours, life ours, death ours; what is we want relations and friends, honour, wealth, and health, is not the all-sufficient God enough? Is not Jesus, in whom dwells all fullness, enough to supply the want of all? . . . Jesus Christ is all and in all; and if Christ be yours, all is yours: God is yours, and the good of both worlds are yours; and what can you desire more.

Secondly, Faith exercised in holy confidence in, and reliance upon God, and Christ, and the promises, will prevent or cure heart trouble. David was cured both these ways, Psalm xxxi. 11-15, viz., by appropriating God to himself, and by trusting in him; "I trusted in thee, O Lord: I said, thou art my God." Psal. xliii. 5. For God is pleased to engage himself to discharge those souls from heart trouble and sinful fear, who trust in him. Psal. xxxvii. 40. Trouble doth disorder the heart, and discompose the mind; but faith in this exercise of it, trusting in the Lord, doth fix and settle the heart; so that then no "evil tidings shall make such a person afraid, for his heart is fixed, trusting in the Lord." Psalm cxii. 7. God hath promised to "keep them in perfect peace, whose minds are stayed on him, because they trust in him." Isa. xxvi. 3. Diffidence is the cause of all disquiet; no true rest can be had, nor quiet to our minds, but by confidence in God. Psalm ii. last. . .

The way, then, whereby faith quieth the soul and cures it of its troubles, is, by raising it above all disquietments, and pitching it solely upon God in Christ, and thereby uniting it to God in Christ; from whence it draws virtue and strength, to subdue whatever troubleth its peace. For the soul is made for God, and never finds rest till it return unto, and settle and center itself upon him again. And that we may thus place our confidence in God and Christ for all supplies, we must most earnestly beg, cry, and seek to God for grace and strength so to do; we must trust in God alone, for all things, and at all times; and thus, by appropriating God to us, and Christ to us, and placing our confidence in them, we may be cured of all our heart troubles.

THE APPLICATION

1. For information. These inferences follow:

First, if faith acted upon God in Christ be such a remedy against heart trouble, then surely faith is a very precious, a very excellent thin; a grace of very great worth and value, and of great use and efficacy: it is precious faith indeed, the very trial of it is more precious than gold. 1Pet. i. 7. Precious for its author, the Lord Jesus; for its object, precious Jesus, and all the exceeding great and precious promises, the purchased inheritance; for its offices, it unites us to Christ, gives us title to eternal life; it supports under all afflictions, prevents or cures all heart troubles; and precious for its end, which is the salvation of our souls. Eph. iii. 17; Heb. ii. 39; 1Pet. i. 9.

. . . Faith unfasteneth the heart from the creature, showing the soul the vanity of it, and carries the soul unto God and Christ, showing it God's all-sufficiency, and Christ's all-fulness: for faith believes what God in his word hath revealed of both. It is the great design of God, in all the troubles he sends upon his people, effectually to teach them the exceeding vanity of the creature, to embitter the things of this world to them, to wean their hearts from them, to bring earthly things out of request with them, to make them see that there is no true contentment nor solid satisfaction for the soul to be found in them, and to make them see where true happiness and contentment is to be had, even in God and in Christ alone, for whom their souls were created, redeemed, and sanctified. . . . Naturally, our hearts hang loose from God, and cleave to the creature, and when the creature fails, our hearts are troubled; but faith takes off the heart from the creature, and settles it upon God in Christ, where it finds rest; and this is the great service it doth us. All the great and famous things which those worthies did, and all the hard and heavy things they suffered, mentioned in Heb. xi., were all done by the power of Faith, v37, &c. The settling of our hearts upon God in Christ, trusting all there, is the best means to cure our heart trouble; and thus faith doth, and therefore it is precious.

Secondly, It follows from the promises, that the want of faith in God and in Christ is the great cause of all our heart troubles, despondencies, and disquietness. Could we but act our faith strongly on God and Christ, as our God and Christ, our troubles would be prevented or cured; for by faith the soul looks up to God in Christ, through the promises, looking off from all other supports, unto God for all supplies, for the removing of all evil felt or feared, and not for the obtaining of all good promised and needed; and by this exercise of faith, the soul is raised up above all discouragements and disquietments; but where this faith is wanting, or the lively exercises of it suspended, there the soul sinks under heart trouble. . . .

Thirdly, Hence, also, we may clearly see the absolute necessity of getting faith in God and in Christ, and of acting it, and living by it; there is no living quietly and comfortably without it, no standing under our burdens, no bearing with patience and cheerfulness our losses and crosses without this faith; no joy and peace but by believing: by faith we stand.

Fourthly, Then the things of the world are not to be trusted to, nor trusted in, for comfort in time of trouble. Nothing but God and Christ is to be trusted in, and trusted to, and there is enough in them to support and comfort us, as hath been showed; but no confidence is to be put in the creature: there is a curse upon such confidence, but a blessing on them that trust in God. No trusting in friends, riches, gifts, or anything; for so to do is idolatry, to give that to the creature which is due to God alone.

Fifthly, Hence we see the reason why so many faint in the day of adversity, and sin under trouble; and others use unlawful means to prevent trouble, or to get out of it. It is because they want this faith in God and Christ; and for want of it, too many miscarry under affliction.

The second use is, by way of exhortation to all the disciples of Christ, in the words of the text, Let not your hearts be troubled, but believe in God, and believe in Christ. You must get and act faith in God and Christ: this is the only preventative, the only remedy against heart trouble. Our Lord, in this text, commands it and commends it: we must needs get faith above all gettings; next to Christ we must get faith, for we cannot have Christ without faith; go to God for it, it is his work, his gift; yea, it is his operation; yea, the same power that raised up Jesus from the dead, must be put forth upon a soul to work faith. Eph. i. 19, 20. . . . because of that infinite distance between God and us, we can never come to believe in him, until our hearts be renewed by the power of grace, and this divine grace of faith infused into them. Therefore must we go to God and Christ, and put up strong cries and prayers to God to work faith in us, and never give over, until it be wrought in us.

And having got faith, we must act and exercise it upon God in Christ . . .

As God offers, so faith receives . . .

In order, then, to obtain solid comfort in all our distresses, let us carefully look whether these acts of faith have really passed upon our souls. Have we thus actually, understandingly, and sincerely believed in God, and in Christ? Have we unfeignedly entered into covenant with God in Christ? Can we conclude that God is our God in Christ, by our being his? If we be entirely his, he is ours for certain. 1John iv. 19; Cant. [Song of Songs] ii. 16. If we place all our happiness in him. Psal. lxxiii. 25. If we give him the throne in our hearts, subjecting our whole selves to his government, making

God in Christ all our love, our trust, joy, desire, delight, fear, our all, cleaving to him alone, and above all, depending upon him as our chief good, contenting ourselves with him as all-sufficient for us, resigning up ourselves to his good will, to be, to do, and to suffer what he will: if we can and do engage ourselves to sincere obedience, that none of his commandments be grievous to us: if in all things we give Christ the pre-eminence; if we have received the Spirit of Christ, as Rom. viii. 9; Gal. iv. 6, which joins us to his, and makes us one spirit with him, and which is a spirit of adoption whereby the soul, seeing his interests in God as his Father, can freely go to God in all his straits. If we have the graces of the Spirit, as "love, meekness, patience, humility," &c. If we have a resemblance of our father in us, a likeness of disposition to God and Christ, the image of God, the life of Christ manifest in us, if we do side with God, and his cause, in evil times, so that we are willing to part with all things for Christ's sake, and at his call; if it be thus with us in the main bent and constant sincerity and integrity of our souls, our consciences in the sight of God bearing us witness that thus it is with us, then may we, upon good grounds, conclude that God, the all-sufficient God is ours,, and Christ Jesus who is all fullness, is ours, and then our hearts should not be troubled. . . If the great God be ours, and the Lord Jesus be ours; if we have no husband, nor wives, nor sons, daughters, nor health, nor wealth, we have enough to content and satisfy our souls forever.

But to draw to a conclusion, that there may be an effectual cure of all our heart trouble, whatever our distress may be, let us labour to act faith on Christ, in considering and believing. . . and all within the confines of this text, ver. 2, 3.

First, let Christ's disciples labour to believe what Christ is, and who he is. . . To believe all things that are written of Christ, is not enough; but to believe in him, is by faith to receive him for our only Lord and saviour, John i. 12; Col. ii. 6, and "actually, unreservedly, unfeignedly, and heartily," to give up our whole selves unto him, taking him for our absolute Lord, our head, our treasure, and our all; and believing he is all that to us that he is. . .

if we be Christ's . . . all the gifts, graces, labours, prayers of all gospel ministers, all gospel ordinances are ordained and designed for our good, Eph. iv. 11-13, for the gathering of us in, and for the perfecting and building of us up in Christ Jesus, until we all come to heaven. The world is ours: the good and the evil of it, the bitter and the sweet of it, the comforts and the crosses of it, the gains and the losses of it, the love and the hate of it, the smiles and the frowns, the friends and foes in it; all is designed for, and shall further promote our spiritual and eternal welfare. Life is ours. All the troubles, sicknesses, pains, evil tidings, persecutations, dissappointments, losses of relations, shame, reproach, or whatever attende this mortal life, shall be sanctified and blessed to us for our good. Yea, death is ours: that shall be our advantage, our gain; that shall put a full end and period to all our sin and suffering, and be a door of entrance for us into glory in our Father's house. Our things present, our present tears, sorrows, miseries, infirmities, &c., shall be so ordered and overruled by the wisdom and love of our Father, that they shall all help us onward to heaven. And things to come are ours: all that glory to be revealed, that saints' everlasting rest that is prepared for the people of God; that crown of righteousness, of glory, and of life; that kingdom of glory, that unspeakable, that inconceivable state of happiness and blessedness which Christ our Lord hath purchased by his blood – all this is ours also. . . What cause hath such a soul to be dejected, whatever crosses or losses do befall him? Is there not enough in Christ, in the promises, in the purchase of Christ? Is there not enough in heaven, in all that glory, to quiet, content, and fully satisfy our souls? O my beloved! (and O my base and faithless heart!) it is our base unbelief that doth us all the mischief, that spoils our peace, that hinders our comfort, and makes us walk so heavily. . .

. . . Now, it is not very hard to know whose we are, whether we be Christ's or our own, Christ's or the world's, Christ's or the devil's. . Whose are we? Put this question seriously to our hearts, in the sight of God, Whose am I? whose image do I bear? By whose spirit am I actuated? Who hath my heart, my chief love, and delight? Have we unfeignedly given up ourselves to Christ? Have we actually entered into covenant with him, taken him for our head and husband? Have we passed over, and surrendered up our whole selves to Christ: our souls, bodies, tongues, time, talents, estates, liberties, relations, and all to Christ? Have we done sincerely? Then we have received Christ upon his terms. If we be Christ's, and not our own, and live unto Christ, and not to ourselves, Rom. xiv. 9; 1Cor. vi. 20; Gal. ii. 20, and are content that Christ should dispose of us and ours as he pleaseth, and are always labouring to be more and more like him, and still longing for more and more communion with him, &c.; then may we, upon good grounds, conclude that Christ is ours. If we be his, he is ours. Secondly, Let us believe in Christ and believe where he is. As to his essential presence, he is in heaven, at the Father's right hand, making continual intercession for us to the father. . .

And as to his spiritual and providential presence, he is always with his people on earth; he is in his people: Christ in you the hope of glory. Col. i. 27. . .

Thirdly, Believe in Christ; believe what he hath told us: "In my Father's house are many mansions; if it were not so, I would have told you: I go to prepare a place for you." John xiv. 3. . . if there were not such a blessed state, and glorious place for you, my disciples, in the other world, after all your sufferings in this, I would have told you so. For I have told of the many troubles you must endure in this world; and for your comfort, I am now telling you what good things you shall shortly enjoy above in my Father's house, where is all joy, peace, rest, and consolation. There are many mansions, no prisons, chains, nor fetters, but glorious dwellings, enough to hold all the saints that ever were, and that ever shall be in the world, where they shall enjoy full and free communion with the blessed trinity, and with one another; perfect liberty without any restraint or remove for ever: believe this, and let not your hearts be troubled.

I go to prepare a place for you. I have purchased this most glorious place for you, by my blood: I have promised it to you;

now I go away to take possession of it for you, in your name and stead. . . and in the meantime, he is preparing us by his word and Spirit, by afflictions and deliverances, for that glorious place. Hence he is called the "forerunner, who is for us entered into that within the veil." Heb. vi. 20. So that, as sure as Christ himself ascended, and went into the highest heavens, so sure shall all his disciples, all true believers ascend, and enter into heaven also; because he went thither himself, to prepare heaven for them, by taking possession of it in his human nature for us, as our head and Saviour . . . If we could believe that Christ hath prepared a place in heaven for us, and that heaven will make amends for all our sufferings in the way thither; and if we could keep the eye of our faith upon that "recompense of reward, that far more exceeding and eternal weight of glory," 2Cor. iv. 16-18, we should bear up bravely under our sufferings, and not have our hearts troubled.

Let us then look more heavenward, more to our father's house: let us have our conversations more in heaven, and set our affections more upon things above; upon that blessed state and place above; and know, "that when Christ, who is our life, shall appear, we shall appear with him in glory." Col. iii. 1, 2, 4. Believe this, and be comforted.

Certainly we are too much taken up with, and too solicitous about our earthly tabernacles: these houses of clay, whose foundation is in the dust, crushed before the moth. We are always minding the diseases, distempers, and dangers, of our bodies, those old crazy, tottering houses, the prisons of our souls; we mind earthly places too much, but too little those heavenly places in Christ Jesus, Eph. ii. 6, where we shall shortly sit with him. . .

Lastly, to prevent and cure all our heart trouble; let us labour to believe what Christ hath promised here in the text, ver. 3, "I will come again and receive you to myself, that where I am ye may be also." . . . I will not stay long from you; my heart is still towards you while I am absent, therefore I will come quickly. Rev. iii. 11. I will come to you with my messenger, death; though it be the king of terrors in itself, and a grim porter; yet, by my coming with it, it shall be to you the king of comforts: I will come with it, by my Spirit, to strengthen you, to look it in the face, to apply to you the virtue of my death, and thereby to take out the sting of it; and I will come to you by my angels, to secure your souls through the regions of devils, into my Father's house. . . This prevented David's fear. Psal. xxiii. 4, "When I walk through the valley of the shadow of death, I will fear no evil, for thou art with me." O welcome death! When Christ comes with it. This bitter cup, of which we must all drink, is brought to us by the hand of our dearest Lord: this last stroke is given by the hand of love: it is a taking us home to our Father's house; this last enemy hath Christ conquered for us: because his children are "partakers of flesh and blood, he likewise took part of the same, that through death (that is, his own death) he might destroy him that had the power of death, that is the devil, and deliver them, who, through fear of death, were all their lifetime subject to bondage." Heb. ii. 14. Jesus knew what death was, he himself had the pangs of death upon him; sin, the sting of death, was laid on him; and the law, which is the strength of sin, the curse of the law was upon him; but now for us, who believe in Jesus, the sting and strength of death is taken out; and when we die, we shall die in the Lord . . . O that we would make sure of our union with Christ! And then let us believe, that he will come with death, to translate our souls out of these earthly tabernacles, these prison-houses, these houses of bondage (wherein our poor souls have been fettered and chained, cloyed and clogged with corruptions and temptations, kept at a distance, and absent from the Lord, and in which they have been groaning for deliverance) into the glorious liberty of the sons of God, in their Father's house, and shall ever be with the Lord. 1Thess. iv. 17.

Secondly, I will receive you to myself. O sweet promise! This is all the hope, all the desire, all the longing, thirsting, breathing, of poor believers, viz., that Christ would take them to himself. This is the sum of all their prayers and labours, that they may be fitted for Christ, and then that Christ would take them to himself. Well, saith Christ, work and wait a little longer; do and suffer a little more; act your faith and patience a little longer, and I will come to you, and take you home to myself, where your soul shall be at rest for ever. The saints, while they are here, at home in the body, they are absent from the Lord; they see but in part, darkly, and know but in part, very imperfectly, and enjoy but a little, a very little, of God and Christ. Oh how sweet are a few drops, a few glimpses and glances of divine love now to a poor soul! The least cast of Christ's eye, the least beam of his loving-kindness, the least intimation of his favour, the least hint of his goodness, how refreshing to a poor believer! But when Christ shall receive them to himself, they shall "then see him as he is, shall be like him, and shall be satisfied with his likeness." 1John iii. 2, 3: Psalm xvii. 15. Then they shall see him whom their souls love, face to face; and then will Jesus open to them all the treasures of his love and grace, to their everlasting consolation. They shall then be admitted into the glorious presence of the great God, and our Saviour Jesus Christ, "in whose presence is fullness of joy, and at whose right hand are pleasures for evermore." Psalm xvi. 11. When the world shall cast them out, and their habitations shall cast them out, and shall know them no more; yea when their houses of clay shall be broken down and dissolved, and can hold them no longer, then will Jesus, blessed Jesus receive them to Himself. . . "I will receive you to myself," into the nearest union and communion with myself; and therefore be not unwilling to part with your dear relations; be not afraid to be separated from your bodies, your old friends, for when these earthly tabernacles are dissolved, immediately I will receive you to myself, which is best of all. You shall then enjoy the fruits of all my sufferings, death, resurrection, ascension, and intercession; and the fruits of all your own labours, prayers, tears, and sufferings; and shall find that I am faithful in making good all my promises, and that your labour was not in vain in the Lord; then shall there be no more any distance between you and me for ever. Comfort yourselves, and comfort one another with these words: "believe this, and let not your hearts be troubled."

Thirdly, "That where I am, ye may be also;" and what more can be desired? . . . O admirable, astonishing dignity, that blessed Jesus will advance his poor saints unto at that day! This high and wonderful honour shall all his saints have; they shall now receive the kingdom prepared for them, and that crown of glory, of righteousness, and of life, which Christ hath purchased for them, perfectly freed now from all sin and sorrow, and stated in an unchangeable state of happiness and blessedness. What cause have we, then, to grieve for our dear relations, whom Christ hath taken to himself, and placed in the Father's house . . . could we but firmly believe these promises of our Lord, and act our faith in meditating fixedly on them, and on Jesus in them, applying and appropriating them, and Christ in them, to our own souls, considering and pondering on them, until our hearts be warmed, and our affections stirred and kindled with them; acting also, hope, love, joy, desire, delight, hunger, thirst, panting, breathing; pouring out our hearts in prayer to God for his Spirit to bring home these promises to our souls in power, fixing them upon our hearts, and helping us to lay hold on them, and upon Christ in them, and resigning up our whole souls to Christ in them, steadfastly relying on his goodness and faithfulness, and trusting in him: I say, could we but do so, and in the strength of God betrust our whole selves, and all our concerns, thus with Christ, and live in the lively exercises of faith thus on God and on Christ, we should find this to be heart's ease to us in all our heart trouble. "Behold, I lay in Sion a chief corner stone, elect, precious; and he that believeth in him shall not be confounded." 1Pet. ii. 6.

> Let all heart trouble cease,
> Let nought disturb your peace,
> Who faith in God profess,
> And in his Son no less.
> > For in his Father's house
> > Are many mansions sweet,
> > Christ hath prepar'd for us,

The Pilgrim Way

When we're for them made meet.[167]

What a challenge to do, to live, believing, thinking and therefore being as Bunyan has written! But take heart, unless we are all to be as the thief on the cross next to Christ who believed in who and what Christ was and entered into paradise that same day we are given time, time to be, to sojourn here in this classroom, time to allow ourselves to be sanctified, to become more and more Christ-like, more fit for heaven and most if honest will tell you it is not a breeze to so live, it takes time.

After some forty years of having a public teaching ministry, I can affirm, that preaching the Scriptures is infinitely easier that living them. Phrases like "practice what you preach" and "don't just talk the talk, walk the walk" underline the challenge before us, as do the words of the apostle James, "Prove yourselves doers of the word, and not merely hearers who delude themselves" (1:22).[168]

---

[167] *Heart's Ease in Heart trouble* p821-800
[168] Bill Crowder Seeing *the Heart of Christ* Discovery House 2018 p22

Robyn Crothers

Part 3: A Lifestyle to Maintain

. . . having your conduct honourable among the Gentiles, that when they speak against you as evildoers, they may, by your good works which they observe . . 1Peter 2:12

Third, to live as pilgrims, Peter tells of a lifestyle to maintain. 'Keep your behaviour excellent among the Gentiles', says verse 12. This word 'behaviour' means conduct, way of life or lifestyle. It points to the overall flavour of our lives. The words 'excellent' means good in the sense of beautiful or attractive. Our lives should be marked by 'good deeds' which conform to God's Word, but which also, in a lesser sense are viewed by even a godless culture as attractive. The world should look at the lives of Christians and admit, even if they don't accept Christ or the Bible, that we are good people.[169]

Do you remember back in Part One where we looked at how our mindset affects our behaviours, how what we think routinely, or not think but just do out of habit is what we become? How we defined a lot of words resulting in us realising how God in saving us has given us so much, enabling us to fulfil his desires for us, giving us himself in fact?

How we are to put off the old man, starving the old nature and ceasing to sow anything from that old life, yet put on the new man, feeding him, sowing good seeds protecting them from any form of attack using Philippians 4:8 as a weed identifier so we can reap a good harvest of much righteous, holy fruit to share?

Determining to be of a disciplined mind, flint-faced, caring for this new man by soaking him in the word and refusing to worry but instead pray, training him to be a profitable servant of his Father and equipped and ready to endure as an innocent grief and suffering when it comes because of our loyalty and love to the Father? Of holiness and a love of which our world is slowly dying from its lack, having the hope of eternity with the Father and being able to rest from travelling and warring as encouragements to keep going?

---

[169] Sermon *The Daily Battle: proving to be true pilgrims*

Then in Part Two we found our new selves at war with our old selves and what a war it is!

For to reap holiness one has to sow holiness and all things lovely while starving, crucifying or uprooting all weeds, everything that belongs to that other life with an almost fierce determination to abstain from allowing anything to infect this most precious crop, hating anything that could contaminate it, taking care not to become weary by forgetting to feed yourself and rest in the presence of the master or by becoming entangled in a weight that he did not desire for you which hinders your joy, a fullness of joy and pleasures now and for eternity which he supplies to enable – along with armour- and encourage you in your daily tasks while warring.

You do? Great!

Now all we have to do is tie all that we have considered into a picture of what our common lifestyle or walk as pilgrims will look like.

> 'Walk' is a word Paul regularly uses for 'live', as did the Old Testament writers. . . This image of putting one foot in front of another as you move steadily from your starting point toward your destination is in fact a brilliant picture of how human life should be lived.[170]

'The Reformers . . . protested vigorously against the dichotomy between the sacred and the secular and its implicit devaluation of creation. When we carry out our vocation in obedience to God's commands, wrote Martin Luther, then God himself works through us to his purposes. And this partnership with God includes all legitimate forms of work, not just spiritual vocations. Luther totally rejected the notion that monks and clergy were engaged in holier work than shopkeepers and housewives. "Seemingly secular works are a worship of God," he wrote, "and an obedience well pleasing to God."

---

[170] *God's Will* p141

The division into sacred and secular had not only made secular work second-best but also held secular workers to a lower standard of devotion and spirituality. The Reformation challenged that concept, insisting that no believer is exempt from the highest spiritual standards. Looking through the biblical lens, Luther wrote, we see that "the entire world [is] full of service to God, not only the churches but also the home, the kitchen, the cellar, the workshop, and the field of the townsfolk and farmers."' [171]

Right, well here goes, keep your imagination working to visualize the life I am going to get you to picture by bombarding you firstly with a heap, and I do mean a heap, of questions and ideas. Are you ready?

Is your lifestyle showing anyone watching that you treasure God above all else, that he comes first? Are you honouring his glory? Revering his holiness? Admiring his greatness? Praising his power? Seeking his truth? Esteeming his wisdom? Treasuring his beauty? Savouring his goodness? Trusting his faithfulness? Believing his promises? Obeying his commands? Respecting his justice? Fearing his wrath? Cherishing his grace? Prizing his presence? Loving his person? Do I exhibit in my life a love to Christ and thankfulness for grace which shows the worth of the price he paid for my rescue or does the way I live display this price as being of no value to me, having no meaning for me?

Do I display goodness – habitual actions which reflect an inward disposition . . . the concept of helping but also of rebuking, correcting and disciplining[172] – or am I seen rightly as a hypocrite, cursing man yet blessing God or blessing man and cursing God? Could I be accused of wearing masks; do I appear as one type of person at the football and another at a work function and yet another in church?

---

[171] Charles Colson and Nancy Pearcey *How Now Shall We Live* Tyndale House Publishers 1999 p388 Quote from Martin Luther, as quoted in Ryken, *Work and Leisure*, 95, 97, 135.

[172] *Quiet Times for Couples* January 25th p32

Does my behaviour or works display my faith in God, my belief in his sovereignty?

Do the choices I make show that I have been freed from the penalty, power and presence of sin? Is my life increasingly holy, am I displaying an ongoing sanctification, a personal and practical holiness, an increase yielding to the Spirit within? Do I make lifestyle choices that show I believe that God's wrath has been turned away from me by Christ's propitiation? Do I show the truth of having the divine nature within, can I be accused of exhibiting Christ like behaviours, characteristics? Is my nature, the way I live visibly different, new when compared to what I used to be? Do I look forward to being glorified, do I view death as a friend that sends me home, that removes me from evil? Do I pray? Always? Do I crave 'direct intercourse with God'?

Is there a stench, or even a whiff of lewdness, lustings, drunkednesses, revellings, drinking parties, or abominable worshiping, idolizing of anything but God floating around my lifestyle?

Does the way I am living show that I fear God or man?

Do I detest evil, pride, arrogance, evil ways and perverse mouths? How do I react to suffering, to hassles, interruptions or inconveniences, to pain, to disease? Do I complain and grumble, do I wonder why me and demand answers from God or accuse him? Does it look as if I see trials as a reason for joy because faith tested will produce patience, endurance and perseverance, that any trial is for my long term good? Do I live as blessed when enduring temptation? Do I wonder why this (trial) and kick and complain loudly against it, demanding my rights or am I content to humble myself under the caring and loving hand of God and accept it? Do I blame God for temptations or give Satan the credit? Do I face life looking like I believe God will never leave, or forsake me? That he is enough?

Do I look as if I am crucifying sins or playing with them? Sins like distrust and disobedience because even my legitimate good desires have not been met by God when I wanted and how I wanted, or presumptive sins because I desire distinction, or the sin of pride from the desire for power? Sins that separate, disrupt or sever relationships like greed, telling and spreading lies by gossiping, unlawful anger, theft, laziness, unreliability, unloyalty?

Am I more weary of my problems than my sins?

Am I living as an ambassador, does my life represent the truth about my Father to those around me? Do I keep the laws of the land that do not conflict with my Father's? Or do I show disrespect to them and those who maintain the laws?

Am I vigilant about protecting my new mindset? Do I consider what my eyes and ears may witness, or how my heart could be damaged in situations? What do I daydream about? If I choose to do this, will it be beneficial, physically, spiritually and mentally now and in the long term? Will it trap me into a way of being that will cause me or my neighbour a problem? Will it hurt another, hinder them from seeing the truth of God or enable them to remain in their sin? Will it delight God, honour him or grieve him? (based on 1Corinthians 6:12, 8:13, and 10:31)

Is my lifestyle like Christ's? Am I joyfully serving even those I'd normally prefer not to be around? Am I obedient to God or my desires? Am I steadfast, flint like with no thought of not continuing on the path God has set out for me, even if it is taking me into hardship, even death? Am I aware of other's needs that I pass on this path, do I stop and serve them out of love? Does my life show that I am faithful, virtuous, knowledgeable, and able to control myself, persevering, goodly, kind and loving? (See 2Peter 1:5-7) Am I disciplined? Am I living, running with certainty? Or do I allow fears, anxieties or misplaced shame to fell me? Can others see that I love God supremely and neighbour be they enemy or friend as myself? Is my proclaimed faith seen by my love, is my so proclaimed unmerited, undeserved and unearnable love being expressed in service, good works toward my fellow man? What does my marriage look like? Am I exhibiting gentleness, showing the Holy Spirit's taming of myself of my temper, negative or critical attitude, tongue, impulsive behaviours, sinful desires, making me considerate towards others and submissive towards God?[173]

Do I always refuse to play God? Or am I happy to tell God what he should do to fix a problem and when it will be best to do so?

Is my life one of faith and love, full of contentment with no dissatisfactions or worries? How corrupted is my thinking about God? Are my thoughts about him, my knowledge of him based primarily on the Bible or what others say? Is my understanding of love likewise based? Do I believe it to be loving when a person of the opposite sex states that they cannot wait for marriage (or that they don't believe in having to do something so old-fashioned beforehand) to have sex because they are so in love with me? Are there sinful pleasures, covetousness or materialism, pride or boasting of self rather than Christ in my life that I could be accused of?

Am I aware of being in Satan's sights because my lifestyle is bugging him, because it is pleasing God? Am I a slave to righteousness or sin? Which activity gets most of my time: screen (as in television, internet, phone and other social media including printed, yep showing my age), time for self which includes exercise or reading, studying the Bible and praying? What is the motive behind my answer? Which activity if done from the right motive has eternal value? Do I deliberately flee, abstain, shut off or refuse to read anything that seeks to display any form of sexual immorality as normal and good for society, or that sexually arouses me? Am I displaying the fact that I am abiding in Christ, that I have my armour on, standing fast in obedience, relying on him and not self?

---

[173] Ideas taken for this sentence from *Quiet Times for Couples* January 27th p 34

Does my life display that I am driven by God's word, promises, truth or my feelings and emotions? Am I dealing with the important firstly or giving into the urgent? Am I sharing my burdens or soldiering on believing myself to be like God? Do I rightly know myself? Which influence has the most oomph, God or the world in the way I view me and live as a result? Have I answered all these questions as honestly as I could?

How did you go?

James L. Snyder writes that 'your passion for God will determine your lifestyle. You cannot say you believe in God and then exhibit behaviours that are in conflict with the holy character and nature of God . . . Christianity is *not* a religion where you adhere to certain rules, regulations, and rituals. Christianity is a passion for God that can only be satisfied as we come to Jesus Christ'[174]

Question: How do the gospels portray those who follow Jesus?
Answer: Matthew 4:18-22, 'And Jesus, walking by the Sea. . . saw two brothers. . . "Follow Me . . ." They immediately left their nest and followed Him. Going on from there he saw two other brothers . . . in the boat with . . . their father, mending their nets. He called them, and immediately they left the boat and their father, and followed Him.'

> "They forsook all, and followed him" – We cannot refrain from citing here the beautiful remark of Trench (*Notes on the Miracles*): "But what was that "all" which "they forsook" . . . It was their all, and therefore, though it might have been but a few poor boats and nets, it was much. And the forsaking consists not in the more or less that is forsaken, but in the spirit in which it is left . . . for it is the worldly affection which holds him, and not the world . . . The apostles might have left little when they left their possessions, but they left much, when they left their desires.[175]

---

[174] *Delighting in God* Introduction by James L. Snyder p10
[175] *Fleetwood's Life of Christ* comment from Pictorial Bible p174

This life style should be righteous, honourable, loving and light filled (which means being holy) yet salty and not necessarily easy or comfortable, and always fully covered by the mantle of prayer, just like Jesus' life. But O, how I have written and rewritten this section. There is just too much to say, to cover. So much that a pilgrim should be displaying in their life and so much that should never ever be seen. So please read your Bible, study it, meditate and pray about what God thru his Spirit shows and teaches you as you do so. Use others' writings and commentaries to help but not to replace your time in God's living book, his how-to-become, live, maintain and persevere-manual for all pilgrims for then and only then will you have a true, complete and correct view of this lifestyle. But you have bought this book and I have to attempt write something helpful and God honouring so here goes –

Differences, sovereignty and decisions

Simply by observation you can see that lifestyles are as individual as we are. There are so many variables that can influence why we chose to live, be, as we do. Some are under our control, most are not, and then there are the different stages of maturing or ages as well. Yet here we have Peter telling us that as pilgrims we are all to have a common yet peculiar lifestyle, a pattern of behaviours, which is to be maintained, continued throughout our sojourning in this world regardless of culture, class, financial situation, race or gender. Paul Windsor once said that pilgrims need to 'recover the importance of being different rather than relevant'[176] to the world. This is only possible because we are united with all and any other pilgrim, walking in unity (not conformity which is to wear a mask, to assume an acceptable look outwardly which does not come from within and which is not pleasing to God), having the same Father, the same saviour and the same Spirit who unites us all into one body, one family.

---

[176] From notes taken during one of the Belgrave Heights Conventions of 2017

But yes, we are different apart from this and those differences, another's or our own, frequently cause us problems especially when we start the comparison game to make ourselves feel better, above another, and when Satan starts playing this game with us it is to make us feel inadequate and useless, a waste of God's space. Back when we were considering what mindsets we should adopt about ourselves I quoted from Bridges comments on Psalm 139, what follows are further thoughts about this psalm –
'James Hufstetler is again helpful to us when he said, "You will never really enjoy other people, you will never have stable emotions, you will never lead a life of godly contentment, you will never conquer jealously and love others as you should until you thank God for making you the way he did."
. . . we also need to thank Him for those so-called positive abilities and traits we do have. . . Paul's words to the Corinthians apply to all of us: "For who makes you different from anyone else? What do you have that you did not receive" (1Corinthians 4:7) All of us receive whatever ability, learning, riches, station in life, rank or influence we have from God to be used by us for His glory. . .
Who you are is not a biological accident. *What* you are is not a circumstantial accident. God planned both for you. . .
The fact that God ordained our days for us should also give meaning to every day, not just the special or exciting days of our lives. Every day is important for us because it is a day ordained by God. If we are bored with life there is something wrong with our concept of God and His involvement in our daily lives.' [177]

Question: Does being happy in your own skin affect the way you live? Do you clamber out of bed every morning greeting the day with a mood of eager childlike discovery and adventure (at least in attitude if the bod is a tad stiff and uncompliant)?
Answer: Accepting ourselves is accepting God's rightful sovereignty over us. I am sure you can think of many ways we are refusing to accept both who and what we are in today's world,

---

[177] *Trusting God* p159, 160-1, 162-3, 165, 167

some may seem trivial while others require major surgery and drugs with long-term unknown consequences but all arise from non-acceptance of God's good and loving sovereignty.

How about practicing being thankful for today because it has not gone as *you* had planned but as your *Father* had?

And I wonder how our acceptance of others may change if we viewed them through this lens of God being sovereign? In Jesus' time parents of disabled children and the child as well were considered to have committed some awful sin and God was punishing them as a result (John 9:1-3), yet this was not God's thinking.

Bridges writes that 'Confidence in God's sovereignty in the lives of people should . . .keep us from becoming resentful and bitter when we are treated unjustly or maliciously by others. Bitterness usually stems not so much from the other person's actions as from the effects of those actions on our lives . . But God never allows people to make decisions about us that undermine His plan [or will] for us . . . Why then do we suffer . . . struggle . . . when someone else's decision or action adversely affects us? Is it not because it is *our* plans that have been dashed, or our pride that has been wounded?[178]

. . . *all* expressions of nature, *all* occurrences of weather, whether it be a devastating tornado or a gentle rain on a spring day, are acts of God. . . Not only do we sin against God when we complain about the weather, we also deprive ourselves of the peace that comes from recognizing our heavenly Father is in control of it. [I wonder how the world's extreme emphasis on so called 'climate change', the fear this is bringing to many especially children and how puny man can fix it sits?][179]

. . . So don't be afraid; you are worth more than many sparrows (Matthew 10:31) According to Jesus, God does exercise His sovereignty in every minute events – even the life and death of an

---

[178] Ibid. p61-2
[179] Ibid. p88,89

almost worthless sparrow. And Jesus' whole point is: If God so exercises His sovereignty in regard to sparrows most certainly He will exercise it in regard to His children. [180]

Pastor Baker, in his book on Job, says, "I have long since quit seeking the answer to that question in my own life . . God owes me no explanation. He has the right to do what He wants, when He wants, and how He wants. Why? Because He's God . . .Job didn't need to know why these things happened as they did – he just needed to know Who was responsible and Who was in control. He just needed to know God, . . .

Job 42:3. . . When he saw God in His great majesty and sovereignty, he repented of his arrogant questioning in "dust and ashes". He stopped asking and simply trusted.'[181]

Though we are one body God the Father deals with us, sees us as individuals who are individually united to his Son. However, you will find no neon signed personal, individually named Biblical direction in the scriptures, no flashing 'Attention Joe Blow/ Jane Doe you must do_____. Right now!'

This despite Paul telling us that 'All Scripture is given by inspiration of God, and is profitable for doctrine, for reproof, for correction, for instruction in righteousness, that the man [or woman] of God may be complete, thoroughly equipped for every good work,' (2Timothy 3:16-17).

Question: So how is one supposed to know what God desires of them in a certain time or place?

Answer: Tozer's comments on this verse of 1Peter I thought were helpful here. He writes, 'As usual, God lays it down here in a broad precept; He does not give the details. He says, 'Have your conversation honest among the Gentiles'. Other translations have it as 'seemly, good and right; beyond reproach and upright; let your conduct be seemly. Let it be honest, let it be good and right, let it be beyond reproach, let it be upright'. . . The application is

---

[180] Ibid. p19
[181] Ibid. p119, 122

left to the circumstance, the time and the individual. God never tells us anything that will enable us to get along without Him . . . He lays down broad principles and then allows the moment, the situation, the circumstances, the individual and the context to determine how those principals shall be applied. . . The application of it takes the living presence of the Holy Ghost . . . God says, 'Here is the rule book; here are the precepts for righteousness. Do not get puffed up now, because you are a weak person and situations change like the chance of circumstance, so you will never quite know how to orientate yourself. You lean on Me hard, you trust Me constantly, you pray all the time, because otherwise you will not know how to make that precept apply in the hour when you need it . . . if you were to memorize the whole Bible by heart, you would still need the presence of God and the living influence of the Holy Ghost living within you to enable you to live even a tiniest verse of that Bible. . . We . . . like . . to be able to point and say, 'There's my religion, look at that, isn't that solid. . . We like to get hold of our verses and then say, 'I know how to run my life.' God says, 'No, My child, you only know the broad outline. The details must be filled in be prayer and faith and humility. . . The broad percept He lays down here for the attitude of the Christian (be honest, seemly, good, right and beyond reproach and upright) there are no details given, but this is the beating heart of it. This is first, because it is indispensable. You can know all the rules in the book but unless you live a life that is honest, and seemly and beyond reproach, it will mean nothing to the Gentiles.'[182]

Along with this broad percept of seemly conduct or honest conversation we have been looking at in 1Peter there are many, many others throughout the scriptures. For example:
1Peter 2:1-2 we read, '. . . lay aside all allice, all deceit, hypocrisy, envy, and all evil speaking . . . desire the pure milk of the word that you may grow.'

---

[182] *Living as a Christian* p131-133

Hebrews 13:5, 'Let your conduct be without covetousness; be content with such things as you have. For He Himself has said, 'I will never leave you nor forsake you.''

Zechariah 7:9-10, 'Thus says the LORD of hosts: Execute true justice, show mercy and compassion, everyone to his brother. Do not oppress the widow or the fatherless, the alien or the poor. Let none of you plan evil in his heart against his brother.'

And then there is Micah 6:6-8, 'With what shall I come before the LORD, and bow myself before the High God? Shall I come before Him with burnt offerings, with calves a year old? Will the LORD be pleased with thousands of rams, ten thousand rivers of oil? Shall I give my firstborn for my transgressions, the fruit of my body for the sin of my soul? He has shown you, O man, what is good; and what does the LORD require of you but to do justly, to love mercy, and to walk humbly with your God?' of which we are going to consider briefly with thanks to Charles Swindoll who writes 'Micah's words [in the first two verses] state exactly what many, to this day, wonder about [a life that is] pleasing to God. Teachers and preachers have made it so sacrificial . . . so complicated . . . so extremely difficult. To them, God is virtually impossible to please. Therefore, religion has become a series of long, drawn-out, deeply painful acts designed to appease this peeved Deity in the sky who takes delight in watching us squirm.

Micah erases the things on the entire list, replacing the complicated possibilities with one of the finest definitions of simple faith . . . *God likes it Simple.* He does not look for big-time, external displays. He does not require slick public performances. He does not expect gigantic acts of self-sacrificial heroism, seventy-hour work weeks of ministry, a calendar of exhausting activities, an endless number of church meetings, massive dedication that proves itself in going to the most primitive tribe hidden away in the densest jungle of the world. STOP! . . .

Go back and look at how you have complicated what God said so simply. What is required? Slow down and read the list aloud:

> To do justice
> To love kindness

To walk humbly with your God.' [183]

In fact, there are so many good behaviours listed – all showing pictures of Christ Jesus' attitude and lifestyle – as well as the undesirable bad ways of living, so many guidelines, what if I do not take you on a journey looking at the many precepts but instead just consider the one I believe to be the principle, the one which colours every conduct of a pilgrim's life? Just one to make it really simple, well here goes –

> A pilgrim's lifestyle is based on the foundation
> of love and is maintained by love.

Love and holiness

No disrespect meant to the more learned Mr. Tozer but I believe love to be first on the list of indispensables, the true beating heart from which all others flow because this is our good God's heart and you will understand why holiness has been added to the heading a little further on.

Jesus tells his disciples and us in John 13:34-35 and 15:9-12 the following, 'A new commandment I give to you, that you love one another; as I have loved you, that you also love one another. By this all will know that you are My disciples, if you have love for one another . . . As the Father loved Me, I also have loved you; abide in My love. If you keep My commandments, you will abide in My love, just as I have kept My Father's commandments and abide in His love. These things I have spoken to you, that My joy may remain in you, and that your joy may be full. This is My commandment, that you love one another as I have loved you.'

> Love is the very basis of the Christian life, for Christians are "rooted and founded in love" (Eph.3:17). Love is both soil and rock, the root from which everything grows, the foundation on which everything is built.[184]

---

[183] *Simple Faith* p138-9

[184] Leon Morris *Testaments of Love A study of Love in the Bible* William B. Eerdmans Publishing Company 1981 p183

We have already looked at the sorts of love talked about in the Bible and its importance but it is a big subject and there is great need so we are going to consider it again from varied sources. And it is your turn to strain your brain instead of me. As you continue to read on please consider how living this way of love will make your lifestyle different from those around you.

1John 4:8, 19, 'He who does not love does not know God, for God is love. . . We love Him because He first loved us.'

To speak of knowing God without knowing love is clearly ridiculous.

Morris writes that 'C. H. Dodd (1884-1973) . . . comes to this conclusion about the statement 'God loves'

> [It] might stand alongside other statements, such as 'God creates', 'God rules', 'God judges; that is to say, it means that love is *one* of His activities. But to say 'God is love' implies that all His activity is loving activity. If He creates, He creates in love; if He rules, He rules in love; if He judges, He judges in love. All that He does is the expression of His nature, which is – to love.[185]

Question: All his good activity is loving activity; it may be sovereign but loving? What about his wrath?

Answer: Yes, all that our God does, all that he thinks, says, or is, is loving, regardless of who it is directed to. Remember that all God does to you before you become a pilgrim is so that you may turn and become his child and all he does afterwards is so that you may grow and endure. The triune God is sinless therefore good and so his love is not tainted by sin but pure good. This is hard to get our heads around for while here on this fallen earth we are all tainted with sin to one degree or another, blood covered believers still have the old man to deal with, while unbelievers are naked having not accepted any covering for theirs.

> God's integrity is such that he takes sin seriously; his whole nature is antagonistic to it. The fact that he loves so deeply means that he is necessarily opposed to all that is evil in the

---

[185] Ibid. p136-7

beloved, to all that degrades them and causes suffering. Precisely because he loves them he will be angry with them.[186]

We even see Jesus acting out of anger, a holy anger for what was happening was giving lie to his Father's character by keeping the gentiles out of the temple area that was for them, not to mention dishonest merchants swindling desperate worshipers.

John 2:13-21 tells us of his first Passover when he began his ministry: '. . . And He found in the temple those who sold oxen and sheep and doves, and the money changers doing business. When He had made a whip of cords, He drove them all out . . . and poured out the changes' money and overturned the tables . . . "Take these things away! Do not make My Father's house a house of merchandise!"'

Then in Matthew 21:12-17 we can read of Jesus cleaning out the temple again but this time it is the day after his donkey ride into Jerusalem and before he was the Passover lamb; 'Then Jesus went into the temple of God and drove out all those who bought and sold . . . "It is written, 'My house shall be called a house of prayer,' but you have made it a 'den of thieves.'"'

The temple in Christs' time, built by Herod was one of the world's wonders, attracting many visitors. It contained the temple itself which only the priests could enter and was surrounded by three outer courts, one for Israelite men, one for Israelite men and women and the furthest from the temple itself was where the gentiles, any non-Jew could be and pray which became rather difficult when it was turned into a gigantic market where you haggled over prices for sacrifices and temple currency.

Christ cares for the purity of our worship now as then and desires unhindered access for all who thirst to worship him. The temple had become closed to the nations when it was meant to be a light that drew them, as the nation of Israel was meant to have done.

---

[186] Ibid. p177

'These merchants, and the priests who allowed their presence, cared nothing for true worship as long as they could make money and keep up the rituals. Our Saviour hated this sacrilege, which kept the nations from learning about the living God in His sanctuary' [187] and this would eventually result in its destruction like the previous temple because his warnings of coming judgement that would begin with the house of God again went unheeded, (Jeremiah 7 and Isaiah 56).

What loving parent (believing or not) has not been angry at the bad behaviour of their child? God is no different. Remember he disciplines his child for the child's benefit, to restore, redirect and bring them to maturity, not for his convenience.

> This is what God has done for rebellious mankind: he pardons their sins against himself at his own cost . . . the depth of God's love is to be seen precisely in the way in which it bears the wounds inflicted on it by mankind and offers full and free pardon.[188]

While here on this earth rebellious mankind does enjoy the good gifts of God, rain, sunshine, nature, relationships, work, money and what it can buy, entertainments, sport etc. but that will all change on their passing into eternity. An eternity without God's love and caring attention if they have not become pilgrims before death.

Now going back to 1John 4:19, 'We love Him because He first loved us . . .'

F. D. Maurice (1805-1872) makes an insightful comment on this verse, writing that we 'Let no one cheat you of the simple force of these words by persuading you to understand the Apostle as saying that we love God out of *gratitude* for the love He shows to us. Some . . . are wont to talk much of the motives, to which, they say, a man's nature is subjected; this motive of gratitude, they

---

[187] https://www.ligonier.org Jesus Cleanses the Temple
[188] *Testaments of Love* p.176 Quote from I. Howard Marshall *The Epistles of John* Grand Rapids 1978 p.215

affirm, is one of the chief . . . .I say they have no right to impute these notions to the Apostle, to make him put *motives* in the place of *God* . . . *They* would make me the slave of a certain set of influences which I feel I ought to control. *He* [St. John] represents God as acting upon me that I may be free . . .

We should clearly understand this point. John is not speaking of our love as an imitation of what we see in God, nor is he referring to gratitude or some kindred emotion. He is saying that God's love is creative: it produces it's like in believers.

This is all of a piece with the way the New Testament writers see the Christian life. Christians have been born again (Jn 3:5, 7f.), they have been converted (Matt. 18:3), they have been buried with Christ in baptism so that they walk in newness of life (Rom. 6:4); their old selves have been crucified (Rom. 6:6), and they have put off their old natures (Eph. 4:22; Col. 3:9). They have been crucified with Christ (Gal.2:19) and raised with him (Col 3:1); they live by faith in the Son of God (Gal.2:20). They have put on the new man (Eph. 4:24; Col.3:10); they have been renewed in the spirit of their mind (Eph.4:23; cf.Rom.12:2). And there is much more. The New Testament envisages a thoroughgoing change when people become Christians, a change brought about by the power of God within them. The first part of the fruit of the Spirit produces is wholehearted love (Gal.5:22). Paul points out that "the love of Christ constrains us" (IICor.5:14), and goes on to refer to the cross. The cross shows us the self-sacrificing love that has made us Christians, the kind of love that is looked for from us. This kind of love is not the achievement of the natural man. True, the natural man feels certain kinds of love, but *agapē*, love as the New Testament writers understood it, is not among them. It is brought about in man by God himself, a most important part of the transformation that turns a worldly man into a Christian.' [189]

That I may be free . . . Remember what we have been freed from and what we have been freed for because of this love? True

---

[189] *Testaments of Love* p173-5

freedom cannot co-exist with fear as John writes in 1John 4:18, 'Love contains no fear – indeed fully developed love expels every particle of fear, for fear always contains some of the torture of feeling guilty.' (J. B. Phillips translation)

Living in grace, in loving relationship with God instead of relationship based on obligated duty motivated by fear of reprisals if one stuffs up and the resultant guilt, frees pilgrims from self-focus, self-protection allowing us to be, well free, free to love, free to be what God had always intended us to be holy, free from sin.

Titus 2:11-12, 'For the grace[love] of God that brings salvation has appeared to all men, teaching us that, denying ungodliness and worldly lusts, we should live soberly, righteously, and godly in the present age'

1John 3:18, '. . let us not love in word or in tongue, but in deed . .'

2Corinthians 5:14, 'For the love of Christ compels us . . .'

The same love of God that bought and gave us our salvation also gives everything needed for us to leave our old un-loving-bound-by all sorts of fears real and imagined-way of life behind and have a holy lifestyle of good works, loving humanity as he does. If Christ's love does not irresistibly urge us on to such a life style of visible freely lovingly good works, we are no better than the demons.

Reeves writes, '. . . the truth is that God is love because God is a Trinity. . .. Christianity is not primarily about lifestyle change: it is about knowing God. . . who God has revealed himself to be: not first and foremost Creator or Ruler, but Father. . . Before he ever created, before he ever ruled the world, before anything else, this God was a Father loving his Son. . .Our definition of God must be built on the Son who reveals him. . . love is not something the Father *has*, merely one of his many moods. Rather, he *is* love. He could not not love . . . the word 'grace' is really just a shorthand way of speaking about the personal and loving kindness out of which, ultimately, God gives *himself*. . . For Calvin, salvation was not about getting some *thing* called 'grace' – it was about freely receiving the Spirit, and so the Father and the Son. . . For the way the Father makes known his love is precisely through giving his Spirit. . . The Father's love is primary. The Father is the loving head . . . in his love he will send and direct the Son, whereas the Son never sends or directs the Father . . . as the apostle Paul observes in 1 Corinthians 11:3 . . . the shape of the Father- Son relationship (the headship) begins a gracious cascade, like a waterfall of love: as the Father is the lover and the head of the Son, so the Son goes out to be the lover and the head of the church. . . That dynamic is also to be replicated in marriages, husbands being the heads of their wives, loving them as Christ the Head loves his bride, the church. He is the lover; she is the beloved. Like the church then, wives are not left to earn the love of their husbands; they can enjoy it as something lavished on them freely, unconditionally and maximally. For eternity, the Father so loves the Son that he excites the Son's eternal love in response; Christ so loves the church that he excites our love in response; the husband so loves his wife that he excites her to love him back. Such is the spreading goodness that rolls out of the very being of this God. . . By the Spirit I (slowly!) begin to love as God loves, with his own generous, overflowing, self-giving love for others. . . the Spirit is not about bringing us to a mere external performance for Christ, but bring us actually to love him and find our joy in him. And any performance 'for him' that is not the expression of such love brings him no pleasure at all. . . What we love and enjoy is foundationally important. It is far more significant than our outward behaviour, for it is our desires that *drive* our behaviour. . the Spirit's first work is to set our desires in order, to open our eyes and give us the Father's own relish for the Son, and the Son's own enjoyment of the Father.

The Heidelberg Catechism (1563) captures this brilliantly when it asks: 'What is the coming-to-life of the new man? Answer: 'It is wholehearted joy in God through Christ and a delight to do every kind of good as God wants us to.' The Spirit of the Father and the Son would never be interested in merely empowering us to 'do good'. His desire (which is the desire of the Father and the Son) is to bring us to such a hearty enjoyment of God through Christ that we delight to know him, that we delight in all his ways, and that *therefore* we want to do as he wants and we hate the thought of ever grieving him. . . . 'Love the Lord your God' and 'Love your neighbour as yourself.' For that is being like this God – sharing the love the Father and the Son have for each other, and then, like them, overflowing with that love to the world.'[190]

Question: So, all this world needs is 'love sweet love'[191]? None of those Old Testament 10 I-shall-not's, just love towards everyone? None of those churchy religious 'have to's'? Great, no chance of being labelled as a legalist then. But why then would anyone hate us for being loving?

Answer: Yes, the world needs love, but not necessarily the love this song was talking about, it is starving for *agapē* love, unconditional love that does not fear speaking or living the truth, God's truth.

Leviticus 19:1-18, 'And the LORD spoke to Moses, saying, "Speak to all the congregation of the children of Israel, and say to them: 'You shall be holy, for I the LORD, your God am holy. Every one of you shall revere his mother and his father, and keep My Sabbaths: I am the LORD your God. Do not turn to idols, nor make for yourselves molded gods: I am the LORD your God, and if you offer a sacrifice of a peace offering to the LORD, you shall offer it of your own free will. It shall be eaten the same day you offer it, and on the next day. And if any remains until the third day, it shall be burnt in the fire. And if it is eaten at all on the third day, it is an abomination. It shall not be accepted. Therefore everyone who eats it shall bear his iniquity, because he has profaned the hallowed offering of the LORD; and that person shall be cut off from his people.

---

[190] Michael Reeves *The Good God Enjoying Father, Son and Spirit* Paternoster 2012 p vii, 2, 3, 4, 8, 11, 10, 76, 79, 80 & 95

[191] Song *Love sweet love* written by Burt F. Bacharach/ Hal David Artist: Jackie DeShannon released 1965

When you reap the harvest of your land, you shall not wholly reap the corners of your field, nor shall you gather the gleanings of your harvest. And you shall not glean your vineyard, nor shall you gather every grape of your vineyard; you shall leave them for the poor and the stranger: I am the LORD your God. You shall not steal, nor deal falsely, nor lie to one another. And you shall not swear by My name falsely, nor shall you profane the name of your God: I am the LORD. You shall not cheat your neighbour, nor rob him. The wages of him who is hired shall not remain with you until morning. You shall not cause the deaf, nor put a stumbling block before the blind, but shall fear your God: I am the LORD. You shall do no injustice in judgement. You shall not be partial to the poor, nor honour the person of the mighty. In righteousness you shall judge your neighbour. You shall not go about as a talebearer among your people; nor shall you take a stand against the life of your neighbour: I am the LORD. You shall not hate your brother in your heart. You shall surely rebuke your neighbour, and not bear sin because of him. You shall not take vengeance, nor bear any grudge against the children of your people, but you shall love your neighbour as yourself: I am the LORD.'"

Commenting on this section of scripture Richards wrote –

> What do we learn? Perhaps the surprising fact that holiness and love are identical twins!
>
> The truest expression of holiness is showing love for others in simple, practical ways. Caring for the poor. Being fair to the well-to-do and needy alike. Doing nothing that might harm another. Loving others as ourselves.
>
> It is this kind of life God calls us to live daily. And this, the simple and practical living out of love, is holiness.[192]

As you keep reading, try interchanging these two ideas of *love* and *holiness* wherever you meet them and see if there is any change of meaning with what you are reading or if they are indeed twins.

---

[192] *The 365 Day devotional commentary* January 28 Leviticus 18-22 p83-4

Bridges writing on holiness comments, 'Farming is a joint venture between God and the farmer. The farmer cannot do what God must [send rain], and God will not do what the farmer should do [prepare the soil and plant the seed]. We can say just as accurately that the pursuit of holiness is a joint venture between God and the Christian. No one can attain any degree of holiness without God working in his life, but just as surely no one will attain it without effort on his own part. God has made it possible for us to walk [live] in holiness. But he has given to us the responsibility of doing the walking; He does not do that for us, Heb. 12:14 ['Pursue peace with all people, and holiness, without which no one will see the Lord']. The word *pursue* suggests two thoughts: first, that diligence and effort are required; and second, that it is a lifelong task . . . holiness is a process, something we never completely attain in this life. Rather, as we begin to conform to the will of God in one area of life, He reveals to us our need in another area. That is why we will always be pursuing – as opposed to attaining – holiness in this life.[193]

To be holy is to be morally blameless. It is to be separated from sin and, therefore, consecrated to God. The word signifies "separation to God, and the conduct befitting those so separated."

Perhaps the best way of understanding the concept of holiness is to note how writers of the New Testament used the word. In 1Thessalonians4:3-7, Paul used the term in contrast to a life of immorality and impurity. Peter used it in contrast to living according to the evil desires we had when we lived outside of Christ (1Peter1:14-16 ['as obedient children, not conforming yourselves to the former lusts, as in your ignorance; but as He who called you is holy, you also be holy in all your conduct, because it is written, "Be holy, for I am holy."']) John contrasted one who is holy with those who do wrong and are vile (Revelation 22:11["he who is unjust, let him be unjust still; he who is filthy, let him be filthy still; he who is righteous, let him be righteous

---

[193] *The Pursuit of Holiness* p13-15

still; he who is holy, let him be holy still."']) To live a holy life, then, is to live a life of conformity to the moral precepts of the Bible and in contrast to the sinful ways of the world. It is to live a life characterized by the "[putting] off of your old self, which is being corrupted by its deceitful desires . . . and [putting] on the new self, created to be like God in true righteousness and holiness" (Ephesians 4:22,24).'[194]

Paul writes in 1Thessalonians 3:11-4:12, some of which we have previously considered, the following words, 'Now may our God and Father Himself, and our Lord Jesus Christ, direct our way to you. And may the Lord make you increase and abound in love to one another and to all, just as we do to you, so that He may establish your hearts blameless in holiness before our God and Father at the coming of our Lord Jesus Christ with all His saints. Finally then, my brethren, we urge and exhort in the Lord Jesus that you should abound more and more, just as you received from us how you ought to walk [live] and to please God; for you know what commandments we gave you through the Lord Jesus. For this is the will of God, your sanctification: that you should abstain from sexual immorality; that each of you should know how to possess his own vessel in sanctification and honour, not in passion of lust, like the Gentiles who do not know God; that no one should take advantage of and defraud his brother in this matter, because the Lord is the avenger of all such, as we also forewarned you and testified. For God did not call us to uncleanness, but in holiness. Therefore he who rejects this does not reject man, but God, who has also given us His Holy Spirit. But concerning brotherly love you have no need that I should write to you, for you yourselves are taught by God to love one another; and indeed you do so toward all the brethren who are in all Macedonia. But we urge you, brethren, that you increase more and more; that you also aspire to lead a quiet life, to mind your own business, and to work with your own hands, as we have commanded you, that you may walk

---

[194] Ibid p19-20

properly toward those who are outside, and that you may lack nothing.'

J. Packer writes of this section of scripture that, 'Paul has some practical things to say about holiness and sanctification – the former meaning a state of being set apart for God, the latter the event or process whereby this apartness comes about.

Holiness is not optional. Sanctification is God's will for all Christians. It is a matter of obeying instructions which come with God's call to salvation; it starts with the heart and is then expressed in conduct.

Holiness entails avoiding sexual immorality. The right course is to marry 'in holiness and honour', respecting my partner as a person made in God's image and the marriage relationship as God's own ordinance of a lifelong bond. Using myself to please myself rather than my partner, clandestine adultery, and overt wife-swapping are among the things Paul condemns.

Holiness involves loving action toward both Christians and non-Christians. Holiness is more than abstaining from evil; Christian love is the way separation to the Christian God must show itself.

Holiness requires willingness to work, so as to be independent. Sponging and scrounging have no place in the true life of faith.

Holiness involves minding my own business, and not being a nosey gossip. How down-to-earth Paul is!' [195]

Did you discover that love and holiness have much in common, that they cross over boundaries of black and white definitions, blurring the edges? I hope so, for this is the love and holiness all pilgrims possess and strive for because they have received God's love and holiness for themselves and so they have within themselves this love and holiness to give out, live out for others to observe and thirst for.

> O soul, consider this deeply: it is the life of a Christian that carries more conviction and persuasion than his words. Though, like an angel, you talk of Christ, of the gospel, of the

---

[195] James Packer *Your father Loves You. Daily insights for knowing God* Harold Shaw Publishers 1986 March 6

doctrines of grace, and of heaven; yet if you indulge devilish tempers, and live under the power of any sinful lusts and passions, you will hereby harden others against the things of God, and prevent their setting out in the ways of God. Study and pray to be a consistent walker in the ways of holiness, else all is but windy profession, and airy talk. O how much harm is done to Christ's cause by the unholy walk of many professors.[196]

Bridges writes that 'The world around us constantly seeks to conform our minds to its sinful ways. It is earnest and pressing in its endeavours. It will entice and persuade us (Prov1:10-14) When we resist, it will ridicule and abuse us as 'old-fashioned' and 'puritanical' (1Pt 4:4) . . .

If holiness, then, is so basic to the Christian life, why do we not experience it more is daily living? Why do so many Christians feel constantly defeated in their struggle with sin? Why does the Church of Jesus Christ so often seem to be more conformed to the world around it than to God?

At the risk of oversimplification, the answers to these questions can be grouped into three basic problem areas.

Our first problem is that *our attitude toward sin is more self-centered than God-centered.* We are more concerned about our own 'victory' over sin than we are about the fact that our sins grieve the heart of God . . . God wants us to walk in *obedience* – not victory. Obedience is orientated toward God; victory is oriented toward self . . .This is not to say God doesn't want us to experience victory, but rather to emphasize that victory is a by-product of obedience . . .

Our second problem is that we have misunderstood *'living by faith'* (Galatians 2:20) to mean that no effort at holiness is required on our part . . . sometimes we have even suggested that any effort on our part is 'of the flesh' . . . We must face the fact that we have a personal responsibility for our walk of holiness . . .

---

[196] *The Pilgrim's Progress* comment by Mason p93

Our third problem is that *we do not take some sin seriously* . . .
Isn't insistence on obeying the letter of the law nit-picking legalism? . . . In commenting on the more minute Old Testament dietary laws God gave to the children of Israel, Andrew Bonar said, "It is not the importance of the thing, but the majesty of the Lawgiver, that is to be the standard of obedience. . . Some, indeed, might reckon such minute and arbitrary rules as these as trifling. But the principle involved in obedience or disobedience was none other than the same principle which was tried in Eden at the foot of the forbidden tree. It's really this: Is the Lord to be obeyed in *all* things whatsoever He commands? Is He a holy Lawgiver? Are His creatures bound to give implicit assent to His will?' Are we willing to call sin 'sin' not because it is big or little, but because God's law forbids it?' [197]

Legalism, those top 10 and persecution

There are many religious practices described in the Old Testament that were made obsolete with the coming of Jesus, the one they foreshadowed. As an example, pilgrims no longer need to sacrifice perfect lambs, goats, bulls or pigeons as these practices have been annulled by Christ's sacrifice of himself once for all.

But the ten commandments, the moral law for how to treat God, family and neighbour has never been made obsolete. These laws are love and holiness being worked out in life, being seen, practical visible holiness. They were given *after* the Israelites and others who escaped with them had followed God's direction and Moses' leading from the Passover night in Egypt and then through the Red Sea. It was by obedience and trust that they walked on a dry seabed and on to Mount Sinai where they entered into a covenant relationship with God.

Colson writes that 'The only way to live a rational and healthy life is to ascertain the nature of these divine laws and ordinances and then use them as the basis for how we should live. We tend to understand this principle very well when it comes to the physical

---

[197] *The Pursuit of Holiness* p 19-23

order. We know that certain laws exist in the physical world and that if we defy these laws, we pay a steep price. Ignoring the law of gravity can have very unpleasant consequences if we happen to be walking off the edge of a cliff. To live in defiance of known physical laws is the height of folly.

But it is no different with the moral laws prescribing human behaviour. Just as certain physical actions produce predictable reactions, so certain moral behaviour produces predictable consequences. Adultery may be portrayed as glamorous by Hollywood, but it invariably produces anger, jealousy, broken relationships, even violence. Defiance of moral laws may even lead to death, whether it is the speeding drunk who kills a mother on her way to the store or the drug addict who contracts and spreads AIDS. No transgression of moral law is without painful consequences.

If we want to live healthy, well-balanced lives, we had better know the laws and ordinances by which God has structured creation. And because these are the laws of our own inner nature, Kuyper notes, we will experience them not as oppressive external constraints but as "a guide through the desert," guaranteeing our safety.

This understanding of life's laws is what Scripture calls wisdom. "Wisdom in Scripture is broadly speaking, the knowledge of God's world and the knack of fitting oneself into it," says Calvin College professor Cornelius Plantinga. A wise person is one who knows the boundaries and limits, the laws and rhythms and seasons of the created order, both in the physical and the social world. "To be wise is to know reality and then accommodate your-self to it." By contrast those who refuse to accommodate to the laws of life are not only immoral but also foolish, no matter how well educated they may be. They fail to recognize the structure of creation and are constantly at odds with reality: "Folly is a stubborn swimming against the stream of the universe . . . spitting into the wind . . . coloring outside the lines"'[198]

In Exodus 20:1-17, (see also Deuteronomy 5:1-22) God says,
'I am the LORD your God who brought you out of the land of Egypt, out of the house of bondage.
You shall have no other gods before Me.
You shall not make for yourself a carved image – any likeness of anything that is in heaven above, or that is in the earth beneath, or that is in the water under the earth; you shall not bow down to them nor serve them. For I, the LORD your God, am a jealous God, visiting the iniquity of the fathers upon the children to the third and fourth generations of those who hate Me, but showing mercy to thousands, to those who keep My commandments.
You shall not take the name of the LORD your God in vain, for the LORD will not hold him guiltless who takes His name in vain.
Observe the Sabbath day, to keep it holy, as the LORD your God commanded you. Six days you shall labour and do all your work, but the seventh day is the Sabbath of the LORD your God. In it you shall do no work: you, nor your son, nor your daughter, nor your male servant, nor your female servant, nor your ox, nor your donkey, nor any of your cattle, nor your stranger who is within your gates, that your male and female servant may rest as well as you. And remember that you were a slave in the land of Egypt, and the LORD your God brought you out from there by a mighty hand and by an outstretched arm; therefore the LORD your God commanded you to keep the Sabbath day.
Honour your father and mother, as the LORD your God has commanded you, that your days may be long, and that it may be well with you in the land which the LORD your God is giving you.
You shall not murder.
You shall not commit adultery.

---

[198] *How Now Shall We Live?* p 16-17 Quotes from Abraham Kuyper Christianity: A Total World and Life System (Marlborough, N.H.: Plymouth Rock Foundation, 1996), 41 and Cornelius Plantinga Jr., "Fashions and Folly: Sin and Character in the 90s," (presented at the January Lecture Series, Calvin Theological Seminary, Grand Rapids, Michigan, January 15, 1993), 14-15

You shall not steal.
You shall not bear false witness against your neighbour.
You shall not covet your neighbour's wife; and you shall not desire your neighbour's house, his field, his male servant, his female servant, his ox, his donkey, or anything that is your neighbour's.'

Packer and Nystrom write that 'God's law is the applicatory interpretation of the Bible as a whole. . . In Hebrew the word for law is *torah*, which primarily means . . . domestic instruction, the kind of admonishing, authoritative yet affectionate, that a faithful father gives his children and others in the household of which he is the head. . .

The law of God, then, as we meet it in Scripture, is first and foremost a law of loyalty and love toward the God of grace, with whom all believers are in covenant. Legalism is no part of this picture. Legalism (that is, looking to law-keeping to secure a status with God) was the basic perversity of the Pharisees . . .

We might paraphrase the Decalogue [the ten commandments] in positive and Christian terms with something like this: "You shall worship your covenant God exclusively and wholeheartedly, according to his own self-revelation, regarding him with consistent reverence and setting aside regular time for rest and worship in his honour; you should respect those who have nurtured you, and labour to sustain the family unit; you must do all you can to safeguard the life, sexual purity, property, reputation, and well-being of all you meet; and knowing that your God watches over you, you are to be content with what you have." . . . Jesus linked attitude and action in all law-keeping.

. . the law . . . is, in the words of James, 'the law of liberty' (James 1:25, 2:12) – that is the path of *freedom* . . . Freedom exists when not only have we been freed *from* whatever oppressed us, but are also now enjoying the state of dignity, happiness, fulfilment, and contentment that we were freed *for* . . . (John 8:31-2 and Gal5:1). Jesus explains that the freedom he gives his followers as they engage with his Word is freedom from sin's dominion for the life as a child of God, at home with one's Father (John 8:34-6). So freedom is a supreme gift, inasmuch as it covers both our forgiveness and acceptance (justification, adoption and freedom from final condemnation) and also the anchoring of us in the life of enjoying, serving and pleasing our heavenly Father. The gift thus changes both our status and our state in relation to God. Constant batterings from circumstances outwardly and fears and temptations inwardly make the life of freedom a constant struggle for us, as anchored boats are tossed and made to strain at their cables by stormy seas. But our anchor holds, our freedom remains, and our deep joy and contentment in the knowledge of being limitlessly loved by the Father, the Son and the Holy Spirit continue within us as we labour to hold steady. This is a quality of life that only believers know.

. . . As God the Father and Jesus Christ the Lord do not change, so orthodoxy and orthopraxy (right belief and right practice) are always essentially the same. What was morally right and good yesterday remains morally right and good today, and what was morally wrong in the past does not become morally right in the present.'[199]

Bridges adds, 'God's law has not become optional because of His grace, merely advisory to keep us from getting hurt as we go through life . . . What has changed is our *reason* for obedience, our *motive* . . . Under a sense of legalism, obedience is done with a view to meriting salvation or God's blessing on our lives. Under grace obedience is a loving response to salvation already provided in Christ and the assurance that having provided salvation God will also through Christ provide all else that we need. . . The only obedience acceptable to God is constrained and impelled by love, because 'love is the fulfilment of the law' (Rom 13:10) God's law as revealed in His Word prescribes our duty, but love provides the correct motive for obedience. We obey God's law not to be loved but because we are loved in Christ.

. . . the moral law is a transcript – a written reproduction – of the moral character of God and that 'God is love' . . . [and so] we

---

[199] *God's Will* p 94, 98, 95, 99, 100

cannot distinguish between law and love. Both express the character of God . . . love provides the motive for obeying the commandments of the law, but the law provides specific direction for exercising love . . . the classic description of love given by Paul in 1 Corinthians 13:4-7:

Love is patient, love is kind. It does not envy, it does not boast, it is not proud. It is not rude, it is not self-seeking, it is not easily angered, it keeps no record of wrongs. Love does not delight in evil but rejoices with the truth. It always protects, always trusts, always hopes, always perseveres.

Paul did not give a dictionary definition of love; instead he described it in terms of specific attitudes and actions toward one another . . . Leviticus 19 is basically an amplification of the Ten Commandments as originally set forth in Exodus 20. Let's consider verses 11-18 of Leviticus 19 . . . [but] let's paraphrase those verses using the format . . . which Paul used in 1Corinthians 13 . . .

Love does not steal, it does not lie, it does not deceive. Love does not profane God's name. It does not defraud nor rob its neighbour. It does not hold the wages of a hired man overnight. Love does not curse the deaf, nor put a stumbling block in front of the blind.

Love does not pervert justice, nor show partiality to the poor or favouritism to the great. Instead, it judges its neighbour fairly. Love does not slander another, nor do anything that endangers his life.

Love does not hate its brother, nor seek revenge, nor bear a grudge, but rather treats its neighbour as itself.

[I suggest that you read over this again but this time keep in mind such activities as drink-driving or using your mobile phone while driving, buying that new outfit not to impress your spouse but your boss, not following through on a promise to a neighbour, gossiping about your over-the-fence neighbour in a manner that degrades or belittles him or her in the eyes of the one you are talking to, taking that piece of equipment from work as you need it at home, not filling out your income tax truthfully, living as though Santa is what Christmas is all about, the kind of entertainment you enjoy, if you're a business owner what your OH&S standards are like, how you treat your children, or another's .]

We can see from this paraphrase that the various expressions of God's moral law, wherever they occur in Scripture, are simply a description of love in action.

Leviticus 19 also helps us understand who our neighbour is. He is the hired man, the deaf, the blind, the poor, the great, the person whom we are tempted to lie to, or steal from, or slander. He is the person who has wronged us and against whom we are tempted to hold a grudge. Our neighbour is even the person whose life we might endanger by reckless behaviour. We can easily say our neighbour is anyone with whom we come in contact . . .

The principle of love is not a "higher principle" over God's moral law. Rather, it provides the motive and the motivation for obedience, while the law provides the direction for the biblical expressions of love.' [200]

> Love inevitably leads to obedience; obedience is evidence of the presence of love.[201]
>
> By denying that there are universal God-taught prohibitions, we enmesh love in perplexities. . . Law is love's eyes; love is law's heart.[202]

Just a thought, many words ago you would have read about saying 'No' to taking on more jobs and giving yourself permission to just be and rest, enjoying God and all that he has given you without stressing. God has commanded this type of rest, one day out of every seven.

<u>Question</u>: Does the world allow us this much time out from the busyness of living our lives, do you allow yourself?

---

[200] Jerry Bridges *Transforming Grace Living Confidently in God's unfailing Love* Navpress 1991 p98-102

[201] *Testaments of Love* p162

[202] *Your Father Loves You* November 18

The Pilgrim Way

<u>Answer</u>: Lucado writes that '. . . Life can get so loud we forget to shut it down. Maybe that's why God made such a big deal about rest in the Ten Commandments . . .

Of the ten declarations carved in the tablets, which one occupies the most space? Murder? Adultery? Stealing? You'd think so. Certainly each is worthy of ample coverage. But curiously, these commandments are tributes to brevity. God needed only five English words to condemn adultery and four to denounce thievery and murder.

But when he came to the topic of rest, one sentence would not suffice. . . God's message is plain: "If creation didn't crash when I rested, it won't crash when you do".

Repeat these words after me: It is not my job to run the world.

A century ago Charles Spurgeon gave this advice to his preaching students:

> Even beasts of burden must be turned out to grass occasionally; the very sea pauses at ebb and flood; earth keeps the Sabbath of the wintry months; and man, even when exalted to God's ambassador, must rest or faint, must trim his lamp or let it burn low; must recruit his vigour or grow prematurely old . . . In the long run we shall do more by sometimes doing less.

The bow cannot always be bent without fear of breaking. For a field to bear fruit, it must occasionally lie fallow. And for you to be healthy, you must rest. Slow down, and God will heal you. he will bring rest to your mind, to your body, and most of all to your soul. He will lead you to green pastures.'[203]

Many years ago, when I was a baby Christian just beginning to totter along on my pilgrimage, I was accused by a more seemingly mature Christian of having a legalistic mentality simply because I refused to lie and state I could not at this time be considered for

---

[203] Max Lucado (born 1955) *Travelling Light Releasing the burdens you were never intended to bear The Promise of Psalm 23* p41-3 Quote from Helmut Thielicke *Encounter with Spurgeon* trans. John W. Doberstein reprinted by Baker Book House 1975 p220

Jury duty. It hurt a lot. I studied a lot. I am not legalistic, but honest. Here is some of what I read at that time –

'Legalism is first of all anything we do or don't do in order to *earn* favour with God [e.g. get saved]. It is concerned with rewards to be gained or penalties to be avoided. This legalism we force on ourselves.

Second legalism insists on conformity to *manmade* religious rules and requirements which are often unspoken but are never the less very real . . . it requires conformity to the 'do's and don'ts' of our particular Christian circle . . . it is conformity to how other people think we should live instead of how the Bible tells us to live . . . as Christians we can't seem to accept the clear biblical teaching in Rom 14 that God allows equally godly people to have differing opinions on certain matters. We universalize what we think is God's particular leading in our lives and apply it to everyone else . . . "putting God in a box". We are insisting that He must surely lead everyone as we believe He has led us. We refuse to allow God the freedom to deal with each of us as individuals – we are legalists. We must not seek to bind the consciences of other believers with the private convictions that arise out of our personal walk with God. . . spiritual disciplines (regular private devotions, studying the Bible, memorizing Scripture, meeting with a group for Bible Study or prayer meeting for example) are provided for our good not for our bondage. They are privileges to be used not duties to be performed . . . promote them as benefits, not as duties. Perhaps stop talking about being 'faithful' to have a quiet time with God each day as if we are doing something to earn a reward . . . better to talk about the *privilege* of spending time with the God of the universe and the importance for our own sake of being consistent in that practice . . . encourage the use of spiritual disciplines and help others succeed in them <u>but</u> should never require them as a condition of acceptance – either by God or by us . . . remember grace understood and embraced will always lead to commitment. But commitment required will always lead to legalism.' [204]

Wright points out that 'In the Old Testament, obedience to the law was not just an arbitrary duty, 'because rules is rules'. A frequent motivation is the encouraging assurance that it is for our own good. This is the thrust of the exhortations in Deuteronomy.

The LORD commanded us to obey all these decrees and to fear the LORD our God *so that we might always prosper and be kept alive.* (6:24, and see also 4:40, 5:33, 30:15-20, etc.)

The assumption behind this kind of motivation is that God, as the creator of human beings, knows best what kind of social patterns will contribute to human wellbeing. His laws were not meant to be negatively restricting, but to provide the conditions in which life can most truly humane and beneficial. Obedience therefore brings blessing, not as a reward, but as a natural result. Just as physical health is not some kind of bonus of Brownie badge for good behaviour. It is simply the natural product of sensible living in the way our bodies were designed to. . .

It is very important to see that the law was given for people's sake, not for God's sake. Of course, it is true that our obedience makes God happy. But the purpose of the law was not to make *him* happy, but *us*. That is what the Psalmists recognized when they exclaim things like 'O how I love your law', or say they prefer it to gold or honey. They could see that obedience to God's law, far from being the dry crust of stale legalism we might imagine, was actually the surest route to personal fulfilment and satisfaction, genuine freedom, and social harmony and prosperity. The law was a gift of grace, a blessing, a treasure, one of the many privileges God had entrusted to Israel – for their own good and then for the blessing of the rest of humanity.' [205]

---

[204] *Transforming Grace* p 129, 135, 136-7

[205] Christopher J. H. Wright (born 1947) *Knowing Jesus through the Old Testament* IVP 1992 p205-07

And lastly a word on being disliked or even hated because we act in love. There has been no man walk this earth who has and does love more than our Christ Jesus and yet remember what they did to him!

Jesus told his disciples "Do not think that I came to bring peace on earth. I did not come to bring peace but a sword. For I have come to set a man against his father, a daughter against her mother, and a daughter-in-law against her mother-in-law; and a man's enemies will be those of his own household. He who loves father or mother more than me is not worthy of me. And he who loves son or daughter more than Me is not worthy of Me. And he who does not take his cross and follow after me is not worthy of me. He who finds his life will lose it, and he who loses his life for My sake will find it. He who receives you receives Me, and he who receives me receives Him who sent Me. . . . he shall by no means lose his reward." (Matthew 10:34-42)

Yet knowing his disciples, knowing his teachings on how the gospel was going to divide loved ones like a sword, causing great pain he also spoke of how no disciple of his would ever lose that which really mattered, no follower would be a loser as a result.

'Now as He was going out on the road, one came running, knelt before Him, and asked Him, "Good Teacher, what shall I do that I may inherit eternal life?" . . . [This rich young ruler went on to claim he had kept commandments No. 5-10 since his youth but no mention was given of No. 1-4.] Then Jesus . . . said to him, ". . . sell whatever you have and give to the poor, and you will have treasure in heaven; and come, take up the cross, and follow Me." But he was sad at this word, and went away sorrowful, for he had great possessions. . . Then Peter began to say to Him, "See, we have left all and followed You." So Jesus answered and said, "Assuredly, I say to you, there is no one who has left house or brothers or sisters or father or mother or wife or children or lands, for My sake and the gospel's who shall not receive a hundredfold now in this time – houses and brothers and sisters and mothers and children and lands, with persecutions – and in the age to come, eternal life."' (Mark 10:17-22, 28-30)

What have you or I in this life that has more value, that is more worthwhile having even briefly, very briefly than eternal life? And what of this life now? Well, as I sit in my back pew of a Sunday morning and look around, I see and know my brothers, my sisters, my mothers, my children, my family that my God has given me for his gospel has divided me from the others. O and yes, he has even given me a house and lands as in a garden as well![206] But I am well aware that this is not necessarily so for all pilgrims while in this world.

In 2018, Open Doors, a worldwide ministry to the persecuted church, says that on average *every month* 255 Christians are killed, 104 are abducted, 180 Christian women are raped, harassed, or forced into marriage, 66 churches are attacked, and 160 Christians are imprisoned without trial.

How is it that those who persecute Christians know whom to target? It's because the Christians are living lives that testify to their faith in Jesus Christ . . . When they are persecuted, they do what Jesus did: '[He] committed Himself to Him who judges righteously' (1Peter 2:23) In faith and practice, always imitate Jesus – especially when your faith is opposed by others. By 2020 over 260 million Christians are living in places around the world where they experience high levels of persecution; that's 1 in every 9 in the last year! Over the last ear. 2,883 were killed for their faith, 9,488 churches and other Christian buildings were attacked, 3,711 believers were detained without trial, arrested, sentenced or imprisoned. Women experience 'double persecution', one for being Christian, one for being a woman.[207]

J. C. Ryle once said that 'Persecution is like the goldsmith's hallmark on real silver and gold; it is one of the marks of a converted man.'

The question of why this is so has caused many disputes, ideas and books to be written, some of which I have read.

---

[206] I wish to give credit for these thoughts to the Rev. Philip Burns' sermon 19:1:20 *Sent out to serve the King Part5 The Gospel Divides* 19.1.20

[207] From https://www.opendoorsusa.org/christian-persecution

This world is fallen so are most of the people in it. God is real and he is sovereign. The restraining presence of the Holy Spirit, for now means this world is not as bad as it could be. Satan is defeated and, on a leash, held by God. I have some answers but not enough, I am not God. For now, my job, my work and yours, is to believe in Christ whom God sent, full-stop (John6:28-29), regardless of the circumstances we find ourselves in while in this world. There may be an answer when we are glorified and completely sin-free, but then we may not need one.

Before we leave this section though let's briefly consider prayer and its place in being loving, loving towards God, others and ourselves. God gave us the ability to communicate with him and all relationships if they are to survive need regular open, honest communication between the parties involved. God recorded all that he has spoken to humanity down through the ages, all that he needs us to know in the Bible. His loving gift to us of prayer is the way for all pilgrims to communicate back. We, to live this lifestyle of a pilgrim need prayer, we need to know how to use our new mindset, how to use the armour, and to confess, repent and get up and going again. If you do not feel the need to pray to God almost as much as you feel the need to eat and drink you are heading onto dangerous ground.

> A habit has been defined as an act repeated so often it becomes involuntary. There is no new decision of mind each time the act is performed. Jesus prayed. He loved to pray. Often praying was His way of resting. He prayed so often it became part of His life. It was to Him like breathing – involuntary. . . Fenelon cried, "In God's name I beseech you let prayer nourish your souls as your meals nourish your body. Let your fixed seasons of prayer keep you in God's presence through the day, and His presence frequently remembered as though it be an everfresh spring of prayer." [208]

---

[208] Dick Eastman (born 1944) *No easy Road* Chosen Books 1971 quote from somewhere within chapter 5 (I no longer have this book)

Paul wrote, 'Rejoice always, pray without ceasing, in everything give thanks: for this is the will of God in Christ Jesus for you.' (1Thesseloians 5:16-8)

The call on a pilgrim to love has never changed, nor the command to be holy. The reality of having to face some form of persecution at one stage or another in our pilgrimage here has never abated but in fact is set to increase as the day approaches. And so, the pilgrims' need to be in full armoury and in constant contact with his or her victorious captain will never diminish during our sojourning. But take heart pilgrim, only the call to love will be required when we arrive home, for there we will be holy thru and thru.

Joyful cross carrying

It was Christ himself who told his disciples (then and now) after Peter's announcement that he was 'The Christ of God' (Luke 9:20) what this Christ would have to endure and as a result all disciples, followers, pilgrims as we read in Luke 9:23-26, '. . . If anyone desires to come after me, let him deny himself, and take up his cross daily, and follow Me. For whoever desires to save his life will lose it, but whoever loses his life for My sake will save it. For what profit is it to a man if he gains the whole world, and is himself destroyed or lost? For whoever is ashamed of Me and My words, of him the Son of Man will be ashamed when He comes in His own glory, and in His Father's, and of the holy angels.'

<u>Question</u>: What is this cross we are being called to take up? What has it to do with my lifestyle?

<u>Answer</u>: I have read many explanations of this cross, some that make the prospect of carrying it bearable to consider and others that cause you to halt and consider. The cross is not a thorn used by God to keep our perspective of ourselves aright but two huge beams of timber that we are to carry till our sojourning is over. It is a burden, a weight which must be carried not discarded. The Jews of Christ's time would have thought of the cross as a form of

punishment, a slow cruel death as we have seen previously, not as a piece of jewelry. A far better biblical scholar than I has the answer that I believe fits but it is not comfortable, it rasps against our self-serving, self-centered old nature causing all sorts of perceived miseries and wounds.

> [The Cross] was something [Christ] took up voluntarily, not something that was imposed on Him; it involved sacrifice and suffering; it involved Him in costly renunciations; it was symbolic of rejection by the world. And it is to cross-bearing of this nature that the disciple is always called. It involves a willingness to accept ostracism and unpopularity with the world for His sake. We can evade carrying the cross simply by conforming our lives to the world's standards.
>
> Contrary to expectation, taking our cross and following Christ is not a joyless experience, as the saintly Samuel Rutherford knew: 'He who looks at the white side of Christ's cross, and takes it up handsomely, will find it just such a burden as wings are to a bird.'
>
> If the disciple is unwilling to fulfil this condition, Jesus said, 'He cannot be my disciple.'[209]

Question: Why did Christ take up his cross? Why did he who created the universe, who could hold all his creation in the palm of his hand, the heavens and all their stars, the seas and all their creatures, the dry lands and their flora and fauna and humans, male and female, why did he voluntarily become an embryo within Mary's womb, dependent on her blood supply, cared for by hands and hearts he had made to only take up the cross?

Answer: Love. Love for the Father and love for all that his Father loved.

Question: Lifestyles marked by joy (or happiness or blessings as some translations use) while daily cross carrying not to mention being at war, how can this be?

---

[209] J. Oswald Sanders (1902-1992) *The Joy of Following Jesus* Moody Press 1990 p21-22

<u>Answer</u>: This joy is not a grim determination on our part with gritted teeth; it has nothing to do with being stoic. This joy is experienced within if not always seen outwardly by others, yet it is a joy from without self. It is a joy despite outward circumstances yet is a joy that our carelessness, ingratitude and willful sins can dampen and destroy. It is a joy from God because of God and the love he has poured into us and continues to do so. It has nothing to do with the world or its joys which are fleeting and dependant on circumstances. And it is complete, a fullness, a contentment that comes from a rested satisfaction of and in the triune God that can wipe out the need for anything in place of its giver if we wrap ourselves in him. It is a joy that comes wrapped with hope and peace, a joy that heals and energizes us onwards. It is a joy all pilgrims have during their sojourning in all of its fullness yet there is more to experience when our walk here is over. It is a joy we have to fight to feel, it is not necessarily one of laughter or exuberance effervescence but when you feel it deep within, a quiet, solid contentment and peace with life, it makes the sky bluer and the day lighter and you may surprise yourself with a desire to laugh! If you have this deep joy others can see something different about you that they will desire, hunger for. If you have lost it you know it and grieve and strive to get it back!

David wrote Psalm 51 when the prophet Nathan confronted him on his sin against God by committing adultery with Bathsheba and then murdering her husband. It is a prayer of repentance and verse 12 says, 'Restore to me [David] the joy of Your salvation, and uphold me by Your generous Spirit' and verse 8 reads, 'Make me hear joy and gladness that the bones You have broken may rejoice.'

For David, and for all pilgrims, a driving force behind all that we do, all that we live for, our life, our behaviours should come from our joy, our delight of having an intimate relationship with the one and only God over all of creation who rejoices over us with song (Zephaniah 3:17), a relationship based on love.

Piper tells us that 'This is Augustine's [354-430 A.D.] understanding of grace. *Grace is God's giving us sovereign joy in God that triumphs over joy in sin. . .* Loving God, in Augustine's mind, is never reduced to deeds of obedience or acts of willpower. He never makes the mistake of quoting John 14:5 ('If you love Me, you will keep My commandments') and claiming that love *is* the same as keeping Christ's commandments, when the text says that keeping Christ's commandments *results from* loving Christ. '*If* you love, *then* me you will obey.' Nor does he make the mistake of quoting 1 John 5:3 ('for this is the love of God, that we keep His commandments; and His commandments are not burdensome') and overlook the point that loving God means keeping his commandments *in such a way* that his commandments are not burdensome. Loving God is being so satisfied in God and so delighted in all that he is for us that his commandments cease to be burdensome. Augustine saw this. And we need him badly today to help us recover the root of all Christian living in the triumphant joy in God that dethrones the sovereignty of laziness and lust and greed. . .

What follows from Augustine's view of grace as the giving of a sovereign joy that triumphs over 'lawless pleasures' is that the entire Christian life is seen as a relentless quest for the fullest joy in God. He said, "The whole life of a good Christian is a holy desire." In other words, the key to Christian living is a thirst and a hunger for God. . .

Augustine's doctrine of delight in God is the root of all Christian living. He brings it to bear on the most practical affairs of life and shows that every moment in every circumstance we stand on the brink between the lure of idolatry and the delight of seeing and knowing God . . . For example, his chief rule on using the things of the world so that they are gratefully received as God's gifts but do not become idols is expressed in this prayer: "He loves thee too little who loves anything together with thee, which he loves not for thy sake." He illustrates:

Suppose, brethren, a man should make a ring for his betrothed, and she should love the ring more wholeheartedly than the betrothed who made it for her . . . Certainly, let her love his gift: but, if she should say, "The ring is enough. I do not want to see his face again" what would we say of her? . . . The pledge is given her by the betrothed just that, in his pledge, he himself may be loved. God, then, has given you all these things. Love Him who made them.

Instead of minimizing the greatness and the beauty of this world, Augustine admired it and made it a means of longing for the City of which this is all a shadow. "From His gifts, which are scattered to good and bad alike in this, our most grim life, let us, with his help, try to express sufficiently what we have yet to experience." . . . Augustine's relentless focus on the City of God did not prevent him from seeing the beauties of this world and enjoying them for what they are – good gifts of God pointing us ever to the Giver and the superior joys of his presence. We need to heed the unremitting call of Augustine to be free from the ensnaring delights of this world, not because they are evil in themselves, but because so few of us use them as we ought: "If the things of this world delight you, praise God for them but turn your love away from them and give it to their Maker, so that in the things that please you may not displease him.". . .

This note of sobering, triumphant joy is a missing element in too much Christian (especially Reformed) theology and worship. Maybe the question we should pose ourselves is whether this is so because we have not experienced the triumph of sovereign joy in our own lives. Can we say the following with Augustine?

How sweet all at once it was for me to be rid of *those fruitless joys* which I had once feared to lose! . . . *You drove them from me*, you who are the true, the *sovereign joy*. You drove them from me and took their place . . . O Lord my God, my Light, my Wealth, and my Salvation.

Or are we in bondage to the pleasures of this world so that, for all our talk about the glory of God, we love television and food and sleep and sex and money and human praise just like everybody else? If so, let us repent and fix our faces like flint toward the

Word of God. And let us pray: O Lord, open my eyes to see the sovereign sight that in your presence is fullness of joy and at your right hand are pleasures forevermore (Psalm 16:11). Grant, O God, that we would live the legacy of Sovereign Joy.[210] If we want to make people glad in God, our lives must look as if God, not possessions, is our joy.'[211]

So, how joy filled and free does your life look?
To be honest I don't believe I have any obvious joy for another to see and desire when I am among people and yet. . .
There was a time when I did not want to live, I had no hope or joy that made me want to get up and face another day, then Christ shook my life apart. The very spot I had once considered turning the steering wheel to the wrong side of the narrow country road into the oncoming semi became the spot where becoming aware of the brilliant hue of blue that the sky was – since when had it ever been so blue? – and noticing the velvety green paddocks and antics of newborn lambs I startled myself by laughing out aloud for the sheer joy of being alive. I could not remember the last time I'd even felt like laughing let alone actually doing so. A lot of years have passed since then. The level of feel-able (as opposed to knowing) joy has fluctuated yet never really left, it just got hid under some rubbish for a while. It is still very good to be truly alive but it will even be better when I get to see my Christ face to face.
Being happy to be alive, happy, truly contented with your life can show in many ways. There are a lot less stress buttons for starters. You can walk at a slower pace (unless trying to shift unwanted weight) and enjoy counting how many little ducklings are trying to fit under those small protective wings or watch the clouds forming and then dissolving, joining to make mythical creatures instead of rushing to the next thing, your voice is patient when answering a three-year old's hundredth "But why?" and you can smile more or even laugh out loud – that really

---

[210] John Piper *The legacy of Sovereign Joy* 2000 Crossway. p57-8, 62-3, 70-2, 73-4
[211] John Piper *Don't waste your life*. Crossway 2003 p111

makes people notice – and your face begins to get more smile lines than frown ones, giving you a look that invites conversation. Contented joy gives you more time to enjoy life for several reasons. You may be able to think of more. You don't need to be as others, you don't have to have a table like the magazines tell you in their Christmas editions (yes, as I am writing this section December has arrived), a sandwich around the lake and a sleep does as much for you (even more as there will be less for the scales to register), you don't need as much stuff for you know the lie behind 'the one with most toys wins' so you don't have as much endless work to do like dusting, washing, insuring, stressing over how to divide up a mountain of stuff in the will or a high paying, high stress job so you can get the stuff in the first place, and you no longer have the need to compare, measure yourself against another.

Joy is a stress killer, though take care as stress can be a joy dampener. Being a stress killer, would not this joy help you to have better times with your spouse, your children, other people in neighborhood or at work? Would not that be something that others would like?

Does that give you a different slant to consider if your life shows joy? I hope so, because every pilgrim does have it somewhere within as they have Christ inside. It just may need a good dusting.

'True Christian joy', wrote Tozer, 'is the heart's harmonious response to the Lord's song of love.' [212]

James L. Snyder believed that what Tozer wanted to get across to the readers of his book 'Delighting in God' was 'simply that your passion for God will determine your lifestyle.' [213]

Piper writes that 'Enjoying God supremely is one way to glorify him. Enjoying God makes him look supremely valuable. . . . God created me – and you – to live with a single, all-embracing, all-transforming passion – namely, a passion to glorify God by

---

[212] *The Knowledge of the Holy* p109
[213] *Delighting in God* Introduction p10

enjoying and displaying his supreme excellence in all the spheres of life. Enjoying and displaying are both crucial. If we try to display the excellence of God without joy in it, we will display a shell of hypocrisy and create scorn or legalism. But if we claim to enjoy his excellence and do not display it for others to see and admire, we deceive ourselves, because the mark of God-enthralled joy is to overflow and expand by extending itself into the hearts of others. . . Life is wasted when we do not live for the glory of God. And I mean *all* of life. . . That is why the Bible gets down into the details of eating and drinking, 'Whether you eat or drink, or whatever you do, *do all to the glory of God*' (1 Corinthians 10:13). We waste out lives when we do not weave God into our eating and drinking and every other part by enjoying and displaying him. . .
Jonathan Edwards [1703-1758] preached of this glory of God and us glorifying Him in a sermon 'with this main point: 'The godly are designed for unknown and inconceivable happiness.'. . .
[The] glory of God [does not] consist merely in the creature's perceiving his perfections: for the creature may perceive the power and wisdom of God, and yet take no delight in it, but abhor it. Those creatures that do so, don't glorify God. Nor doth the glory of God consist especially in speaking of his perfections: for words avail not any otherwise than as they express the sentiment of the mind. Tis glory of God, therefore, [consists] in the creature's admiring and rejoicing [and] exulting in the manifestation of his beauty and excellency . . . The essence of glorifying . . . God consists, therefore, in the creature's rejoicing in God's manifestations of his beauty, which is the joy and happiness we speak of. So we see it comes to this at last: that the end of the creation is that God may communicate happiness to the creature; for if God created the world that he may be glorified in the creature, he created it that they might rejoice in his glory: for we have shown that they are the same. . .
Love has to do with showing a dying soul the life-giving beauty of the glory of God, especially his grace. . . we show God's glory in a hundred practical ways that include care about food and clothes and shelter and health. That's what Jesus meant when he said,

"Let your light shine before others, so that they may see your good works and give glory to your Father who is in heaven" (Matthew 5:16).

Every good work should be a revelation of the glory of God. What makes the good deed an act of love is not the raw act, but the passion and the sacrifice to make God himself known as glorious. Not to aim to show God is not to love, because God is what we need most deeply. And to have all else without him is to perish in the end. The Bible says that you can give away all that you have and deliver your body to be burned and have not love (1 Corinthians 13:3). If you don't point people to God for everlasting joy, you don't love. You waste your life. . .

God calls us to pray and think and dream and plan and work not to be made much of, but to make much of him in every part of our lives. . . .'[214]

Fleetwood writes that 'The principle of love to God will be also fruitful of every good work . . . All the best things we can do, if destitute of this principle, will prove to be only the result of self-deception and hypocrisy, or done merely to procure the esteem of men. Without love, a narrowness of soul will shut us up within ourselves, and make all we do to others only as merchants, who, trading for their own advantages, and care nothing for the interests of their neighbours. It is love only that opens our hearts to consider other persons, and to love them on their own account, and on account of the God who made us, and who is love.'[215]

1 Corinthians 13

Morris writes that 'Herman Ridderbos [1909-2007] stresses the importance of the fact, that for Paul, love "unfolds itself in a great many "forms of love." He proceeds,

---

[214] *Don't Waste your Life* p 28, 31-2, 30-31, 34-5, 38 & 49.
[215] *Fleetwood's Life of Christ* p481-484

> In addition to love, Paul speaks, for example, of peace . . , steadfastness . . , kindness . . , goodness . . , faithfulness . . , gentleness . . , compassion . . , humility . . , forbearing . . , forgiving . . , thinking about what is true . . , just . . , honourable . . , pure . . , lovely . . , sweet-sounding . . , obligingness . . .
>
> Of all these concepts and descriptions, some are more, others less "specifically Christian". These virtues, however, even though they occour in the same terms in the non-Christian Greek ethic, in Paul's epistles are always brought under the viewpoint of brotherly communion and the upbuilding of the church, and not, as in the Greek ethic, under that of character formation; they are always understood, therefore, as the fulfilment of the requirement of love . . .

Many of the absolute references to love seem to show that love is a way of life, the only way for Christians. "Walk in love," we read, "even as Christ also loved us." (Eph 5:2). Walking is a metaphor that Paul in particular uses frequently. It indicates steady and persistent – if unspectacular – progress. . . love is not a virtue that can be practiced alone. One may hope without other people, or believe, but one cannot love in isolation. . .' [216]

So, let's have a closer look at Paul's picture of the love found in 1Corinthians 13 that we are to have flowing out of our hearts indwelt by Christ. [217]

- *Love suffers long and is kind* (v.4)

The Greek for *suffers long* meant *long-tempered*, the quality of having a long fuse. This is describing 'that quality of self-restraint in the face of provocation that does not hastily retaliate or promptly punish.'

It is a patient loving intent 'even when experiencing serious heartache'. The Greek for *kind* here means to *show oneself*

---

[216] *Testaments of Love* p210-11, 232, 233-4.

[217] I wish to give credit to Bill Crowder *What is Real Love?* Discovery Series 1Corinthians 13:4-8 RBC Ministries 1997 for some of the definitions, wording and ideas in this section.

useful, to act benevolently. It is a kindness that is generous and useful. Therefore, we could say that a love which suffers long and is kind, is a love that shows patient restraint and choses to be kind, generous and useful instead of bitter and retaliatory.
Proverbs 10:12, 'Hatred stirs up strife, but love covers all sins.'
Lucado writes, 'The Greek word used here for *patience* is a descriptive one. It figuratively means 'taking a long time to boil'. Think about a pot of boiling water . . . The utensil may have an influence but the primary factor is the intensity of the flame. Water boils quickly when the flame is high. It boils slowly when the flame is low. Patience 'keeps the burner down'. . . . Patience isn't naïve. It doesn't ignore misbehaviour. It just keeps the flame low. It waits. It listens. It's slow to boil. This is how God treats us. . . Patience is a fruit of his Spirit. It hangs from the tree of Galatians 5:22. Have you asked God to give you some fruit? . . . And while you're praying, ask for understanding. 'Patient people have great understanding' (Prov. 14:29). Could it be your impatience stems from a lack of understanding? . . .
'Love is kind', writes Paul.
Nehemiah agrees: 'You are God, ready to pardon, gracious and merciful, slow to anger, abundant in kindness' (Neh.9:17 NKJV).
David agrees, 'Your lovingkindness is better than life' (Ps.63:3 NASB) . . .
In the original language, the word for kindness carries an added idea . . . chiefly it refers to an act of grace. But it also refers to a deed or person who is 'useful, serviceable, adapted to its purpose'. *Kindness* was even employed to describe food that was tasty as well as healthy . . . Isn't kindness good *and* good for you?? Pleasant *and* practical? . .
The Bible says, 'Whoever is wise will observe these things, and they will understand the lovingkindness of the LORD' (Ps. 107:43 NKJV.) Hasn't God been kind – pleasantly useful – to you? And since God has been so kind to you . . . can't you be kind to others? . . .
Kind hearts are quietly kind. They let the car cut into traffic and the young mum with three kids move up in the checkout line.

They pick up the neighbour's trash can that rolled into the street. And they are especially kind at church. They understand that perhaps the neediest person they'll meet all week is the one standing in the foyer or sitting on the row behind them in worship. . . .

. . . mercy is the deepest gesture of kindness. Paul equates the two. 'Be kind to one another, tender-hearted, forgiving one another, even as God in Christ forgave you' (Eph 4:32NKJV) . . .
Kindness at home. Kindness in public. Kindness at church and kindness with your enemies . . . Someone else needs your kindness. . . You.
Don't we tend to be tough on ourselves? And rightly so. Like the young couple at the wedding, we don't always plan ahead. Like Zacchaeus, we've cheated our share of friends. We've been self-serving. And like the woman with the illness, our world sometimes seems out of control.
But did Jesus scold the couple? No. Did he punish Zacchaeus? No. Was he hard on the woman? No. He is kind to the forgetful. He is kind to the greedy. He is kind to the sick.
And he is kind to us. And since he is kind to us, can't we be a little kinder to ourselves? . . . He knows everything about you, yet he doesn't hold back his kindness toward you. Why don't you be kind to yourself? He forgives your faults. Why don't you do the same? He thinks tomorrow is worth living. Why don't you agree? He believes in you enough to call you his ambassador, his follower, even his child. Why not take his cue and believe in yourself?' [218]

- *Love does not envy* (v.4)

The Greek used here means *to earnestly covert, have desire, move with envy.* To intently covert something that belongs to another which God has not seen fit to endow you with is not at all loving, especially if involves murderous thoughts as well. It is a

---

[218] Max Lucado A *Love Worth Giving Living in the overflow of God's Love* W Publishing group 2002 p14-5, 17, 26-31

thought that says God is not enough. It is discontentment with what he has given you.

Galatians 5:26, 'Let us not become conceited, provoking one another, envying one another.'

Envy possesses a power sufficient to blind the understanding and harden the heart. [219]

Lucado writes, 'My job was not to question [God] but to trust him 'Don't be jealous . . . Trust the LORD and do good' (Ps 37:1, 3 NCV). The cure for jealousy? Trust. The cause of jealousy? Distrust. . . . What are the consequences of envy?

Loneliness tops the list. Solomon says, "Anger is cruel and destroys like a flood, but no one can put up with jealousy!" (Prov 27:4 NCV) Who wants to hang out with a jealous fool? . . . Sickness is another consequence. The wise man also wrote, "Peace of mind means a healthy body, but jealousy will rot your bones" (Prov 14:30).

Violence is the ugliest fruit. 'You want something you don't have, and you will do anything to get it. You will even kill!' (James 4:2 CEV) 'Jealousy', informs Proverbs 6:34, 'enrages a man' (NASB). The Jews used one word for jealousy, qua-nah. It meant 'to be intensely red'. . .have you seen such envy? . . . on your face?

. . . Stop listing what you want, and start trusting God to provide what you need.'[220]

- *Love does not parade itself, is not puffed up* or as the NIV reads, 'Love is patient, love is kind. It does not envy, it does not boast, it is not proud' (v.4). The Greek translated here as *parade* means to *boast or brag, puffed up* is to *inflate, to be proud, haughty, arrogant.* The picture I get is of one very overdressed in finery, including flounces and puffy laces and outrageous colours to make a grand entrance that no one will miss or that of an

---

[219] *Fleetwood's Life of Christ* comment from Dr Campbell's Expository Bible p145
[220] *A Love Worth Giving* p37-8

insignificant puffer fish caught and landed on the beach swelling itself up in the hope that you will respect it and step away.
Lucado reminds us to –
> *Put others before yourself.*
> And then:
> *Accept your part in his plan.*

True humility is not thinking lowly of yourself but thinking accurately of yourself. The humble heart does not say, "I can't do anything." But rather, "I can't do everything. I know my part and am happy to do it."
When Paul writes, '*consider* others better than yourselves' (Phil 2:3 NIV emphasis mine), he uses a verb that means 'to calculate', 'to reckon'. The word implies a conscious judgement resting on carefully weighed facts. To consider others better than yourself, then, is not to say you have no place; it is to say that you know your place. 'Don't cherish exaggerated ideas of yourself or your importance, but try to have a sane estimate of your capabilities by the light of the faith that God has given to you' (Rom 12:3 PHILLIPS).
> And finally:
> *Be quick to applaud the success of others.* [221]

- *Love does not behave rudely, does not seek its own, is not provoked, thinks no evil* or, 'It is not rude, it is not self-seeking, it is not easily angered, it keeps no record of wrongs' (v. 5 NIV).

1Corinthians 10:24, 'Let no one seek his own, but each one the other's well-being.'
The Greek translated *rudely* can mean *an indecency, an action that is unseemly, that shames*. To *seek its own* from the Greek involved could imply *a demand for something one thinks is due them*. *Provoked* is *to be exasperated, stirred up*. *Thinks no evil* means *to keep no accounts of evil, no grudge stewing*. So, this is a love that does not become irritated nor shame another, keep grudges or demand a 'thank-you'.
Love is also even-tempered. We have already seen that it is 'long-tempered' (v.4), and here is a related characteristic – that it is not

---

[221] Ibid p48-9

easily provoked. Phillips translates this as "It is not touchy", which gives us a good idea of what Paul means. It is easy to be so concerned with getting our own way that we become irritated with people, well-meaning and otherwise, who frustrate our best intentions. But the person infused with God's love takes such frustration in stride, accepting it as part of life.

Karl Barth comments, '... The neighbour can get dreadfully on my nerves even in the exercise of what he regards as, and what might well be, his particular gifts. And he can then provoke and embitter and in some degree enrage me. Love cannot alter the fact that he gets on my nerves, but as self-giving (and this perhaps with salutary counter-effects on my poor nerves) it can rule out *a limine* my allowing myself to be 'provoked' by him – i.e., forced into the position and role of an antagonist.' [222]

F.F. Bruce noticing Heb. 10:24, 'And let us consider one another in order to stir up love and good works' comments, 'But here love is provoked in the sense of being stimulated in the lives of Christians by the considerateness and example of other members of their fellowship.' [223]

Lucado writes that 'The Greek word for *rude* means shameful or disgraceful behaviour.

God calls us to a higher, more noble concern. Not, 'What are my rights?' but 'What is loving?'

Do you have the right to dominate a conversation? Yes, but is it loving to do so?

Do you have the right to pretend you don't hear your wife speaking? I suppose so. But is it loving?

Is it within your rights to bark at the clerk or snap at the kids? Yes. But is it loving to act this way? . . .

People can be so rude. We snatch parking places. We forget names. We interrupt. We fail to show up. Could you use some courtesy? . . . Receive the courtesy of Christ. He's your groom.

---

[222] *Testaments of Love* p247 Quoted from *Church Dogmatics*, IV,2, Edinburgh, 1958, 834
[223] Ibid. p233

Does not the groom cherish the bride? Respect the bride? Honour the bride? Let Christ do what he longs to do.

For as you receive his love, you'll find it easier to give yours. As you reflect on his courtesy to you, you'll likely to offer the same. .

Paul writes; 'Do nothing from selfishness or empty conceit, but with humility of mind regard one another as more important than yourselves; do not *merely* look out for your own personal interests, but also for the interests of others' (Phil 2:3-4 NASB) . . . The word the apostle uses for *selfishness* shares a root form with the words *strife* and *contentious*. It suggests a self-preoccupation that hurts others. A divisive arrogance. . . *Selfishness is an obsession with self that excludes others, hurting everyone.*

Looking after your personal interests is proper life management. Doing so to the exclusion of the rest of the world is selfishness. The adverb highlighted in verse 4 is helpful. . . Desire success? Fine. Just don't hurt others in achieving it. Wish to look nice? That's okay. Just don't do so by making others look bad. Love is not selfish. . .

Love builds up relationships; selfishness erodes relationships . . . Can we get our eyes off of self? . . . According to Scripture, we can.

'Therefore if there is any encouragement in Christ, if there is any consolation of love, if there is any fellowship of the Spirit, if any affection and compassion, make my joy complete by being of the same mind.' (Phil 2:1-2 NASB)

Paul's sarcasm is thinly veiled. Is there any encouragement? Any consolation? Any fellowship? Then smile!

What's the cure for selfishness?

Get your self out of your eye by getting your eye off your self. Quit staring at that little self, and focus on your great Saviour. . .

Isn't that the work of the Cross? A smaller 'I' and a greater Christ? Don't focus on yourself; focus on all you have in Christ. Focus on the encouragement in Christ, the consolation of Christ, the love of Christ, the fellowship of the Spirit, the affection and compassion of heaven. . . We deserve a lava bath, but we've been given a pool of grace.

Yet to look at our faces you'd think our circumstances had made only a 'slight improvement'. "How's life?" someone asks. And we who've been resurrected from the dead say, "Well, things could be better." . . . Are you so focused on what you don't have that you are blind to what you do? Have you received any encouragement? Any fellowship? Any consolation? Then don't you have reason for joy? . . .

> You have a ticket to heaven no thief can take,
> An eternal home no divorce can break.
> Every sin of your life has been cast to the sea.
> Every mistake you've made is nailed to the tree.
> You're blood-bought and heaven-made.
> A child of God – forever saved.
> So be grateful, joyful – for isn't it true?

What you don't have is much less than what you do.

Why did Cain kill Abel? . . . What made him so mad?

Anger in and of itself is not a sin. The emotion was God's idea. . It's possible to feel what Cain felt without doing what Cain did. . According to the apostle, love is not:

> 'touchy' (TLB)
> 'irritable' (NLT)
> 'quick tempered' (CEV)
> 'quick to take offense' (NEB)
> 'easily angered' (NIV)
> and love 'doesn't fly off the handle' (MSG).

'The LORD accepted Abel and his gift, but he did not accept Cain and his gift. So Cain became very *angry* and felt *rejected*' (Gen 4:4-5, emphasis mine).

Interesting. This is the first appearance of Anger in the Bible. . . and look who is in the front set with him – Rejection. . . .

The fire of anger has many logs, but according to biblical accounts, the thickest and the hottest block of wood is rejection . . .

Through Christ, God has accepted you. Think about what this means. . .

Rejections are like speed bumps on the road. They come with the journey. . . You're going to get cut, dished, dropped, and kicked around. You cannot keep people from rejecting you. But you can keep rejections from enraging you. How? By letting [God's] acceptance compensate for their rejection.

When others reject you, let God accept you. He is not frowning. He is not mad. He sings over you. Take a long drink from his limitless love, and cool down. . . .

What if you took every thought captive? What if you refused to let any trash enter your mind? What if you took the counsel of Solomon: 'Be careful what you think, because your thoughts run your life' (Prov. 4:23) . . .

You are driving to work when the words of your co-worker come to mind. He needled you about your performance. He second guessed your efficiency . . . You begin to wonder. *I didn't deserve any of that. Who is he to criticize me? Besides, he has as much taste as a rice cake. Have you seen those shoes he wears?*

At this point you need to make a choice. *Am I going to keep a list of these wrongs?* You can. . . Or you can do something else. You can take those thoughts captive. You can defy the culprit. Quote a verse if you have to: 'Bless those who persecute you; bless and do not curse' (Rom 12:14 NIV) . . . Anger at your parents is keeping you awake. You want to sleep, but this afternoon's phone call won't let you. As always, all they did was criticize.

No compliments. No applause. Just pick, pick, pick

Why aren't you . . . ? When will you . . . ? Why don't you . . . ? Grrr. .

Remember . . . You are not a victim of your thoughts. You have a vote. You have a voice. You can exercise thought prevention. You can also exercise thought permission. . .

It's not enough to keep no list of wrongs. We have to cultivate a list of blessings. The same verb Paul uses for *keeps* in the phrase 'keeps no list of wrongs' is used for *think* in Philippians 4:8: 'Whatever is true, whatever is honourable, whatever is just, whatever is pure, whatever is lovely, whatever is gracious, if there is any excellence, if there is anything worthy of praise, think about these things.' (RSV) *Thinking* conveys the idea of pondering –

studying and focusing, allowing what is viewed to have an impact on us.

> Rather than store up the sour, store up the sweet.
> You want to make a list? Then list his mercies . . .

Stand face to feet with the form of your crucified Saviour and pray, "Jesus, if you can forgive me for hurting you, then I can forgive them for hurting me." You didn't deserve to be hurt by them. But neither did you deserve to be forgiven by him.' [224]

- *Love does not rejoice in iniquity, but rejoices in the truth* or 'Love does not delight in evil but rejoices with the truth' (v6 NIV).

This is a love that congratulates those who love and live the truth, but not those who do unrighteousness.

Morris writes that 'Paul combines a negative and a positive assertion in his assurance that love 'does not rejoice on the basis of unrighteousness but rejoices with the truth' (v.6). We unhesitatingly accept this idea, yet we have trouble putting it into practice. The unhappy truth is that we do tend to rejoice in the misfortunes of others. Certainly many of our jokes prove this point (and think of what happens to our clowns!). Newspapers' reporting feeds our appetites for catastrophe in a similar way. Seldom does good make headlines, but evil often does. And the fact that newspapers [and women's magazines] continue to sell shows that in general we approve of this pattern – particularly when people or groups we dislike meet with misfortune. Examples of this abound in every society.[55] [[55]Lewis Smedes explains the way of the world in these terms: "We will enjoy our disgust so much that we would be furious were we to be deprived of it . . . Life without an occasional scandal would rob us of the joy of indignation and disgust. A well-ordered world must have some evil.]

The poor are not displeased when the rich are in trouble, while the rich take calmly the trials of the poor. The political party in government regards with equanimity the troubles of the

---

[224] *A Love Worth Giving* p 55, 58, 64-5, 67-9, 73-5, 81, 83, 90-1

opposition, and the opposition returns the compliment with interest. But Paul is saying that, natural though this reaction may be, it is not a loving one. Love is not happy when things go badly for others; it does not rejoice in unrighteousness.'[225]

And Lucado asks if we 'Want to separate the fake from the factual, the counterfeit from the real thing? Want to know if what you feel is genuine love?

Ask yourself this: *Do I encourage this person to do what is right?* For true love 'takes no pleasure in other people's sins but delights in the truth.' (1Cor. 13:6 JB) . . .

Love doesn't ask someone to do what is wrong. . . *If you find yourself prompting evil in others, heed the alarm.* This is not love. And if others prompt evil in you, be alert. . . *Here's an example.* A classic one. A young couple are on a date. His affection goes beyond her comfort zone. She resists. But he tries to persuade her with the oldest line in the book: "But I love you. I just want to be near you. If you loved me. . ."

That siren you hear? It's the phony-love detector. This guy doesn't love her. He may love having sex with her. He may love her body. He may love boasting to his buddies about his conquest. But he doesn't love her. True love will never ask the 'beloved' to do what he or she thinks is wrong.

  Love doesn't tear down the convictions of others.
    Quite the contrary.

'Love builds up' (1Cor 8:1). 'Whoever loves a brother or sister lives in the light and will not cause anyone to stumble.' (1John 2:10) 'You are sinning against Christ when you sin against other Christians by encouraging them to do something they believe is wrong.' (1Cor 8:12 NLT)

Do you want to know if your love for someone is true? If your friendship is genuine? . . . Ask yourself: Do I influence this person to do what is right? . . .

If you want to be doubly sure, however, ask the next question.
  Do I applaud what is right? . . .

---

[225] *Testaments of Love* p248

You want to plumb the depths of your love for someone? How do you feel when that person succeeds? Do you rejoice? Or are you jealous? And when he or she stumbles? Falls to misfortune? Are you really sorry? Or are you secretly pleased?
Love never celebrates misfortune. Never.' [226]

- *Love bears all things, believes all things, hopes all things, endures all things* or 'It always protects, always trusts, always hopes, always perseveres' (v.7 NIV).

Galatians 6:2, 'Bear one another's burdens, and so fulfil the law of Christ.' From the Greek the meaning of *bare*, is *to cover with silence, suffer*; *believes* is *to have faith in, upon or with respect to a person, commit to trust*; *hopes*, is *to expect or trust*; and *endures*, is *to remain, abide, persevere or take patiently*. You could say this is a love that silently suffers the sorrow of seemingly not being enough, while in expectant trust the loving one takes this patiently having faith that in the end love will triumph regardless of circumstances.

> Accepting with contentment whatever circumstances God allows for me is very much a part of a holy walk.[227]
>
> Paul lists four positive achievements of love (v.7). Most understand the first to mean love "endures all things". The verb (*stegō*) primarily indicates 'covering', and in a secondary sense 'warding off by covering'. This latter meaning suggests endurance.[228]

I wonder...

In Genesis 3, do you remember how God killed, shed the first blood of his good creation to cover the nakedness and shame of rebellious Adam and Eve, to cover their sin from his wrath foreshadowing the time of Christ's sacrifice when his blood would cover those who would humble themselves and accept his gift but those found without this covering will experience God's wrath at

---

[226] *A Love Worth Giving* p99-100
[227] *The Pursuit of Holiness* p72
[228] *Testaments of Love* p249

the end of time when the final judgement day comes, when God's loving endurance of humanity's sin finally ends. So, to date God has endured our sin for around 6000 years. Now that is a long time to endure!

Morris tells us that 'What Paul is saying is that love will always give the benefit of the doubt, because it can never assume that the worst is true. . . 'hopes all things'. The world looks for the downfall of people and assumes that they cannot survive trials. Love . . . sees that men fail, but it can never take failure as the last word . . . love never regards such trials as insurmountable. Love does not lash out in wild rebellion against life's difficulties – love always hopes. Love knows that God will ultimately triumph through these trials.

Paul's final assurance is that love 'endures all things'. Paul's verb (*hypomenō*) is one that indicates an active, vigorous endurance, not a passive, resigned acceptance of all that happens. It is used, for example, to describe the solider in a keenly contested conflict who battles on undismayed. He does not allow the difficulties of the moment to rob him of strength and purpose; he fights on unflinchingly. So it is, Paul says, with love. Love's endurance is a positive acceptance of life with all its difficulties, not a passive acquiesce in things as they are. Love does more than put up with life's hardships; it grows and develops as it struggles against them. Love sees problems positively – as valuable tests that refine and prove its worth.'[229]

Lucado writes, '*Agape* love 'bears all things, believes all things, hopes all things, endures all things' (13:7 NKJV).

This is the type of love that Paul prescribes for the church in Corinth. Don't we need the same prescription today? Don't groups still fight with each other? Don't we flirt with those we shouldn't? Aren't we sometimes quiet when we should speak? And don't those who have found freedom still have the harder time with those who haven't? Someday there will be a

---

[229] Ibid. p250-1

community where everyone behaves and no one complains. But it won't be this side of heaven.

So till then what do we do? We reason. We confront. We teach. But most of all we love.

Such love isn't easy. Not for you. Not for me. Not even for Jesus. Want proof? Listen to his frustration: "you people have no faith. How long must I stay with you? *How long must I put up with you?*" (Mark 9:19 NCV) . . . To know Jesus asked such a question reassures us. But to hear how he answered it will change us.

How long must I put up with you?

"Long enough to be called crazy by my brothers and a liar by my neighbours. Long enough to be run out of my town and my Temple. Long enough to be laughed at, cursed, slapped, hit, blindfolded, and mocked. Long enough to feel warm spit and sharp whips and see my own blood puddle at my feet."

How long? "Until the rooster sings and the sweat stings and the mallet rings and a hillside of demons smirk at a dying God."

How long? "Long enough for every sin to so soak my sinless soul that heaven will turn in horror until my swollen lips pronounce the final transaction: 'It is finished.'"

How long? "Until it kills me."

Jesus bore all things, believed all things, hoped all things, and endured all things. Every single one. . .

Paul employed a rich word here. Its root meaning is 'to cover or conceal'. Its cousins on the noun side of the family are *roof* and *shelter*. . . The Theological Dictionary of the New Testament is known for its word study, not its poetry. But the scholar sounds poetic as he explains the meaning of protect as used in 1Corinthians 13:7. The word conveys, he says, 'The idea of covering with a cloak of love.' . . . Your finest cloak of love . . . came from God. Never thought of your Creator as a clothier? Adam and Eve did. . . He dresses us with himself. 'You were all baptized into Christ, and so you were all clothed with Christ' (Gal.3:26-27) . . .

We hide. He seeks. We bring sin. He brings a sacrifice. We try fig leaves. He brings the robe of righteousness. And we are left to sing the song of the prophet: 'He has covered me with clothes of salvation and wrapped me with a coat of goodness, like a bridegroom dressed for his wedding, like a bride dressed in jewels' (Isa.61:10) . . .

Know anyone who needs a cloak of love?

Have you ever heard anyone gossip about someone you know? Ever seen human jackals make a meal out of a fallen friend? "Well, I hear that she . . ." "Oh, but didn't you know that she . . ." "Let me tell you what a friend told me about him . . ." "Then all of a sudden it's your turn. Everybody is picking your friend apart. What do you say?

Here is what love says: Love says nothing. Love stays silent. 'Love covers a multitude of sins' (1Peter 4:8 NASB). Love doesn't expose. It doesn't gossip. If love says anything, love speaks words of defence. Words of kindness. Words of protection. . .

Know anyone who could use some protection?

Of course you do. Then give some.

Pay a gas bill for a struggling elderly couple.

Promise your kids that, God being your helper, they'll never know a hungry day or a homeless night.

Tell your husband that you'd do it all over again and invite him on a honeymoon.

Make sure your divorced friends are invited to your parties.

And when you see a wounded soul, shivering and shaken on a gurney of life, offer a lab coat and leave the rose. . .

A cloak of love. A rose of gratitude.

Have you been given the first? Then take time to give the second.'[230]

- *Love never fails.* (v.8)

---

[230] *A Love Worth Giving* p 114, 118, 121, 123-125

The Greek for *fails* here is interesting, at least I think so. It means *to be driven out of one's course, to lose, become inefficient, to fall away, to be cast off.*

Lucado writes, 'The verb Paul uses for the word fail is used elsewhere to describe the demise of a flower as it falls to the ground, withers, and decays. It carries the meaning of death and abolishment. God's love, says the apostle, will never fall to the ground, wither, and decay. By its nature, it is permanent. It is never abolished...

Our love depends on the receiver of the love... The receiver regulates our love.

Not so with the love of God. We have no thermostatic impact on his love for us. The love of God is born from within him, not from what he finds in us... God's love does not hinge on yours. The abundance of your love does not increase his. The lack of your love does not diminish his. Your goodness does not enhance his love, nor does your weakness dilute it...

... Love is a fruit of the Spirit of God. 'The Spirit produces the fruit' (Gal. 5:22 NCV).

And, this is so important, you are a branch on the vine of God. 'I am the vine, and you are the branches' (John 15:5 NCV). Need a refresher course on how vines function? What is the role of the branch in the bearing of fruit? Branches don't exert a lot of energy. You never hear of gardeners treating branches for exhaustion. Branches don't attend clinics on stress management. Nor do they groan and grunt: "I've got to get this grape out. I've got to get this grape out. I'm going to bear this grape if it kills me!"

No, the branch does none of that. The branch has one job – to receive nourishment from the vine. And you have one job – to receive nourishment from Jesus. 'I am the Vine, you are the branches. When you're joined with me and I with you, the relation intimate and organic, the harvest is sure to be abundant. Separated, you can't produce a thing' (John 15:5 MSG)...

His job is to bear fruit. Our job is to stay put. The more tightly we are attached to Jesus, the more purely his love can pass through us.

Let's rewrite 1Corinthians 13:4-8 . . . Not with your name or Jesus' name but with both. Read it aloud with your name in the blank

    Christ in _____ is patient, Christ in _____ is kind. Christ in _____ does not envy, Christ in _____ does not boast, Christ in _____ is not proud. Christ in _____ is not rude, Christ in _____ is not self-seeking, Christ in _____ is not easily angered, Christ in _____ keeps no record of wrongs. Christ in _____ does not delight in evil but rejoices with the truth. Christ in _____ always protects, always trusts, always hopes, always preserves. Christ in _____ never fails.

Will we ever love like that? . . . No.

This side of heaven only God will. But we will love better than we have.

When kindness comes grudgingly, we'll remember his kindness to us and ask him to make us more kind. When patience is scares, we'll thank him for his and ask him to make us more patient. When it's hard to forgive, we won't list all the times we've been given grief. Rather, we'll list all the times we've been given grace and pray to become more forgiving. We will receive first so we can give later. . .'[231]

That is a lot to take in. I've read and reread so many times now looking for errors and I'm sure I will have missed some but I still have not got my head around all that I have read.

But there is more . . .

We have forgotten the opening verses 1-3, 'Though I speak with the tongues of men and angels, but have not love, I have become sounding brass or a clanging cymbal. And though I have the gift of prophecy, and understand all mysteries and all knowledge, and though I have all faith, so that I could remove mountains, but have not love, I am nothing. And though I bestow all my goods to

---

[231] Ibid. p161-4

feed the poor, and though I give my body to be burned, but have not love it profits me nothing.'

This introduction to all we have considered is extremely important. This intro is all about motive.

I may be doing amazing good works for Christ, making a great noise and attracting much acclaim and attention and persecution that may even lead to me being burnt at the stake like Faithful was, but my noise probably will not have an eternal impact a true pilgrim would wish for.

Erdman proclaims that 'there is no virtue in merely making one's self miserable. Suffering self-inflicted because of such unworthy motives as pride or stubbornness or anger or desire for unstinted applause is utterly and shamefully profitless. Apart from love, self-sacrifice is vain.' [232]

I may be the most wise-of-God-things since Solomon and have enough faith that I know mountains will leave their place at my very word but without love all I will do is get up peoples' noses for it will all be about me and because me cannot handle this as I'm not God it will destroy me. Others may gain from my selfish-less burn-out service but I will not gain, I will lose.

Richards writes that 'A person can serve selflessly, and if he or she "has not love", Paul said, "I gain nothing." The text doesn't say that a person who serves "but has not love" is ineffective. . . He or she may have spectacular gifts, and build a giant church where thousands are saved. . . What Paul said was that while others may benefit from service rendered without love, whatever I do "I gain nothing." . . . If you or I serve in order to gain recognition, or because we fear we won't otherwise be accepted, or even because we feel it's our duty, our service will help others; but not us. We'll struggle with dissatisfaction and loneliness. We'll still feel empty and unfilled.

---

[232] *Testaments of Love* p244 Quote from Charles Erdman 's *Paul's Hymn of Love* New York 1928 p 32

But if we serve others out of love – ah, then we truly are filled! We gain satisfaction. We gain joy. We gain future rewards. And we gain the inner serenity that comes with knowing we have pleased the Lord.'[233]

Contented (marital) submission

'*agape* gives, whereas pride asserts itself.' [234]

I do not believe, that anyone without *agapē/hesedh* in their lives, in their hearts can submit to another including a spouse. When you are full of self, full of pride you cannot humble yourself and submit rightly out of love for you cannot do so freely.

<u>Question</u>: "Submission?" I hear a woman groan. A woman, for most men I have known in my past would be struggling to hide their glee about this command, completely missing the command for them as a result.

<u>Answer</u>: I suppose we should not be surprised at how we have allowed Satan to twist the picture of submission as well as that of a husband's love even in the mind of many a pilgrim, for there is still far too much of the world's ideas within us.

Our Lord Christ submitted to his head, his Father but did he appear oppressed and used against his will by God? And yes, I do know Father/Son relationships are not like a marriage between one man and one woman but the command to submit is given to all pilgrims regardless of sex or marital status as we read in Ephesians 5:8b and 21 (which comes before 22, and we will consider later), '. . . Walk as children of light . . . submitting to one another [mutual submission comes first] in the fear of God', for our submission is to be as Christ's is.

The family unit of one husband married to one wife with or without children as God desires, the primary building block of society has been eroding slowly for a long time but so much rapidly lately that it is seen by many to be an unneeded out-dated

---

[233] *The 365-day Devotional Commentary* October 20th True Spirituality p930-1

[234] *Testaments of Love* p245

oddity, and who needs the opposite gender or any gender for that matter.

I believe we have to show by our lives the lie of this thinking, to make this so labeled 'outdated institution' very much desired and valued again for the good of all society as well as individuals, so we are going to consider (using a Bible commentary) some of what scripture and not the world has to say on this subject, on how it should be lived out, on what it means to be married.

My second husband has been walking as a pilgrim far longer than I and lives out what you are going to read and have read (not always perfectly but better that I could have ever dreamed). This marriage is vastly different from the first, it is a marriage of life, of deep loving friendship and respect, not one of paper and contempt.

I hope your imagination is engaged as well as your intellect to see the picture of the marital relationship that God desires between pilgrims for the world to observe and how different it looks when compared to what our western society sees as a better, more modern, way of partnering or co-habituation.

1Peter 3:1-7 comes after 2:11-12, (yes, as before I know this is obvious but many really seem to forget how to count when it comes to certain verses), "Beloved, I beg you as sojourners and pilgrims, abstain from fleshy lusts which was against the soul, having your conduct honorable among the Gentiles, that when they speak against you as evildoers, they may, by your good works which they observe, glorify God in the day of visitation.' where verse 13 says 'Therefore submit yourselves to every ordinance of man for the Lord's sake . .' and verse 18, 20, 23, 'Servants, be submissive to your masters . . . this is commendable before God . . but [Christ] committed Himself to Him who judges righteously' and *now* after another two verses Peter writes 3:1-7, 'Wives, likewise, be submissive to your own husbands, that even if some do not obey the word, they without a word, may be won by the conduct of their wives, when they observe your chase conduct accompanied be fear. Do not let your adornment be merely outward – arranging the hair, wearing gold, or putting on fine apparel – rather let it be the hidden person of the heart, with the incorruptible beauty of a gentle and quiet spirit, which is very precious in the sight of God. For in this manner, in former times, the holy women who trusted in God also adorned themselves, being submissive to their own husbands, as Sarah obeyed Abraham, calling him lord, whose daughters you are if you do good and are not afraid with any terror. Husbands, likewise, dwell with them with understanding, giving honor to the wife, as to the weaker vessel, and as being heirs together of the grace of life, that your prayers may not be hindered.'

First note the opening address of 3:1-7 is to the wife and it follows on from what has been said beforehand and that she is not being told to be submissive to men but to her own husband. We are told that as pilgrims we are to submit each to another regardless of sex or marital state as noted earlier, but the submission a married couple practice will be slightly different due to the different degree of intimacy within this relationship. But it is still a *likewise* submission, a similar submission for both wives and husbands to that previously discussed, that of Christ's submission. Tidball's write that 'Paul's reasons . . . are theological but Peter's are pragmatic . . . he is not writing to Christian couples, but to Christian wives, some of whom were married to unbelieving husbands. . . Peter knows that 'actions speak louder than words'. His concern is a missionary one and he instructs wives to avoid causing their husbands to build up defenses against the gospel because of the way they treat them, but rather to behave in such a way as to remove any barriers So, while they may have made an independent decision to follow Christ, in all other respects they should defer to their husbands and fulfil the role expected of a wife. Moreover they should do so not merely in terms of grudging obedience but of a submissive spirit. Peter's reference to *the purity and reverence of your lives* (literally, 'purity in fear') suggests, however, that their submission has a limit and should not go as far as reneging on their faith in Christ. Wherever else Peter speaks of reverence (literally, 'fear') in 1 Peter it is to speak of having reverence for God as opposed to fearing men. . . To be true daughters of Sarah, Christian wives need to model themselves on her by living morally upright lives with confidence, and not give way to fear of how their unbelieving husbands might respond.

Twin tributaries flow into the New Testament's teaching on marriage to create one stream. One tributary emphasizes the equality of women and men in marriage, and the other the respect for the sense of order that is inherent in creation and the new creation, which was all too imperfectly reflected in the Greco-Roman world in which Paul lived. The tributaries flow happily into one, without opposing each other with cross currents. They run together because of Christ who, though 'head over everything' and 'head of the church', the community of the new creation, taught submission and modelled it. Where submission is mutual and where each partner defers to the other there is no tension between equality and accepting one's place in a structured order. . . While particular ways of applying biblical truth may pass, what remains is that order is created in the community of the new creation by mutual love, mutual submission, mutual deference and by giving up the will to power.'[235]

Piper adds that '1Pt 3:1-6 is for wives with unbelieving husbands: a picture of what submission is NOT
  1. Submission is not agreeing on everything.
  2. Submission does not mean leaving your brain at the
altar. The wife should not be the most 'let's'. Leadership does not mean you do not listen; it doesn't even mean always getting the last word. Good leadership often says, "You were right, I was wrong." Leadership is taking initiative. In general, . . . leadership means a bent toward initiative under which women thrive, not dictation, never listening.

---

[235] Derek (born 1968) and Dianne Tidball *The Message of Women Creation, Grace and Gender* IVP 2012 p243, 244, 246, 247, 248

3. Submission does not mean you do not try to influence your husband – especially to win him over to the gospel.

4. Submission is not putting the will of the husband before the will of Christ. Christ is her Lord now, and *for the Lord's sake*, she will submit to the husband, but he is not her Lord. Therefore, whenever she must choose between the two, she chooses Jesus . . . she would say it not with a haughty or arrogant attitude, but rather with a winsome, submissive, longing one. He will be able to discern in her a longing that he not do that *so that* she could enjoy him as her leader.

5. Submission does not mean getting all of her spiritual strength through her husband.

6. Submission does not mean living or acting in fear. Submission is the calling of a wife to honour and affirm her husband's leadership and to help carry it through accordingly to her gifts.'[236]

In regards to 1Peter 3:3-4 and 7, where Peter is first speaking to wives then comes a warning word to husbands Wright comments that 'Many husbands rejoice when they read . . . a quiet spirit. They equate this quality with not talking or giving an opinion . . .' The Greek word for quiet really means a tranquillity which comes from within and causes no disturbance to other people. When a woman possesses this inner peace and tranquillity, she doesn't have to prove herself to her husband or to anyone else. She is strong and knows it. She is strong and yet doesn't feel compelled to use her strength to control or dominate others. There is an inner contentment and satisfaction which is not based on accomplishments, position of authority, ability to direct or control family members, or the recognition of others.

A wife's inner peace, strength, confidence, and tranquillity come from relying and depending on God. She draws her strength and wisdom from God. When this happens . . . the results begin to be obvious . . . She is free of anxious competitiveness and aggressiveness to prove her worth and

---

[236] John Piper *What submission is NOT* Feb 26 2016 desiringgod.com

value. She knows what tranquillity is because of the affirmation given her by God. . .

The King James Version . . . instructs husbands, "Dwell with them [wives] according to knowledge." The original language for being considerate means seeking to know, to inquire, or investigate. The implication here is for a husband to become an explorer and set out on a lifetime expedition to discover his wife's likes, dislikes, needs, the way in which she would like her needs met, her love language, her strengths, weaknesses, moods, her sense of timing, and fears, and then take all this into consideration when he interacts with her. No husband is a mind reader, so it is helpful when wives share their specific likes and dislikes . . . A wife deeply appreciates her husband when he really listens to her rather than merely tolerating her viewpoint. When a husband is learning to respond to his wife from his heart, his challenge is to attempt to see things from his wife's perspective and to understand her uniqueness.

And whenever it is obvious to a wife that her husband is making this his goal, it is helpful that she recognize his attempts and affirm him for seeking to live according to God's Word. . .

. . . A wife is not necessarily physically fragile, but she is to be handled with care in many ways. A husband is called by God to develop an attitude of respect in his heart for his wife. . . to give her a place of honor and see [her] as having value. She needs to be convinced that her husband thinks she is special. And in most cases . . . with her sensitive intuition, will know if the response is genuine or not.

. . . This has nothing to do with her intelligence, work ability, or spiritual life. . . The statement about weakness was intended to alert a husband to respect and be concerned about his wife's welfare.

Husbands, here are some suggestions for showing respect:
- Don't allow anyone to speak to your wife in a damaging or disrespectful way.

- Value her opinion and listen to her even when she disagrees with you.
- Walk into a room *with* her instead of *ahead* of her.
- Be careful to meet her needs in a group setting instead of leaving her alone while you talk with other men.
- Compliment her in public and in private.
- Be sensitive to her emotions and past hurts. Don't intrude in those areas, but support her instead.'[237]

Ephesians 5:22-29, 33, 'Wives, submit to your own husbands, as to the Lord. For the husband is head of the wife, as also Christ is head of the church; and He is the savior of the body. Therefore, just as the church is subject to Christ, so let the wives be to their own husbands in everything. Husbands, love your wives, just as Christ also loved the church and gave Himself for her, that he might sanctify and cleanse her with the washing of water by the word, that He might present her to Himself a glorious church, not having spot or wrinkle or any such thing, but that she should be holy and without blemish. So husbands ought to love their own wives as their own bodies; he who loves his wife loves himself. For no one ever hated his own flesh, but nourishes and cherishes it, just as the Lord does the church . . . let each one of you in particular so love his own wife as himself, and let the wife see that she respects her husband.'

Remember what Christ gave up for the church, how he is her saviour, and sanctifier, how he makes her clean, whole and holy, how he feeds her with his flesh and blood and cherishes her? This is how a husband is to be toward his wife. It is interesting to note that what a man struggles to do, that is what he is told to be and the same goes for the woman. Women are very good at loving anything but respecting? Men however are good respecters of things or people they consider worthy but loving, being romantic, sensitive, soft or gentle?

---

[237] *Quite Times for Couples* July1st p198, June 2nd p167, July 2nd p199.

In Ephesians 5:22 and 25 Paul gives some very simple and clear commands for wives and husbands, he writes not for wives to love and husbands to rule, both of which each party is good at doing but, 'Wives submit to your own husbands, as to the Lord . . . Husbands, love your wives, just as Christ also loved the church and gave Himself for her'; both of which neither party can do without God. H. D. McDonald explains the significance of this command –

> The call to husbands to love their wives was no less revolutionary than what Paul has to say about relationships in general. This declaration raises the wife to the position of co-partner. She is no longer a chattel; a thing to be used. Only as this statement is read in the light of 1Corithians 13 is its full significance understood. There is no question there of another's inferiority and one's own superiority. All that is gone – lost in love. And when the standard of the love as here stated is taken seriously – even as Christ loved the church – then the position of the wife in relation to the husband is all the more close and all the more intimate.[238]

Wright asks us to 'Please remember these verses [Ephesians 5:22, 23, 25, 26, 28, 29] were directed toward wives, and were never meant for husbands to quote to their wives! . . . There are a number of things that submission does not require of a wife. It does not mean that she is a slave or a nonperson without a thought, wish, or desire of her own. She does not have to put on blinders and ignore the faults or behaviours in her husband which may contradict God's Word.

It does not mean denying her giftedness and talents. In fact, there will be many occasions in which a wife has greater wisdom, insight, or ability than her husband . . . Submission simply means arranging oneself under the authority of another. Because of abilities and giftedness, this can shift back and forth between partners . . .

---

[238] *Testaments of Love* p226

A husband expresses love to his wife by regarding her as a completely equal partner in everything that concerns their life together. He asserts his leadership to see that this equal partnership works. Loving headship affirms and defers; it encourages and stimulates. Loving headship delights to delegate without demanding. But a husband must remember that he bears the responsibility before God for the maintenance of a healthy marriage. . .

The King James Version translates the verb *feeds* as *nourisheth*. This word broadens our understanding of a husband's responsibility. He must nourish his wife mentally, physically, emotionally, and spiritually. As one author puts it:

When a man makes provision for his wife to be the best-educated, most well-adjusted, and most spiritually mature woman she can possibly be, he is fulfilling his mandate to nourish her as he would his own body. To do less (especially if his motive is selfish or self-protective) is to ignore the example of Christ, who has selflessly provided for and encouraged the development and exercise of each believer's giftedness. A husband should want his wife to be all that she can be. It is part of loving her sacrificially.'[239]

Colossians 3:17-20, 23-24, 'And whatever you do in word or deed, do it all in the name of the Lord Jesus, giving thanks to God the father through Him. Wives, submit to your own husbands, as it is fitting in the Lord. Husbands, love your wives and do not be bitter toward them. Children, obey your parents in all things for this is well pleasing to the Lord. . . And whatever you do, do it heartily, as to the Lord and not to men, knowing that from the Lord you will receive the reward of the inheritance; for you serve the Lord Christ.'

New Testament scholar Dr Paula Gooder points out that 'the Greek verb for submission, *hupotasso*, is used in the key submission passages in Ephesians and Colossians in the passive

---

[239] *Quiet Times for Couples* January 7th & 8th p14-15, February 3rd p 42 quote is by Nancy Groom *Married Without Masks* Navpress 1989 p.98,99

voice. In the active form the verb means to subject someone else – that is to force their submission. But in the passive it means to choose to submit yourself. This was as counter-cultural then as it is now. . . So there is in the Bible's teaching a counter-cultural call for all of us to challenge the "me-first" instinct and instead to live lives of servant-hearted submission. . . C. S. Lewis wrote: "True humility is not thinking less of yourself, but thinking of yourself less." In the same way, submission is not self-loathing nor does it ignore self-care and self-value. Rather it is a decision to yield to someone else and to put their interests ahead of your own . . . we only submit to someone out of a desire to please Jesus . . . (Acts 4:19-20).'[240]

1Corinthians 7:3-5a, 'Let the husband render to his wife the affection due her, and likewise also the wife to her husband. The wife does not have authority over her own body, but the husband does. And likewise the husband does not have authority over his own body, but the wife does. Do not deprive one another except with consent for a time . . .'
Considering the 1 Corinthians 7, Ephesians 5 and 1Peter 3 verses we have already looked at for this section on contented marital submission the Tidballs write, 'Paul's words display a remarkable symmetry abought the rights and duties of the husband and the wife. Both are called to fulfil their marital duties to their partners and both are said to have authority over their partner's bodies. Neither has precedence in their relationship. The rights do not fall on one side and the duties on the other. Intimacy is completely mutual. . . the obligation Paul sets out is an obligation to give love, not demand it. . . As Bailey explains,

> The marital relationship is now presented as a positive 'right' that each partner is expected to *give as a gift* to the other. The husband and wife are equal in this regard. Neither partner is to demand those rights, rather each is to *give gifts* to the other. Gifts given in love are always seen by

---
[240] Krish Kandiah What *is biblical submission*? 5:4:16 christanitytoday.com.

the giver as valuable, otherwise they would not be given. Furthermore, by definition, a gift is always offered as a result of free choice. If it is coerced, it is not a gift.

The surprising element in this is the equal status given to the wife. The common understanding was that the wife was the property of the husband and the assumption was that he had authority over her body, but not vice versa. By saying they have authority over each other's bodies, Paul is giving remarkable right of control to the wife over the husband. He is no longer free, as would have been thought normal in the ancient world, to fulfil his sexual desires as he chooses, but is restrained by a prior obligation. The common assumption that it was acceptable for a man, but not a woman, to commit adultery is overturned by Paul's saying. . .

The primary motivation for mutual submission is respect for Christ. . . A refusal to live in this way is in effect to disrespect him.

Within each pair of relationships mentioned there is, in fact, a third partner, Christ himself. . . All that follows needs to be read through the lens both of Christ's presence in the relationship and of his position as Saviour and Lord. He who came to serve, not be served and 'who made himself nothing' is the pattern for all relationships and his teaching governs them all. His life of grace, love and 'self-abasing service' defines the qualities which are to be evident and the behaviour which is to be practiced. His presence will encourage the household to relate in humility, service, patience, forgiveness and love to one another. On the other hand, whatever is incompatible with him is ruled out for both partners, whether it is self-seeking assertiveness on the part of the weaker partner or abusive authoritarianism on the part of the household head.

In general [submission] has to do with 'order', and so 'a proper social ordering of people' which was prized in the ancient world as the antidote to chaos and anarchy. . . The term did not carry any of the negative overtones that it often carries today and did not imply inferiority on the part of the one submitting, since people were caught in a complex web of relationships in which they might play different roles.

Submission was not to be identified with obedience, even if on occasions this is how it would have demonstrated itself. Wives are not told to obey their husbands, unlike the children, who are told to obey their parents. 'Paul avoids the nuances of "obedience" and "ruling",' Craig Keener believes, 'but he does not mind calling wives to submit or husbands to love, because this was the behaviour that should indeed characterize all Christians'. One can obey without submitting since submission is a broader and different concept which defines the attitude of heart and mind, and requires one to let go of being in control or a desire to be dominant. . . As the church has voluntarily submitted herself to Christ so the wife is invited to voluntarily submit herself to her husband. The husband is never commanded to make her submit and the issue here is not about a husband exercising authority over the wife. . . since submission is mutual, and since Christ himself defines it, this is not a license for the husband to demand obedience, to require that the wife act sinfully or submit to abuse. Paul roots his understanding of the male headship of the family here not in any creation mandate but by analogy with Christ's headship of the church *of which he is the Saviour*. So this is a new creation principle not just the old one, and Christ serves as the pattern for male headship in the family, as is explained further is verses 25-33. Christ became the Saviour of his church by himself voluntarily submitting his body to torture and death, as verse 25 states, not be being self-assertive, or self-protective, nor by standing on his status and demanding obedience, but by sacrificial self-giving love.

When women in the Christian household submit to their husbands they might expect to be met with a reciprocal submission, patterned on Christ himself, rather than an arrogant authoritarianism which has been moulded by the non-Christian values of their culture. . . [Paul's] vision for each marriage partner 'is counter-cultural to the core' and 'would have been difficult for couples in the Roman world to live out apart from the enabling grace of God, as it still is. . . . in submitting to Christ, the church submits to 'a beneficial and loving rule that enables growth'. In submitting to her husband, the Christian wife may expect to encounter the same...'[241]

All you have just read on submission does not mean that by being obedient to God's call on you to be submissive will mean life goes well for you here or with your marriage. Christ was perfectively submissive as a man to those he had created who were in positions of God-given authority over him – parents, teachers, high priests, political powers of the day – despite this submission resulting in him being subjected to the unjust control and power of sinful men. Christ's Father however was well pleased with his Son's actions and God is well pleased with pilgrims behaving submissively likewise.

To constantly and continually live this lifestyle of pilgrims, to live like Christ, the suffering servant of Isaiah, submissive to God's will, self-disciplined, loving yet angry at all that hindered people from knowing God, to persevere in loving rightly or being holy is only possible by knowing and abiding, remaining in a trusting dependent and obedient vine-like relationship with the God who is love.

Morris writes 'But 'modern man loves those he conceives to be 'the sons of light' (i.e., those of whom he approves) and hates 'the men of the pit' (those of whom he disapproves). His love is selective and it centers of himself. He cannot conceive of love in the Christian sense as anything other than impractical idealism – an idealism of which he does not approve.

If it were not so tragic it would be funny that modern man dismisses Christianity and the Christian way of love on the ground that it does not work. Will anyone in his right mind claim that any of the modern alternatives do work? Certainly the stress on the self-centered life does not lead to blissful happiness; only fierce competition results when self-absorbed people confront each other. People try to get the better of each other, and in this sad process laws are broken, rights are violated – and police forces

---

[241] *The Message of Women* p236, 237, 239-243

grow larger. Crimes multiply, crimes of violence being the most 'popular', because violence is the simplest way for the physically strong to get their own way. The result is that everybody loses. We lose by the depredation we suffer, and we lose by the increased taxes we pay to support the protection we have come to need so much. The more self-centered our society becomes, the more crimes we commit, the more police we need, and the more jails we fill. There is scarcely the need to elaborate the point because life in any modern city is a vivid illustration of the truth that selfishness leads ultimately to suffering – for everyone. Where is there a system that works better than the way of Christian love?'[242]

So, pilgrim walk, have a lifestyle deeply stained with the hue of *agapē/hesedh* love, for as pilgrims we are called to walk differently from the world around us. Just wondering, do you know what the opposite to being loving towards someone is? It is being indifferent, not the feeling of hate. Can you understand why this is true?

Something else which would make a pilgrim's way of life stand out from the masses would be a life careless of others opinions, a life which did of not need to be like other lives, free from doing the comparing and stressing out that you don't measure up and how the way of being a pilgrim could cause undeserved suffering. The how to do this, I believe is found in the context of 1Pt 2:19-24, '. . . but [Jesus] committed Himself to Him who judges righteously . . .'

> What a release this is. To simply trust ourselves to God, to remember that He judges justly, and to leave our case in His hands.
>
> Was Jesus wise to do so? Yes, for out of the innocent suffering of the Saviour God worked our salvation. The suffering of Jesus was not meaningless; it was permitted that through it good might come. If we would but commit ourselves into God's hands, we can be sure that not only

---

[242] *Testaments of Love* p278-9

justice will be done for us, but also that our suffering will serve the cause of grace. [243]

How different would our lifestyles be if we were only concerned about what the righteous loving judge thought about us and did not allow ourselves to consider another's commending or condemning judgement or even our own when looking at our way of being – taken that we are, to the best of our understanding at the time, doing our very best at being Christ like?

Whose praise would, should mean more to us; man's or God's? Who loves us more with a good and true love, a holy love? Who, wanting only what is good for us, can judge or discipline us rightly from love's view, not expediency? Who are we as pilgrims actually meant to be serving, doing for? Comparing and judging are not how we should be seen living.

Sophie de Witt writes, 'We [especially women] spend our lives making . . . comparisons: measuring ourselves against others. How do you feel when you compare and come off worse?

Inadequacy, despair, self-pity [because of] envy, anxiety, insecurity, guilt, bitterness, grumbling . . . These feelings are all symptoms of looking-up comparison.

[Wouldn't] the treatment for looking-down symptoms simply to get ourselves a life which means that, when we compare ourselves to others, we come off better?

Not really . . . Here are the symptoms of looking-down comparisons: pride, arrogance, superiority, inverted superiority, entitlement, insecurity and anxiety.

Whether we look down or up, CCS [Compulsive Comparison Syndrome] makes it all about us: about our goodness, or our lack of goodness. Either way, it ultimately destroys our relationship with God.

There is a way to live which allows us to be at peace with ourselves;' to love others; and to enjoy life with God. The Bible calls that experience 'contentment'.

---

[243] *The 365-day Devotional commentary* p1111-2

To be 'blessed' is to enjoy significance, security and satisfaction in this world, without dilution, disappointment or death.

Where does this blessing come from? From the One who designed the world; from God Himself.

Our significance does not come from which family we're born into, who we married, what we do Monday to Friday or how we serve on a Sunday. It comes from being made by God, to know God.

Measuring ourselves against others, desiring a better position, is a direct result of us taking God's place at the centre of the world and looking for blessing in things that are not our Creator. The reality of CCS shows that our hearts are rejecting God's loving rule in our lives. In a world where 'I' am at the centre instead of God, CCS will be a constant companion. It has to be.

In the end, the treatment for CCS is wonderfully challengingly simple.

Let God be God.

The gospel is not: be good enough, and Jesus will bless you. It is: the perfect Jesus has blessed you; now enjoy becoming more like Him.

[Considering Proverbs 31:10-31, please read for yourself at some stage.] This lady is, first and foremost, 'a wife of noble character' (v10), not a wife of noble *deeds*.

The most important thing about this lady is that she feared the LORD, which is Proverbs language for having a right recognition and respect for God. She was a woman who let God be God in her life, who kept Him at the centre. A woman who knew that her gifts of charm and beauty and, presumably, energy, business savvy, wisdom, forward planning, budget-balancing, and so on were 'deceptive' and 'fleeting'; that they were not what brings true blessing now, nor in the future. . . She has let God be her God, at the centre of her life; and she is using the circumstances

He's given her and the abilities He's given her, to serve Him. She's content.'[244]

God is not like us – yea I know, big understatement – he sees all, knows all, he alone has the big picture about everything past, present and future, including motives and he alone is fully righteous. We humans do not and as pilgrims though God sees us as righteous as because of his Son's blood, we will not be fully righteous till our pilgrimage is ended here, yet we consider ourselves suitably qualified to pass judgement on everything and everyone whatever, whenever, wherever.

Question: Is this loving?
Answer: Jesus commanded us not to condemn another as we read in Matthew 7:1-2, 'Judge not, that you will be not judged. For with what judgement you judge, you will be judged; and with the measure you use, it will be measured back to you.'

He goes on to warn us that if we are going to judge a pilgrim brother to ensure we have no undealt with sin in us first or we will not see clearly enough to assist and edify him: verses 3-5, 'And why do you look at the speck in your brother's eye, but do not consider the plank in your own eye? Or how can you say to your brother, 'Let me remove the speck from your eye'; and look, a plank is in your own eye? [A reasonably difficult job considering that your plank would hinder you from getting physically close enough to another to remove a speck.] Hypocrite! First remove the plank from your own eye, and then you will see clearly to remove the speck from your brother's eye.' Jesus then wraps up this small but concise section on judging another by warning us pilgrims about judging then advising one who is not a pilgrim: verse6, 'Do not give what is holy to the dogs; nor cast your pearls before swine, lest they trample them under their feet, and turn and tear you in pieces.'

A pilgrim cannot expect or presume that a lover of the world would appreciate God-honouring advice on how to better

---

[244] Sophie de Witt *Compared to her . . . How to experience true contentment* thegoodbook company 2012 p10, 17-18, 38, 39, 44, 45, 51, 57, 75, 89, 90.

themselves or their lives, at the very least they won't thank you for being a busy-body and a-know-it-all, at the very worst they could take a swing at you to knock you down to their level or lower. Pray for them to be born again and wait and wait and pray and . . .

Paul also had a similar view on this form of judgement as he wrote in 1Corinthians 4:2-5, 'Moreover it is required in stewards [servants of Christ and overseers of the mysteries or gospel of God as in verse1 which all pilgrims are in a way] that I should be judged by you or by a human court. In fact, I do not even judge myself. For I know of nothing against myself, yet I am not justified by this; but He who judges me is the Lord. Therefore judge nothing before the time, until the Lord comes, who will both bring to light the hidden things of darkness and reveal the counsels [motives] of the hearts. Then each one's praise will come from God.'

Being fully and truly satisfied with God, with his love, with him, just him, brings a contentment the world has no idea exists. It is frankly difficult for me to describe with words, it is peace, joy, a settled- ness, a future hope, it is God himself because he and he alone truly is enough. And this makes life very simple, not easy but simple.

> . . . To like our condition, to be pleased and satisfied with it, and with the holy will of God in it; that is, to be content, content with sickness, poverty, shame, prison, loss of relations and friends, &c. In a word, when our wills lie even with God's will, (as in reason they should,) and our minds lie even with our conditions, then have we inward peace, and tranquillity, quietness, and contentment, and never till then; and then sickness is as good as health, and poverty is as good as riches, and a prison, &c.[245]

A contented person will find it easier that a discounted one to be humble and meek in thought and deed. Packer writes of these

---

[245] *Heart's Ease in Heart Trouble* Jn xiv. 1, 2, 3 p839-840

two ways of living, being, telling us that 'Humility, a brother-virtue to self-control, is the opposite of pigheaded pride. Humility reveals itself in at least two ways: acceptance of things you cannot change, and acceptance of correction in areas of your life where you can change – and where you need to.

Meekness [which actually takes great strength] accepts things the way they come at us; it doesn't quarrel with God when discerning aspects of his providence. Instead, meekness acknowledges that God knows what he is doing and that he makes all things work together for those who love him – even if at this present moment things do not appear to be working well at all. A person who is meek accepts the way that God orders things.'[246]

Bunyan's pilgrims and Vanity Fair

A traveller doesn't live according to the customs and standards of the foreign country. For the sake of not offending the locals, he may temporarily adopt some of their customs. As citizens of heaven, we may adopt some of the ways of earth, if they are morally neutral, in order not to offend the natives. But we live according to different standards than they do, namely those of God's Word.[247]

Considering this let's see how Bunyan's pilgrims went and how others viewed their efforts.

Jesus instructs his disciples and the multitude following him in Matthew 7:13-14, to 'Enter by the narrow gate; for wide is the gate and broad is the way that leads to destruction, and there are many who go in by it. Because narrow [strait] is the gate and difficult is the way which leads to life, and there are few who find it.'

Scott writes 'Christian being admitted at the strait gate, is directed in the narrow way. In the broad road every man may choose a path suited to his inclinations, shift about to avoid difficulties, or accommodate himself to circumstances; and he will

---

[246] *God's Will* p130-1

[247] Sermon *The Daily battle: proving to be true pilgrims*

be sure of company agreeable to his taste. But Christians must follow one another in the narrow way, along the same track, surmounting difficulties, facing enemies, and bearing hardships, without any room to evade them: nor is any indulgence given to different tastes, tastes, habits, or propensities. It is therefore, a straitened, or as some render the word, an afflicted way; being indeed a habitual course of repentance, faith, love, self-denial, patience, and mortification to sin and the world, according to the rule of the holy Scriptures. Christ himself is the way, by which we come to the Father and walk with him; but true faith works by love, and 'sets us in the way of his steps' Ps lxxxv.13. This path is also straight as opposed to the crooked ways of wicked men, Ps cxxv.5; for it consists in a uniform regard to piety, integrity, sincerity, and kindness; at a distance from all the hypocrisies, frauds, and artifices, by which ungodly men wind about, to avoid detection, keep up their credit, deceive others or impose on themselves. The question proposed by Christian [Are there no turnings or windings by which a stronger man may lose his way?] implies that believers are more afraid of missing the way, than encountering hardships in it: and Good-will's answer, which many ways *butted* down on it, or opened into it, in various directions, shows that the careless and self-willed are extremely liable to be deceived: but it follows, that all these ways are crooked and wide; they turn aside from the direct line of living faith and holy obedience, and are more soothing, indulgent, and pleasing to corrupt nature, than the path of life; which lies straight forward, and is everywhere contrary to the bias of the carnal mind.' [248]

This *narrow way* of living however takes all pilgrims through the world, through Bunyan's Vanity Fair, exposing them to every delight for every individual to get bogged in and take their eye off the goal' of entering the Celestial City.[249]

---

[248] *The Pilgrim's Progress* comment by Scott p63

[249] Notes from Gables' sermon series on Pilgrim's Progress #40 Vanity Fair– the *Description* 2.9.99, and I wish to give credit for ideas on the following several pages coming from this message and *#41 Vanity Fair – reaction to a Christian Influence* 2.11.99

Vanity Fair according to Rev. Jim Gables, is the City of Destruction but with its gay clothes on, all its allurements, bright lights etc. This is the world's attempts to convince itself that all is very fine thank you without God as they endlessly seek for joy, happiness and love from the created instead of the creator.

Scott comments that 'Christianity does not allow men to 'bury their talent in the earth', or to put 'their light under a bushel': they should not 'go out of the world', or retire into cloisters and deserts, and therefore they must all go through this fair. Thus our Lord and Saviour endured all the temptations and sufferings of this evil world; without being at all impeded or entangled by them, or stepping in the least aside to avoid them. The age is which he lived peculiarly abounded in all possible allurements; and he was exposed to such enmity, contempt, and sufferings, as could never be exceeded or equaled. But 'he went about doing good'; and his whole conduct, as well as his indignant repulse to the tempter's insolent offer, hath shown emphatically his judgement of all earthly things, and exhibited to us 'an example that we should follow his steps.' [250]

This fair in the township of Vanity was set up by Beelzebub, Apollyon and Legion with their companions when they saw that the way which the Pilgrims had to take to reach the Celestial City lay through this town.

[A] fair wherein should be sold all sorts of vanity; and that it should last all year long; therefore at this fair are all such merchandise sold, as houses, lands, trades, places, honours, performers, titles, countries, kingdoms, lusts, pleasures, and delights of all sorts, as whores, bawds, wives, husbands, children, masters, servants, lives, blood, bodies, souls, silver, gold, pearls, precious stones, and what not.

And moreover, at this fair is at all times to be seeing juggling, cheats, games, plays, fools, apes, knaves, and rogues, and that of every kind. Here are to be seen too, and that for nothing, thefts,

---

[250] *The Pilgrim's Progress* comment by Scott p140-1

The Pilgrim Way

murders, adulterers, false swearers, and that of a blood red-colour.

Now these pilgrims [Christian and Faithful] . . . must needs go through this fair. Well, so they did; but behold; even as they entered into the fair, all the people in the fair were moved; and the town itself, as it were, in a hubbub about them; and that for several reasons, for,

First, The pilgrims wore clothes with such kind of raiment as was diverse from the raiment of any that traded in that fair. The people, therefore, of the fair made a great gazing upon them: some said they were fools, 1Cor. iv 9,10; some, they were bedlams; and some, they were outlandish men.

Secondly, And as they wondered at their apparel, so they did likewise at their speech; for few could understand what they said: they naturally spoke the language of Canaan; but they that kept the fair were the men of this world: so that from one end of the fair to the other they seemed barbarians each to the other.

Thirdly, But that which did not a little amuse the merchandisers was, that these pilgrims set very lightly by all their wares; they cared not so much as to look upon them; and if they called upon them to buy, they put their fingers in their ears, and cry, "Turn away mine eyes from beholding vanity", Ps.cxix.37; and look upwards, signifying that their trade and traffic was in heaven.[251]

<u>Question</u>: Did you notice the three things that set these two pilgrims apart from the citizens of Vanity Fair? In today's real world should these same three things still set pilgrims apart from citizens of this world? Does being loving have anything to do with these differences?

<u>Answer</u>: Keep reading and see how you would answer my dear reader.

1. Raiment or clothing

---

[251] Ibid. p140-3

In Bunyan's times those who called themselves Christian did apparently wear a kind of uniform making their clothing distinctly different from what non-Christians wore. Jim Gables wonders if we as pilgrims should not choose to expose or enhance certain body parts with the desire to draw attention to them. I have observed that one can too easily get into a heated discussion if one, especially a male minister, tries to suggest that another's clothing, especially a woman's, is not really appropriate for a Christian to be seen in.

Question: So, what is appropriate? And why is it and something else not?
Answer: I've had some interesting discussions with my husband who I have known for nearly 20years now about this subject. I have not always liked what he has had to say but when he has got me to understand how a male sees, thinks and feels rather than a female – though maybe if we were really honest ladies we are not that different in some instances – my attitude towards female clothing did slowly change. Men (most anyway, women also to a degree but usually not as instantly as touch is more the button for them) are sexually aroused primarily by what they see.
Not too sure about this? Why or how do you think pornography is so dangerously and destructively rampant and making a fortune for the evil ones creating and publishing these pictures?
Job had made a vow never to look at a woman in that way as we read in Job 31:1, 'I have made a covenant with my eyes; why then should I look upon a young woman?'
King David does not seem to have done the same, or if he had he forgot one spring evening as we learn reading 2Samuel 11:2-4, 'Then it happened one evening that David arose from his bed and walked on the roof of the king's house. And from the roof he saw a woman bathing, and the woman was very beautiful to behold. So David sent and inquired about the woman . . . Then David sent messengers, and took her. . .' The woman got pregnant. David arranged the murder of her husband then married her, it's hard to say no to a King. God being God did turn this sad state of affairs around into something good but that did not save David or the

woman Bathsheba from the resultant painful circumstances that they would have live with.

Why do you as a woman dress (this also includes the showering, face and nail painting, the tanning cream, hair do, jewelry selection, perfume and whatever else you think you have to do in addition to some sort of body cover-up which today seems to be involving less fabric and is preferably see through) as you do? Honestly?

I wonder if you can say there is never a thought in your mind about how a certain male (not necessarily your husband either if you are married) may think when he sees you at least occasionally when you are considering what's in your robe for an evening out or even going to a sports event during the day, or can you?

Mind you I also don't think the men out there are all innocent either. You cannot tell me that those jeans which are tighter than the pantyhose I wear are comfortable guys or those tops that reveal bulging muscles – when I am feeling frozen despite being so rugged up, I look like the Michelin man – are what you would really prefer. Are you aware that most male fragrances actually extinguish your natural female attracting odour, so why use something so strong that you smell like a chemical factory after showering? Examine your motives. God already knows what they are. Both sexes should dress in a way that their society or culture would consider displayed a morally pure nature rather than a fashionable edgy one, though I know that to find such clothing in shops, even for children or teenagers is getting harder.

Back in the 1Peter 3 verses earlier you read Peter's fashion advice to female pilgrims, 'Do not let your adornment be merely outward – arranging the hair, wearing gold, or putting on fine apparel – rather let it be the hidden person of the heart, with the incorruptible beauty of a gentle and quiet spirit, which is very precious in the sight of God.' Some sermons can get pew sitters rather warm if this passage is not presented as clearly as it should be.

Peter is writing to his time, his culture about 'the nature of true feminine beauty. While some Christians down the years have thought that Peter was advocating that Christian women should dress in a drab or dowdy fashion, avoid cosmetics, and show little care for the way they presented themselves, this is not Peter's point. . . Peter is exhorting Christian women 'to avoid appearing morally improper by the standards of their culture.[252]

2. Speech

When I first went back into a church – over 20yrs ago now – I wish I had taken my dictionary, so many words were used that I really did not fully understand. The *language of Canaan* in Pilgrim's Progress refers to spiritual speech. Pilgrims must omit certain words from their speech. Words that the world throws around like dust as Jim Gables says. A pilgrim's main choice of subject matter should also be different, especially when with other pilgrims. We are living in the world therefore sport, weather and politics are of valid interest but our main interest surely should be around God and our walk as a result.

I want us to consider a Greek word that the KJ version of the Bible uses in 1Peter 2:12 and how the NKJ uses this same word. Are you up for another of my word searches?

1Peter 2:12 in the KJ reads, 'Having your conversation honest among the Gentiles that whereas they speak against you as evildoers they may by your good works which they shall behold . .'

The Greek word *anastrŏphĕ* (#391) is translated *conversation* in the verse we are considering and is from the word *anastrĕphō* (#390) which means to overturn; also to return; by implication to busy oneself, i.e. remain, live: - abide, behave self, have conversation, live . . .

---

[252] *The Message of Women* p244-5

In the NKJ *anastrĕphō* is translated as *conduct* in 2Cor 1:12, 'For our boasting is this: the testimony of our conscience that we conducted ourselves in the world in simplicity and godly sincerity, not with fleshly wisdom but by the grace of God . .' and in Ephesians 2:3, 'among whom also we all conducted ourselves in the lusts of our flesh . . .'

And so is *anastrŏphĕ* in the NKJ as we can read in Ephesians 4:22, 'that you put off, concerning your former conduct, the old man . .' and 1Peter 1:15, 'but as He who called you is holy, you also be holy in all your conduct'.

I find it interesting that a word translated as *conduct* can also mean *have conversation*. Have you ever considered that having a conversation over the back fence with your neighbour, or at work with a colleague, a part of your conduct, what you do, a part of your lifestyle, your walk as a pilgrim that we are called to examine? Maybe we need to begin to consider our words and their tone of delivery more carefully for it is far easier to not light a fire than put one out.

Paul advised us in Colossians 4:5-6 to 'Walk [live] in wisdom toward those who are outside, redeeming the time. Let your speech always be with grace, seasoned with salt, that you may know how you ought to answer each one.'

In Matthew 5:13-16 Jesus tells us we 'are the salt of the earth; but if the salt loses its flavour, how shall it be seasoned? It is then good for nothing but to be thrown out and trampled underfoot by men. You are the light of the world. A city that is set on a hill cannot be hidden. Nor do they light a lamp and put it under a basket, but on a lamp stand, and it gives light to all who are in the house. Let your light so shine before men, that they may see your good works and glorify your Father in heaven.'

Question: How does salt season our words? What has it got to do with how we live other than how we like our chips?

Answer: Other than making porridge taste good or making you thirsty if there is too much on those chips, I was stuck for inspiration so I did a bit of Google research and learnt quite a bit, so bear with me as I share . . .

Of the annual global production of around two hundred million tonnes of salt, about 6% is used for human consumption. Salt is essential for life in general and as saltiness is one of the basic human tastes it is an essential nutrient which gives flavour, texture and colour enhancement to foods we eat as well as being a food preservative and a binding agent by causing the gelatinization of protein.[253]

Other uses include water conditioning 12%, de-icing highways 8%, and agricultural use 6%. The rest (68%) is used for manufacturing and other industrial processes. Sodium chloride is one of the largest inorganic raw materials used by volume. Its major chemical products are caustic soda and chlorine; these are used to make PVC, plastics and paper pulp for example.

As a flux it removes iron and other metal contaminates from molten aluminum.

It is used to precipitate out the saponified products in the manufacture of soaps and glycerin.

As an emulsifier it is used in the production of synthetic rubber.

In the firing of pottery when salt is added to the furnace it vaporizes before condensing onto the surface of the ceramic material, forming a strong glaze.

It can be added to drilling fluid to provide a stable 'wall' when working in sands or gravels for example, to prevent the hole from collapsing.

It is also a mordant in textile dying, regenerates resins in water softening and used in the tanning of hides.[254]

Indulge me for a moment as I attempt to consider these many qualities of salt in regards to our conversations as pilgrims. . .

A salted conversation could be said to be a conversation that hastens to provide all with essential nourishment for the maintaining of life yet is not boring but improved on compared to

---

[253] Bethany Moncel *Six functions of salt in food* www.thespruceeats.com
[254] https://en.m.wilkipedia.org

worldly talk. It unfreezes relationships and communication, softening, promoting a blending of personalities and ideas, stabilizing, strengthening, cleansing – for no stain of past wrong doings remain to hinder its other work, improving the moral conditions and toughing all against worldly influences, preserving, binding and creating a thirst for such words as this type of talk is firmly fixed, unwavering as anchored to the foundation of love.
How about having a go yourself and see what you can come up with?
Swindoll has some additional insights, writing that, 'When salt becomes contaminated by dirt, sand, and other impurities, Jesus said it becomes 'good for nothing. (Today if somebody is shiftless or lazy or does a poor job, we say that person is 'good for nothing'. That saying comes from Jesus' words.) . . . Jesus says to shine for the world . . . You say your environment is dark? What an opportunity! . . . You've got the light! Now be careful . . . don't shine a big blinding beacon right into your co-worker's eyes. He needs light, but just enough in the right places. And salt? Don't dump a truck load on him. Just a little please. Too much salt ruins the food just as too much light blinds the eyes. . . 'Good works' sounds a clarion call. Just live a different life. . . "Don't' make it complicated," says Jesus. "Simply let your light shine."' [255]

Paul writes in Ephesians about righteous and unrighteous speech instructing us to 'be renewed in the spirit of [our] mind . . . and that [we] put on the new man which was created according to God, in true righteousness and holiness. Therefore, putting away lying, 'Let each one of [us] speak truth with his neighbour' . . . Let no corrupt word proceed out of your mouth, but what is good for necessary edification, that it may impart grace to the hearers. And do not grieve the Holy Spirit of God, by whom you were sealed for the day of redemption. Let all bitterness, wrath, anger, clamour [loud quarrelling], and evil speaking be put away from you, with all malice. And be kind to one another, tender-hearted, forgiving

---

[255] *Simple Faith* p58, 63, 64

one another, even as God in Christ forgave you. Therefore be imitators of God . . . walk in love . . . But fornication and all uncleanness or covetousness, let it not even be named among you, as is fitting for saints; neither filthiness, nor foolish talking, nor coarse jesting, which are not fitting, but rather giving of thanks' (4:23-5:4).

Question: How do you suppose the Holy Spirit feels when he hears the Father's name God used as a swear word? Why don't people use the name of another god, a little g one?

Answer: The word *blaspheme* originally meant to speak evil of any one, to injure by words, to blame unjustly. When applied to God, it means to speak of him unjustly, to ascribe to him acts and attitudes which he does not possess or to speak impiously or profanely. It also means to say or do anything by which his name or honour is insulted, or which conveys an *impression* unfavourable to God. It means also, to attempt to do or say a thing which belongs to him alone, or which he only can do. (as Christ was accused of in John x.33.)[256]

How much of our conversation is just foolish talk, just talk to fill in the silence or dirty jokes to impress the crowd usually at the expense of some woman? Can you imagine what it would be like if we removed this sort of unrighteous speech and the tone it is usually spoken with from our lips? What if we had the power to remove it from our television programs including the 'suitable for children' ones and the advertising? I might be able to watch instead of having to press the off button.

How often do we just converse about subjects just as the world does? For example, how do you feel about growing older? Have you ever thought what you are showing of your feelings about this by the way you talk of it?

> How sad that we talk of growing old in the same way as the world does. We [pilgrims] are not moving toward death but from death toward greater and greater life. We are not finishing our lives, we are just beginning our lives – for we

---

[256] *Fleetwood's Life of Christ* p364 comment from Barnes on the Gospels

have him, his very gift of life, and we will have that for eternity.[257]

3. Thought very little of what the Fair offered

This, Jim Gables points out was the difference that offended the citizens of Vanity the most, for they were completely disinterested in all that was on offer. Pilgrims are to 'buy truth and also wisdom and instruction and understanding (Proverbs 23:23), things of substance that the world has no appetite for. By not participating in or purchasing what the world offers and the pleasures it loves you will find yourself exposed to persecution of some sort Gables warns, as they see us as dishonouring or degrading their choice of lifestyle in our refusal.

Here for sale all year round were every vain thing, all which came with a deceiving promise that it will satisfy the self and allow it to boastfully parade itself for all to admire such as whatever we hope may fill or hide the emptiness inside, or the fact that we are just a breath, a vapour that is here then gone.

A house on a block of land is not to be scorned but houses and lands? How many does one actually need?

Can a bought spouse give love freely, unconditionally? Perhaps, as this will depend on the motive for buying her and what sort of love is being considered.

I find the idea of viewing lives, blood and bodies with the view of purchasing the one or more that pleases repulsive enough without considering a soul. And yet across our world evil people are buying and selling at a profit these very items. The black market for body organs to transplant into those who are rich and desperate is very much alive and flourishing. Babies are stolen for those willing to pay to adopt them, and are you aware that every 26 seconds a child somewhere in the world is stolen, or sold by

---

[257] Roger C. Palms *Enjoying the Closeness of God Know the Pleasure of Being His Friend*. World Wide Publications 1989 p238

parents who want a new fridge into the illegal sex markets that feed the growing demand of depraved persons? [258]

There was also much to see in this fair which did not take your money but may have taken your soul unbeknown to you. In today's world most of us would see no harm in watching a juggler preforming, games, plays or apes. But maybe Bunyan was not thinking of a chess game or a football match and I am not sure what plays were about or how they were done in his time but I would not like to watch some of todays as a pilgrim. Swan Lake in the nude – No thanks!

I enjoy visiting the zoo and watching the animals but what of the deformed human caged for the people's leering and jeering entertainment in the 1600's? Have you read about the Elephant Man, Joseph Carey Merrick (1862-1890) of England for one example?

How much free-to-air television or screen do you view? I find there is less and less that I am comfortable with and can justify watching or hearing as so much that is on offer is only about knaves, rouges, thefts, murders, adulterers and false swearers. The presentation may be different but the content does not seem to have really changed much from Bunyan's time.

Jumping forward in Bunyan's tale we find Christian and his companion arriving at a 'delicate plain, called Ease, where they went with much content . . . Now at the farther side . . . was a little hill, called Lucre, and in that hill a silver mine; which some . . had turned aside to see; but going too near the brim of the pit, the ground being deceitful under them broke, and they were slain: some also had been maimed there, and could not to their dying day be their own men again . . .

Scott comments that, 'When the church enjoys great outward peace . . . professors are peculiarly exposed to the temptation of seeking worldly riches and distinctions . . . and many of them are more disconcerted and disposed to murmur . . . The love of money is not always connected with the desire of covetously

---

[258] Destiny Rescue www.destinyrescue.org

hoarding it: it often arises from a vain affection of gentility, which is emphatically implied by the epithet bestowed on Demas (*gentlemanlike*). The connections that professors form in a day of ease and prosperity, and the example of the world around them (without excepting some of those who would be thought to love the gospel), buy into a style of living that they cannot afford . . . An increasing family ensures additional expense; and children genteelly educated naturally expect to be provided for accordingly. Thus debts are contracted, and gradually accumulate; it is neither so easy or so reputable to retrench, as it was to launch out; and numerous tempters induce men thus circumstanced to turn aside to the hill Lucre; that is, to leave the direct path of probity and piety, that they may obtain supplies to their urgent and clamorous necessities. Young persons, when they first set out in life, often lay the foundation for innumerable evils, by vainly emulating the expensive style of those in the same line of business, or the same rank in the community; who are enabled to support such expenses, either by extensive dealings, or by means that ought not to be used. Besides the bankruptcies which continually originate from this mistaken conduct, it is often found, that fair profits are inadequate to uphold that appearance which was at first needlessly assumed; and so necessity is pleaded for engaging in those branches of trade, or seizing on those emoluments, which the conduct of worldly people screen from total scandal, but which are evidently contrary to the word of God, and the plain rule of exact truth and rectitude, and which render their consciences very uneasy. But who can bear the mortification of owning himself poorer than he was thought to be? . . . Professors in these circumstances are as likely to embrace Demas's invitation, as either By-ends, Money-love, or Save-all; and if they be 'not drowned in destruction and perdition,' will 'fall into temptation and a snare, and pierce themselves through with many sorrows.' Men should therefore consider, that it is as unjust to contract debts for superfluous indulgences, or to obtain credit by false appearances of affluence, as it is to defraud by any other

imposition; and that this dishonesty makes way for innumerable temptations to more disgraceful species of the same crime: not to speak of its absolute inconsistency with piety and charity.' [259]
Love does not . . .
Nothing that is offered to us by the world can be compared to having a relationship with God the creator and Father. It is and will be worthwhile to keep our eyes focused on eternity with him rather than on things that disappear as the morning dew heated by the noonday sun.
Now backtrack with me to Vanity Fair and discover how Christian and Faithful are faring. [260]

Christian and Faithful were charged with causing trouble and placed in a cage in the town's central square. In Bunyan's time this was a punishment often used; you were a spectacle and pass-byers would throw rotten fruit at you. Today it's not rotten fruit but words chosen by the media that humiliate you and stain your character; different weapons with same result. However, our two pilgrims behaved so well under this punishment that some town folk began to wonder at and question their punishment, increasing the hubbub.

If you read through the book of Acts in the Bible you learn of the apostles and followers of Christ after his ascension. In 17:6b we read of what others thought of these men for they too cried out to the city rulers, 'These who have turned the world upside down have come here too.' Gables says that 'wherever the apostles went there was either a revival or a riot!'

Because of the increasing disturbance in Vanity Lord Hate-good, the town judge after a court hearing, charged Christian and Faithful with being 'enemies to and disturbers of the town's trade; that they had made commotions and divisions in the town, and

---

[259] *The Pilgrim's Progress* comment by Scott p163-4
[260] *The Pilgrim's Progress* p143-153 and credit for ideas expressed in this section to Gables' sermons # *41 Vanity Fair – Reaction to a Christian Influence* 2.11.99, *#42 Vanity Fair – Christian's reaction to persecution* 2.12.99, *#43 Vanity Fair –Truth of God on Trial* 2.13.99, *#44 Vanity Fair- Death of Faithful* 2.14.99

had won a party to their own most dangerous opinions, in contempt of the law of their prince.'

There were three witnesses for this court case, Envy representing the spirit of the person that deep down envies the character of a Christian – the truth of God – but does not want to have to endure what Christians have to endure to have such a character, Superstition representing those not interested in the truth of God but in the customs of men in the religion of God, the superstitions, as a result they cannot stand having a true believer in their community as they declare that their worship is in vain and disrupt the way of life these are comfortable with and then there is Pick-think who represents a person that speaks because he is seeking a favour from someone in power. Bunyan's jury characters (as with all his characters) had names that personified vices or sins. For example, there was Mr. Blind-man who clearly saw that this man Faithful was a heretic, in error of the way God should be served and worshiped.

Faithful found he was unable to remain silent, he was faithful to his calling, faithful to God but not to the desires of the world regardless, he was tortured and burnt at the stake. Christian was released and set on his way alone.

Gables notes that the extent of persecution that you will encounter as a Christian will be determined by the influence or number of Christians that are in your community.[261]

Scott comments that, 'The presence of real Christians in those places, where a large concourse of worldly men is collected, must produce a disturbance and effervescence. The smaller the number is of those whose actions, words, or silence protest against the prevalence of vice and irreligion, the fiercer the opposition that will be excited.

A pious clergyman, on board a vessel, where he was a single exception to the general ungodliness that prevailed, once gave

---

[261] Notes from Gables' sermon series on Pilgrim's Progress #41 *Vanity Fair – Reaction to a Christian Influence* 2.11.99

great offence by silently withdrawing when oaths or unseemly discourse made his situation uneasy, and he was called to account for so assuming a singularity! Believers, appearing in character among worldly people, and not disguising their sentiments, will meet with this opposition, which more accommodating professors will escape. The believer's avowed dependence on the righteousness and attainment of Christ for acceptance, gives vast offence to those who rely on their own good works for justification: his conformity to the example and obedience to the commandments of the Redeemer, render him a precise, unfashionable, uncouth character, in the judgement of those who "walk according to the course of this world": and they will deem him insane or outlandish for his oddities and peculiarities. His discourse, seasoned with piety, humility, seriousness, sincerity, meekness and spirituality, so different from the "filthy conversation of the wicked" and the polite dissimulation of the courtly, that they can have no intercourse with him, or he with them; and if he speaks of the love of Christ and the satisfaction of communion with him, while they "blaspheme the worthy name by which he is called", they must be as barbarians to each other. But above all, the believer's contempt of worldly things, when they interfere with the will and glory of God, forms such a testimony against all the pursuits and conduct of carnal men, as must excite their greatest astonishment and indignation; while he shuns with dread and abhorrence as incompatible with salvation, those very things to which they wholly addict themselves without the least remorse! When the scoffs of those, who "think it strange that they will not run with them to the same excess of riot," extant from them a more explicit declaration of their religious principles, it may be expected that the reproaches and insults of their despisers will be increased; and then all the mischief and confusion which follow will be laid to their charge. "There were no such disputes about religion before they came" to "turn the world upside down;" "they exceedingly troubled the city," town or village, by their pious discourse and censorious example. This Satan takes occasion to excite men to persecute the church, when he fears lest the servants of God should successfully disseminate their principles; persecuting princes and magistrates, his "most trusty friends" are deputed by him to molest and punish their peaceable subjects, for conscientiously refusing conformity to the world, or for dissenting from doctrines and modes of worship, which they deem as unscriptural. Thus the most valuable members of the community are banished, imprisoned, or murdered; multitudes are tempted to hypocrisy; encouragement is given to time-servers to seek secular advantages by acting contrary to their conscience; the principles of sincerity and integrity are generally weakened or destroyed by multiplied prevarications and false professions; and numerous instruments of cruelty and oppression are involved in this complication of atrocious crimes... In Fox's Martyrs we meet with authenticated facts that fully equal this allegorical representation; nay, "The Acts of the Apostles" give us the very same view of the subject. The contempt, injustice, and cruelty, with which persecutors treat the harmless disciples of Christ, makes way for the exhibition of that amiable conduct and spirit which accord to the precepts of Scripture, and the example of persecuted prophets and apostles; this often produces the most happy effects on those who are less prejudiced, which still more exasperates determined opposers; but, however, frequently occasions a short respite for the persecuted, while worldly people quarrel about them among themselves. And even if greater severity be at length determined on, in order to deter others from joining them, perseverance in prudence, meekness, and patience, amidst all the rage of their enemies, will bear testimony for them in the consciences of numbers; their religion will appear beautiful, in proportion as their persecutors expose their own odious deformity: God will be with them to comfort and deliver them; he will be honoured by their profession and behaviour, and many will derive the most important advantage from their patent sufferings and cheerful fortitude in adhering to the truths of the gospel. But when believers are put off their guard by ill-usage; when their zeal is rash, fierce, contentious, boasting, or disproportionate; when they are provoked to render "railing for railing", or to act contrary to the plain precepts of Scripture; then they bring guilt on their consciences, stumble their brethren, harden the hearts and open the mouths of opposers, dishonouring God and the gospel, and gratify the great enemy of souls; who malignantly rejoices in their misconduct, but is tortured when they endure sufferings in a proper manner.' [262]

Gables goes on to council pilgrims by asking, what has Faithful taught us? Be faithful to your Christian calling regardless. Be faithful to God not to the world and its desires. You as a believer are immortal until God's purposes are fulfilled in you. Nothing can harm you or take your life until God's purposes are fulfilled by you but when his purposes are finished then you shall be ushered out . . . until that time occurs for one not even the devil himself shall frustrate or hinder the purposes of God in your life. You are immortal. Satan cannot take your life without permission . . . It does not mean that God's purposes for every one of us is going to result in an old life, that we shall see grey hairs . . . God gives us life. He determines when it ends. Be faithful unto death. Hopeful, Bunyan's newest character who will accompany Christian the rest of the way came into being by witnessing the behaviour, words and sufferings of Christian and Faithful. He told Christian that many more would be coming out of Vanity and joining them on the pilgrimage. One dies and out of the ashes comes a new Christian. Be more concerned about your ministry than your life. [263]

Hopeful joins Christian on his pilgrimage following the torture and burning at the stake of Faithful and as they journey onwards, they meet with a character by the name By-ends.

By-ends informing the two pilgrims that he is from the Town of Fair-speech, and his kindred are Lord Turn-about, Lord Time-

---

[262] *The Pilgrim's Progress* comment by Scott p142-3
[263] Notes from Gables' sermon series on Pilgrim's Progress #44 *Vanity Fair – Death of Faithful* 2.14.99

server, Lord Fair-speech, Mr Smooth-man, Mr facing-both-ways, Mr Any-thing and the parson Mr Two-tongues requests their company on his journey to the Celestial City.

During the ensuing conversation By-ends agrees that "It is true we somewhat differ in religion from those stricter sort, yet but in two small points: First, we never strive against wind and tide; Secondly, we are always most zealous when religion goes in his silver slippers; we love much to walk with him in the street, if the sun shines, and the people applaud him."

After further talking Christian says, "If you will go with us you must go against wind and tide; the which, I perceive, is against your opinion; you must also own religion in his rags as well as when in his silver slippers, and stand by him too when bound in irons as well as when he walketh the streets with applause.

By. You must not impose, nor lord it over my faith; leave me to my liberty, and let me go with you.

Chr. Not a step further, unless you will do in what I propound as we. Then said By-ends, I shall never desert my old principles, since they are harmless and profitable . . .

Looking back later one of the two pilgrims saw Mr Hold-the World, Mr Money-love and Mr Save-all, men that had been once aquainted with Mr By-ends "for in their minority they were school-fellows, and were taught by one Mr Gripeman, a schoolmaster in Love-gain, which is a market town in the county of Coveting . . . . This schoolmaster taught them the art of getting either by violence, cozenage, flattery, lying, or by putting on a guise of religion . . ." join him.

Mr Money-love asked about the two who were still in view.

By. They are a couple of far countrymen, that after their mode are going on pilgrimage.

Money. Alas! Why did they not stay, that we might have had their good company? For they, and we, and you, Sir, I hope, are all going on pilgrimage.

By. We are so indeed; but the men before us are so rigid, and love so much their own notions, and do also so lightly esteem the opinion of others, that let a man be ever so godly, yet if he jumps not with them in all things they thrust him quite out of their company.

Save. That's bad; but we read of some that are righteous over much, and such men's rigidness prevails with them to judge and condemn all but themselves; but I pray what and how many were the things wherein you differed?

By. Why they, after their headstrong manner, conclude that it is their duty to rush on their journey all weathers; an I am for waiting for wind and tide. They are for hazarding all for God at a clap, and I am for taking all advantages to secure my life and estate. They are for holding their notions, though all other men be against them; but I am for religion in what, and so far as the times and my safety will bear it. They are fore religion when in rags and contempt; but I am for him when he walks in his golden slippers in the sunshine, and with applause.[264]

These four continue conversing, discussing how to use religion as a cloak for gain in the world, gain finically or socially.

Scott comments that they 'only attend to religion when they can gain by it; they cut and shape their creed and conduct to suit the times, and to please those among whom they live; they determine to keep what they have at any rate, and to get more, if it can be done without open scandal . . . God permits Satan to bait his hook with some worldly advantage, in order to induce men to renounce their profession, expose their hypocrisy, or disgrace the gospel; and they, poor deluded mortals! Call it "an opening of providence". The Lord indeed puts the object in their way, if they will break his commandments in order to seize upon it: but he does it to prove them, and to show whether they most love him or their worldly interests; but the devil thus tempts them, that he may "take them captive at his will". The arguments . . . are only valid on the supposition that religion is a mere external appearance, and has nothing to do with the state of the heart and affections; and in short, that hypocrisy and piety are words

---

[264] *The Pilgrim's Progress* p153-8

precisely of the same meaning . . . the answer of Christian, though somewhat rough, is so apposite and conclusive, that it is sufficient to fortify every honest and attentive mind against all the arguments . . . arguments . . . in support of their ingenious schemes and assiduous efforts to reconcile religion with covetousness and the love of the world, or to render it subservient to their secular interests.'[265]

Now to return to the conversation of our four travellers –

By. . . . Suppose a man, a minister or a tradesman, &c., should have an advantage lie before him, to get the good blessings of this life, yet so as that he can by no means come by them, except, in appearance at least, he becomes extraordinary zealous in some points of religion that he meddled not with before – may he not use this means to obtain his end, and yet be a right honest man?

Money. . . . as it concerns a minister . . . Suppose a minister, a worthy man, possessed but a very small benefice, and has in his eyes a greater, more fat and plump by far; he has also now an opportunity of getting of it, yet so as by being more studious, by preaching more frequently and zealously, and, because the temper of the people requires it, by altering of some of his principles . . . His desire of a greater benefice is lawful; this cannot be contradicted, since it is set before him by providence . . . I conclude, then, that a minister that changes a small for a great should not, for so doing, be judged as covetous; but rather, since he is improved in his parts and industry thereby, be counted as one that pursues his call, and the opportunity put into his hand to do good. . . now . . . the tradesman . . . suppose such a one to have but a poor employ in the world; but by becoming religious he may mend his market, perhaps get a rich wife, or more and far better customers to his shop . . . To become religious is a virtue, by what means soever a man becomes so . . . the man that gets these by becoming religious, gets that which is good, of them that are good, by becoming good himself; so then here is a good wife,

---

[265] Ibid. comment by Scott p159-60

and good customers, and good gain, and all these by becoming religious, which is good: therefore, to become religious to get all these is a good and profitable design.
The others so applauded Mr Money-love's statement and believing that 'no man was able to contradict it and because Christian and Hopeful were yet in call, they jointly agreed to assult them with this question . . . and bid them to answer it if they could. Then said Christian, Even a babe in religion may answer ten thousand such questions. For it be unlawful to follow Christ for loaves, as it is, John vi., how much more is it abominable to make of him and religion a stalking-horse to get and enjoy the world? Nor do we find any other than heathens, hypocrites, devils, and witches, that are of this opinion. . .. [see Genesis xxxiv. 20-24, Luke xx. 46, 47, Acts viii. 18-23] . . . and your reward will be according to your works. [266]

> Love should always move slowly in receiving a report, but ever deal faithfully when it is plain that men are not what they profess to be. [267]

I wonder what your thoughts about these three points were. I believe that in principle they are still very relevant for pilgrims of today and the future to consider and apply to their walk because they will always set us aside from the world as they reflect our Father's loving ways, desiring better for us than we actually do. For example, to dress modestly is loving yourself and honouring your Father. You are saying that there is more to you than being an object to lust after and that you are strong enough to be different. By not selling yourself to the first bidder you are loving others by challenging them to consider that there is a better way to be and showing them what that is and that it is truly worthwhile to pursue.

The seven walks of living

---

[266] Ibid. p159-162
[267] Ibid. p157

The Pilgrim Way

In Paul's letter to the Ephesians there are seven ways God calls us to walk as pilgrims which we are going to now look at with thanks to D. L. Moody.

I. *The walk of obedience.* (Ephesians ii:1-2 [And you He made alive, who were dead in trespasses and sins, in which you once walked according to the course of this world, according to the prince of the power of the air, the spirit who now works in the sons of disobedience])

We are obeying something or other all the time – either our own carnal nature or God. The essence of sin is obedience to our own lusts and desires, and disobedience to God. Did you ever notice that everything but man obeys God? . . . That is where all the trouble, and all the wretchedness, and misery, and woe come, and there will never be peace in your soul and mine until we are willing to obey God . . . As someone has put it, 'Do *as* God commands and do *all* God commands.' Partial obedience is not enough. If the doctor's prescription were changed a little it might mean death.

II. *Walk worthy of the vocation wherewith ye are called.* (Ephesians iv:1 [I, therefore, the prisoner of the Lord, beseech you to walk worthy of the calling with which you were called])

More depends upon my walk than upon my talk. Don't forget that. Talk is very cheap nowadays. 'We talk cream and live skim milk' . . . Some people talk like angels, and live like devils. Some people, when they are away from home, are angelic, and yet they are like snapping-turtles at home. . . we are called to represent the 'King of Kings, and Lord of Lords'. Therefore let us walk worthy.

III. *Walk in love* (Ephesians v:2 [And walk in love, as Christ also has loved us and given Himself for us, an offering and a sacrifice to God for a sweet-smelling aroma])

Jude says, 'Keep yourself in the love of God'. I believe that if the disciples of Jesus Christ would keep themselves in the love of God for thirty days their number would double in no time. If this world is ever to be conquered, it will be conquered by love, and there is no way to preach love like living it in our actions. If we are full of love, we will be full of forgiveness; we will be clothed with humility. '*Keep* yourselves in the love of God.'

. . . In the early church nothing astonished the pagans so much as the life of love lived by the Christians. "Behold, how they love one another," they said; "they love each other without knowing each other." If you have not that spirit of love you have not really the Christ of the Bible in your heart, because God is love, and when we are born of God we get God's Spirit. When we have that Spirit, it will be natural for us to love . . .

Andrew Murray [1828-1917] has said that most Christians are ready to pray for the Holy Ghost for power in service, but that we seldom pray for Him as the Spirit of love. We have almost forgotten that love is the first fruitage of the Spirit's indwelling. Love is the fulfilling of the law. When sin entered, it broke the bands of love, and we found the spirit of hatred leading Cain to murder his brother. Oh, for a baptism of love, uniting us altogether in one Spirit!

. . . Are you walking in love? If not, make up your mind that you will do it from now on. Move into the thirteenth chapter of First Corinthians. Many people take an occasional journey into that chapter, but few live there. . .

  IV. *Walk circumspectly* (Ephesians v:15 [See then that you walk circumspectly, not as fools but as wise])

The eyes of the world are upon us. They don't read the Bible, but they read you and me, and we talk more by our walk than in any other way. We are 'living epistles, known and read of all men.' I can walk a lie. I can walk dishonestly. I can walk crookedly, and make other people stumble over me. . .

An old divine, trying to illustrate this passage . . . describes a cat walking on a brick wall covered with sharp pieces of glass. The cat goes along, putting his feet down very cautiously, so as not to cut his feet. Let us keep in mind that the eyes of the world are upon our acts . . .

Many a person who is engaged in active Christian work, or who takes a leading part in the prayer meeting, is so faulty in his daily walk as to be a stumbling-block to others. Sometimes the last people to be favourably impressed by professing Christians are those who know them in their home life. This is all wrong. Test yourselves, therefore, and see if you indulge in any questionable habit, anything in your example and influence that is likely to lead astray those who read your conduct.

V. *Walk not as other gentiles walk* (Ephesians iv:17 [This I say, therefore, and testify in the Lord, that you should no longer walk as the rest of the Gentiles walk, in the futility of their mind])

God expects a difference when we become His. The world expects a difference, and the church of God expects a difference between one that professes to be a child of light and one that is a child of darkness; and if there is not a difference in your life since you have become a Christian, then I am afraid that you have not become a real one.

The course of this world is away from God; therefore I must go against the current of the world, if I am a child of God . . . The church will have a convincing testimony and will become a power in the world when it is separated from the world; but as long as it is hand and glove with the world, it cannot have power. . .

You say, "I will walk as I please."

You can do it. You can take a course away from God, but it will bring you into bondage and darkness.

VI. *Walk as children of light* (Ephesians v:8 [For you were once darkness, but now you are light in the Lord. Walk as children of light])

Put off the ways of darkness. Put off the works of darkness.

. . . Let the Word of God into your heart and it will dispel the darkness. . . We are children of the day, children of the light; we have been born of His Spirit, and He brings light and peace. I believe that nothing is going to light up the dark places of the world like the old Book. Men talk about the light of nature, but we do not find that civilization has made any progress where the light of Christ and the Bible has not come. . .

VII. *Let us walk in good works* (Ephesians ii:10 [For we are His workmanship, created in Christ Jesus for good works, which God prepared beforehand that we should walk in them])

I learned a motto in England which I am going to pass on to you: 'For our Lord Jesus Christ's sake, do all the good you can, to all the people you can, by all the means you can, in all the places you can, as long as ever you can.' . . .

You know that very often one little act of kindness will live a good deal longer than a most magnificent sermon. . .

Let us walk the walk of good works. Find something to do, and do it every day, and you will never backslide, and you won't be asking, "Have I got to give up this and that?" Christ will give you something better than anything you give up. Oh, may God baptize us all with the spirit of love and the spirit of work!

If we walk with God, we will not be asking, What is the harm of this and that? The question will be, What is the *good*? If a thing does not help us we will give it up for something better.

Right here I want to say that I don't see how any Christian man or woman can touch the Sunday newspapers. . . The time has come when the nation should rise up and cry aloud to God to stop this iniquitous thing. It is doing more harm to-day than any other one thing in literature. You can get along without it one day in the week, and I believe you are dishonouring God by having anything to do with it. If persons would rather read the Sunday newspaper than the Bible, if they cannot get along without the opera and the theatre, God have mercy upon them . . . A man or a woman never lets down the standard without losing more than they gain.

Keep the standard high and let God have the first place, and then He withhold no good thing from you: Let the world call you a bigot . . . If the world has nothing to say against you, Jesus Christ will probably have nothing to say for you. [268]

This was written over a hundred years ago. Then it was the emergence of the Sunday newspaper and other Sunday entertainments that Moody was so vocal against as they took

---

[268] D. L. Moody (!837-1899) *Short Talks The seven 'Walks' of Ephesians* and *Fellowship with God* p56-7 The Moody Press 1990 p 36-47.

time therefore hearts away from that old Book. What is there in today's world that is doing this? Work, sport, shopping, multiple forms of media – I mean, how many television channels can you watch, or magazines can you read? and that's without considering the internet? So much that tries to pull us away, numb, deafen and blind us to our real need and its only answer, O pilgrim please take care where you decide to place your feet!

Heed forgetfulness

Our relationship with the triune God gives and enables pilgrims to live and maintain this peculiar lifestyle of a sojourner. Yet as we are also to work at maintaining this relationship, we are going to consider now what could happen if we don't and how we are helped to maintain it.

Question: What happens if we become forgetful, neglectful of this relationship? (What happens with any other relationship?) What is the result when it is not just one who has become careless but a whole society, a whole nation?

Answer: Forgetful, careless, neglectful, these words may not sound as loudly as the next phrase but they are pictures of it – rebellious disobedience towards the Lord God, our creator and saviour – and should pull us up sharply.

We have considered persecution of various forms in this book and the letter to the Hebrews was written for pilgrims who were suffering hard persecutions, so hard that many were considering abandoning their journey. It is interesting to note that the author did not concentrate on their suffering but on sin. He did not advise his readers on how to react when faced with the choice between their faith in Christ or their life, but on what happens prior, the many small seemingly insignificant decisions of years past which have slowly and quietly eroded their once firm foundation.

The author of Hebrews is looking at what can stop a pilgrim reaching the Celestial City and the rest that God has promised, and it is not the persecution that we fear. We do not wake up one morning and decide we will start to sin any more than a husband will suddenly decide to commit adultery, stuff happens slowly, a little missed here, a little slip there, usually unseen by most, beforehand.

David Williams spoke of three steps discussed in the letter to the Hebrews.

1. Drifting from the message of the gospel.

Hebrews 2:1-4, 'Therefore we must give the more earnest heed to the things we have heard, lest we drift away. For if the word spoken through angels proved steadfast, and every transgression and disobedience received a just reward, how shall we escape if we neglect so great a salvation, which at the first began to be spoken by the Lord, and was confirmed to us by those who heard Him. God also bearing witness both with signs and wonders, with various miracles, and gifts of the Holy Spirit, according to His own will?'

Drifting is easy, there is no effort required, a dead dog can drift down the Yarra with no problem. It is associated with neglect. Neglecting to speak up, or acting in a manner that would bring God glory in a certain circumstance, choosing instead to go to the toilet, or simply not picking up your Bible every day to read and pray and allowing a day to become a month and a month to become a year. The cure is to pay careful attention to the gospel, to study your Bible, to live it.

2. Disconnecting from the Christian community.

Hebrews 10:23-25 and 32-35, 'Let us hold fast the confession of our hope without wavering, for He who promised is faithful. And let us consider one another in order to stir up love and good works, not forsaking the assembling of ourselves together, as is the manner of some, but exhorting one another, and so much the more as you see the Day approaching. . . But recall the former days in which, after you were illuminated [enlightened], you endured a great struggle with sufferings: partly while you were made a spectacle both by reproaches and tribulations, and partly while you became companions of those who were so treated; for you had compassion on me in my chains, and joyfully accepted the plundering of your goods, knowing that you have a better and an enduring possession for yourselves in heaven. Therefore do not cast away your confidence, which has great reward.'

Christians, pilgrims need each other for only they know what it is to stand against the flesh, the devil and the world, only they can support and edify each other in Christ. If you are beginning to stray, drift from the path you are more likely to decrease your attendance at church or fellowship gatherings, prayer meetings because these force you to see what is happening. There is a challenge in verse 32. Will you or I choose to publicly support someone who is being publicly exposed, who is facing opposition for their Christianity? Will I choose to support on Facebook, write in to the local paper, or visit a pilgrim brother or sister who is in jail?

3. Disobeying the gospel, disobeying God which is sin.

Hebrews 3:12-14, 'Beware, brethren, lest there be in any of you an evil heart of unbelief in departing from the living God; but exhort one another daily, while it is called "Today", lest any of you be hardened through the deceitfulness of sin. For we have become partakers of Christ if we hold the beginning of our confidence steadfast to the end.'

Persecution cannot stop you, in fact all persecution can do is get you there quicker than you had planned, like Bunyan's character Faithful. Persecution has no power to harden your heart, to make you carless of the things of God, only sin has this power. There are several warnings throughout Hebrews that tell us it is our sin that will take pilgrims off the narrow way, the King's highway. We should be more concerned about sin than any suffering we may have to face. [269]

---

[269] I wish to give credit to David Williams for his three steps and ideas I took from the outline and my notes at the Belgrave Heights Summer Convention 2019/20 message given by him on the 28.12.2019 titled *Preparing for Tomorrow*

Let's consider Paul's letter to the Romans, read the complete letter sometime but for now I want you to see something which shows I believe that Paul understood how easy it is for pilgrims to be forgetful. This letter has been divided into sixteen chapters at a much later stage, as with all scripture to make it easy to find what is being said, read or studied. At the beginning of the twelfth chapter in the first verse there is a *therefore*, which is followed by verse two – *be transformed by the renewing of your mind* – which we considered in Part 1.

"Why the therefore Paul?" we could ask.

Can you hear him answer, "Because of all I have said since beginning this letter to you what follows next is logical, is expected."

Paul had much to say before he began these last four chapters teaching ethics, teaching what was expected of pilgrims, how we are to be as pilgrims, how we are to walk therefore the first seventy-five percent of the letter was taken up with teaching us how God is, teaching pilgrims of the undeserved mercy and grace lavished upon us by a God who loves.

Paul 'knows – not the least from his own experience – that there is no greater incentive to holy living than a contemplation of the mercies of God.' [270]

To fight against forgetfulness try spending a regular set-apart time studying what Yahweh has done for us pilgrims and pray for help to make what we read, what we come to know of God, stick.

According to Wright, 'Knowing God means knowing what *God* has done, knowing it was done *for me*, and knowing the *response* I should make.' [271]

Is this not what the gospel teaches us? What the Bible shows and teaches? He goes on to tell us that 'the knowledge of God [became] lost [according to the book titled Hosea in the Old Testament] because the people [the nation of Israel]

---

[270] I wish to give credit for the ideas expressed in this paragraph as well as the quote to John Stott's *The Message of Romans* Inter-varsity Press 1994 p320-1

[271] Christopher J. H. Wright *Knowing God the Father through the Old Testament* Monarch Books 2007 p157

persistently failed to acknowledge God's gifts, to walk in God's ways, and to teach God's laws. . .

. . . Israel is addressed as a wife whose unfaithfulness has been exposed and denounced:

> Their mother has been unfaithful
> > And has conceived them in disgrace.
> She said, 'I will go after my lovers,
> > who give me my food and my water,
> > my wool and my linen, my oil and my drink.'
> She has not acknowledged that I was the one
> > who gave her the grain, the new wine and the oil,
> Who lavished on her silver and gold –
> > which they used for Baal.
> Therefore I will take away my grain when it ripens,
> > and my new wine when it is ready.
> I will take back my wool and my linen,
> > intended to cover her nakedness.
> > > (Hosea 2:5, 8-9)

. . . . this did not mean that Israel no longer even knew the name of Yahweh. It means they refused to acknowledge him in one of his most basic activities – the regularity and fruitfulness of the created order and the fertility of the land that he himself had given to them.

Ingratitude to God for all his good gifts leads to losing the knowledge of God. When we are tempted to attribute to other causes whatever measure of blessing comes our way in life, or even to claim credit for it ourselves, then we are on the dangerous road of forgetting the Lord.

> Hear the word of the Lord, O people of Israel;
> > for the Lord has an indictment
> > against the inhabitants of the land.
> There is no faithfulness or loyalty,
> > and no knowledge of God in the land.
> Swearing, lying, and murder,
> > and stealing and adultery break out;

> bloodshed follows bloodshed.
> Therefore the land mourns,
> and all who live in it languish;
> together with the wild animals
> and the birds of the air,
> even the fish of the sea are perishing.
> (Hosea 4:1-3, NRSV)

What happens when a whole people refuses to know the God who is their saviour, husband and father? What Hosea observes is a complete moral collapse of society and accompanying detrimental ecological effects. . . No knowledge of Yahweh leads to breakdown of all trust and commitment. . . Once even the caricature of deity loses any imperative grip on the social conscience, then the bonds of social truthfulness, trust, love, mutual commitment and kindness, all begin to dissolve under the acids of ego-centric skepticism.

Instead of such godly characteristics, observes Hosea, the land is filled with the dismal fruit of moral disorder, the breaking of almost all the commandments in the second table of the Decalogue: abusive and violent language; public and private untruthfulness; crimes against life and property; a culture of rampant violence. No knowledge of God leads to no restraints on evil. Paul's searing commentary on this in Romans 1 and 2 expands Hosea's diagnosis of eight-century Israel into a penetrating analysis of the human condition, once the suppression of the knowledge of God has worked like poison through human society.

The knowledge of God [is] restored through repentance. . .

Hosea reminds us that fine words are not enough. God seeks specific repentance over named sins, based on clear-eyed recognition and wholehearted renunciation of them . . . We cannot claim to know God while colluding in injustice, cruelty and the idolizing of money, sex and power. . .

To forget someone is relational, not just cognitive. If one person says of another, 'You've forgotten me', it means that the other person has lost any sense of commitment or obligation; the shared history no longer means anything; the love has died; the relationship holds no further personal investment. So it was between Israel and God [and it is] only by the breath-taking love and grace of God [that we are] transported from betrayal, adultery and martial breakdown (as Hosea's metaphor for Israel's sin, in which is mirrored our own) to covenant intimacy, ethical integrity and eternal security [as seen in Hosea 2:19-20, '"I will betroth you to Me forever; Yes, I will betroth you to Me in righteousness and justice, in lovingkindness and mercy; I will betroth you to Me in faithfulness, and you shall know the LORD."'] The New Testament teaches us that we already have the inauguration of this new covenant in the crucified and risen Christ, and the Bride of Christ awaits the Bridegroom's return to consummate the relationship in the kind of perfection that Hosea and other prophets glimpsed and stammered to express.

But though these are future realities to which we look forward with eager anticipation, they are vitally relevant to how we live now. For we are called to know God here and now. . . God longs to be known by us, as saviour, as father, as husband. We run terrible risks of forfeiting the knowledge of God when we refuse to recognize his gifts, fail to live by his standards, and neglect the teaching of his words and ways. . . There is, Hosea would say, a sweetness greater than even the most loving human marriage when we return to the love that sought us and bought us, woos us and wins us.'[272]

In the second part of Pilgrim's Progress we follow the pilgrimage of Christian's wife Christina and their four sons James the least, Joseph, Samuel and Matthew with a neighbour named Mercy.

After stopping at the Interpreter's house, they are sent on their way with a guide and bodyguard named Mr. Great-Heart. As they journey on together Great-heart says to Samuel as they draw closer to a certain place, "Your father had the battle with Apollyon at a place yonder before us, in a narrow passage just beyond

---

[272] Ibid. p161, 163-6, 169, 175, 178-9

Forgetful Green. And indeed, that place is the most dangerous place in all these parts; for is at any time pilgrims meet with any brunt, it is when they forget what favours they have received, and how unworthy they are of them." [273]

Mason comments, 'O pilgrims, attend to this! Pride and ingratitude go hand in hand. Study, ever study, the favours of your Lord; how freely they are bestowed upon you, and how utterly unworthy you are of the least of them. Beware of Forgetful Green. Many, after going some way on pilgrimage, get into this green, and continue here, and talk of their own faithfulness to grace received, the merit of their works, and a second justification by their works. . . they forget that they are still sinners, poor, needy, wretched sinners, and that they want the blood of Christ to cleanse them, the righteousness of Christ to justify them, and the spirit of Christ to keep them humble, and to enable them to live by faith upon the fullness of Christ to sanctify them, as much as they did when they first set out as pilgrims. O 'tis a most blessed thing to be kept mindful of what we are, and of the Lord's free grace and unmerited goodness to us!' [274]

God knows us better than we know ourselves, he knows that we are prone to forgetfulness which is no helping hand for maintaining this lifestyle and so he gave us three things to help us pilgrims of the New Testament age to remember him by. He gave us his completed written word, the Bible, his church, fellowship gatherings of like-minded pilgrims and he gave us communion, the Lord's supper on his last night, his last meal with his disciples before his crucifixion as we read of in Paul's comments and instructions in 1Corinthians 11:23-28, 'For I received from the Lord that which I also delivered to you: that the Lord Jesus on the same night in which He was betrayed took bread; and when He had given thanks, He broke it and said, "Take, eat; this is My body which is broken for you; do this in remembrance of me." in the same manner He also took the cup after supper, saying, "This cup

---

[273] *The Pilgrim's Progress part 2* p321

[274] *The Pilgrim's Progress Part 2* comment by Mason p317

is the new covenant in My blood. This do, as often as you drink it, in remembrance of Me." For as often as you eat this bread and drink this cup, you proclaim the Lord's death till He comes. Therefore whoever eats this bread or drinks this cup of the Lord in an unworthy manner will be guilty of the body and blood of the Lord. But let a man examine himself, and so let him eat of the bread and drink of the cup.'

Question: How do you approach communion? Where do your thoughts go during this sacrament? (Please don't ask me this question.)

Answer: The language of this quote may be quaint, but I found its message challenging. Do I think and feel like it is advised here, do I reverence the remembering of my Lord God and saviour like this? Do you?

Fleetwood writes, 'Was it not then an instance of our Saviour's wisdom and benevolence, by uniting us together at the sacrificial offering of his body and blood, to urge the putting away of all bitterness, anger, evil-speaking, and revenge, and to inspire us with compassion and love? . . .

When we actually join in communion, we should be careful that our affections be properly directed and warmly engaged. Not to allow our hearts to be drawn away by the vanities and cares of this world, for this is a direct violation of the ordinance; and, therefore, we should be extremely careful to maintain a right frame of mind at that time. We should study to abstract our thoughts as much as possible from every passing event in the world around, every terrestrial consideration, indeed, of any kind whatever, and to have our thoughts, our very souls of a truth, fervently employed in the solemn service. Retire, oh my soul, each of us should say, from this scene of things here below; from all its pleasures and all its pursuits, and hold holy communion with our Almighty Father, and with our blessed Redeemer, by the aid of the Spirit being given to us. Meditate upon that infinite grace of Omnipotence, which formed the amazing plan, that displayed pardon, peace, and endless happiness, to so underserving a creature as thou art. Recollect that surprising condescension and tenderness of thy compassionate Redeemer, which induce him to bring down from heaven salvation to the sons of men. Call to mind the encouraging instructions he offered, the charming pattern he exhibited, the hard labours and sufferings he endured in the course of his ministry; especially remember the ignominy, the reproaches, the agonies he endured when he hung on the cross, and purchased for thee eternal mercy. Think upon these affecting subjects till thine heart is filled with sorrow for thine iniquities: till thy faith becomes lively, active, and dutiful; till thy gratitude, and love are elevated to the highest; till thy obedience is rendered uniform, steady, and complete. Hast thou, O my God, thou Parent of universal nature! – hast thou so illustriously manifested thy compassion for sinners, as not to spare thine own Son? Hast thou sent the Saviour into the lower world, in order to raise the children of men to immortality, and to that glory and bliss which shall never end? And am I now in thy presence on purpose to celebrate this institution, who requireth me to commemorate the death of the great Messiah: to declare my public acceptance of his excellent revelation, and my regard to my Christian brethren? May then the remembrance of his beneficence dwell upon my mind, and upon my heart for ever and ever! May I consider and comply with the institution of his gospel; and may the sentiments of kindness and charity towards all my fellow-mortals, and fellow-disciples, reign in my breast, with increasing purity, with increasing zeal!

Such is the state of mind we ought to be in, and such that which should possess our souls, when we partake of this sacred ordinance; but it will signify little to entertain these views at that time only, unless the effects of them are apparent in our future conduct and conversation; for a transient flow of our affections, or displays of our immediate delight, were not only intended in this institution.

Jesus did not ordain it as a ceremony or charm, but as a proper method of establishing our hearts in the fear and love of God, who gave his only beloved Son to die for wretched sinners.

The Pilgrim Way

Though ye have, therefore, O Christians! Obeyed the Redeemer's command in this appointment, and found your best sympathies greatly incited towards him, yet this is not the whole required at your hands: it will justly be expected that you should live to the honour of your divine Master. As you have solemnly professes your faith in him, and your love towards him, the reality of your faith and love should be demonstrated by walking more strictly in the way of his precepts, and by abounding in that heavenly character and temper which his spotless example so engagingly recommends. Thus only will the sacrament of the Lord's Supper become subservient to the most beneficial purposes. Thus only will it be instrumental in qualifying us for sharing in the dignity and felicity possessed by our exalted Saviour.

May, therefore, all the followers of the immaculate Jesus, by uniting together at his sacred table, advance from holiness to holiness, till they arrive at the regions of eternal felicity!' [275]

So, let us as pilgrims make a habit of using what our loving good Father has provided us with to maintain his desired lifestyle before unbelievers and believers, persevering to the end, not forgetting or neglecting his gift of prayer which must cover all.

As this third part comes to a close, are you thinking that all this sort of sounds perhaps a nice way to live but very naïve, way beyond the reality of real life, real living in this world and so practically unworkable? I once thought the same, I don't anymore.

Consider this snippet of how Bunyan reasoned within himself, how he faced twelve years of incarceration in a time when prisons had no luxuries, where food had to be brought by those outside if they had any and bribes paid for needed medicines to be allowed.

327. But notwithstanding these helps [God's grace, conviction, instruction and understanding, more time to read Scriptures and meditate and pray, how to face death and to live upon God] I

---

[275] *Fleetwood's Life of Christ* p545-8

found myself a man encompassed with infirmities; the parting with my wife and poor children, hath often been to me in this place, as the pulling the flesh from the bones, and that not only because I am somewhat too fond of these great mercies, but also because I should have often brought to my mind the many hardships, miseries, and wants that my poor family was likely to meet with, should I be taken from them, especially my poor blind child . . .

328. . . . I must venture you all with God, though it goeth to the quick to leave you. Oh! I saw in this condition I was as a man who was pulling down his house upon the head of his wife and children; yet, thought I, I must do it . . .

329. . . . these two Scriptures, "Leave thy fatherless children, I will preserve them alive, and let thy widows trust in me" And again, "The Lord said, verily it shall go well with thy remnant; verily I will cause the enemy to entreat thee well in the time of evil," &c.
Jer xlix II; Chap xv. II.

330. I had also their consideration, that if I should venture all for God, I engaged God to take care of my concernments: but if I forsook him in his ways, for fear of any trouble that should come to me or mine, then I should not only falsify my profession, but should count also that my concernments were not so sure, if left at God's feet, while I stood to and for his name, as they would be, if they were under my own care, though with the denial of the way of God. This was a smarting consideration, and that was, the dread of the torments of hell, which I was sure they must partake of, that for fear of the cross, do shrink from their profession of Christ, his words and laws, before the sons of men. I thought also of the glory that he had prepared for those that in faith, and love, and patience, stood to his ways before them. These things, I say, have helped me, when the thoughts of the misery that both myself and mine, might, for the sake of my profession, be exposed to, have lain pinching on my mind.

336. . . . Thus was I tossed for many weeks, and knew not what

to do; at last this consideration fell with weight upon me, "That it was for the word and the way of God that I was in this condition; wherefore I was engaged not to flinch an hair's breadth from it.[276]

> If a man would live well, let him fetch his last day to him, and make it always his company and keeper.[277]

---

[276] *Grace Abounding to the Chief of Sinners: a brief relation of the exceeding mercy of God in Christ, to his poor servant, John Bunyan. A Brief Account of the Author's Imprisonment* The Pilgrims Progress and other selected Works p807-10

[277] Interpreter, a John Bunyan character in The Pilgrim's Progress

Robyn Crothers

Interlude 2: Take heed before that day

Luke chapter 13 starts with a discussion which arose when some seemed to believe that bad things – like being killed by Pilate whilst sacrificing in the temple, or being killed on a work site only happened to people who were the worst of sinners.
Jesus refutes this, teaching that they and we should not be concerned about how death comes for it surely will come if Christ does not return first, but about being in a right relationship with him beforehand. It is in this context that Jesus teaches the following parable which we are going to consider using extracts from Bunyan's discourse on it followed by some other writers.
Luke 13:6-9, '. . . "A certain man had a fig tree planted in his vineyard, and he came seeking fruit on it and found none. Then he said to the keeper of his vineyard, 'Look, for three years I have come seeking fruit on this fig tree and find none. Cut it down; why does it use up the ground?' But he answered and said to him, 'Sir, let it alone this year also, until I dig around it and fertilize it. And if it bears fruit, well. But if not, after that you can cut it down.'"'
This parable is a warning for all those who profess to love Christ in word but not in life. Bunyan wrote a *brief and plain discourse* on this parable giving it the title, *The Barren Fig-tree, or, The Doom and Downfall of the Fruitless Professor.*

A certain man had a fig-tree planted in his vineyard . . . Observe, then, that it is no new thing if you find in God's church barren fig-trees, fruitless professors, even as here you see is a tree, a fruitless tree, a fruitless fig-tree in the vineyard. Fruit is not so easily brought forth, as a profession is got into. It is easy for a man to clothe himself with a fair show in the flesh, to word it, and say, Be thou warmed and filled with the best; it is no hard thing to do these, with other things: but to be fruitful, to bring forth fruit to

God, this doth not every tree . . . John xv.2, "Every branch in me that beareth not fruit, he taketh away," assert the same thing . . . .

Had a fig-tree . . . The foolish virgins also went forth of the world with the other, had lamps, and light, and were awakened with the others; yea, had boldness to go forth, when the midnight cry was made, with the other; and thought that they could have looked Christ in the face, when he sat upon the throne of judgement, with the other; and yet but foolish, but barren fig-trees . . . Matt.viii. 22,23, "Many", said Christ, "will say unto me in that day," this and that, and will also talk of many wonderful works; yet behold, he finds nothing in them but the fruits of unrighteousness: they were altogether barren and fruitless professors. . .

Had a fig-tree planted in his vineyard . . . He doth not say, "he planted a fig-tree", but there was a fig-tree there . . . "And when the king came in to see the guests, he saw there a man that had not on a wedding-garment. And he said unto him, Friend, how comest thou in hither, not having on a wedding-garment?" Matt. xxii. 11, 12. . . . "How comest thee hither?" my Father did not bring thee hither; I did not bring thee hither; my Spirit did not bring thee hither . . . John x.1., "He that cometh not in by the door, but climbeth up some other way, the same is a thief and a robber." . . .

And he came and sought fruit thereon and found none . . . untimely fruit . . . fruit too soon . . . These professors are those light and inconsiderate ones that think nothing but peace will attend the gospel; and so anon rejoice at the tidings, without forseeing the evil: wherefore, when the evil comes, being unarmed, so not able to stand any longer, they die, and are withered and bring forth no fruit . . . Matt. xiii. 20, 21. . . . fruit too late . . . The missing of the season is dangerous; staying till the door is shut is dangerous. Many there be that came not till the flood of God's anger is raised, and too deep for them to wade through. "Surely in the floods of great waters they shall not come nigh unto him." Psal. xxxii.6 . . .

Barren fig-tree, seeing thou art a professor, and art got into the vineyard, thou standest before the Lord of the vineyard as one of the trees of the garden; wherefore he looketh for fruit from thee, as from the rest of the trees in the vineyard; fruit, I say, and such as may declare thee in the heart and life, one that hath sound profession of repentance, By thy profession thou hast said, I am sensible of the evil of sin. Now then, live such a life as declares that thou art sensible of the evil of sin. By thy Profession thou hast said, I am sorry for my sin: why then, live such a life as may declare this sorrow. By thy profession thou hast said, "I am ashamed of my sin," Psal.xxxviii.18; yea, but live such a life, that men by that may "see thy shame for sin." Jer.xxi.19. By thy profession thou sayest, I have turned from, left off, and am become an enemy to every appearance of evil. 1Thess.v.22. Ah! But doth thy life and conversation declare thee to be such a one? Take heed, barren fig-tree, lest thy life should give thy profession the lie . . .

You have some professors that are only saints before men, when they are abroad, but are devils and vipers at home; saints by profession, but devils by practice; saints in word, but sinners in heart and life. These men may have the profession, but they want the fruits that become repentance.

Barren fig-tree, can it be imagined that those that paint themselves, did ever repent of their pride? Or that those that pursue this world, did ever repent of their fleshly lusts? Where, barren fig-tree, is the fruit of these people's repentance? Nay, do they not rather declare to the world, that they have repented of their profession? Their fruits look as if they had. Their pride saith, they have repented of their humility; their covetousness declareth, that they are weary of depending upon God; and do not thy actions declare that thou abhorrest chastity? Where is thy fruit, barren fig-tree? Repentance is not only a sorrow, and a shame for, but a turning from sin to God. Heb. vi., it is called, "Repentance from dead works." Hast thou that godly sorrow that worketh "repentance to salvation, never to be repented of?"

2Cor.vii. 10,11. How dost thy show thy carefulness, and clearing of thyself; thy indignation against sin; thy fear of offending; thy vehement desire to walk with God; thy zeal for his name and glory in the world? And what revenge hast thou in thy heart against every thought of disobedience?

But where is the fruit of this repentance? Where is thy watching, thy fasting, thy praying against the remainders of corruption? Where is thy self-abhorrence, thy blushing before God, for the sin that is yet behind? Where is thy tenderness of the name of God and his ways? Where is thy self-denial and contentment? How dost thou show before men the truth of thy turning to God? "Hast thou renounced the hidden things of dishonesty, not walking in craftiness?" 2Cor.iv.2. Canst thou commend thyself "to every man's conscience in the sight of God?" . . . .

Thou professest to believe thou hast peace in another world; hast thou let go this, barren fig-tree? Thou professes thou believest in Christ: is he the joy and the life of thy soul? Yea, what conformity unto him, to his sorrows and suffering? What resemblance hath his crying, and groaning, and bleeding, and dying, wrought in thee? Dost thou "bear in thy body the dying of the Lord Jesus? And is also the life of Jesus made manifest in thy mortal body"? 2Cor. iv. 10,11. Barren fig-tree, "show me thy faith by thy works. Show, out of a good conversation, thy works, with meekness of heart." James ii. 18, and iii.13. . .

What degree of heart-holiness? For "faith purifies the heart." Acts xv.9. What love to the Lord Jesus? For "faith worketh by love." Gal.v.6. . . . Doust thou walk like one that is bought with a price, with the price of precious blood? . . . as the apostle saith, "we should walk worthy of God", that is, so as we may show in every place, that the presence of God is with us, his fear in us, and his majesty and authority upon our actions. Fruits meet for him, such a dependence upon him, such trust in his word, such satisfaction in his presence, such a trusting of him with all my concerns, and such delights in the enjoyment of him that may demonstrate that his fear is in my heart, that my soul is wrapped up in his things, and that my body, and soul, and estates, and all, are in truth, through his grace, at his disposal, fruit meet for him.

. . . how many willingly offer themselves in all ages, and their all, for the worthy name of the Lord Jesus, to be racked, starved, hanged, burned, drowned, pulled in pieces, and a thousand calamities. . . Hast thou fruit becoming the care of God, the protection of God, the wisdom of God, the patience and husbandry of God? It is the fruit of the vineyard, that is either the shame or the praise of the husbandman. . . The question is not now, What thou thinkest of thyself, nor what all the people of God think of thee, but what thou shalt be found in that day when God shall search thy broughs for fruit.

Then said he, &c. . . God cries out that his patience is abused, that his forbearance is abused . . . "I am weary with repenting" Jeremiah xv. 6. . . Barren fig-tree, thou hast had time, seasons, ministers, afflictions, judgements, mercies, and what not! And yet hast not been fruitful: thou hast had awakenings, reproofs, threatenings, comforts . . . patterns, examples, citations, provocations and yet hast not been fruitful. . . He hath not done without a cause all that he hath done, and therefore he looketh for fruit . . . "Behold the axe is laid to the root of the trees; every tree, therefore, that bringeth not forth good fruit, is hewn down and cast into the fire." Matt. iii. 10.

And he, answering, said unto him, Lord, let it alone this year also, till I shall dig about it, and dung it; and if it bear fruit, well; and if not, then after that thou shalt cut it down. These are the words of the dresser of the vineyard, who, I told you, is Jesus Christ (for he made intercession for the transgressors). And they contain a petition presented to an offended justice, praying that a little more time and patience might be exercised towards the barren cumber-ground fig-tree. . . Here is astonishing grace indeed! . . . Lord, a little longer. Let us not lose a soul for want to means. I will try . . . If I do any good to it, it will be in a little time . . . Barren fig-tree, see how the Lord Jesus, by these very words, suggesteth the cause of thy fruitlessness of soul. The things of this world lie too close to thy heart; the earth with its things have bound up thy roots; thou art and earth-bound soul . . . "If any man love the world, the love of the Father is not in him;" how then can he be fruitful in the vineyard? . . . how then can the professor that hath . . . a root wrapped up in such earthly things, as the lusts, and pleasures, and vanities of this world, bring forth fruit to God? . . . Lord, I will loose his roots, I will dig up this earth, I will lay his roots bare; my hand shall be upon him by sickness, by disappointments, by cross providences; I will dig about him until he stands shaking and tottering, until he be ready to fall; then, if ever, he will seek to take faster hold. Thus, I say, deals the Lord Jesus oft-times with the barren professor; he diggeth about him, he smiteth one blow at his heart, another blow at his lusts, a third at his pleasures, a forth at his comforts, another at his self-conceitedness; this is the way to take bad earth from the roots, and to loosen his roots from the earth. Barren fig-tree, see here the care, the love, the labour, and way, which the Lord Jesus, the dresser of the vineyard, is fain to take with thee, if haply thou mayst be made fruitful . . . "I will dig about it and dung it;" I will bring it under an heart-awakening ministry . . . I will visit it with heart-awakening, heart-warming, heart-encouraging considerations . . . I will strive with him by my Spirit, and give him some tastes of the heavenly gift, and the power of the world to come. I am loth to lose him for want of digging . . . "When I say to the wicked, O wicked man, thou shalt surely die; if he then do that which is lawful and right, if he walk in the statutes of life, without committing iniquity, he shall surely live, he shall not die." Ezek. xxxiii. 14,15. . .

Gospel means applied, is the last remedy for a barren professor: if the gospel, if the grace of the gospel will not do, there can be nothing expected, but cut it down. . . Heb. xii. 25, "See that ye refuse not him that speaketh. For if they escaped not who refused him that spoke on earth, much more shall not we escape if we turn away from him that speaketh from heaven."[278]

Also commenting on Luke 13:8-9, Johnson writes –
The vineyard-keeper intercedes, urging the owner to give the fig tree one last opportunity. . . He promises to give it special attention for yet another year. . . These activities represent additional gracious opportunities to bear fruit through repentance provided by Christ's incarnation and earthly ministry. Israel was ripe for judgement already, Jesus is saying. Yet one final and particularly unambiguous opportunity for repentance was given. No mere prophet was sent, but the Son of God Himself. . . While the parable underscores the lesson of repentance, it also places emphasis on the patient mercy of God. Both for Israel and for us, Jesus represents God's final opportunity . . . We must not foolishly think that we've gotten away with evil and we will not be judged. No, reckoning is delayed because God is merciful. He is patient towards us, not being willing that any should perish but that all should come to repentance (2Pet. 3:9) . . .

But in the end, judgement delayed is not judgement cancelled. A final opportunity will pass and then our day of reckoning will follow. . .

The day of opportunity passed for Israel. The time came when it was too late. So it is for all of us. God is patient. He graciously provides many opportunities to repent and bear fruit. But in the end a day of reckoning comes. This can happen in this life, when God gives us over, or abandons us, to our sin (Rom. 1:24ff), or on the day of our death, when we find ourselves standing before our maker, either in Christ, or alone without a mediator.

Ryle finds this parable to be 'peculiarly humbling and heart-searching'. It is both 'lit by grace and packed with warnings', Barclay adds. Consequently it calls us to search our souls for the

---

[278] *The Barren Fig-tree, or, The Doom and Downfall of the Fruitless Professor* The Pilgrim's Progress and other selected Works p671-701

fruit of repentance. Is God getting a return on His investment in us? Have I turned from the pursuit of sin? Have I cultivated a loathing of evil and a hunger and thirst for righteousness? Have I developed a love for the word of God, the people of God, and the worship of God? Am I pursuing holiness? Do I have a zeal for good works? Am I characterized by love in my dealings with my neighbours? These are the fruits that are 'in keeping with repentance' (Luke 3:8).

Let's put it another way. For what am I living? For most people life is about pleasure, prestige (or Fame), and power [and all without any kind of pain I'd add]. They crave and pursue these things. They have bought the lie. Why am I a Christian? Because there is a holy God to whom I must be reconciled. Yet it is beyond my power to affect that reconciliation myself. Only in Christ can that reconciliation occur. And I am a Christian because there is more to life than the benefits of this world. All that the world offers is vanity and striving after the wind. True life is found in serving, pleasing, honouring, and glorifying God, and making Him known. This is the fruit that Jesus seeks.[279]

When will the happy time come, in which Christians shall form themselves on these important maxims of their great Master! When shall they be known to be his disciples, by the candour of their sentiments, the equality of their conduct, and the beneficence of their actions, as well as by the articles of their faith, and the forms of their worship! Let us all apply these changes to ourselves, in the dear and awful name of Him that gave them.

What can be more dreadful to us than to think not being severely judged by that God, without whose hourly forbearance and gracious indulgence we are all undone? Let us then exercise that mercy which we need; and to form our minds to this most

---

[279] Terry L. Johnson The *Parables of Jesus* Christian Focus 2007 p364-5

reasonable temper, let us often be thinking of our own many infirmities, and be humbling ourselves before God on account of them.

Animated by the gracious invitations and the precious promises, let us make our daily addresses to his throne, asking, that we may receive; seeking, that we may find; and knocking, that the door of mercy may be opened to us.

On the whole, let us remember that we ourselves are at last to be tried by the rule by which we are here directed to judge of others, even by the fruits which we produce. May God by his grace make the tree good, that the productions of it may be found to his glory and the refreshment of all around us, that we may not be "cut down as cumberers of the ground, and cast into the fire!"

The way of life which our blessed Redeemer has marked out for us, may indeed to corrupt nature appear rugged and narrow, and the gate strait through which we are to pass; but let us encourage ourselves against all these difficulties, by considering that "immortal life and glory" to which they infallibly lead. Then shall we, doubtless, prefer the most painful way of piety and virtue, though with yet fewer companions than we might reasonably expect, to all those flowery and frequented paths of vice which "go down to the chambers of death." [280]

'"For God so loved the world that He gave His only begotten Son, that whoever believes in Him should not perish but have everlasting life. For God did not send His Son into the world to condemn the world, but that the world through Him might be saved . . . For as the Father raises the dead and gives life to them, even so the Son gives life to whom He will . . . But you are not willing to come to me that you may have life." (John 3:16-17, 5:21, 40).

---

[280] *Fleetwood's Life of Christ* comment from Dr Campbell's Expository Bible p166-7

Robyn Crothers

Part 4:
A Day to Remember

> . . . *they may, by your good works which they observe, glorify God in the day of visitation.* 1 Peter 2:12b

Fourth, to live as pilgrims, *there is a day to remember*. Peter says that those who observe our good deeds will 'glorify God in the day of visitation'. [281]

On the day he visits us, the day of visitation . . .

Question: Which day are you meaning Peter? What makes *a* day *the* day, for us, for God?

Answer: Consider, my dear reader what makes *a* day become *the* day for you, a birthday, anniversary, remembrance days like Anzac Day, Easter, Christmas, personal and private days or those of national or world importance? Is it not the who, what or why that turns a day into one worth remembering, thinking of, looking forward to or even dreading that makes it *the* day?

Our days are numbered, time is measured here. We have calendars, time schedules, work days and holidays, days of joy and days of mourning, days important only to one and days important to hordes. But our God is outside time. He existed in eternity past and he exists in a future eternity, our time frame, our measuring of time is not his, as Peter reminds us in 2Peter 3:8 'that with the Lord one day is as a thousand years and a thousand years as one day'.

God visits his world for many reasons. To rescue us from eternal sinfulness and death, or just to rescue as we read in Psalm 106:4b, 'Oh, visit me with your salvation' and Genesis 50:24, 'And Joseph said to his brethren, "I am dying; but God will surely visit you, and bring you out of this land to the land of which He swore to Abraham, to Isaac, and to Jacob"' ; to provide as we read in Psalm 65:9a, 'You visit the earth and water it, You greatly enrich it'; and

---

[281] Sermon *The Daily Battle: proving to be true pilgrims*

to punish for sin as Exodus 32:34b, "'Nevertheless, in the day when I visit for punishment, I will visit punishment upon them for their sin'" tells us and for not realizing the time when Jerusalem and her people could have avoided the Lord's wrath as a weeping Jesus in Luke 19: 42-44 tells us, "'If you had known, even you, especially in this your day, the things that make for your peace! But now they are hidden from your eyes. For days will come upon you when your enemies will build an embankment around you, surround you and close you in on every side, and level you, and your children within you, to the ground; and they will not leave in you one stone upon another, because you did not know the time of your visitation.'"

God visits us when we are born again. He visits and abides within by his Spirit changing us, filling us with good works and light to display the truth of his gospel. Perhaps when an unbeliever becomes a believer, they will recall the influence of a passing pilgrim and give thanks for them as well as their own salvation thus glorifying God. Perhaps an unbeliever being grateful for some aide from a known pilgrim gives thanks, thus unknowingly glorifying God. Perhaps . . .

Does it matter, really matter, which visit and how glory is given because regardless we as pilgrims are still called to live continually and consistently as kingdom children, ambassadors till we are called home. We are called to good works for anything that is not good will give lie to our profession and the character of our Father, never glorifying him.

However, God does have his own *the* days marked on his calendar and he has informed us of them in his scriptures.

The first *the* day, began when he spoke saying "Let there be light." In fact, with creation we have seven *the* days, six days of evening and mornings and one day, the seventh where God 'rested from all His work' which as yet has not had an evening, has not ended (Genesis 1:1-2:3). Adam and Eve lived in this eternal state of rest, tending and keeping Eden's garden (Genesis 2:15) and walking with their Lord till they rebelled against him. Mankind ever since has been born outside of that rest, grieving him greatly and so 'when the fullness of the time had come, God sent forth His Son, born of a woman, born under the law to redeem those who were under the law, that we might receive the adoption as sons' (Galatians 4:4-5).

This fullness of time came many generations after Adam. After having his many servants, prophets, priests and judges beaten, stoned and killed rather than heard and obeyed, God became silent for four hundred years after his last Old Testament prophet Malachi till the coming of his promised herald, John the Baptist who announced the Son, the heir's coming.

The promise of being able to enter into God's rest remains for those who obey, those who believe, who have faith, and *the* day to do so is *today*, 'Today, if you will hear His voice' and 'not harden your' heart (Hebrews 3:7-4:13). But as a grieved Jesus told Jerusalem *today* ends, *the* day of grace ends heralding *the* day that will end time as we understand it.

As we do not yet have hindsight to look back over this day there are many varying and conflicting ideas about eschatology (the study of end things, the end of time) of scripture and some become rather hot, red and pugnacious with their pet theories. I know what I believe and why but here is not the place for that discussion especially when I do not believe that what is still mysterious and veiled is what is most important for if it was God would have clearly explained. What does matter is what is written and that causes enough difficulty with trust and obedience without worrying about the rest. We are to watch, be ready, be found at our post doing his will with our wedding garment on, being steadfast in our believing and faith in trusting all that Christ has shown us and being obedient to him in that to the end of our pilgrimage regardless of others and our circumstances.

In the NKJ and the NIV version of the Old Testament there seems to be two main words that are translated with the idea of being visited by God.

- *pâqad* (#6485) is a primary Hebrew root meaning to

visit with friendly or hostile intent and so by analogy to oversee, muster, change, care for . . . avenge . . . commit . . . do judgement. This visitation is in many senses chiefly official, to account for or give a reckoning. This is the word that was translated in the earlier readings from Psalm 106:4b, Genesis 50:24, Psalm 65:9a and Exodus 32:34, a few pages back.

However, in Genesis 21:1-2 we see a slightly different understanding of this word, an official visit to care for, to bless the world, 'And the LORD visited Sarah as He had said, and the LORD did for Sarah as he had spoken. For Sarah conceived and bore Abraham a son in his old age, at the set time of which God had spoken to him.'

- *p^{e}quddâh* (#6486) is from this primary root but is

translated mostly with the idea of punishment in view, a chiefly official visitation to pass judgement on account of deeds done or omitted, a visitation of reckoning.

This word first appears in Numbers 16 where a large group of men rose up against Moses and Aaron's leadership over them.

Verses 28-32 read, 'And Moses said: "By this you shall know that the LORD has sent me to do all these works, for I have not done them of my own will. If these men die naturally like all men, or if they are visited by the common fate of all men, then the LORD has not sent me. But if the LORD creates a new thing, and the earth opens its mouth and swallows them up with all that belongs to them, and they go down alive into the pit, then you will understand that these men have rejected the LORD." Now it came to pass, as he finished speaking all these words, that the ground split apart under them, and the earth opened its mouth and swallowed them up . . .'

In Isaiah 10:3 we hear God asking, '"What will you do in the day of punishment, and in the desolation which will come from afar? To whom will you flee for help? And where will you leave your glory?"'

Hosea 9:7 reads, 'The days of punishment have come; the days of recompense have come. Israel knows! The prophet is a fool, the spiritual man is insane, because of the greatness of your iniquity and great enmity.'

In the New testament where Jesus spoke more about hell than heaven the amount of word usage for the idea of God visiting for punishment or judgement is a little different which I find slightly surprising.

The Greek word *ĕpiskŏpē* (#1984) appears only twice, Luke 19:44 which we also looked at a few pages back and 1Peter 2:12 which is the focus of this forth part. It means to inspect mostly to offer relief and so by implication the superintendence of someone and specifically means the visitation of a bishop, a person given an official position by God within the Christian church (Titus 1:5-9).

It comes from *ĕpiskĕptŏmia* (#1980), to inspect, go see, select as in Acts 7:23, 'Now when he [Moses] was forty years old, it came into his heart to visit his brethren, the children of Israel' or as in Christ's speech explaining the way of his judgement of individuals in Matthew 25:36, "I was naked and you clothed Me; I was sick and you visited Me; I was in prison and you came to Me."

So, considering all that you have just read, what conclusion have you come to about what day Peter is talking of?

'What is 'the day of visitation'? Either it refers to God's visitation in saving these pagans, or it refers to the future day of judgement. Most commentators take it to mean that these pagans who slander Christians will glorify God when they later get saved as a result of observing the Christians' good works. I don't interpret the phrase in that way because Peter doesn't make it clear that all (or even most) of these pagans will be converted by seeing our good works. In the context, he is saying that God will vindicate the Christian's righteous behaviour, apart from what happens to those who persecute us. Thus I take the day of visitation to refer to the future day of judgement.

How, then, will pagans glorify God in that day? Some will be converted before that day because, humanly speaking, they observed the good deeds of Christians whom they persecuted. This they will glorify God for His saving grace and for the

faithfulness of His people. Others will stand before God with every excuse for their unbelief and rebellion knocked out from under them. At that point God will be vindicated and their once-defiant knees, too, will bow and their once-proud tongues then will confess that 'Jesus Christ is Lord to the glory of God the Father.'
For us, the point is that as pilgrims, we keep that great day of visitation in view. We live now knowing that one day everyone must stand before God, either for commendation or condemnation. Thus we should seek to live with that day in view, so that we will hear, "Well done, good and faithful servant!" And as we live with that day in view, we should seek to persuade those who are on the road to condemnation to receive God's mercy before it is too late.'[282]

> The darkness grows thicker around us, and godly servants of the Most High become rarer and more rare. Impiety and licentiousness are rampant throughout the world, and we live like pigs, like wild beasts, devoid of all reason. But a voice will soon be heard thundering forth: 'Behold, the bridegroom cometh!' God will not be able to bear this wicked world much longer, but will come, with the dreadful day, and chastise the scorners of his Word.

Does that sound like a statement by one of today's preachers?
It was said by Martin Luther, who lived from 1483 to 1546. If Luther felt that the Lord's return was near in his day, what should we think today? [283]

Question: What is this future day of judgement?
Answer: 'Then I [John] saw a great white throne and Him who sat on it, from whose face the earth and the heaven fled away. And there was found no place for them. And I saw the dead, small and great, standing before God, and books were opened. And another book was opened, which is the Book of Life. And the dead were judged according to their works, by the things which were written

---

[282] Sermon *The Daily Battle: proving to be true pilgrims*
[283] *With the Word* p835-6

in the books. The sea gave up the dead who were in it, and Death and Hades delivered up the dead who were in them. And they were judged, each one according to his works. Then Death and Hades were cast into the lake of fire. This is the second death. And anyone not found written in the Book of Life was cast into the lake of fire. Now I saw a new heaven and a new earth, for the first heaven and the first earth had passed away . . . "And behold, I [Jesus] am coming quickly, and My reward is with Me, to give to every one according to his work."' (The Revelation of Jesus Christ 20:11-21:1a, 21:12)

When the promised baby of virgin birth, whose arrival was mostly unnoticed by the world and his people, grew to be a man he rode a donkey into Jerusalem, as a King coming in peace. But when Christ Jesus returns upon a white horse as King and judge at the end of our history, the end of time, every eye in the world shall see him coming. His arrival will be as unmissable, it will be loud and sudden, startling all out of their preoccupation with living life as a thief startles a home owner in the night. All those living, those in heaven, those in the graves and those without graves will be raised to kneel and acknowledge his lordship regardless if they were a pilgrim or unbeliever, to the glory of God.

Peter tells us that 'the heavens will pass away with a great noise, and the elements will melt with fervent heat; both the earth and the works that are in it will be burnt up' for this is what by the word of God they have been reserved for since their preservation by the same word after the flood (2Peter 3:10).

After this all humanity will stand before his throne and his final judgement will begin, forever separating the tares from the wheat, the goats from the sheep.

'And the kings of the earth, the great men, the rich men, the commanders, the mighty men, every slave and every free man, hid themselves in the caves and in the rocks of the mountains, and said to the mountains and rocks, "fall on us and hide us from the face of Him who sits on the throne and from the wrath of the

Lamb! For the great day of His wrath has come, and who is able to stand?"' (The Revelation of Jesus Christ 6:15-17)

Remember back when we looked the pilgrim's armour in Ephesians 6:10-18, and we considered what it was to stand? Well, here is another aspect of what to stand means.

> Who then will be able to stand? Only those who have confessed their sin and quit it. Those who have given up their trinkets; those who have quit loving the world; those who have given up the hope that anything down here is permanent; and those who hate their sin as God hates it; they will stand in that day. 'Therefore,' David wrote, 'the ungodly shall not stand in the judgement, nor sinners in the congregation of the righteous' (Ps.1:5). No one who has not put his trust in Christ and forsaken the world shall be able to stand in that day.
>
> Who shall be able to stand? The one who has put his trust in Christ, the one who has forsaken the world, the one who has overcome. What did he overcome? He overcame the temptation to quit. . . if God takes away everything I have, I will love Him anyhow. I will praise Him even if He slays me. We have to overcome, because the overcomer will be able to stand in that day, that terrible, terrible day.[284]

Matthew 25:31-46 records Jesus speaking of this separation of the sheep and goats, '"When the Son of Man comes in His glory, and all the holy angels with Him, then He will sit on the throne of His glory. All the nations will be gathered before Him, and He will separate them from one another, as a shepherd divides his sheep from the goats. And He will set the sheep on His right hand, but the goats on the left. Then the King will say to those on His right hand, "Come, you blessed of My Father, inherit the kingdom prepared for you from the foundation of the world: for I was hungry and you gave Me food; I was thirsty and you gave Me drink; I was a stranger and you took me in; I was naked and you

---

[284] A. W. Tozer Preparing *for Jesus' Return Daily live the Blessed Hope* compiled and edited by James L. Snyder BethanyHouse 2012 p130-1

clothed Me; I was sick and you visited Me; I was in prison and you came to me."
Then the righteous will answer Him, saying, "Lord, when did we see You hungry and feed You, or thirsty and give You drink? When did we see You a stranger and take You in, or naked and clothe You? Or when did we see You sick, or in prison, and come to You?" And the King will answer and say to them, "Assuredly, I say to you, inasmuch as you did it to one of the least of these My brethren, you did it to Me." Then He will also say to those on the left hand, "Depart from me, you cursed, into the everlasting fire prepared for the devil and his angels: for I was hungry and you gave Me no food; I was thirsty and you gave Me no drink; I was a stranger and you did not take me in, naked and you did not clothe me, sick and in prison and you did not visit Me."
Then they also will answer Him, saying, "Lord, when did we see You hungry or thirsty or a stranger or naked or sick or in prison, and did not minister to You?" Then He will answer them, saying, "Assuredly, I say to you, inasmuch as you did not do it to one of the least of these, you did not do it to Me."
And these will go away into everlasting punishment, but the righteous into eternal life."'
Scott writes, '. . . in order to show that they are indeed the persons for whom this inheritance was prepared, he will next make known their good works, as the effect of their faith and love . . . It is impossible that human language can express greater encouragement to self-denying, assiduous, laborious, and expensive charity to poor Christians, for the sake of our common Lord, than is contained in this declaration. We must not, however, suppose that acts of liberality, from whatever motive, will constitute a man's title to eternal felicity; and there cannot be a more fatal delusion than this too common, but groundless inference, from this and a few similar texts. For many who are liberal, humane, and compassionate in some instances, live habitually in the practice of those sins, of which it is expressly said, that "they who do such things shall not inherit the kingdom

of God." And as none but believers are the brethren of Christ, so love to Christ must be the motive of the liberality and kindness here spoken of. So that these actions will be produced as evidences of the excellency and efficacy of justifying faith and the love of Christ, of a person's having been a real believer, and not a mere professor, and to show that there is a propriety in the Lord's honouring him in heaven, who thus proved himself his zealous friend on earth.[285]

Perhaps the true reason why the grand inquiry shall rest so much on the performance of duties is, that men too frequently consider their neglect a matter of no greater consequence, but dread the commission of crimes. And hence, while they can keep themselves free from the latter, they easily find excuses for the former. And as there is not a more pernicious error with regard to religion and morality than this, Jesus thought proper to give such an account of the judgement as should prove a solemn caution to all . .

. . . piety and charity cannot subsist separately; piety, and its origin, faith, always producing charity; and charity, wherever it subsists, necessarily pre-supposing piety.

The connexion between piety and charity will evidently appear, if it be considered, that no man can be truly benevolent and merciful without having those dispositions. Consequently, he must have benevolence in God, he must love God; for piety, or the love of God, is nothing else but the regard we cherish towards God on account of his perfections.

Piety and charity being thus essentially connected together, it is abundantly sufficient to examine the conduct of men with regard to either of those graces. In the parable, the inquiry is represented as turning upon the duties of charity, perhaps, because in this there is less room for self-deceit than in the other. It is common for hypocrites, by pretending zeal in the externals of religion, to make specious pretences to extraordinary piety, and

---

[285] *Fleetwood's Life of Christ* comment by Scott p521

at the same time are totally deficient in charity: are covetous and unjust, and consequently destitute of all love for their Creator. Yet none can assume the appearance of charity but by feeding the hungry, clothing the naked, relieving the distressed, and preforming other benevolent offices to their brethren.

The works of charity may indeed, in some particular cases, flow from other principles than those of a pious and benevolent disposition, as from vanity, or even views of interest; but then it should be remembered, that a common degree of hypocrisy will hardly engage men to undertake them; they are by far too weighty duties to be sustained by those false principals, and, therefore, are seldom counterfeited. Consequently, wherever a genuine, and a permanent charity is found, we may conclude that there reigns the love of God.

Hence we learn that all pretences to goodness, without a principle of grace wrought in the heart, avail nothing in reference to man's eternal salvation . . . since . . . the duty we owe to God is the same in kind with that we owe to man in like circumstances, it follows, that true morality can never exist where piety is wanting; and that those who pretend to morality, and are destitute of piety, are as unsound in their creed as they are in their practice.'[286]

> The moral man came to the judgement,
> But self-righteous rags would not do;
> The men who had crucified Jesus
> Had passed off as moral men, too;
> The soul that had put off salvation,
> "Not tonight; I'll get saved by and by,
> No time now to think of religion!"
> At last they had found time to die. [287]

---

[286] Ibid. p522-3
[287] *Preparing for Jesus' Return* p133 quote from last verse of *I Dreamed of that the Great Judgement Morning* by Bertram H. Shadduck (1869-1950)

When this day of final judgement is completed, life as we know it will change dependent on our view of God and his Son and eternity will begin where time as we understand it will cease.

Question: How long is eternity?
Answer: When my friend Alison was dying, we used to talk together often about dying, death, heaven for she was also a pilgrim, and eternity. I still have my jar of sand from that time.

Do you remember being at the beach and having the sand stick to you, having sandy sandwiches as a result? Do you remember what those tiny grains looked like on your hand? Did you ever try to count them? Can you imagine trying to now?

If a single grain represented a hundred years and you counted every grain of sand in this earth, that's all the beaches, all the rivers, all the deserts, and all that are under the dirt and waters – well eternity would not have even started. Where do you want to spend your eternity my dear reader?

O and if you are like me and think that spending eternity on fluffy clouds playing a harp is boring, don't stress, heaven will never be boring, ever. Yes, it is a place of delightful rest but that does not equal boredom, or even sleeping but rest from everything sinful. Heaven is a place of busyness. Work, productive service with no taint of sin, will be a delight not the drudgery of laborious toil but work like a child sees it, as the satisfying fun of playing.

Lutzer writes, 'Our death is but the passing from one degree of loving service to another; the difference is like that of the unborn child and the one who has entered into the experiences of a new life.' [288]

Mind you being bored for eternity on a fluffy cloud with a harp would be heaven on steroids compared to hell.

The sheep's homecoming

As pilgrims, as wheat that fell on good soil and produced fruit, little or much, or sheep who know the Shepherd's voice and enter

---
[288] Ibid. p67

thru him, who are abiding in him and whom the Father loves and so has made their home within, who are building on the solid sure foundation of Christ's work for and in them, who have bowed the knee and taken him as their Lord and loved him over and above all else before our time was up, for those who have their wedding garments on and are waiting in readiness, there is no judgement day to fear or feel shame over, of condemnation and punishment but one of reward, of hearing our beloved say, "Well done, good and faithful servant . . . enter into the joy of your lord", and of finally being able to see him as he is, face to face and enter into our promised inheritance and rest. (Matthew 13:8, 23; John 10:3-4, 7-9, 15:10, 14:23; Luke 6:47-48; Philippians 2:10-11, Luke 14:26-27; Matthew 22:8-13, 25:1-13, Luke 21:34-36; John 3:16-18, 5:24; 1John 2:28, Matthew 25:21, 23 1John 3:2 and 1Peter 1:3-5.)
We have been following Bunyan's characters through their pilgrimage and so it seems only appropriate to share as well the moments when Christian's and Hopeful's pilgrimage comes to an end and they enter into the Celestial City.

As Christian and Hopeful draw near to the Celestial City they are met by 'two men in raiment that shone like gold, also their faces shone as the light.' After answering several questions put to them by these men they were informed that they had 'but two difficulties more to meet with, 'and then you are in the city.' Christian then and his companion asked the men to go along with them; so they told them they would. But, said they, you must obtain it by your own faith. So I saw in my dream that they went on together till they came in sight of the gate.

Now I farther saw, that betwixt them and the gate was a river; but there was no bridge to go over, and the river was very deep. At the sight therefore of this river, the pilgrims were much stunned; but the men that went with them said, You must go through, or you cannot come at the gate . . . The pilgrims then especially Christian, began to despond in their minds, and looked this way and that, but no way could be found by them, by which they might excape the river. Then they asked the men if the waters were all of a depth? They said, No; yet they could not help them in that case; For, said they, you shall find it deeper or shallower, as you believe in the king of the place.

They then addressed themselves to the water, and entering, Christian began to sink, and crying out to his good friend Hopeful, he said, "I sink in deep waters . . .

Then said the other, Be of good cheer, my brother; I feel the bottom and it is good. Then said Christian, Ah! My friend, the sorrow of death hath compassed me about, I shall not see the land that flows with milk and honey. And with that a great darkness and horror fell upon Christian, so that he could not see before him. Also he in great measure lost his senses, so that he could neither remember or orderly talk of any of those sweet refreshments, that he had met with in the way of his pilgrimage. But all the words that he spake still tended to discover that he had horror of mind, and heart – fears that he should die in that river, and never obtain entrance in at the gate. Here also . . . he was much in the troublesome thoughts of the sins that he had committed, both since and before he began to be a pilgrim . . . Hopeful therefore had much ado to keep his brother's head above water; yea sometimes he would be quiet gone down, and then, ere a while would rise up again half dead. Hopeful did also endeavour to comfort him, saying, Brother, I see the gate, and men standing by to receive us; but Christian would answer, It is you, it is you they wait for; you have been hopeful ever since I knew you. And so have you, said he to Christian. Ah, brother, said he, surely if I was right, he would now rise to help me; but for my sins he hath bought me into the snare and hath left me. Then said Hopeful, My brother, you have quiet forgot the text where it is said of the wicked, "There are no bonds in their death, but their strength is firm; they are not troubled as other men, neither are they plagued like other men." These troubles and distresses that you go through in these waters are no sign that God hath forsaken you; but are sent to try you, whether you will call to mind that which heretofore you have received of his goodness, and live upon him in your distresses. . . . "Be of good cheer, Jesus Christ maketh thee whole." And with that Christian brake out with a loud voice, Oh, I see him again! And he tells me, "When thou passest through the waters, I will be with thee; and through the rivers, they shall not overflow thee." Isa. xliii. 2. Then they both took courage, and the enemy was after that as still as a stone. . . thus they got over.'

They were met and escorted up the hill by the two shining men of before, who talked of the inexpressible beauty and glory of the place they were heading for '. . . There you shall not see again such things as you saw when you were in the lower region upon the earth, to wit, sorrow, sickness, affliction, and death . . . You must there receive the comforts of all your toil, and have joy for all your sorrows; you must reap what you have sown, even the fruit of all your prayers and tears, and sufferings for the King by the way. Gal. vi. 7, 8. . . There also you shall serve him continually with praise, with shouting, and thanksgiving, whom you desired to serve in the world, though with much difficulty, because of the infirmity of your flesh.' As they got closer to the gate they were met by a great company including trumpeters welcoming the two pilgrims with much shouting and trumpeting. As the city came into view 'they thought they heard all the bells therein to ring, to welcome them thereto' also.

'Now, when they were come up to the gate, there was written over it in letters of gold, "Blessed are they that do his commandments, that they may have right to the tree of life, and may enter through the gates into the city." Rev. xxii. 14.

. . . Now I saw in my dream that these two men went in at the gate; and lo! As they entered they were transfigured . . . Then I heard in my dream that all the bells in the city rang again for joy, and that is was said unto them, "Enter ye into the joy of your Lord."[289]

---

[289] *The Pilgrim's Progress* p227-234

Scott writes, 'The dreaded pangs that precede the awful separation of those intimate associates, the soul and the body; the painful parting with dear friends and every earthly object; the gloomy ideas of the dark, cold, and noisome grave; and the solemn thought of launching into an unseen eternity, render Death the king of terrors. Faith in a crucified, buried, risen, and ascended Saviour; experience of his faithfulness and love in times past; hope of an immediate entrance into his presence, where temptation, conflict, sin, and suffering, will find no admission; and the desire of perfect knowledge, holiness, and felicity, will reconcile the mind to the inevitable stroke, and sometimes give a complete victory over every fear: yet if faith, and hope be weakened, through the recollection of any peculiar misconduct, the withholding of divine light, and consolation, or some violent assult of the tempter, the believer will be peculiarly liable to alarm and distress . . . constitution has considerable effecy upon the mind; and some men, like Christian, are in every stage of their profession, more exposed to temptations of a discouraging nature, than to ambition, avarice, or fleshly lusts . . . The Lord, however, is no man's debtor; none can claim consolation as their due; and, though a believer's experience and the testimony of his conscience may evidence the sincerity of his faith and love, yet he must disclaim to the last every other dependence than the righteousness and blood of Christ, and the free mercy of God in him.'[290]

> Ah, Christian! None can conceive or describe what it is to live in a state separate from a body of sin and death . . . If Jesus be so sweet to faith below, who can tell what he is in full fruition above? This we must die to know. [291]

Towards the end of Part 2 of Pilgrim's Progress we read that 'when Mr. Standfast had thus set things in order, and the time being came for him to haste him away, he also went down to the

---

[290] Ibid comment by Scott p227
[291] Ibid comment by Mason p231

river: Now there was a great calm at that time in the river; wherefore Mr. Standfast, when he was about half way in, stood a while and talked to his companions that had waited upon him thither: and he said, This river has been a terror to many: yea, the thoughts of it also have often frightened me: now, methinks, I stand easy; my foot is fixed upon that on which the feet of the priests that bore the ark of the covenant stood, while Israel went over this Jordan. Josh. iii. 17. The waters, indeed, are to the palate bitter, and to the stomach cold; yet the thoughts of what I am going to, and of the conduct that waits for me on the other side, doth lie as a glowing coal at my heart. I see myself now at the end of my journey; my toilsome days are ended. I am going to see that head that was crowned with thorns, and that face that was spit upon for me. I have formerly lived by hearsay and faith; but now I go where I shall live by sight, and shall be with him in whose company I delight myself. I have loved to hear my Lord spoken of; and wherever I have seen the print of his shoe in the earth, there I have coveted to set my foot too. His name has been to me as a civet box; yea, sweeter than all perfumes. His voice to me has been most sweet; and his countenance I have more desired than they that have most desired the light of the sun. His words I did use to gather for my food, and for antidotes against my faintings. He has held me, and has kept me from mine iniquities; yea, my steps have been strengthened in his way . . .'[292]

1John 4:17 tells us that as sheep, 'Love has been perfected among us in this: that we may have boldness in the day of judgement; because as He is, so we are in this world.'

Moody when meditating upon the preciousness of Christ's blood and the context that it is mentioned in by Peter in 1Peter 1:18-9 which says, 'knowing that you were not redeemed with corruptible [perishable] things, like silver or gold, from your aimless conduct received by tradition from your fathers, but with

---

[292] *The Pilgrim's Progress Part II* p396

the precious blood of Christ, as of a lamb without blemish and without spot' wrote–

And it is precious because it is going to *give me boldness in the day of judgement.* Isn't that good?

Do you know I pity these people who live all their life-time under the bondage of death. If I am behind the blood of the Son of God, judgement is already passed; it is behind me; it is not before me. Know ye not that ye shall judge the world? People live in constant dread of the great white throne judgement. When that comes, I am going to be with Christ on the throne, I am not going to be judged! That day is passed to the true child of God. "He was wounded for our transgressions, He was bruised for our iniquities", and is God going to demand payment twice? I am going to have boldness in the day of judgement.[293]

I have done much reading for this book and being challenged yet also strangely encouraged I have shared many pieces with you my dear reader. Even in my lifetime the views of our western culture and society surrounding suffering, the process of dying and death itself have radically changed and as I believe not for the better you are going to be further exposed to much older-than-I thinking; thinking that is rare outside of Christian circles especially but sadly becoming rare within as well. How many people do you know that though grieving, even deeply, speak of death as a loving stroke from a loving Lord?

1Peter 1:3-5 says, 'Blessed be the God and Father of our Lord Jesus Christ, who according to His abundant mercy has begotten us again to a living hope through the resurrection of Jesus Christ from the dead, to an inheritance incorruptible and undefiled and that does not fade away, reserved in heaven for you, who are kept by the power of God through faith for salvation ready to be revealed in the last time.'

---

[293] *Short talks* The *Precious Blood* p92

What follows is a short extract of a piece written by Thomas Brooks originally for a private funeral service which would have gone far longer than a message, if any, given at today's funerals.

. . . I could heartily wish that you and all others concerned in this sad loss, were more taken up in minding the happy exchange that she hath made, than with your present loss. She hath exchanged earth for heaven, a wilderness for a paradise, a prison for a place, a house made with hands for one eternal in the heavens, 2Cor. v. 1,2. She hath exchanged imperfection for perfection, sighing for singing, mourning for rejoicing, prayers for praises, the society of sinful mortals for the company of God, Christ, angels, and the spirits of just men made perfect, Heb. xii. 22-24; an imperfect transient enjoyment of God for a more clear, full, perfect, and permanent enjoyment of God. She has exchanged pain for ease, sickness for health, a bed of weakness for a bed of spices, a complete blessedness. She hath exchanged her brass for silver, her counters for gold, and her earthly contentments for heavenly enjoyments.

And as I desire that one of your eyes may be fixed upon her happiness, so I desire that the other of your eyes may be fixed upon Christ's fullness. Though your brook be dried up, yet Christ the fountain of light, life, love, grace, glory, comfort, joy, goodness, sweetness, and satisfaction is still at hand, and always full and flowing, yea, overflowing John i. 16, Col. i. 19, ii. 3. As the worth and value of many pieces of silver is contracted in one piece of gold, so all the sweetness, all the goodness, all the excellencies that are in husbands, wives, children, friends, &c, are contracted in Christ; yea, all the whole volume of perfections which is spread through heaven and earth, is epitomised in Christ; Ipse unus erit tibi omnia, quia in ipso uno bono, bona sunt omnia, saith Augustine, one Christ will be to thee instead of all things else, because in him are all good things to be found.

The inheritance reserved for believers till they come to heaven, is a pure undefiled and incorruptible inheritance . . . cannot be defiled nor blemished with abuse one way or another. Other inheritances may, and often are, with oaths, cruelty, blood, deceit, &c. The Greek . . . signifies a precious stone, which, though it be never so much soiled, yet it cannot be blemished nor defiled; yea, the oftener you cast it into the fire, and take it out, the more clear, bright, and shining it is. All earthly inheritances are true gardens of Adonis, where we can gather nothing but trivial flowers, surrounded with many briers, thorns, and thistles . . . Oh the hands, the hearts, the thoughts, the lives that have been defiled, stained, and polluted with earthly inheritances!

. . . This inheritance is kept and secured to us by promise, by power, by blood, by oath; and therefore must needs be sure . . . Christ hath already taken possession of it in their names and in their rooms . . . But earthly inheritances they are not sure, they are not secure . . . How many are kept out, and how many are cast out, of their inheritances, by power, policy, craft, cruelty.

. . . It is a permanent, a lasting, inheritance . . . It is an inheritance that shall continue as long as God himself continues. . . A believer's inheritance, his glory, his happiness, his blessedness, shall be as fresh and flourishing after he hath been many thousand thousands of years in heaven as it was at his first entrance into it. Earthly inheritances are like tennis-balls, which are bandied up and down from one to another, and in time worn out, 1Tim. vi. 17. . . When this world shall be no more, when time shall be no more, the inheritance of the saints shall be fresh, flourishing and continuing.

. . . It is the freest inheritance. It is an inheritance that is free from all vexation and molestation . . . This inheritance flows from free love, and is freely offered. . . There is nothing, there is not the least thing about this inheritance that is purchased or paid for by us . . . it is all of grace.

. . . here every child is an heir to all, and hath right to all. In earthly inheritances, the more you divide, the less is everyone's part; but this inheritance is not diminished by the multitude of possessors, nor impaired by the number of co-heirs; it is as much to many as to a few, and as great to one as to all . . .

It is a soul-satisfying inheritance . . . As one master satisfies the servant, and as one father satisfies the child, and as one husband satisfies the wife, so one God, one Christ, one inheritance, satisfies the believing soul . . . But now all other inheritances they cannot satisfy the heart of man . . . the world deludes a man, and puts cheats upon him; it promises a man pleasure, and pays him with pain; it promises profit . . . and pays him with loss; loss of God, of Christ, of peace of conscience, of comfort, of heaven, of happiness, of all; it promises contentment, and fills him with torment; - and therefore can never satisfy the soul of man . . .

This life is full of trials, full of troubles, and full of changes. Sin within, and Satan and the world without, will keep a Christian from rest, till he comes to rest in the bosom of Christ. The life of a Christian is a race; and what rest have they that are still a-running their race? The life of a Christian is a warfare; and what rest have they that are still engaged in a constant warfare? The life of a Christian is the life of a pilgrim; and what rest hath a pilgrim, who is still a-travelling from place to place . . . The fears, the snares, the cares, the changes &c, that attends believers in this world, are such that will keep them from taking up their rest here. A Christian hears that word always sounding in his ears, 'Arise, for this is not thy resting-place' Micah ii. 10. A man may as well expect to find heaven in hell, as expect to find rest in this world. It was the complaint of Ambrose . . . What misery do we not undergo in this life? What storms and tempests do we not endure? With what troubles are we not tossed? Whose worth is spared? Man's sorrows begin when his days begin, and his sorrows are multiplied as his days are multiplied; his whole life is but one continued grief; labour wears him, care tears him, fears toss him, losses vex him, dangers trouble him, crosses disquiet him, nothing pleases him; in the day he wishes, Would God it were night, and in the night, Would God it were day; before he rises he sighs; before he washes he weeps; before he feeds he fears; under all his abundance he is in wants, and 'in the midst of his sufficiency he is in straits', Job xx. 22; his heart as Gregory

Nyssene speaks . . . is not so much quietened in those things which it hath, as it is tormented for those things which it hath not. In a word, all the rest we have in this world, is but a very short nap, to that glorious rest that is reserved in heaven for us: Heb. iv. 9, 10. 'There remaineth therefore a rest to the people of God. For he that is entered into his rest, he also hath ceased from his own works, as God did from his.' There remains a rest to the people of God . . . a Sabbath that shall never have end . . . it is an universal rest, Rev. xiv. 13, a rest from all sin, and a rest from all sorrow; a rest from all afflictions and a rest from all temptations; a rest from all oppression and a rest from all vexations; a rest from all labour and pains, from all trouble and travail, from all aches, weaknesses, and diseases. There is no crying out, O my bones! O my back! O my bowels! O my sides! O my head! My heart! Our rest here is only in part and imperfect; here we have rest in one part and pain in another, quiet in one part and torment in another. Sometimes when the head is well, the heart is sick; and sometimes when there is peace in the conscience, there is pain in the bones. Here many return us hatred for our love, and this hinders our rest; here we are apt to create cares and fears to ourselves . . . here we are very apt to give offence, and as apt to take offence, though none be given, and this hinders our rest, 1Cor. x. 32. Sometimes we have rest abroad, and none at home . . Our rest here is imperfect and incomplete, but our rest in heaven shall be most perfect and complete; there the inward and the outward man shall be both at rest . . . it is a rest that none can interrupt. Here sometimes sin interrupts our rest, sometimes temptations . . . sometimes divine withdrawings . . . sometimes the sudden changes and alterations that God makes in our conditions interrupts our rest; sometimes the power, and sometimes the policy, and sometimes the cruelty of wicked men . . . sometimes the crossness of friends, and sometimes the death of friends interrupts our rest . . . Oh! But heaven . . . there is nothing to cloud a Christian's joy, or to interrupt a Christian's rest . . . Here is joy without sorrow, blessedness without misery, health without sickness, light without darkness, abundance without wont, beauty without deformity, honour without disgrace, ease without labour, and peace without interruption or perturbation. Here shall be eyes without tears, hearts without fears, and souls without sin.

... as it is an uninterrupted rest, so it is a peculiar rest ... proper and peculiar to the inhabitants of that heavenly country... Here wicked men have their good things; their peace, their rest, their quiet, &c, their heaven, whilst the people of God are troubled, disquieted on every side, but the day is a-coming wherein the saints shall have rest, and sinners shall never have a good day more ... their torments shall be endless and ceaseless.

Now all veils shall be taken off; and we shall have a clear prospect of God's excellency and glory, of his blessedness and fullness, of his loveliness and sweetness. Now all masks, clouds, and curtains, shall be drawn for ever, that saints may clearly see the breadth, length, depth, and height of divine love, and that they may clearly see into the mystery of the Trinity, the mystery of Christ's incarnation, the mystery of man's redemption, the mystery of providences, the mystery of prophesies; and all those mysteries that relate to the nature, substances, offices, orders, and excellences of the angles, those princes of glory, who still keep their standings in the court of heaven; and all those mysteries that concern the nature, original, immortality, spirituality, excellency, and activity of our own souls, beside a world of other mysteries that respect the decrees and counsels of God, the creation of the world, the fall of Adam, and the fall of angels ... Oh blessed sight! To behold the King of angels, the holy of holies, the God of heaven, the Ruler of earth, the Father of the living! Oh blessed vision and contemplation, where in we shall see God in himself, God in us, and ourselves in God! . . . Here our understandings shall be full of the knowledge of God, our minds full of the wisdom of God, our wills full of righteousness and holiness of God, and our affections full of the love and delights of God. . . In heaven we shall see God face to face, without the interposition of men or means; and this direct and immediate sight of God, is that which makes heaven to be heaven to the saints.

In heaven, your knowledge shall be full, your love full, your visions of God full, your communion with God full, your fruition of God full, and your conformity to God full, and from hence will arise fullness of joy. If all the earth were paper, and all the plants of the earth pens, and all the sea were ink, and if every man, woman, and child, had the pen of a ready writer, yet were they not able to express the thousandth part of those joys that saints shall have in heaven.

. . . now in heaven the joy of the saints shall be constant; there shall nothing fall in to disturb or to interrupt their joy. . . The joy of the saints in heaven is never ebbing, but always flowing to all contentment. The joys of heaven never fade, never wither, never die, nor never are lessened nor interrupted.

If the best and greatest things are reserved for believers till they come to heaven, then make not a judgement of the saints' condition by their present state. . . What though they are now in rags, it will not be long before they are clothed in their royal robes; what though they are now abased, it will not be long before they shall in the sight of all the world be highly advanced; what though they are now under many wants, it will not be long before they shall be filled with all fullness; what though they are now under many trials and afflictions, yet it will not be long before all tears shall be wiped away from their eyes, and their sighing turned into singing, 'and everlasting joys shall be upon their heads'; and therefore do not judge of their condition by their present state.

. . . Surely there is infinitely more in the great and glorious things that are reserved for believers in heaven, to joy and rejoice them, than there can be in all the troubles and trials, afflictions and temptations, that they meet with in this world, to sad, grieve, and deject them. Ah, Christians! The great and glorious things that are reserved in heaven for you, will afford you such an exuberancy of joy, as no good can match, as no evil can overmatch. Witness the joy of the martyrs, both ancient and modern. Oh how my heart leapeth for joy, saith one, that I am so near the apprehension of eternal bliss. [294]

The goat's homecoming

But take heed of what occurs to the person (goat) who has not a pilgrim become before departing this world or has been an unprofitable, fruitless, wasteful one. Pilgrim's Progress does not conclude with our two entering the Celestial City but another character.

Now, while I was gazing upon all these things, I turned my head to look back, and saw Ignorance come up to the river side; but he soon got over, and that without half that difficulty which the other two men met with. For it happened there was then at that place one Vain-hope, a ferryman, that with his boat helped him over: so he, as the other I saw, did ascend the hill, to come up to the gate; only he came alone; neither did any man meet him with the least encouragement. When he was come up to the gate, he looked up to the writing that was above, and then began to knock, supposing that entrance should have been quickly administered to him: but he was asked by the man that looked over the top of the gate, Whence come you? And what would you have? He answered, "I have ate and drank in the presence of the King, and he has taught in our streets." Then they asked him for his certificate, that they might go in and show it to the King; so he fumbled in his bosom for one, and found none. Then said they, You have none; but the man answered never a word. So they told the King, but he would not come down to see him, but commanded the two shining ones, that conducted Christian and Hopeful to the city, to go out and take Ignorance, and bind him

---

[294] Thomas Brooks (1608-1680) *A String of Pearls or The best things reserved till last*. First published in 1657. This extract is taken from the corrected second edition done in 1660 from the Complete Works of Thomas Brooks https://archive.org

hand and foot and have him away. Then they took him up, and carried him through the air to the door that I saw in the side of the hill, and put him in there. Then I saw that there was a way to hell, even from the gates of heaven, as well as from the City of Destruction. So I awoke, and beheld it was a dream.[295]

Vain-hope ever dwells in the bosom of fools, and is ever ready to assist Ignorance. . . He had been his companion through life, and will not forsake him in the hour of death. You see Ignorance had no bands in his death, no fears, doubts, and sorrows, no terror from the enemy, but all was serene and happy. Vain-hope was his ferryman, and he, as the *good folk* say, died like a lamb: ah! But did such lambs see what was to follow, when Vain-hope had wafted them over the river, they would roar like lions.[296]

God won't strip himself of his holiness
and admit an unforgiven sinner into his heaven.[297]

In the gospel of Luke we come to a section where Jesus taught several parables that the Pharisees could hear. Being lovers of money they were not pleased with what they heard and in 16:15 we hear Jesus replying "You are those who justify yourselves before men, but God knows your hearts. For what is highly esteemed among men is an abomination in the sight of God" and a little later (verses 19-31) he tells the following parable –
"'There was a certain rich man who was clothed in purple and fine lines and fared sumptuously every day. But there was a certain beggar named Lazarus, full of sores, who was laid at his gate, desiring to be fed with the crumbs which fell from the rich man's table. Moreover the dogs came and licked his sores. So it was that the beggar dies, and was carried by the angels to Abraham's bosom. The rich man also died and was buried. And being in

---

[295] *The Pilgrim's Progress* p234-5
[296] Ibid. comment by Mason p235
[297] From notes taken listening to Gables' series on Pilgrim's Progress *#72 The Fate of Ignorance* 3.14.99

torments in Hades, he lifted up his eyes and saw Abraham afar off, and Lazarus in his bosom. Then he cried and said, "Father Abraham, have mercy on me, and send Lazarus that he may dip the tip of his finger in water and cool my tongue; for I am tormented in this flame." But Abraham said, "Son, remember that in your lifetime you received your good things, and likewise Lazarus evil things; but now he is comforted and you are tormented. And besides all this, between us and you there is a great gulf fixed, so that those who want to pass from here to you cannot, nor can those from there pass to us." Then he said, "I beg you therefore, father, that you would send him to my father's house, for I have five brothers, that he may testify to them, lest they also come to this place of torment." Abraham said to him, "They have Moses and the prophets; let them hear them." And he said, "No, father Abraham; but if one goes to them from the dead, they will repent." But he said to him, "If they do not hear Moses and the prophets, neither will they be persuaded though one rise from the dead."'

Firstly just to note briefly, Jesus was having a go at the richly over fed Pharisees who avoided those they considered unclean such as the Lazarus' of this world and considered Abraham to be their father though they did not see Jesus as the Christ in the writings of Moses and the prophets, the Old Testament, nor even when he rose from the dead. If you cannot believe by reading scripture you will not believe with seeing miracles.

I would think that as Lazarus was lying at the rich man's gate the rich man would have stepped over or around him to get in or out but now, he expects the one he could not see to serve him. The mangy dogs (dogs in Christ's time were never pets) unlike the rich man saw Lazarus and their licking may have given some short relief from the sores covering his body.

Henry notes that, 'Those offend God, nay, and they put a contempt upon human nature, that pamper their dogs and horses, and let the families of their poor neighbours starve'[298], which is an interesting comment considering today's attitude towards the care for pets and the amount of money this costs, don't you think?

Secondly let us consider their deaths and destinations for our choices and our works in this life fix our eternal destinies. We enter this life with really only guarantee, we have to leave it as we came, with nothing from this world except our memories, regardless of what we may have been granted to accumulate be it material or credential. All humanity is destined to die since Adam and Eve's rebellion but death has never meant ceasing to exist.

> "Every human being," says C. S. Lewis [1898-1963], "is in the process of becoming a noble being; noble beyond imagination. Or else, alas, a vile being beyond redemption" He exhorts us to remember that "the dullest and most uninteresting person you can talk to may one day be a creature which, if you saw it now, you would be strongly tempted to worship, or else a horror and a corruption such as you now meet, if at all, only in a nightmare. . . . There are no ordinary people . . . It is immortals whom we joke with, work with, marry, snub and exploit – immortal horrors or everlasting splendours."[299]

It is what occurs immediately after we have died that shows the differences between a child of the living God of light, the true child of Abraham, and the child of darkness. One has angels and heavenly comforts beyond our present understanding and the other has torments – note that's torment plural – and that's only while in hades which is destined later to be turfed into hell's lake of eternal fire. These then are destined for a second death, and yet even then they do not cease to be, there is still the

---

[298] *Matthew Henry's Commentary* p1476

[299] Erwin W. Lutzer *One Minute After You Die A preview of your final Destination* Moody Press 1997 p9

'experience [of] a conscious afterlife . . . Personhood survives the death of the body.'[300]

The *sheol* of the Old Testament is Hebrew, the *hades* of the New Testament is Greek, but they both are referring to the same place. For the age we are in this is the abode of the departed spirit of the unbeliever not the corpus rotting in the grave. The one in hades could see the state of the blessed one in heaven but the parable does not speak of Lazarus seeing into hades. To be able to see beauty, contentment and rest when you were in torments would only worsen them if that was possible.

But what I want you to see is that after you die here it is too late, the reservation for your dwelling spot in eternity was settled and finalized before your soul departed.

Here is an extract from another of Brooks' funeral sermons for you to consider. In this one he paints a picture of what being in hell would be like compared to heaven.

. . . souls, as you would escape hell, and come to heaven, as you would be happy in life, and blessed in death, and glorious after death, don't spend any more of your precious time in drinking and drabbing, in carding, dicing, and dancing; don't trifle away your time, don't swear away your time, don't whore away your time, do not lie away your time . . . because time is a talent that God will reckon with you for. Ah! Young men and women, you may reckon upon years, many years yet to come, when possibly you have not so many hours to make ready your accounts. It may be this night you may have a summons, and then, if your time be done, and your work to be begun, in what sad cause will you be. Will you not wish that you had never been born? . . . Sirs! Time let slip cannot be recalled. The foolish virgins found it so . . .

I am now young, and in the flower of my days; but who knows what a day may bring forth? . . . an eternity depends upon those few hours I am to breath in this world. Oh! What cause have I therefore . . . to know God betimes, to believe betimes, to repent

---

[300] Ibid. p31, 62

betimes, to get my peace made and my pardon sealed betimes, to get my nature changed, my conscience purged and my interest in Christ cleared betimes, before eternity overtakes me, before my glass be out, my sun set, my race run, lest the dark night of eternity should overtake me, and I made miserable for ever...

Do not say, O young man, that thou art young, and hereafter will be time enough to provide for eternity, for eternity may be at the door, ready to call thee away for ever. Every day's experience speaks out eternity to be as near the young man's back as it is before the old man's face . . . Though there is but one way to come into this world, yet there is a thousand ways to be sent out of this world . . . if you will not hear the voice of God to-day, if you will not provide for eternity to-day, God may swear to-morrow that you shall never enter into his rest. . . It is a very sad and dangerous thing to trifle and dally with God, his word, his offers, our own souls, and eternity . . . Nothing more sure than death, and nothing more uncertain than life . . .

Now if, for all that that hath been said, you are resolved to spend the flower of your days, and the prime of your strength, in the service of sin and the world, then know that no tongue can express, no heart can conceive that trouble of mind, that terror of soul, that horror of conscience, that fear. . . that weeping and wailing, that crying and roaring, that sighing and groaning, that cursing and banning, that stomping and tearing, that wringing of hands and gnashing of teeth, that shall certainly attend you, when God shall bring you into judgement for all your looseness and lightness, for all your wickedness and wantonness, for all your profaneness and baseness, for all your neglect of God, your grieving the Comforter, your trampling under foot the blood of a Saviour, for your despising of the means, for your prizing earth above heaven, and the pleasures of this world, above the pleasures that be at God's right hand.

. . . Oh! How will you wish in that day when your sins shall be charged on you, when justice shall be armed against you, when conscience shall be gnawing within you, when the world shall be a flaming fire about you, when the gates of heaven shall be shut against you, and the flame of hell ready to take hold of you, when angels and saints shall sit in judgement upon you, and forever turn their faces from you, when evil spirits shall be terrifying of you, and Jesus Christ for ever disowning of you; how will you, I say, wish in that day that you had never been born, or that you might now be unborn, or that your mother's womb had proved your tombs! Oh! How well you then wish to be turned into a bird, a beast, a stork, a stone, a toad, a tree! Oh that our immortal souls were mortal! Oh that we were nothing! Oh that we were anything but what we are! . . .

But now to those young men and women who begin to seek, serve, and love the Lord in the primrose of their days, the day of judgement will be to them melodia in aure, jubilum in corde, like music in the ear, and a jubilee in the heart. This day will be to them 'a day of refreshing', a 'day of redemption', a day of vindication, a day of coronation, a day of consolation, a day of salvation . . . Now the Lord will pay them for all the prayers they have made . . . for all the tears they have shed. In this great day Christ will remember all the individual offices of love and friendship shewed to any of his. Now he will mention many things for their honour and comfort that they never minded, now the least and lowest acts of love and pity towards his shall be interpreted as a special kindness shewed to himself. Now the crown shall be set upon their heads, and the royal robes put upon their backs; now all the world shall see that they have not served the Lord for nought. Now Christ shall pass over all their weaknesses, and make honourable mention of all the services they have performed, of all the mercies they have improved, and all the great things that for his name and glory they have suffered.
. . . . .

Sirs! Do not delude and befool your own souls; if you are not as wicked as others, you shall not be as much tormented as others, but yet you shall be as certainly damned as others; you shall as certain to hell as others; you shall as sure be shut out for ever from God, Christ, saints, angels, and all treasures, pleasures, and glories of heaven, as others, except it be prevented by timely repentance on your side, and pardoning mercy on God's. Wilt thou count it madness, young man! in him that is sick, to reason thus? I am not so sick as such and such, and therefore I will not send to the physician; and in the wounded man to say, I am not so desperately wounded as such and such, and therefore I will not send to the chirugeon; and in the trator to say, I am not guilty of so many foul and heinous treasons as such and such, and therefore I will not look after a pardon . . . ? And wilt thou not count it the greatest madness in the world for thee to put off repentance, and thy returning to the Lord in the spring and the morning of thy youth, because that thou art not as sinful, as wicked as such and such. If to have a softer bed, a milder punishment in hell than others, will satisfy thee, then go on; but if thou art afraid of the worm that never dies, and of the fire that never goes out. . . Oh seek and serve the Lord.

. . . To think often of hell, is the way to be preserved from falling into hell. Ah! Young men, young women, that you would often consider of the bitterness of the damned's torments, and of the pitilessness of their torments, and of the diversity of their torments, and of the easelessness of their torments, and of the remedilessness of their torments . . . The sinner's delight here is momentary, that which torments hereafter is perpetual. When a sinner is in hell, dost thou think, young man! that another Christ shall be found to die for him, or that the same Christ will be crucified again for him, or that another gospel should be preached to him? Surely, no.

Ah! Why then wilt thou not betimes return and seek out after the tilings that belong to thy everlasting peace? . . . Ah! Young man, that these occasional hints of hell may be a means to preserve thee from lying in those everlasting flames . . .[301]

---

[301] Thomas Brooks *Apples of Gold for Young men and Women* First published 1657 This extract taken from the 3rd edition corrected from the Complete Works of Thomas Brooks https://archive.org

The fear of hell, of eternal fire and brimstone is an excellent motivator to seek out the Lord and to encourage you to return to the narrow way when you stumble but it will be a love for the triune God and a rightful fear, a reverent respect for him because you have received his everlasting love for you in spite of you and you see and hate the awfulness of sin, your sin especially, that will keep you in a willing reciprocal relationship which results in acceptable clothing, works and service that looks eagerly for his return.

Three Parables but what's the time Mr. Wolf?

I find it hard to imagine hearing something more devastatingly final after ending your sojourning here to have Jesus say "I never knew you; depart from Me" (Matthew 7:21-23). Remember Bunyan's dream did not end with Pilgrim and Hopeful crossing the River and entering the Celestial City with its bells ringing for joy but with the ending of Ignorance's pilgrimage, a final warning of there being 'a direct way to Hell even from the gates of Heaven'.

Jesus warns of this but he used parables to show us how to be fully assured we would not hear those terrible words, 'Depart from Me, I never knew you.'

For Jesus to know you, you have to intimately know (this knowing is the same as the intimate knowing between a husband and wife of one another, and is not confined to a sexual knowledge, as the same wording is used for both) the Jesus of the scriptures, and be in that relationship on his terms not yours, in the way that the scriptures alone can tell you of.

> The whole Scripture is but one entire love-letter, despatched from the Lord Christ to his beloved spouse...

> Ah! Young men, young women! The word of the Lord is a light to guide you, a counsellor to counsel you, a comforter to comfort you, a staff to support you, a sword to defend you, and a physician to cure you. The word is a mine to enrich you, a robe to clothe you, and a crown to crown you. It is bread to strengthen you, and wine to cheer you, and a honeycomb to feast you, and music to delight you, and a paradise to entertain you. Oh! Therefore, before all, and above all, search the Scripture, study the Scripture, dwell on the Scripture, delight in the Scripture, treasure up the Scripture . . .[302]

In the earlier parts of this book we looked at how to be a pilgrim, how to be in a covenant relationship with God, with Jesus so we will not be starting there but it is worthwhile to remember that all those who profess to be pilgrims, who call themselves Christian, who attend church, who even pray and do seemingly very good self-sacrificial works, may be ones that Christ does not know. The church can have many hypocrites sitting in the pews, just ensure you yourself are not one, not a tare, not one of the bad fish caught in the fisherman's dragnet, not one who hears Jesus but does not do Jesus (Matthew 13:24-30, 36-43, 47-50; 7:13-27). Jesus taught many parables but we are going to consider three of them that show how we as pilgrims are expected to be found by Christ when he returns.

1. Have you got your wedding garment?

First up the Father and Son expect to find us properly clothed for our wedding feast and eagerly waiting for him who we claim as our beloved.

The context for the first parable we are looking at in Matthew 22:2-14, is that again Jesus is warning his people, especially the Pharisees and chief priests that they are in imminent danger of losing their claim on God's kingdom to the abhorrent gentiles.

---

[302] Ibid.

However, he also shows those last-minute guests how to be found acceptable to the King and remain at the feast.

"'The kingdom of heaven is like a certain king who arranged a marriage for his son, and sent out his servants to call those who were invited to the wedding; and they were not willing to come. Again, he sent out other servants, saying, 'Tell those who are invited, "See, I have prepared my dinner; my oxen and fatted cattle are killed, and all things are ready. Come to the wedding."' But they made light of it and went their ways, one to his own farm, another to his business. And the rest seized his servants, treated them spitefully, and killed them.'" (v. 2-6)

Can you imagine having had an invite from the Queen , the President of the United States, our Prime Minister, Oprah, or anyone you consider to be a 'somebody' and having at first accepted their invite you do an about face on being informed that all is ready and now is the time to come (how invites were done in Christ's culture was a bit different than ours now) because the weeds are requiring your immediate attention, or that you have just decided to start dieting. The religious elite of Bible times did treat God's messengers, his prophets especially very badly, even killing many.

"'But when the king heard about it, he was furious. And he sent out his armies, destroyed those murderers, and burnt up their city. Then he said to his servants, 'The wedding is ready, but those who were invited were not worthy. Therefore go into the highways, and as many as you find, invite to the wedding.' So those servants went out into the highways and gathered together all whom they found, both bad and good. And the wedding hall was filled with guests.

But when the king came in to see the guests, he saw a man there who did not have on a wedding garment. So he said to him, 'Friend, how did you come in here without a wedding garment?' And he was speechless.' (v 7-12)

Apparently, it was the custom in those days that the host provided all guests with a covering gown. These were simple nondescript robes that covered a person's rank or station within the community and allowed all guests to mingle as equals. Some read that the King was speechless, others that the guest was. Regardless who was, *speechless* still suggests that this guest though having been given a garment to wear had refused to do so, wishing to do things his own way. The King would be speechless at such a flagrant public act of defiance. The guest as he had been discovered among a room packed with obedient guests could also have been speechless. This defiance showed a heart actively rebelling against the King's will and justifies his proclamation that followed. [303]

Then the king said to the servants, 'Bind him hand and foot, take him away, and cast him into outer darkness; there will be weeping and gnashing of teeth,' For many are called, but few are chosen."' (v. 12- 14)

Question: What is the relevance and importance of this wedding garment, that the one without it is cast into hell without any appeal?

Answer: Let's revisit Genesis 3:21, 'Also for Adam and his wife the LORD God made tunics of skin, and clothed them.' The sewn fig leaf clothing that Adam and Eve made themselves could not cover their rebellion against God, only what was God's way, the way that involved the shedding of innocent blood would do.

Isaiah wrote in 61:10 of his book in the Old Testament, 'I will greatly rejoice in the LORD, my soul shall be joyful in my God; for He has clothed me with the garments of salvation, He has covered me with the robe of righteousness, as a bridegroom decks himself with ornaments, and as a bride adorns herself with her jewels.'

In The Revelation of Jesus Christ 19:7-8 we read, 'Let us be glad and rejoice and give Him glory, for the marriage of the Lamb has come, and His wife has made herself ready. And to her it was

---

[303] John Reid (1930-2016) *What the Bible says about providing Wedding Garments for Guests.* www.bibletools.org>RTD>cgg

granted to be arrayed in fine linen, clean and bright, for the fine linen is the righteous acts of the saints.'

> If the gospel be the wedding feast, then the wedding garment is a frame of heart, and a course of life agreeable to the gospel. . .Those, and those only, who have put on the Lord Jesus, and to whom he is all in all, have the wedding garment . . . Those that walk unworthy of their Christianity, forfeit all the happiness they presumptuously laid claim to.[304]

Doddridge writes, 'In order to our partaking of an inheritance among the saints in light, it is necessary that we be made meet for it by the holiness both of our hearts and lives. (Col. i. 12). This is the wedding garment, wrought by the Spirit of God himself, and offered to us by the freedom of his grace. And it is so necessary, that without it we must be separated from the number of his guests and friends, and even, though we had eaten and drank in his presence, must be cast out into outer darkness. (Luke xiii. 26)'

And Fleetwood wrote, 'By the conclusion of the parable, we learn, that the mere profession of the Christian religion will not save a man, unless he carries out his profession, and acts on Christian principles. Let us, therefore, who have obeyed the call, and profess to be the people of God, think often on that solemn day, when the king will come in to see his guests, and when he will scrutinize every soul that lays claim to the joys of heaven. Let us also stand in awe when we think of the speechless confusion that will come over such as have not on the wedding garment, and of the frightful despair amid which they will be consigned to weeping and wailing, and gnashing of teeth; and let us also remember, that to have seen, for a while, the light of the Gospel, and the fair prospect of an eternal hope, will add greatly to the horrors of these gloomy caverns. On the other hand, to animate and encourage all who are now truly living the life of the righteous, and who are realizing to themselves the full enjoyment

---

[304] *Matthew Henry's Commentary* p 1315

of "the life of God in the soul of man," let them look forward in joyful anticipation to that hour which will usher them into everlasting bliss.'[305]

So, how's your garment looking? Have you received it from the Spirit, put it on and kept it on? Or have you tried to cobble one from the created world yourself, that you prefer better, that you consider is better than what the King offers? I mean who wants to be covered by the blood of Christ and look like everyone else? Only those who are wise, for it is foolish to go to hell.

2. Is sleeping a sin?

Matthew 25:1-13 comes just before the chief priests, scribes, and the elders of the people gathered to plot how and when to take their Lord and kill him (26:1-5) and is in part an answer to his disciples questions earlier about when the temple would be destroyed, the sign of his coming and of the end of the age, (24:3). It is a parable that builds on from the previous parable's theme of the division between the unready and the ready professors of Christ.

'"Then the kingdom of heaven shall be likened to ten virgins who took their lamps and went out to meet the bridegroom. Now five of them were wise, and five were foolish. Those who were foolish took their lamps and took no oil with them, but the wise took oil in their vessels with their lamps. But while the bridegroom was delayed, they all slumbered and slept. And at midnight a cry was heard: 'Behold, the bridegroom is coming; go out to meet him!' Then all those virgins arose and trimmed their lamps. And the foolish said to the wise, 'Give us some of your oil, for our lamps are going out.' But the wise answered, saying, 'No, lest there should not be enough for us and you; but go rather to those who sell, and buy for yourselves.' And while they went to buy, the bridegroom came, and those who were ready went in with him to the wedding; and the door was shut. Afterward the other virgins came also, saying, 'Lord, Lord, open to us!' But he answered and

---

[305] *Fleetwood's Life of Christ* Fleetwood's writings and comment by Doddridge p475

said, 'Assuredly, I say to you, I do not know you.' Watch therefore, for you know neither the day nor the hour in which the Son of Man is coming."'

Question: A virginal escort, a wedding at midnight, and not opening the door to some of those involved in the wedding? I don't get it!

Answer: I believe there is an Old Testament event that despite being dressed differently mirrors this parable and I don't think those listening then got it either. But that did not stop the head of this family from obeying the obvious and that was to get to work, do as God told them and be prepared for when it came because once the door was shut it was too late.

Hebrews 11:7 reads, 'By faith Noah, being divinely warned of things not yet seen, moved with godly fear, prepared an ark for the saving of his household, by which he condemned the world and became heir of the righteousness which is according to faith.'

Have a read of the full account of the flood found in Genesis 5:32-9:19. According to Genesis 2:4-6, none living then would have understood what *floodwaters* meant or *rain* as no one would have seen them. Can you imagine the amount of ridicule Noah would have got during the hundred years it took him to build that huge boat and collect all the necessary food as well as all the animal kinds. And God shut the door of the ark as the rain started to fall and the fountains of the great deep broke up. Men ceased to scoff now and desired to have the door opened, but it was too late, only believing Noah and his family had by godly fear and faith prepared for that which they had not fully understood.

All ten virgins had lamps and oil to varying amounts and they all nodded off and slept, this was not the problem.

To sleep is not a sin, but a blessed gift from God for our weary bodies and minds as Psalm 127:2 says, 'It is vain for you to rise up early, to sit up late, to eat the bread of sorrows; for so He gives His beloved sleep.' I'm sure Noah appreciated the rest a good night's sleep gives as he toiled at boat building. In fact, considering this psalm you could conclude that to sleep in this manner is obeying God.

Since the creation of Adam there has been many warnings from God to his people of the coming executions of his judgements because of rebellion against his revealed will. As he has carried out all his promised judgements (though some were delayed briefly because of a time of repentance in the people's hearts) including judging his Son for all sins of all times, I don't think God is going to forget this day of the last, final judgement. It may be delayed but, in the end, it will come upon the world. Since the death of Christ, the people of this world have been given a warning of this coming final judgement. Like Noah we probably don't understand how it will look but there is no misunderstanding its results or what we are expected to be doing to be prepared. To date we have had over two thousand and twenty years to prepare. Are you nodding and unprepared? You have had plenty of warning, will your excuses be sufficient? Were Vain-hope's and Ignorance's?

Our preparation, like Noah's will cause us to be mocked, reviled and persecuted. He did not stop doing what God had commanded and neither should we.

Not being prepared for a long wait and not having any time left to prepare, to have enough light for the remaining distance they had to travel, was the problem for five of these virgins and a warning for us. Being labeled as foolish today does not sound that bad, stupid sounds worse, but this word has been transcribed from the Greek word *mōrŏs* (#3474) from which we get the word moron and means *dull* or *stupid, heedless, blockhead, absurd* and probably comes from a base word which means *cannot see far off*.

When it comes to considering these five virgins' attitude to being prepared for what they had proclaimed they desired, sadly all the meanings of this word apply. They did not consider the far-off possibility of having a long wait, they were only seeing the now. They had faith but no proof, no works. Even the thief crucified next to Christ had works, words that showed he believed who was dying next to him.

The writer of Psalm 119 tells us that God's word, the Bible is our lamp, our light for his path that we are to walk (v.105) and that includes the walk to our physical death.

How well do you know God's word? How obedient are you to it?

Being prepared is how you will never hear Jesus declaring that he does not know you (Matthew 7:21-3).

This parable shows us that you cannot be accepted because of another's readiness, you yourself have to be ready, be prepared. When my husband was very young yet involved in the family's nightly devotions, he decided he would have everything covered when Christ returned as by hanging on to his father's trousers he'd get taken also – cute but not what is taught here. Your loved ones or neighbours cannot hitch a ride on your knowledge of God and your works for him, your relationship with him, only you can. So be careful that having claimed your desire to be in the bridal procession that you don't become sidetracked especially when it takes longer than you thought to attain the hope you eagerly look for, wasting the now God has allotted you with accumulating all sorts of things and stuff, even busying yourself serving as Martha did and have the days slip from your grasp one by one, till there is no more sand in the hourglass left, and with no figs on your tree you find that the door has been shut.

To be prepared is not complicated to understand. Have you understood John 3:16 when reading it quoted in this book? Have you understood what it means to be a pilgrim and how to live as one? And has that head understanding anchored itself firmly into your heart? Then you have understood how to be prepared.

The doing however is not easy, even with armour on, for there are wars on two overlapping fronts that all pilgrims must fight. But we plod on, our many and varied experiences he gives us throughout our life build up our trust. We learn it is safe to fully depend on, to rest in this loving God's sovereignty and to keep obeying him and praying for he does make a true difference. This knowledge is impossible to gain suddenly at short notice for it is a growing over time bank of knowings. So, use your time wisely, building up and growing, deepening your relationship, walk in dependence upon God as Mary sought to do till it becomes habitual. A habit of life that prepares you for that last part of your journey here, your death which may be a time you can only remember and think on what you know of God and pray for you may no longer be physically able enough to do or to read or hear his word. And God being loving and knowing your heart understands if you are no longer mentally able to do anything you would have once so eagerly done.

> Christianity is not a one moment religion. The gospel is not fire insurance. When [you] receive Christ as Savior, [you] receive Him as Lord, for life. Continue then to seek to know God. Continue to grow in your love of God. Continue to serve Christ and His kingdom. Continue to obey the commandments of God. Continue to pursue holiness. Continue in fruitful service to Christ.
>
> Don't stop. Don't quit. Don't backslide. Don't get distracted. Don't lose heart. In this way eschatology [the study of end times, of Christ's return] is a theology of Christian life. In this way the second coming is at the centre of the Christian life and we make constant reference to it. Prepare your soul. Be constantly ready. Live careful, sober, urgent, sensible lives. Be always ready to face Christ. Be always ready for Christ's return. 'Be on the alert,' Jesus says, 'for you do not know the day or the hour.'[306]

Fleetwood wrote, '. . . taking their lamp of Christian profession, go forth . . . The foolish Christians are here represented as contenting themselves with the bare lamp of profession, never thinking of furnishing it with the oil of divine grace, the fruit of which is a life of holiness. Where as the wise, well knowing that a lamp . . . that faith, without love and holiness, will be of no consequence, take

---

[306] *The Parables of Jesus* p390-1

care to supply themselves with a sufficient quantity of divine grace, and to display in their lives the works of love and charity. . . [The next parable like this one] is intended to stir us up to a zealous preparation for the coming of our Lord, by diligence in the discharge of our duty, and by a careful improvement of our souls in the advancement of holiness: and, at the same time, to expose the vain pretenses of hypocrites, and to demonstrate, that mere outward form, without the power of godliness will be of no service in the last day of account.'[307]

3. What is it to you? You use what you have.

The third parable, Matthew 25:14-30 follows on from the last. This parable Henry says 'implies that we are in a state of work and business, as the former implies that we are in a state of expectancy. That showed the necessity of habitual preparation, this of actual diligence in our present work and service.'[308]

'"For the kingdom of heaven is like a man travelling to a far country, who called his own servants and delivered his goods to them. And to one he gave five talents, to another two, and to another one, to each according to his own ability; and immediately he went on a journey. Then he who had received the five talents went and traded with them, and made another five talents. And likewise he who had received two gained two more also. But he who had received one went and dug in the ground, and hid his lord's money.

After a long time the lord of those servants came and settled accounts with them. So he who had received five talents came and brought five other talents, saying, 'Lord, you delivered to me five talents; look, I have gained five more talents besides them.' His lord said to him, 'Well done, good and faithful servant; you were faithful over a few things, I will make you ruler over many things. Enter into the joy of your lord.' He also who had received two talents came and said, 'Lord, you delivered to me two talents;

---

[307] *Fleetwood's Life of Christ* p511, 513
[308] *Mathew Henry's Commentary* p1334

look, I have gained two more talents beside them.' His lord said to him, 'Well done, good and faithful servant; you have been faithful over a few things, I will make you ruler over many things. Enter into the joy of your lord.' Then he who had received the one talent came and said, 'Lord, I knew you to be a hard man, reaping where you have not sown, and gathering where you have not scattered seed. And I was afraid, and went and hid your talent in the ground. Look, there you have what is yours' But his lord answered and said to him, 'You wicked and lazy servant, you knew that I reap where I have not sown, and gather where I have not scattered seed. So you ought to have deposited my money with the bankers, and at my coming I would have received back my own with interest. Therefore take the talent from him, and give it to him who has ten talents. For to everyone who has, more will be given, and he will have abundance; but from him who does not have, even what he has will be taken away. And cast the unprofitable servant into the outer darkness. There will be weeping and gnashing of teeth.'"'

Note first, that these three servants are all under the lordship of the same lord, they belong to him. Though they are entrusted with different amounts of talents they are all expected to do something with what they were given that would give their lord some return on his investing them with his talents to begin with. The two servants who increased what they had been entrusted with received the same commendation even though the amounts achieved were not the same. God does not expect the same results from people as he is the one who has given us our varying abilities and skills.

However, as we saw in Interlude 2, God expects fruit from his people, a return from all that he has bestowed upon and in us and that a non-return over time has consequences.

Secondly, notice that the servant who was only entrusted with one talent *knew* his lord to be a *hard* man.

<u>Question</u>: Why was this opinion of the lord his alone, an opinion that made him afraid of his master, afraid to do anything for him?

Answer: For some reason this servant seems to have a mistaken idea of what his lord was like. I don't think he spent much time reading his Bible, do you? Remember what perfect love does, it casts fear out.

In John 4:34-38 we hear Jesus saying, '"My food is to do the will of Him who sent Me, and to finish His work. . . look at the fields, for they are already white for harvest! And he who reaps receives wages, and gathers fruit for eternal life, that both he who sows and he who reaps may rejoice together. For in this the saying is true; 'One sows and another reaps.' I sent you to reap that for which you have not laboured, others have laboured, and you have entered into their labours.'

In 1Corinthians 3:6 and 8b Paul writes, 'I planted, Apollos watered, but God gave the increase. . . and each one will receive his own reward according to his own labour.'

Paul and Apollos planted and watered using the gospel message, our Lord's good news of salvation by the talents, skills the Lord had given them and he would reward them for the fruit, the increase that he gave. Does that sound like a *hard* man or one full of mercy, grace and charitable love?

> Good thoughts of God would beget love, and that love would make us diligent and faithful; but hard thoughts of God beget fear, and that fear makes us slothful and unfaithful . . .This ill affection toward God arose from his false notions of him. Hard thoughts of God drive us from, and cramp us in his service. Those who think it impossible to please him, and in vain to serve him, will do nothing to purpose in religion.[309]

Question: But what is a talent? Is it money or gifts?
Answer: The talent Jesus was referring to was an ancient unit of mass. Wikipedia tells me that the Babylonians and Sumerians had a system in which there were 60 shekels in a mina [see Luke 19:11-27] and 60 minas in a talent. The heavy common talent,

---

[309] *Matthew Henry's Commentary* p1336

used in New Testament times, weighed around 58:9kg. As a unit of currency, it was valued for that weight of silver and so worth about 6,000 denarii. In ancient times the same amount of silver was often worth more than gold.

How are you at math?

Let's see, in Matthew 20:2 a denarius is a day's wage for a labourer so one talent equaling 6,000 denarii would be around sixteen and a half years' wages for a labourer.

Today in Australia the median hourly wage for a labourer is $22.04, so annually you could earn around $ 44,080. In sixteen and a half years you would have earnt around $727,320. So, you could say that in today's money one talent equals $727,320.

Still with me?

So, two talents would equal $1,454,640. Five talents would equal $3,636,600. Fancy being entrusted with that amount of money to use it as you thought fit with the idea of increasing it over an unknown amount of time.

Question: But is money and increasing it all this parable is about, is this the work our Lord wants from us?

Answer: In John 6:28-9 we read, 'Then they [the crowd of over five thousand people Jesus had fed the previous day] said to Him, "What shall we do, that we may work the works of God?" Jesus answered and said to them, "This is the work of God, that you believe in Him whom He sent."

So, believe in the gospel message, in all that Christ came to do and act on it, trust and obey, increase in holiness, love and good works, increase in your sanctification. To build your muscles up you have to use them, to build yourself up spiritually, to become what God wants you have to use all the resources he gives you, or lose them.

James tells us that God is the giver of all good and every perfect gift (James 1:17) and Paul tells us that there is nothing we have that did not come from God (1Corinthians 4:7), nothing.

So, what are these talents? Are they not things that God has given? What things do you have?

What physical and mental capabilities? What social skills? What hospitality skills? What level of education? What life experiences? Job skills, life skills or experiences, money, house, spare room, garden, car, influence, voice, lawn mower, second language, empathy, vegie patch, patience, single, married, divorced, sewing machine, iron, widowed, kids, no kids, duster, mop and bucket, buried kids, organizational skills, calling, etc. Note that there is no division of secular and spiritual, *all good* gifts are from God.

How are you using your talents to equip the saints for the work of ministry and the building up of any that belong to Christ?

Fleetwood writes 'Such is the parable of the talents, . . . a parable containing the measure of our duty to God, and the motives that enforce it . . . We are to consider God as our Lord and Master, the author and giver of every good gift, and ourselves as his servants or stewards, who have received from him such blessings and natural abilities, as may fit us for the several station and offices of life to which in his providence he hath appointed us. But then we are to observe, that these are only committed to us as a trust or loan, for whose due management we are accountable to the donor. . .

We learn from this instructive parable, that Infinite Wisdom hath intrusted men with different talents, and adjusted them to the various purposes of human life. But though the gifts of men are unequal, none can, with justice, complain; since whatever is bestowed, be it more or less, is a favour entirely unmerited.

Each then should be thankful, and satisfied with his portion; and, instead of envying the more liberal endowments of others, apply himself to the improvement of his own. And it should be attentively observed, that the difficulty of the task is in proportion to the number of talents committed to each . . . Surely then, we have no reason to complain if our Master has laid on us a lighter burden, a less severe and difficult service, than what he has on others. Especially as our interest, in the favour of the Almighty, does not depend on the number of our talents, but on our diligence and application in the management of them . . .

The proper improvement of all God's gifts is the employing them so, as they may best promote his glory and the good of our fellow-men . . . We may cultivate our understandings by learning and study, and extend our knowledge through all the subjects of human inquiry; but if our end be only to gratify our curiosity or our vanity, we are not serving God, but ourselves.'[310]

I have asked before but this is so very important I will ask you and myself again, why are we labouring at doing what we are doing? Who are we living for, who do we want to hear 'Well done' from?

But what's the time Mr. Wolf?

Question: Have you noticed what these last two parables had in common?

Answer: How about a long unknown span of time between the leaving of the King or lord and his returning? We did look earlier at why this delay happens but that does not explain why no arrival time is given. Surely having a date would help with planning our schedule, or would it? How prone are we with the excuse of being too busy with living, with the now, to putting off even important stuff till the last moment believing there will be no consequences, that everything will work out in the long run? Some do this when making decisions about studying for exams, getting bumps, lumps and spots checked, making a will, making a choice about Christ's offer. Do you not, my dear reader, realize that choosing not to make a choice till later is still making a choice, making a choice that it really is not that urgent, that relevant for today even though there is no guarantee you have a tomorrow?

Jesus discusses this in Mathew 24:35-51 which reads, '"Heaven and earth will pass away, but My words will by no means pass away. But of that day and hour no one knows, not even the angels of heaven, but My Father only. But as the days of Noah were, so also will the coming of the Son of Man be. For as in the days before the flood, they were eating and drinking, marrying and giving in marriage, until the day that Noah entered the ark, and

---

[310] *Fleetwood's Life of Christ* p515-8

did not know until the flood came and took them all away, so also will the coming of the Son of Man be. Then two men will be in the field: one will be taken and the other left. Two women will be grinding at the mill: one will be taken and the other left. Watch therefore, for you do not know what hour your Lord is coming. But know this, that if the master of the house had known what hour the thief would come, he would have watched and not allowed his house to be broken into.
Therefore you also be ready, for the Son of Man is coming at an hour you do not expect.
Who then is a faithful and wise servant, whom his master made ruler over his household, to give them food in due season? Blessed is that servant whom his master, when he comes, will find so doing. Assuredly, I say to you that he will make him ruler over all his goods. But if that evil servant says in his heart, 'My master is delaying his coming,' and begins to beat his fellow servants, and to eat and drink with the drunkards, the master of that servant will come on a day when he is not looking for him and at an hour that he is not aware of, and will cut him in two and appoint him his portion with the hypocrites. There shall be weeping and gnashing of teeth.'"
Firstly, note that in the days before the flood life went on as it had for years despite a crazy man building a huge boat because the end for all flesh and the earth was coming. They did not believe it was going to happen till that time arrived and their way of life and lives were taken from them.
It will be the same for this coming time of destruction and loss. There are ample warnings throughout both the Old and New Testaments that this day is coming so watch for it, but even then, we will be surprised when that time breaks into our lives. Like death in a way, for even when you have been waiting for a loved one to die for a time, when they do it still takes you by surprise. One minute the soul is there in the body then it's gone quicker than lightning flashes across the skies and you are left with a shell. The growing incidents of burglaries, road deaths or crimes of

violence fill the media outlets daily but when it happens to you personally you are shocked by the sudden unexpectedness of it actually happening to you.

Secondly note the wise and faithful servant who was put in charge while his master was gone to ensure all in the master's care were fed when and as needed. Some believe this parable is about church rulers, ministers and the like and how they are to feed God's people. I don't necessarily agree that this story is only for them, especially when Peter calls all pilgrims *a royal priesthood* (1Peter 2:9). Old Testament priests offered up sacrifices for themselves and the people to God, prayed to God and taught the people from his word.

The word from which *priesthood* is derived is never used in the NT to describe the Christian ministry, but rather the task of all Christian believers (*cf*. Rev. 1:6) [311]

From Romans 12:1 we learn that as pilgrims we are to present our bodies as *a living sacrifice, holy, acceptable to God,* which is our *reasonable service.* Our bodies, our renewed minds, our talents are all now for God's use to benefit all people, to feed his people and all peoples physically, emotionally and spiritually giving him glory.

In Colossians 3:16-17,23-25, 4:2-3 we read, 'Let the word of Christ dwell in you richly in all wisdom, teaching and admonishing one another in psalms and hymns and spiritual songs, singing with grace in your hearts to the Lord. And whatever you do in word or deed, do all in the name of the Lord Jesus, giving thanks to God the Father through Him. . . And whatever you do, do it heartily, as to the Lord and not to men, knowing that from the Lord you will receive the reward of the inheritance; for you serve the Lord Christ. But he who does wrong will be repaid for what he has done, and there is no partiality. . . Continue earnestly in prayer, being vigilant in it with thanksgiving; meanwhile praying also for

---

[311] *New Bible Commentary* p1376

us, that God would open to us a door for the word, to speak the mystery of Christ . . .'

O we can teach others about God like the Old Testament priests did and we are to pray for ourselves and for others that God's gospel may go forth and to give thanks to God for all things. To be able to do this work we need to soak in His Word, to 'so saturate ourselves with the Word of God that our blood becomes, as Charles Spurgeon said, 'bibline'.[312]
And we need to abide in him, to keep our relationship from the stain of sin by confession and repentance, and communication lines open by a habitual life of always praying, giving thanks. Our prayer life is really the one place in our life where we can practice the presence of the Lord in anticipation of Jesus' soon return.

. . . we must intentionally cultivate the discipline of seeking the face of God daily. This . . .needs to be a passion of our heart and not merely a routine. . .

1. 'Pray until you pray'. . . So many times it is just a mental list, a grocery list, if you please, of what I want God to do for me.

2. 'Pray until you are conscious of being heard.' . . .This is the objective in all true prayer: to come into the conscious presence of the God whom we serve, love and know with confidence that He has heard us.

3. 'Pray until you receive an answer.' . . . Pray till we understand what God is trying to do or say in that area of our life . . . Prayer is a matter of involving ourselves in a personal relationship, one on one, with God.
The whole purpose of these disciplines [confession, time in the Word and prayer] is to daily wean us from the world. . We must come to the place where the world no longer fascinates us but rather we are highly fascinated with the Blessed Hope.[313]
An elderly Christian acquaintance of ours died the morning he was to be discharged from a stay in hospital. He was found dressed

---

[312] *Preparing for Jesus Return* p196

[313] *Preparing for Jesus' Return* p198-9

and sitting in the chair beside his bed, hands folded on top of his open well-worn Bible, head forward and eyes shut. He had died praying. What a way to be found by his master!

Thirdly note the evil servant who cares not for his master's people except to abuse them and oppress them while he pleasures himself with carousing, gluttony and drinking in company I'm sure his master would not be pleased with.

Perhaps as when a mess is made at home, rules ignored or forgotten because the parents are away for a time, only to hear the key in the front door lock turning . . .

This is serious, this is hidden rebellion, hypocrisy. To do this towards parents is not good, to do against God is foolish. To use position and status to gain for self with no thought or regard for those in your care or the heart of the God you claim to serve as this servant did brings no glory to God and no delight eternally for those servants.

My Bible commentary tells us that, 'If the time is unknown, people will be caught unprepared, as *in the days of Noah*. There will be only two groups, the prepared (who are saved) and the unprepared (who are lost). Vs 40-41 illustrate with vivid pictures from everyday life how this basic division will separate those whose situation is otherwise identical. The way to *be ready* is not to try to calculate the date, for that is impossible (just as a *thief* does not announce his time of arrival), but to be always *keeping watch*.

It is, however, impossible to live life on constant alert. So vs 45-51 explain in a parable what 'being ready' means. When *the master* leaves a *servant* in charge during his absence, he does not expect to find him waiting at the door when he return, but rather getting on with the job entrusted to him. Neither of the two servants portrayed has advance knowledge of the master's return; the difference is in the way he finds them behaving. Our 'readiness' for the coming of Jesus is not in excited speculation but in faithful stewardship. . . The reward for faithful service is greater responsibility.'[314]

Spurgeon writes, 'Every Easter we remind ourselves that 'The Lord is risen indeed' (Lk. 24:34). But how often are we reminding ourselves or others that 'behold He cometh!' (Rev. 1:7)?

Beloved, no truth ought to be more frequently proclaimed, next to the first coming of the Lord, than His Second Coming. You cannot thoroughly set forth all the ends and bearings of the first advent if you forget the second. At the Lord's Supper, there is no discerning the Lord's body unless you discern His first coming, but there is no drinking of His cup to its fullness unless you hear Him say, "Till I come" (Rev. 2:25). You must look forward as well as backward.

So must it be with all our ministries; we must look to Christ on the cross and on the throne. We must vividly realize that He, who has once come, is coming again, or else our testimonies will be marred and one-sided. We will make lame work of preaching and teaching if we leave out either event.'[315]

A closing hymn

Well we have had the funeral sermons so we will close with a hymn, just one but one with a message for those left behind.

> Dear ones will give me their last embrace,
> Faces will bend o'er my still cold face,
> Shadows of mourning will fill the place,
> Five minutes after I die.
>> But the sorrowing faces I shall not see,
>> The murmuring voices will not reach me,
>> And where, oh, where will my spirit be,
>> Five minutes after I die?
> Quickly the years of my life have flown,

---

[314] *New Bible Commentary* p937

[315] Charles Spurgeon *The second coming of Christ* Whitaker House 1996 p15

The Pilgrim Way

Gathering treasure I thought my own,
There I must reap from the seed I have sown
Five minutes after I die.
> The chance of salvation I did not lack,
> But then I must stay on my chosen track,
> No room for repentance, no turning back,
> Five minutes after I die.

Now I can stifle convictions stirred,
Now I can silence the Voice oft heard,
But I must face His neglected Word,
Five minutes after I die.
> And mated at last with my chosen throng,
> I must enter eternity, endless long,
> Oh, woe is me, if my soul is wrong,
> Five minutes after I die.

What if I turn from my sin and pride,
Open to Jesus my heart's door wide,
Trusting Him now, and to be my Guide,
Five minutes after I die.
> All heaven to gain when the race is run,
> My loved ones to meet when my work is done,
> Eternity's joy would just begun
> Five minutes after I die.

Fool that I am—a hard word, yet true,
Passing pure chance of a prize in view,
Doing a deed I can ne'er undo,
Five minutes after I die.
> God help me to choose! My eternal state
> Depends on my choosing—I dare not wait,
> The choice must be now: it will be too late
> Five minutes after I die. [316]

---

[316] W. J. Tunley Arr. H. C. A. *Five Minutes after I Die* Heb. ix. 27 Alexander's Hymns No. 3 [ca. 1905] Marshall, Morgan & Scott LTD. No. 207

Do not wait even five minutes before you die, thinking that God does not consider your motives. Do not put off making this one decision, the only one that is *THE* most important you will ever make as it is the only one to have repercussions echoing through out eternity. Do not think you can have the apparent fun of the world and at the last moment choose eternal life insurance. This solely self-driven desire to save your skin is not a reason that God will accept. If you are a pilgrim, having made this choice, keep looking up, keep hanging on, keep remembering, keep being found by him studying his word and praying, keep plodding, keep examining, judging yourself, checking for fruit, for growth, keep putting one foot in front of the other until you are either called home or the beloved returns.

. . . the truth is that we often want to change the consequences of sin, but not the sin itself . . . People ask me to help them sort out the mess of their lives, but they don't really want to change the behaviour that's creating the mess. People want help with debt, but they don't want to change the idolatry of shopping that creates the damaging spending habits. They want help with broken relationships, but they don't want to change the idolatry of self that creates the friction. This is how John Owen puts it:

> A man who only opposes the sin in his heart for fear of shame among men or eternal punishment from God would practice the sin if there was no punishment attending it [writes John Owen]. How does this differ from living in the practice of the sin? Those who belong to Christ, and are obedient to the Word of God, have the death of Christ, the love of God, the detestable nature of sin, the preciousness of communion with God, and a deep-rooted hatred of sin *as sin* to oppose to all the workings of lust in their hearts.

. . . . The New Testament language of repentance is very violent. It includes amputating, murdering, starving and fighting. We need to be violent with sin. If we hold back, it's almost certainly because we don't want to be violent towards something we still love. We need to hate sin as sin and desire God for his own sake. John Owen again:

> Look on him whom you have pierced, and let it trouble you. Say to your soul, 'What have I done? What love, what mercy, what blood, what grace have I despised and trampled on! Is this how I pay back the Father for his love? Is this how I thank the Son for his blood? Is this how I respond to the Holy Spirit for his grace? Have I defiled the heart that Christ died to wash, and the Holy Spirit has chosen to dwell in? How can I keep myself out of the dust? What can I say to the dear Lord Jesus? How shall I hold up my head with any boldness before him? Do I count fellowship with him of so little value that, for this vile lust's sake, I have hardly left him any room in my heart? How shall I escape if I neglect so great salvation?
>
> What shall I say to the Lord? His love, mercy, grace, goodness, peace, joy, consolation – I have despised all of them! I have considered them as nothing, that I might harbour lust in my heart. Have I seen God as my Father, that I might provoke him to his face? Was my soul washed that there might be room for new defilements? Shall I seek to disappoint the purpose of the death of Christ? Shall I grieve the Holy Spirit, who sealed me unto the day of redemption?
>
> Allow your conscience to consider these things every day.

The key to change is continually returning to the cross. . . A cross-centered life means an inevitable and resolute rejection of all self-confidence and self-righteousness . . . When we go to the cross, we see our God dying for us. If you let any other god down, then it will beat you up. . . when you let Christ down, he loves you still. He doesn't beat you up; he dies for you.

Let his love win your love and let that love replace all other affections. The secret of change is to renew your love for Christ as you see him crucified in your place.[317]

---

[317] *You can Change* p137-9 which includes a quote from John Owen's *The Mortification of Sin* abridged and simplified by Richard Rushing Banner of Truth 2004 p59, 78-9.

Finale: the carrot!

When one of our granddaughter's was four, she loved listening to picture story books being read to her. It was one of the few things she would sit still for.
One of her favourites then was 'Clippity-Clop' by Pamela Allen. As the inside cover states, it is about *a little old woman and a little old man, each with a stubborn donkey, each with the same problem. Who will solve it? What would you do?*
The little old man – no I can't draw the pictures for you! – first tries whipping his stubborn donkey which refuses to move. This works but the little old man struggles to keep up with his animal. So next, when he has caught up, he tries enticing the donkey by laying a trail of carrots, a very long trail while softly singing. *"Yummy, yummy yum-yum . . . come, come, come . . ."* This also works, but only for a time for the poor donkey becomes so stuffed with carrots he can neither munch or take another step. So now the little old man, puffing very hard, has to carry his donkey instead of the animal carrying him.
Much to his chagrin the little old woman now streaks past grinning from ear to ear, sitting comfortably upon her donkey.

The picture shows her holding a stick over her donkey's head so that the fat juicy crunchy carrot tied on by string is just out of teeth's reach![318]

Question: What motivates pilgrims to keep going, to keep serving God in this world till we are welcomed home?
Answer: Observation or experience may have taught you that you can only go so far by whipping yourself into gear with 'I musts' or 'I have to's ', fired by emotional zeal, guilt, or the need to keep up with the Christian Joneses or should I say Marthas before you burnout and collapse, which will usually happen way before the finishing line is even in sight.

Then again you will possibly go even less distance by stuffing yourself, your head with information. Flitting from one talk feast to the next, always learning and enjoying the social fellowshipping but never having the time to digest and practice, never coming to a personal knowledge, a heart knowledge of the truth, needing someone else other that God to lean on, to carry you, to pray for you as they are so much better than you, to encourage you, to lift you up yet again until they burn out.

So, what should be the primary motive for a pilgrim, what should entice us to know, remember, and live accordingly in a way that will delight God, and us when we hear "Well done, good and faithful servant, enter into the joy of your Lord"?
Need a hint?

> "Now consider this, you who forget God,
> Lest I tear you in pieces,
> And there be none to deliver:
> Whoever offers praise glorifies Me:
> And to him who orders his conduct aright
> I will show the salvation of God." (Psalm 50:22-23)

Another loud hint is found in a verse of the scripture this book was born from, 1Peter 2:12, 'having your conduct honourable among the Gentiles, that when they speak against you as

---

[318] Pamela Allen *Clippity-Clop* Puffin Books 1994

evildoers, they may, by your good works which they observe, glorify God in the day of visitation.'
Did you see it?

During Faithful's pilgrimage he meets up with Talkative, son of Saywell of Prating-row and they strike up a conversation on how one can tell if there has been a work of saving grace in the heart of a person.
Talkative claims that it can be known when the grace of God is in the heart 'as it causeth there a great outcry against sin . . .'
Faith. Nay . . . I think you should rather say, It shows itself by inclining the soul to abhor its sin.
Talk. "Why what difference is there between crying out against, and abhorring of sin?
Faith. Oh! A great deal. A man may cry out against sin, of policy, but he cannot abhor it but by virtue of a godly antipathy against it. I have heard many cry out against sin in the pulpit, who yet can abide it well enough in the heart, house, and conversation . . . But what is the second thing whereby you will prove a discovery of a work of grace in the heart?
Talk. Great knowledge of gospel mysteries.
Faith. This sign should have been first: but first or last, it is also false; for knowledge, great knowledge, may be obtained in the mysteries of the gospel, and yet no work of grace in the soul. 1Cor xiii. Yea, if a man have all knowledge he may yet be nothing, and so consequently be no child of God. When Christ said, "Do ye know all these things?" and the disciples had answered, "Yes"; he added, "Blessed are ye, if ye do them." He doth not lay the blessing in the knowing of them, but in the doing of them. For there is a knowledge that is not attended with doing: "he that knoweth his Master's will, and doeth it not". A man may know like an angel, and yet be no Christian; therefore your sign of it is not true. Indeed, to know, is a thing that pleases talkers and boasters; but to do, is that which pleaseth God. Not that the heart can be good without knowledge; for without that the heart is nought. There are therefore two sorts of knowledge; knowledge that

resteth in the bare speculation of things, and knowledge that is accompanied with the grace of faith and love, which puts a man upon doing even the will of God from the: the first of these will serve the talker; but without the other the true Christian is not content: "Give me understanding and I shall keep thy law; yea, I shall observe it with my whole heart". Ps. cxix 34. . . . A work of grace in the soul discovereth itself, either to him that hath it, or to standers by. . .To others, it is thus discovered. . . By a life answerable to that confession; to wit, a life of holiness; heart-holiness, family-holiness (if he hath a family), and by conversation-holiness in the world, which in the general teacheth him inwardly to abhor his sin, and himself for that, in secret to supress it in his family, and to promote holiness in the world; not by talk only, as a hypocrite or talkative person may do, but by a practical subjection in faith and love to the power of the word. Ps 1. 23; Ezek. xx. 43; Matt. v. 8; John xiv.15; Rom. x. 9, 10; Phil. iii 17-20.[319]

Are you wondering why I have put this extract from Bunyan's tale in here? It is as Jim Gables says, what we do is important but why we do it is critical. Your motive is far more important than your act of duty. The only acceptable motive for a pilgrim is the glory of God. Why do you, I do things? Why go to church? Why do I obey the commandments? God's glory or yours, mine? Christian here says 'not a step further unless God is the chief end of your life'. [320]

> He has bought us to be His own . . .The obligation resting upon believers as a consequence is that they should *glorify God* . . . The prime motive in the service of the Christian must not be the accomplishing of purposes which seem to him to be desirable, but the glory of God.[321]

Do you recall reading this in a longer quote way, way back in the second part of this book? This, God's glory and our glorying in and

---

[319] *The Pilgrim's Progress* p131-4

[320] Notes from Gables' sermon series on Pilgrim's Progress #45 By-ends companions #1 2.15.99

[321] *The first epistle of Paul to the Corinthians* p104.

glorifying of him, this should be the prime motive behind *all* other motives of the pilgrim.

Question: But what is this *glory of God*? Why should it be our prime motive for service, for how we live as pilgrims?

Answer: My trusty dictionary tells me that glory means the following: exalted renown, honourable fame or adoring praise and thanksgiving, having a resplendent majesty, beauty or magnificence, an effulgence of heavenly light, but let's look at what the original Hebrew that the Old Testament was written in meant.

The Hebrew verb that is translated as *glory* was used to describe the *weight* or *worthiness* of something.

Occasionally it was used in an unflattering manner, in a way you would prefer not to be used about yourself, as seen in Genesis 18:20, 'And the Lord said, "Because the outcry against Sodom and Gomorrah is very great [glorious], and because their sin is very grave"' And in 1Samuel 4:18 where Eli's massive bulk that was a result of his in-glorious greed (1Samuel 3:13, 2:12-16) caused his neck to break when he fell backwards.

But usually the word was used to depict greatness and splendour as in Genesis 31:1, 'Now Jacob heard the words of Laban's sons, saying, "Jacob has taken away all that was our father's, and from what was our father's he has acquired all this wealth.' In the KJ version the last part of this verse reads, '... and of that which was our father's hath he gotten all this glory.'

And Psalm 49:16, 'Do not be afraid when one becomes rich, when the glory of his house is increased.'

The noun form of the word was sometimes translated as honour as in 1Kings 3:13, '"And I [the LORD] have also given you what you have not asked: both riches and honour, so that there shall not be anyone like you among the kings all your days..."'

> The glory of God is the manifest beauty of his holiness, the manifestation of his character, his worth, his attributes... It

is the way he puts his holiness on display for people to apprehend. [322]

As we can see by reading for example the following sections of scripture –

Psalm 19:1, 'The heavens declare the glory of God; and the firmament shows His handiwork' – he is shouting at us. He shouts with clouds . . . blue expanse . . . with gold on the horizons . . . with galaxies and stars. He is shouting, I am glorious, open your eyes. It is like this, only better if you know me.

In Isaiah 6:3 we read, 'And one [seraphim] cried to another and said: "Holy, holy, holy is the LORD of hosts; the whole earth is full of His glory!" but in 2Corinthians 4:4-6 we read, 'whose minds the god of this age has blinded, who do not believe, lest the light of the gospel of the glory of Christ, who is the image of God, should shine on them. For we do not preach ourselves, but Christ Jesus the Lord, and ourselves your bondservants for Jesus' sake. For it is the God who commanded light to shine out of darkness, who has shone in our hearts to give the light of the knowledge of the glory of God in the face of Jesus Christ.'

In Romans 1:18-32, which I hope you will read in its entirety, where Paul is addressing unbelievers there is a couple of verses that are helpful in their warnings. Verses 21and 23 read, '. . . although they knew God, they did not glorify Him as God, nor were thankful, but became futile in their thoughts, and their foolish hearts were darkened . . . and changed the glory of the incorruptible God into an image . . .'

All mankind are made in God's image and are meant to worship, glorify the God who made them. We have a space inside created for this and it cries out to be filled. And trying to fill this void, this hunger or restless searching for that elusive something with anything other than God such as sex, alcohol, illicit drugs, entertainment, relationships, stuff, will be futile long term, for as I have learnt by experience *only* God satisfies this craving, nothing

---

[322] John Piper Sermon *To Him Be Glory Forevermore* preached Dec 17 2006 desiringgod.com

we make from or use of God's creation and attempt to put in his rightful place, this space inside us, will.

What else does this craving, and this helplessness, proclaim but that there was once in man a true happiness, of which all that now remains is the empty print and trace? This he tries in vain to fill with everything around him, seeking in things that are not there the help he cannot find in those that are, though none can help, since this infinite abyss can be filled only with an infinite and immutable object; in other words by God Himself.[323]

Scripture speaks of the glory of God as –

- Belonging to the Father, Son and Spirit. Luke 9:29,32,34-35, 'As He [Jesus] prayed, the appearance of His face was altered, and His robe became white and glistening . . . they [Peter, John and James] saw His glory. . . a cloud came and overshadowed them . . . And a voice came out of the cloud, saying, "This is My beloved Son. Hear Him!"' and 1Peter 4:14, '. . . blessed are you for the Spirit of glory and of God rests upon you . . .'

- A cloud and a fire. In Exodus Moses described the glory this way in various places including 13:21 and 40:34, 38, 'And the LORD went before them be day in a pillar of cloud to lead the way, and by night in a pillar of fire to give them light, so as to go be day and night. . . Then the cloud covered the tabernacle of meeting, and the glory of the LORD filled the tabernacle. . . For the cloud of the LORD was above the tabernacle by day, and fire was over it by night, in the sight of all the house of Israel, throughout all their journeys.' This cloud is described as thick and dark (Exodus 19:9, 16; 20:21) and Moses speaks of it as a cloud that hides in Exodus 33: 22, 20b, '"So it shall be, while My glory passes by, that I will put you [Moses] in the cleft of the rock, and will cover you with My hand while I pass by . . . for no man shall see Me, and live."'

---

[323] Blaise Pascall (1623-1662) *Finding God in Revealing Fundamental Truths of Life* league of Everyday Doxologists www.doxologists.org

- A consuming fire of judgement. Again, in Exodus but this time not as a light for our way but a fire to destroy, to fear as we read in 24:17, 'The sight of the glory of the LORD was like a consuming fire on the top of the mountain in the eyes of the children of Israel.' This is not a different glory but the same.

John the Baptist speaking of the Christ warned his hearers that, '"His winnowing fan is in His hand, and he will thoroughly clean out His threshing floor, and gather His wheat into the barn; but He will burn up the chaff with unquenchable fire"' (Matthew 3:12).

Preaching on Malachi 4:1-2 which says, '"For behold, the day is coming, burning like an oven, and all the proud, yes, all who do wickedly will be stubble. And the day which is coming shall burn them up," says the LORD of hosts. "That will leave them neither root nor branch. But to you who fear My name the Sun of Righteousness shall arise with healing in His wings; and you shall go out and grow fat like stall-fed calves'– 'the main lesson Jonathan Edwards drew from this was that 'That same spiritual Sun, whose beams are most comfortable and beneficial to believers, will burn and destroy unbelievers.' . . . the very glory that is the fragrance of life to some is the smell of death to others. God's purpose is unfathomably kind: he will at the last so spread his life, being and goodness that he will be all in all; he will at the last fill the universe with the light of his wonderful glory. He is all light – but that *is* terrible for those who love the darkness.'[324]

- A person of radiating (this means an outward, not an inward movement) light that gives life, a brightness. Ezekiel writes of his vision of God in the first chapter of his book when he was an exile in Babylon. We will start towards the end of this description at v26 to 28, 'And above the firmament over their heads was the likeness of a throne, in appearance like a sapphire stone; on the likeness of the throne was a likeness with the appearance of a man high above it. Also from the appearance of His waist and upward I saw, as it were, the colour of amber with the

---

[324] *The Good God* p102

appearance of fire all around within it; and from the appearance of His waist and downward I saw, as it were, the appearance of fire with brightness all around. Like the appearance of a rainbow in a cloud on a rainy day, so was the appearance of the brightness all around it. This was the appearance of the likeness of the glory of the Lord.' So . . . I fell on my face.'

Psalm 104:2 tells us that God covers Himself with light like we cover ourselves with clothing. John1:4,9 and 14, 'In Him [Jesus] was life, and the life was the light of men . . . That was the true Light which gives light to every man coming into the world. . . And the Word became flesh and dwelt among us, and we beheld His glory, the glory as of the only begotten of the Father, full of grace and truth.'

This glory, this light that radiates outward, gave life and sustained life even before the earth's sun existed (Genesis 1:3,11-19) and it will be the only source of light for the New Jerusalem (The Revelation of Jesus Christ 21:23, 22:5).

- God's excellency (Isaiah 35:2). This is his goodness, grace and compassion (Exodus 3:18-23) which is above the heavens (Psalm 113:4), yet fills his temple, his place of residence (Exodus 40:34-38, Revelation 15:8, 21:10-11, 22-24, 22:5) and is something God will not give to another (Isaiah 42:8, Exodus 20:35), for he alone is God but as pilgrims who serve as Christ does we will participate, share in his eternal glory (John 17:20, 22, 12:26; Romans 8:17; 1Peter 5:1). It is declared by the heavens (Psalm 19:1, and read Isaiah 40:6-42:9) and is a glory that will go through death with you, unlike the glory of man (Psalm 49).

- Eternal. John 1:14, 17:5 tells us that, '. . . the Word became flesh and dwelt among us, and we beheld His glory, the glory as of the only begotten of the Father, full of grace and truth. . . And now, O Father, glorify Me together with Yourself, with the glory which I had with You before the world began.'

So before Creation began, in eternity past the Triune God had glory and shared this glory. Knowing Jesus and the Father, thinking of the Cross, it is hard to consider this glory as 'something that is not about love... Through Jesus we do not see a proud divine glory, but the glory of inexpressible humility and kindness... He makes Himself known as the compassionate One with the ability to heal, to bring life and rich abundance... What does it [this glory] look like? [Considering John12:23-33 where Jesus speaks of his death] A seed, dying to bear fruit... His glory is inestimably good, overflowing self-giving.[325]

This glory is our uncreated-always-has-been-and-is God's weighty unique nature, his character, his name. It is in fact the sovereign triune God of all that has been created, the great I AM who I AM, himself. And as this God is love, jealous, holy, a just judge, wrathful if need be – someone once described his righteous anger as 'His love turned against all that defiles, ignores and insolently repudiates it'– and all these make up what is his glory. If God did not have this glory, this weight, he would be as all little gods, an idol of our imaginations and preferences and just as useless so all of creation would be completely and eternally undone and lost, in fact we would not even exist.

Question: So why are we to give him glory, to glorify him? What does this mean? How do we do this?

Answer: My trusty dictionary was not much help here to begin with as it told me that to glorify means to 'make glorious, exalt to the glory of heaven; invest with radiance; transform into something more splendid. To try and make a common or inferior thing seem more splendid than it really is' but God is already all these, though he has never been or ever will be common!

However, it did give the definitions of to *extol or praise* and this is what scripture tells us to do, and not because he is needy like us or all other gods but simply because of whom he is. 'Give unto the LORD the glory due to His name' (Psalm 29:2a).

Give the glory *due* to his name. The scriptures are not telling us to give God glory as if he had none and was craving for some like we

---

[325] Ibid. p103-4

do, but to acknowledge the truth, that glory is already an attribute he has had from eternity past and will have to eternity future whether we give him glory or not. We are the losers if we do not glorify him, not God.

Piper tells us that God 'is infinitely jealous for his reputation, "For my own sake, for my own sake I act," says the Lord. 'My glory I will not give to another!' Why [is] God's commitment to his own glory . . . immensely relevant for your life[?] . . . God's zeal to seek his own glory and to be praised by men cannot be owing to his need to shore up some weakness or compensate for some deficiency . . . Since God is unique as the most glorious of all beings and totally self-sufficient, he must be for himself if he is to be for us. If he were to abandon the goal of his own self-exaltation we would be the losers. His aim to bring praise to himself, and his aim to bring pleasure to his people, are one aim. What could God give us to enjoy that would show him most loving . . . *Himself.* If God would give us that which is best and most satisfying, that is, if he would love us perfectly, he must offer us no less that himself for our contemplation and fellowship and joy. Ps. 16:11. . . God is after us to give us what is best – not prestige, wealth or even health in this life, but a full-blown vision of, and fellowship with, himself. *We praise what we enjoy because the delight is incomplete until it is expressed in praise.*

. . . if God is truly for us, if he would give us the best and make our joy full, he must make it his aim to win our praises for himself . . . because he loves us and seeks the fullness of our joy that can only be found in knowing and praising him, the most beautiful of all things . . . The Bible does not say God wants us to give Him glory Isa 43:7. . . it is already an attribute of His. He wants us to acknowledge the truth of this.'[326]

God has revealed himself to us as a God who is passionate to make known the glory of his name – not the pronunciation of it, as if this were magic, but the reality of it – the God who absolutely

---

[326] Piper Sermon *Is God for us or for Himself?* October 23 1984 desiringgod.com

is, the God who is personal and the God who is supremely glorious (Ps. 106:7-8).

> God is most glorified in us when we are most satisfied in him.[327]

This reasoning should also make it plain that God wanting glory, wanting to be honoured for who he is, is not being self-centered, or selfish, or to use Piper's words narcissistic or a megalomaniac, for none of those characteristics belong to Yahweh's way of loving.

> We glorify God when we simply give credit to him for what he is and for what he has done, when we declare him to be as he truly is. [328]

Psalms 135 and 136 are two examples of this sort of praise that naturally rises up from within when we recognise who God is and what he has done for us personally, communally and nationally or even worldwide.

For an example some of 136, 'Oh, give thanks to the LORD, for He is good! For His mercy endures forever. . . To Him who alone does great wonders, for His mercy endures forever; to Him who by wisdom made the heavens, for His mercy endures forever; to Him who laid out the earth above the waters, for His mercy endures forever; to Him who made great lights, for His mercy endures forever–the sun to rule by day, for His mercy endures forever; the moon and stars to rule by night, for His mercy endures forever. . . Who remembered us in our lowly state, for His mercy endures forever; and rescued us from our enemies, for His mercy endures forever; who gives food to all flesh, for His mercy endures forever. Oh, give thanks to the God of heaven! For His mercy endures forever.' (v. 1, 4-9, 23-26) Mercy in this psalm is referring to our God's *hesedh* love.

We understand who Yahweh is most clearly because of Jesus; 'the light of the world . . . is the shining out of the Father's glory'.[329]

---

[327] Piper Sermon Glorifying *God . . . period* July 15 2013 desiringgod.com
[328] *The Good God* p99
[329] Ibid. p103

Jesus did not need anything from us. He served us, giving instead of taking, warning in love and kindness to come out of our darkness and into his light, into his abundant overflowing life before it was too late. (Matthew 20:27-28; John.1: 4-5, 3:17-21, 8:12). And Christ's basic mindset was and is to glorify the Father.

In John 12:27-28a we hear part of Jesus' conversation with two of the disciples, '"Now my soul is troubled, and what shall I say? 'Father, save me from this hour'? But for this purpose I came to this hour. Father, glorify Your name."'

It is in Christ's cross that we see 'the glorification of the glory of God, the deepest revelation of the very heart of God – and it is all about laying down his own life to give life, to bear fruit . . . His glory is inestimably good, overflowing self-giving . . .' [330], never self-focused or centered, never inward focused but a never ending radiating outwardness.

And again, through Christ, we get to understand more of this glory.

John 17:1-5, 'Jesus spoke these words, lifted up His eyes to heaven, and said: "Father, the hour has come, Glorify Your Son, that Your Son also may glorify You, as You have given Him authority over all flesh, that He should give eternal life to as many as You have given Him. And this is eternal life, that they may know You, the only true God, and Jesus Christ whom You have sent. I have glorified You on the earth. I have finished the work which You have given Me to do. And now, O Father, glorify Me together with Yourself, with the glory which I had with You before the world was."'

> This is the way God prays when he is being loving to his people. He prays that his glory be upheld and displayed . . . NOT that our value may be central, but that his glory may be central, and we may see it and savour it for all eternity. . . magnifying the supremacy of God in all things, and being willing to suffer patiently to help see and savour this

---

[330] Ibid. p105

supremacy is . . . the essence of God's love. And it's the essence of your love. Because the supremacy of God's glory is the source and sum of all full and lasting joy. [331]

We glorify God as we depend on him and refuse to be self-sufficient, indeed self-anything and 'work out [our] own salvation with fear and trembling' (Philippians 2:12), in loving grateful obedient relationship to him. We glorify God when we choose to still trust him and be obedient when we cannot understand the why, when we trust in the dark. And we glorify God when we extol and praise the Son, when we believe on the Christ Jesus, (John 5:23, 6:29).

I think of all scripture perhaps the book of Ezekiel shows us why the glory of God is important and why his glory should be our main reason for acting as we pilgrims do.

Wright tells us that 'Not many people in the Old Testament had an equal passion for Yahweh as Ezekiel. The glory of his God was possibly the main driving force of his life and as such Ezekiel like no other prophet showed graphically without any considerations to sensibilities how Yahweh saw our sin and how it affected Him. Ezekiel also shows us salvation from God's point of view, why He saves; that Yahweh's name and reputation should be vindicated and that [He] should be universally acknowledged as God . . . All that really mattered for Ezekiel was that both in Israel and in the world of nations, the glory of God would be revealed, the honour of God's name would be restored, and the truth of God's identity would be known. [At this time in history, a time much like our own, the nations were mocking Israel's Yahweh for they considered him to be of less use than their own gods and Israel's life style and attitude towards him did nothing to lessen this thinking.] The universal acknowledgement of Yahweh as God – that alone was Ezekiel's burning ambition. . . *Israel* would know the reality and power of Yahweh their God when they witnessed his judgement of the nations . . . *the nations* would know the truth

---

[331] John Piper *How Is God's Passion for His Own Glory not Selfishness?* Nov 24 2007 desiringgod.com

about Yahweh when they understand the reason for His judgement of Israel . . . Both 'knowings' would constitute a recognition of Yahweh's *glory*. . . This can be seen in the recurring phrase, at least seventy times; 'Then you [or they] shall know that I am God'; this is really the only knowledge that counts.' [332]

Jim Gables said, 'God's glory is the only legitimate reason, motive for religion for serving God, as anything done for self-reasons will fall short under judgement. Your motive is more important than your actual act of duty. When did your children most please you? Was it when they just did something without nagging, without a bribe? God loves a cheerful giver, a deed done from the heart of his child, because he alone is worthy.' [333]

> Do you serve God to keep his wrath off your back
> or because his laws which display his
> glorious character are worthy of being served?[334]

Ignatius of Loyola (1491-1556) advised, 'Let each remember that he will make progress in spiritual things only insofar as he rids himself of self-love, self-will and self-interest.'

To do that don't we need to focus on something else, and is not Yahweh truly the best for self to focus on?

Job of the book in the Old Testament by his name never got an answer for his questions about his suffering. Instead God declared himself in the thirty-eighth chapter, shifting Job's focus off self and overwhelming him with God's omnipotent glory (have a read of chapters 38 to 42:6). Job never needed an answer when he understood that when even the tiny things that man does not consider as well as the great things are known and addressed by this God of unknowable goodness and power his were too.

You could say that glorifying God is like boasting about God, about the sort of God he is and the Bible actually tells us to do this.

---

[332] Christopher J. H. Wright *The message of Ezekiel* Inter-Varisity Press 2001 p25, 271, 321.

[333] Notes from Gables' sermon series on Pilgrim's Progress #45 By-ends companions #1 2.15.99 and *46. #2* 2.16.99

[334] Ibid *#68. Evaluation of Ignorance and Temporary* 3.10.99

1Corinthians 1:31 in the NKJ reads, '. . . He who glories, let him glory in the LORD'

In the NIV the same verse reads, '. . . Let him who boasts boast in the Lord.'

The Greek word that has been translated here is *kauchaŏmai* (#2744) which comes from some (obsolete) base akin to that of another Greek word meaning to boast and another meaning to *vaunt* either in a good or bad sense. So, its meaning is (make) boast, glory, joy or rejoice.

The new Testament verse we have just looked at is quoted from the Old Testament.

Jeremiah 9:23-24 NKJ reads,

> 'Thus says the LORD:
> "Let not the wise man glory in his wisdom,
> Let not the mighty man glory in his might,
> Nor let the rich man glory in his riches;
> But let him who glories glory in this,
> That he understands and knows Me,
> That I am the LORD, exercising lovingkindness,
> judgement, and righteousness in the earth.
> For in these I delight," says the LORD.'

The NIV version here replaces *glory* with *boast* and *glories* with *boasts* as we saw above for the New Testament.

The Hebrew word is *hâlal* (#1984), a primary root; to *be clear* (originally of sound, but usually of colour); to *shine*; hence, *to make a show*, to *boast*; and thus to *be* (clamorously) *foolish*; to *rave*; cause to *celebrate*; also to *stultify*:– (make) boast (self), celebrate, commend, (deal, make), Fool (-ish, -ly), glory, give (light), be (make, feign self) mad (against), give in marriage, [sing, be worthy for] praise, rage, renowned, shine.

The world likes to boast in and of itself, as most of us do if we are honest and if we believe we have anything worthy of boasting about. What Jeremiah listed in his verses we just read, *wisdom*, *might* and *riches* are still things we boast of today, things of pride, the pride of life, the lust of the eyes and the lust of the flesh. Do

The Pilgrim Way

you not find this to be true? What are you boastful about? Job and pay packet? The number of scalps you have won for the kingdom? Kid's and their academic or sporting abilities? Looks, sexual abilities? The number of bottoms on your church's pews? Car? Wardrobe? House? For does not the one with the most win?

Win what?

Boasting about self is self glorifying self, and for fallen mankind this is a destructive action, for a pilgrim it is dangerously sinful for there is nothing in or of our self which can be boasted about. Only God is big enough to handle being boasted about, being glorified because he alone is without sin so his head does not swell with praise shrinking his brains.[335]

> Boasting in anything other than Christ is fatal. What we boast about is what we are depending on. So boast about depending on, finding your identity in, finding your belonging in, talking about, sharing, celebrating, praising God, the Father, Son and Holy Spirit. Boast about the power of God in the cross and the power of the Spirit in the Word for the main claim the Bible makes is not of its authority but its power. If I believe the Bible has authority but no power, I have to make you believe what it says. But if the Bible has power then I only have to read it and guess who gets the glory? This power of the triune God that worked for us now works in us to transform us so we can will and do as God desires us to, and guess who gets the glory, who truly can be boasted about? Let the one who boasts boast in the Lord.[336]

For me personally having God's glory as my carrot, the basic, primary motive for what I do, wipes out a lot of ideas and choices, making living and working for God much simpler and yet in some ways much harder.

---

[335] I wish to give credit to ideas in this paragraph to things written by Max Lucado in *Travelling Light* p73-4

[336] From notes taken during a lecture by Peter Adams on *The Power of the Gospel, the Power of the Spirit* several years ago.

I don't mind working (though now my body complains much louder than it did 30 years ago), I don't mind organizing or planning, or cooking up a storm to give away (not good for that diet if I keep it all for self). All this seems much easier than getting my spirit or mind and body into order so that it glorifies God yet this is what I understand this verse to be asking I do first, above, before all else for him. This is work no one really sees, unless they are as observant as my friend Flora. This will not bring you as much attention or acclaim, if any, in this world even from the church as some other tasks but that should not be our motive for doing should it?

Question: How do you do good so that God gets the glory as Peter writes in 1Peter 2:12?

Answer: 1Peter 2:12 and the ideas within Matthew 5:16, 4:10-11 show 'more explicitly what it is about the good deeds of Christians that makes them a means to God's glory. In order for God to get glory we have to do good by depending on God's strength. Not mere good deeds, but good deeds done in a spirit that comes from a joyful dependence on God's help – this is what glorifies God. . . needs to be 'about it the spirit of joy and gratitude and humility that comes from being born along on the wings of mercy.' [337]

Remembering our 1Peter2:11-12 verses we learn that it is for the glory of God, for his glorification that we are told we must live, be in the full view of the gentiles, the ones who mock and persecute us while they are having a long hard look at us as we keep on being committed to this way, proving God's way works in all situations, rather than being secluded out of sight from the world's stare.

Jesus says much the same in Matthew 5:16, "'Let your light so shine before men, that they may see your good works, and glorify your Father in heaven.'"

---

[337] John Piper Sermon *How to Do Good so that God gets the Glory* Aug 3 1980 desiringgod.com

The goal of every pilgrim's life should be to so live, so be as God has commanded in his word, that he would get all the glory and as I hope you have realized glorifying God is not merely a once a week act of worship on a Sunday.

It is a peculiar and strange kind of living in this marred fallen yet beautiful world that seeks to advance God, display the reality of God rather than the daily-cross-carrying-self. And from the time that God called the nation of Israel into being it was meant to be this way as we read in In Deuteronomy 4:4-9 we hear Moses saying, "'But you who held fast to the LORD your God are alive today . . . Surely I have taught you statutes and judgements, just as the LORD my God commanded me, that you should act according to them in the land which you go to possess. Therefore be careful to observe them; for this is your wisdom and your understanding in the sight of the peoples who will surely hear all these statutes, and say, 'Surely this great nation is a wise and understanding people. For what great nation is there that has God (or a god) so near to it, as the LORD our God is to us, for whatever reason we may call upon Him? And what great nation is there that has such statutes and righteous judgements as are in all this law which I set before you this day? Only take heed to yourself, and diligently keep yourself, lest you forget . . . and . . . they depart from your heart all the days of your life . . .'"

Wright tells us that 'Obedience to the law was not for Israel's [believers] benefit alone. It is a marked feature of the OT that Israel lived on a very public stage. All that happened in its history was open to the comment and reaction of the nations at large . . . this "visibility" of Israel was a deliberate part of its theological identity and role as the "priesthood" of Yahweh among the nations (cf. Exod. 19:4-6). It could be either positive, as here, when the nations are impressed with the wisdom of Israel's law (cf. 28:10); or negative, as when the nations are shocked be the severity of Israel's judgement when they abandon the ways of their God (28:37; 29:22-28) Either way, faithful or unfaithful, the people of God are an open book to the world, and the world asks questions and draws conclusions. . . . Old Testament law explicitly invites, even welcomes, public inspection and comparison. But the expected result of such comparison is that Israel's law will be found superior in wisdom and justice...

. . . missiologically, these verses articulate a motivation for obedience to the law that is easily overlooked. The point is that if Israel would live as God intended, then *the nations* would notice. Israel existed for the ultimate purpose of being the vehicle of God's blessing the nations. . .The missiological challenge, therefore, is that the ethical quality of life of the people of God (their obedience to the law, in this context) is a vital factor in the attraction of the nations to the living God . . . There is a vital link between the religious claims of the people of God (that God is near them) and their practical social ethic. The world will be interested in the former only when it sees the later . . .

We must conclude . . . by noting that the final thrust of the rhetoric of our text is ethical. For unless Israel would live in accordance with God's law, what value would their incredible historical and religious experience retrain? And furthermore, how would the nations come to know of the uniqueness of Yahweh as the living God and of His saving action in history unless they are drawn be the ethical distinctiveness of God's people (cf. vv.6-8; Peter urged this point upon his readers as the messianic people of God, 1 Pet. 2:9-12)? If God's people abandon their ethical distinctiveness by forgetfulness, idolatry, or disobedience, then not only do they jeopardize their own well-being (v. 40), they also frustrate the broader purposes of the God who brought them into existence by electing love and "out of darkness" by redeeming power.'[338]

The book of Ezekiel contains some very powerful yet confronting word pictures and language that perhaps one would not think to

---

[338] Christopher J. H. Wright *Deuteronomy* New International Biblical Commentary Hendrickson Publishers, paternoster press. 1996 p 47,49, 58

find within a holy book. Yet they show vividly I believe why we should live and maintain this new way of being and yes, it is a reason that glorifies God.

Chapter 16 of Ezekiel gives us a picture story of God's love for Jerusalem, her response of harlotry and his reaction – "'. . . on the day you were born your navel cord was not cut, nor were you washed . . . rubbed with salt nor wrapped . . . No eye pitied you . . . to have compassion on you; but you were thrown out into the open field . . . when I passed by you and saw you struggling in your own blood . . . I said to you in your blood, 'Live!' I made you thrive . . . and you grew . . . but you were naked and bare. When I passed by you again and looked upon you, indeed your time was the time of love; so I spread My wing over you and covered your nakedness. Yes, I swore an oath to you and entered into a covenant with you, and you became Mine," says the Lord GOD. "Then I washed you in water . . . and I anointed you with oil . . . I clothed you with fine linen and covered you with silk. I adorned you with ornaments . . . bracelets . . . a chain on your neck . . . a jewel in your nose, earrings . . . and a crown . . . Thus you were adorned with gold and silver, and your clothing was of fine linen, silk, and embroidered cloth. You ate pastry of fine flour, honey, and oil. You were exceedingly beautiful, and succeeded to royalty. Your fame went out among the nations because of your beauty, for it was perfect through My splendour which I had bestowed on you . . .

But you trusted in your own beauty, played the harlot because of your fame . . . You took some of your garments and adorned multicoloured high places for yourself . . . You have also taken your beautiful jewellery from My gold and My silver, which I had given you, and made for yourself male images and played the harlot with them. You took your embroidered garments and covered them, and you set My oil and My incense before them. Also My food which I gave you . . . Moreover you took your sons and your daughters, whom you bore to me, and these you sacrificed to them to be devoured . . . And . . . you did not remember the days of your youth . . . therefore I stretched out My hand against you . . . Men make payment to all harlots, but you made your payments to all your lovers and hired them to come to you from all around for your harlotry . . . I will gather all your lovers . . . and I will judge you . . . they shall stone you . . . and thrust you through with their swords . . . I will make you cease playing the harlot, and you shall no longer hire lovers . . . I will deal with you as you have done, who despised the oath by breaking the covenant. Nevertheless I will remember My covenant with you in the days of your youth, and I will establish an everlasting covenant with you . . . Then you shall know that I am the LORD, that you may remember and be ashamed, and never open your mouth anymore because of your shame, when I provide you an atonement for all you have done," says the Lord GOD."'

I don't know about you but I can put my name in the place of *Jerusalem* in the above verses and see how God saw and rescued me, loved me and gave gifts to me and how I was not interested in him, just his gifts, without any feeling of *agapē* towards the giver. I can see how he disciplined me and made that old lifestyle cease, how he was right and I was wrong and my grumbling mouth opens less. I am what I am *only* because of God and by knowing this, living this and praising him for it I am glorifying him.

Wright says of this Ezekiel passage '. . . a moving and powerful description, albeit in an unusual form, of the loving grace of God and the boundless generosity which flows from it. The picture of utter human weakness, need and vulnerability that the abandoned newborn evokes emphasizes that the people of God . . Their very existence is dependent on the divine command *Live!* . . The divine rescuer's action . . . sprang from totally self-motivated and unconditional love . . . the woman's beauty was meant to enhance Yahweh's own reputation . . . The message of the imagery for us is that as the people who claim the name of the Lord . . . we live in public view. Where God's people live in God's way, God's name is adorned and beautified, and something of His splendour is witnessed among them . . . that is God's purpose as the New Testament shows. The very existence of the church is for the sake of the greater praise and glory of God, and especially of His redeeming grace. Even the presentation of the church as a bride, cleansed, radiant and beautiful, is recycled from the Old Testament imagery. Do our lives weave the kind of clothing that our Lord would want to be seen in? Do our actions so shine like jewellery that the watching world is led to give glory to our Father, as Jesus exhorted?. . . Peter also combines imagery from temple and priesthood in calling on Christians to live out the practical and ethical implications of their status in the eyes of the nations, so that ultimately they too will come to glorify God (1Peter 2:4-12). The ethical challenge of Christian living has a strong missionary purpose: only as the world sees any difference in the behaviour of God's people will they be drawn to acknowledge the God whose people we claim to be.' [339]

So, the gentiles, the nations are watching, considering if this God of mine, ours is real and worth believing in. Seeing if he does make a real and lasting difference to life here and now, if the hope he offers exceeds all that they have trusted so far. They are watching for us to slip up or do something they can ridicule us for and conclude that our God makes no difference.

A life that looked good for a while, that was challenging or attractive to the onlookers for a moment but then became as theirs, proves to be no more helpful or hopeful than their ways or was even worse, says what about our truly glorious God?

He's not big enough to be of any difference or help?

So, my fellow pilgrims heed the way you walk and keep at it, maintain your God-empowered lifestyle, persist in this way so you are found finishing well on your day of visitation.

Dance to the one true piper, remembering he alone is good, loving and for you at all times as it is his nature and he cannot

---

[339] *The message of Ezekiel* p133- 136.

deny himself, be anything else. And as he provides all for you, for all your needs there is very little luggage you actually need to pack and carry. Note that is *needs* not *wants* for *want* drags you down into the filth of the world's ever grasping greedy never satisfied womb that enslaves and destroys. We were not created for this.

Being pilgrims, Christian, returns us to what we were meant to be, and places God where he should be, giving him glory and allowing us to be free of so much than weighs us down. We may not be able to pack light to begin with but as we journey forwards and our knowledge of the person and character of the triune God deepens and connects our brain (logic) with our hearts (our will, passion) we will find a lot of what we thought was necessary becomes discarded for we will learn that GOD alone IS truly ENOUGH for every need, every situation, everything on our journey and that's the way it was always meant to be and we will rest.

Bridges writes, 'John said that God is love, and this is how he showed His love, by sending His Son to die for us [see 1John 4:9-10] Our greatest need is not freedom from adversity. All the possible calamities that could occur in this life cannot in any way be compared with the absolute calamity of eternal separation from God. Jesus said no earthly joy could compare with the eternal joy of our names written in heaven (see Luke10:20). In like manner, no earthly adversity can compare with that awful calamity of God's eternal judgement in hell.

So when John said that God showed His love by sending His Son, he was saying God showed His love by meeting our greatest need – a need so great that no other need can even come close to it in comparison. . .

We are meant to feel the pain of adversity, but we must resist allowing that pain to cause us to lapse into hard thoughts about God . . . seek to reason through the truths of God's love in times of heartache, pain, and disappointment . . . If God's love was sufficient for my greatest need, my eternal salvation, surely it is sufficient for my lesser needs, the adversities I encounter in this life.' [340]

Humanity's greatest need today is not to strip supermarket shelves bare and hoard toilet paper because of some virial pandemic but to be as feverishly zealous as in their panicked fear for toilet paper and noodles to seek God and his salvation, their real need. O that they would fall over one another in eagerness to get not to the supermarket but to their God!

The pilgrim way is the way of Christ. As pilgrims we have a new mindset akin to his, we have the same war to fight, the same life principles to live by, the same how-to-manual, and we have the same glorious hope in that day as he. The pilgrim way is God's way, the way of the cross. The only true and right way. The only way to be truly and eternally alive. And so, as a pilgrim know that 'We should have our eyes on the horizon but our boots on our feet'[341] heading along the way, his highway with the song of praise on our lips.

What way are you going my dear reader?

Mason writes 'At the close of this excellent book [Bunyan's *The Pilgrim's Progress*], let me address one word, reader, to your soul and mine. What think we of a pilgrim's life, and a pilgrim's death? His life begins with the knowledge of Christ, and ends by dying in him, and eternally enjoying him. And, all through life, the pilgrim looks to, and lives upon Christ. Blessed beginning! comfortable living! joyful dying!

Now have we part and lot in this matter? Is Christ our life? The life of our souls? If he is, we shall live by faith upon him, rely on his atonement, glory in his righteousness, rejoice in his salvation, desiring to have done with all sin, and to be dead to self-righteous confidence; and in heart, lip, and life, studying to glorify him, by devoting ourselves to him, looking, longing, and waiting for his

---

[340] *Trusting God* p134, 137

[341] Jonathan Lamb. Speaker at Belgrave Heights Convention Melbourne

coming to receive us to himself, that where he is, there we may be also!

As many as live by their faith, and walk according to this rule, peace be on them, from the holy, blesses, and glorious TRINITY. Amen.' [342]

> O wond'rous grace, unask'd, divine, and free,
> Lodg'd in the womb of vast eternity!
> Maturing time unfolds the amazing plan,
> Completes and opens what love first began.
>
> GILES[343]

To glorify God, let's give him the last word on doing, living the pilgrim way –

Of making many books there is no end, and much study is wearisome to the flesh. Let us hear the conclusion of the whole matter: Fear God and keep His commandments, for this is man's all. For God will bring every work into judgement, including every secret thing, whether good or evil. Ecclesiastes 12:12b-14.

---

[342] *The Pilgrim's Progress Part 11* comment by Mason p396
[343] *The Holy War* p434

The Pilgrim Way

www.ingramcontent.com/pod-product-compliance
Lightning Source LLC
Chambersburg PA
CBHW030144100526
44592CB00009B/105